# The Enigma of Isaac Babel

# The Enigma of Isaac Babel

*Biography, History, Context*

## Edited by Gregory Freidin

Stanford University Press

Stanford, California

Stanford University Press
Stanford, California

Printed in the United States of America on acid-free, archival-quality paper

Library of Congress Cataloging-in-Publication Data

The enigma of Isaac Babel : biography, history, context / edited by Gregory Freidin.
p. cm.
Includes bibliographical references and index.
ISBN 978-0-8047-5903-8 (cloth : alk. paper)
1. Babel', I. (Isaak), 1894–1941—Criticism and interpretation—Congresses. 2. Russian literature—Jewish authors—History and criticism—Congresses. 3. Russian literature—20th century—History and criticism—Congresses. 4. Authors, Russian—20th century—Biography—Congresses. I. Freidin, Gregory.
PG3476.B2Z657 2009
891.73'42—dc22
2008020027

Typeset by Bruce Lundquist in 11.5/15 Adobe Garamond Pro

# Contents

## Part Three: Babel in the World of Letters and On Stage

# Preface

**THE DEAN** of the Odessa mobsters Froim Grach liked Benya Krik. "Benya speaks little," he told the council of thieves when asked to size Benya up, then added, "But he speaks with zest. He says little but you feel you want him to say something more" ("How It Was Done in Odessa," 1923). Maxim Gorky liked Isaac Babel and thought him better than Nikolay Gogol. Gorky's praise of Babel is echoed by the fictional elder gangster promoting his brilliant protégé. Literature and gangland raids, literature and violence, literature and the Russian Revolution, Russian literature and the Jews—welcome to the world of Isaac Babel.

What Froim Grach said about Benya Krik encapsulates Isaac Babel and his legacy. A rather small body of work is all that has survived of Babel's writings. But most of it is zesty and brilliant, leaving generations of readers gasping for more. The words are spoken by a gangster, an outlaw, with a slight local accent (Odessa) and lightly damaged Russian syntax, revealing the speaker to be a little more comfortable in Yiddish than Russian. The words of praise coming from one gangster about another are composed tongue-in-cheek, for they mark a sly intrusion by an outsider into the very serious world of Russian letters, suggesting, perhaps, that the gangster's words mean the opposite of what they say, or the opposite of the opposite, or something in-between the opposite and the same. Was the statement just an aside to shape the character of the story as a man of few words but plenty of action? Or was this a joke, ostensibly about the gangster's verbal parsimony, but made at the expense of the torrents of prose contained in Russia's nineteenth-century "baggy monsters"? Or was the marginality of the master of verbal economy, in fact, a claim to legitimacy in the upside-down revolutionary world? Was the slight Yiddishism of the phrasing a refreshing estrangement device, or was it an oblique claim by a marginal culture on a place of honor at Russian culture's high table?

The riddle of Babel is lodged inside an enigma, and it is definitely wrapped in irony—irony that is irreducible. A reader chasing the ultimate meaning of an ironic statement is not unlike the proverbial dog chasing its tail, but the questions prompted by Froim's laconic tirade allow the reader to see the world anew, to clear the air of drudgery, and to get rid of the cobwebs of received ideas—be they about life, art, revolution, violence, masculinity, Russian literature and culture, not to mention the Jews. Which is why one wants to hear something more from Isaac Babel. More, however, is not easily obtained because the author, like his creation Benya Krik, was on paper a man of few words and was unusually circumspect and sometimes misleading about his art and life. Babel was not even forty-six when he was executed in the Lefortovo Prison in Moscow, and his manuscripts and correspondence, which he kept under lock and key in a small chest, along with whatever other papers he had in his two houses at the time of his arrest, traveled with him to prison and to this day have not recovered.

**AMONG MODERN RUSSIAN AUTHORS** as well as the larger pool of stars of European modernism, Isaac Babel makes the most tantalizing case. He achieved world fame as he turned thirty with his cycle of stories about the Russian civil war; he was admired as the author of the no less famous, comical, and Rabelaisian *Tales of Odessa*; he set the pattern and tone for stories about Jewish childhood with the quartet of tales *Story of My Dovecote*; he left two powerful, enigmatic plays, *Sunset* and *Maria* (in which the Maria character never appears), and a scattering of newspaper reporting and promising stories—fragments of larger, unfinished cycles. The intensity of his readers' sentiment in Russia and elsewhere, and particularly in the United States, stands in reverse proportion to the extant volume of his work.

This collection, then, represents an attempt by a community of international scholars to tease out "something more" about Isaac Babel. This is a propitious time. Since the fall of the Soviet Union and the opening of the archives, we have come to know more about his works and days, his milieu, the history of his time, and various contexts that frame his writings. We have aimed at a multidimensional view of the man and his legacy, hence the division of this volume into the three somewhat overlapping parts.

The first part, "Attempting a Biography," brings together essays by two Babel experts for whom Babel has come to be inseparable from his biographical context. Patricia Blake sketches out her portrait of Issac Babel using as a backdrop the early days of her biographer's journey—an American writer researching a book on Babel's life and death in Moscow during the cold war as she herself was being watched by the Soviet secret police. Gregory Freidin, who discovered Babel early in his youth and heard many stories about him from Babel's old friend, the sculptor Ilya Slonim, looks for the autobiographical "message in a bottle" in Babel's own writing, especially the little-understood play *Maria* as well as the stories of the 1920s and 1930s leading up to it. The result is a patchwork of historical fact and fiction from which the complicated and contradictory figure of Issac Babel begins to emerge.

The second part, "Babel in the Context of Russian History," attempts to locate Babel's legacy in the shifting sands of the political, cultural, and social circumstances of the Russian Revolution, a period that stretched from 1917 all the way to Babel's death in 1940. Historian Oleg Budnitskii offers a new and intriguing context for reading Babel's *Red Cavalry* and his civil war Diary: the history of the Red Army's attitudes toward the Jews, with a special focus on Semyon Budenny's First Cavalry Army for which Babel served as a reporter, propagandist, and staff officer in the Polish campaign in 1920. A longtime Babel expert, Carol Avins, examines Babel's work, especially his story "The Road," in the context of the written record of the Jewish experience of the Russian Revolution and offers a fresh reading of one of the most enigmatic stories of Babel's career. A literary scholar and linguist, Michael S. Gorham, offers yet another historical context for understanding Babel—the struggle for the authoritative postrevolutionary language of state, which ultimately came to dominate public discourse in Russia. His juxtaposition of Babel's *Red Cavalry* and Furmanov's *Chapaev* goes a long way toward explaining Babel's "silence" in the 1930s, when the "Furmanov model," a paired language of command adopted by the top-down ideological party state, came to dominate the print media as well as the officially sanctioned Soviet letters. A fascinating view of Babel's evolution as a writer and stylist in his interaction with the body of Russian and Soviet Russian literature emerges from the chapter by the world's foremost expert on Soviet Russian literature, especially the 1920s and 1930s, Marietta Chudakova. Contrary to the prevailing view of Babel as a sui generis author with a limited genealogy in Russian letters and practically no following among Soviet Russian writers, Chudakova convincingly demonstrates that Babel, in fact, had a tremendous impact on Soviet Russian prose, which absorbed elements of his style even as it diluted its intensity and pungency to "safe" consumption levels. Paradoxically or not, Babel, too, found himself caught up in the "taming of Babel": as the author of his 1937 story, "The Kiss," Chudakova suggests, he was coming close to resembling his own Soviet epigones.

"Babel in the World of Letters and On Stage" is largely devoted to the examination of Babel's writings in contexts that are specifically literary. Alexander Zholkovsky examines the device of the "debut" in Babel's prose and compares it to its uses in Nabokov, Chekhov, Andreev, and Sholom Aleichem, among others. Robert Alter focuses on the emergence of a modern literary sensibility, juxtaposing the aestheticizing gaze implied in Flaubert's *le style indirect libre* with Babel's first-person narrator who, in Victor Shklovsky's famous quip, could speak "in the same voice about stars and gonorrhea." Zsuzsa Hetényi (Budapest), a Babel expert of long standing, inventories the world of Babel's childhood stories and examines them in the context of the Jewish childhood archetype in twentieth-century European and American literary tradition. Elif Batuman (Stanford) explores an important thematic leitmotif in Babel's writings—refusal to be a clerk—in terms of her own ingenious theory of literary double accounting, showing Babel's deep kinship with Flaubert and Cervantes. The eminent Babel scholar, Efraim Sicher (Beer–Sheva) contextualizes Babel's writings in the contemporary Yiddish and Hebrew literature, drawing our attention to another instance of Babel's "double bookkeeping": the subtexts in his writings that could only be appreciated by a certain trilingual segment of his audience, namely, those who were conversant in all the three languages in use by the Jews of the Russian empire: Russian, Yiddish, and Hebrew. Finally, in the concluding essay of the collection, Carl Weber (Stanford), who directed the Stanford production of *Maria*, shares his thoughts both on his direction of the play and the special concerns of a director producing the work for the twenty-first-century American audience.

**EARLIER VERSIONS** of most of these essays were solicited for and presented at the Isaac Babel Workshop at Stanford University in February–March, 2004. The workshop was attended, among others, by Babel's two daughters, the late Nathalie Babel and Lydia, and Lydia's mother, Babel's companion in the last years of his life, Antonina Nikolaevna Pirozhkova. The workshop included the exhibition "Isaac Babel: A Writer's Life," put together with the generous support and assistance of the Hoover Institution Libraries and Archives, and the U.S. premiere of Babel's play *Maria*. The centerpiece was the international conference that lent the title to the present volume.

The conference papers have been revised for this publication, and two papers were written expressly for this volume: "Staging Babel's *Maria*—For Young American Audiences, Seventy Years After" by Carl Weber and "*Pan Pisar*': Clerkship in Babel's First-Person Narration" by Elif Batuman, who has chronicled the Babel Conference and Workshop in her now famous essay, "Babel in California" (*N+1* 2 [2005]).

Elif Batuman rendered invaluable help to the editor at the earlier stages in the preparation of this volume for publication. I owe a debt of gratitude to Martha Kelly, Irina Erman, and Luke Parker, who have aided me in shepherding the manuscript through its later editorial stages. The title of the volume was suggested to me by my Stanford colleague, historian Steven Zipperstein, who, along with Gabriella Safran, my Slavic Department colleague, have helped me to broaden my view of Isaac Babel and sustain my interest in his life and art over the last decade. Thanks are also due to Stanford's Division of Literatures, Cultures and Languages, and its head, Roland Greene, for supporting this publication.

*Gregory Freidin, Stanford University, 2007*

# Contributors

**ROBERT ALTER** is Class of 1937 Professor of Hebrew and Comparative Literature at the University of California at Berkeley. His twenty-two published books include a variety of studies of the European and American novel and of literary aspects of the Bible. His two most recent books are *Imagined Cities: Urban Experience and the Language of the Novel* and *The Book of Psalms: A Translation with Commentary*.

**CAROL J. AVINS**, Associate Professor of Russian Literature at Rutgers University, is the author of *Border Crossings: The West and Russian Identity in Soviet Literature, 1917–1934* and co-translator of Irina Ratushinskaya, *Beyond the Limit*. Her work on Isaac Babel includes the Introduction and annotations to his *1920 Diary*. The article in this volume is part of a larger project on Babel's stories and the transformations of his time.

**ELIF BATUMAN** received a doctorate in Comparative Literature from Stanford University in 2007, and is the author of *The Possessed: Adventures with Russsian Books and the People Who Read Them* (New York: Farrar, Straus and Giroux, 2010).

**PATRICIA BLAKE** is an associate of the Davis Center for Russian and Eurasian Studies at Harvard. She is the editor of four books of contemporary Russian fiction and poetry in English translation, and has edited a collection of essays, *Writers in Russia*, by her longtime collaborator, the late Max Hayward. Much of her career has been spent as a reporter and writer for *Life* and *Time*. She is currently completing a biography of Isaac Babel.

**OLEG BUDNITSKII** holds the degree of *Doctor of Historical Sciences.* He is Senior Fellow at the Institute of Russian History, Russian Academy of Sciences, and Academic Director of the International Center for Russian and East European Jewish Studies in Moscow. He is editor-in-chief of *Arkhiv evreiskoi istorii* (Archive of Jewish History), and author or editor of over 150 publications (including twelve books), among them *Rossiiskie evrei mezhdy krasnymi i belymi, 1917–20 (Russian Jews between the Reds and the Whites, 1917–20)* (Moscow: ROSSPEN, 2005); *Terrorism v rossiiskom osvoboditel'nom dvizhenii: ideologiia, etika, psikhologiia (Terrorism in the Russian Liberation Movement: Ideology, Ethics, Psychology)* (Moscow: ROSSPEN, 2000); co-editor, *Rossiia i rossiiskaia emigratsiia v vospominaniiakh i dnevnikakh: anno-tirovannaia bibliografiia (Russia and the Russian Emigration in Memoirs and Diaries: An Annotated Bibliography,* 4 vols. (Moscow: ROSSPEN, 2003–2005); and editor, *"Strictly Personal and Confidential!" B. A. Bakhmetev and V. A. Maklakov: Correspondence 1919–51,* 3 vols. (Moscow and Stanford: ROSSPEN and Hoover Institution Press, 2001–2002). He has received grants from, among others, the Fulbright Program, IREX, the American Council of Learned Societies, the Open Society Institute (Soros Foundation), the Vidal Sassoon International Center for the Study of Antisemitism, the Russian Endowment for the Humanities, and the Skirball Fellowship from the Oxford Centre for Hebrew and Jewish Studies.

**DR. MARIETTA CHUDAKOVA** is the author of more than 300 works on the history of 20th-century Russian literature, including monographs on Yuri Olesha (*Masterstvo Yuriia Oleshi* [1972]), Mikhail Zoshchenko (*Poetika Mikhaila Zoshchenko* [1979]), Mikhail Bulgakov (*Zhizneiopisanie Mikhaila Bulgakova* [1988, 1989]), and most recently a collection of works on the history of Russian literature of the Soviet period (*Literatura sovetskogo proshlogo* [2001]). She is a member of the Union of Russian Writers as well as the editorial boards of the journals *Novy mir* and *Chelovek.* In 1994–2000, Chudakova served on the Presidential Clemency Board of the Russian Federation. She lives in Moscow.

**GREGORY FREIDIN**, Professor of Slavic Languages and Literatures at Stanford University, is the author of a critical-biographical study of the poet Osip Mandelstam, *A Coat of Many Colors* (University of California Press, 1987), editor and contributor of *Russian Culture in Transition* (*Stanford Slavic Studies* 7, 1993), co-editor and contributor of *Russia at the*

*Barricades* (M. E. Sharpe, 1994), editor of the Norton Critical Edition of *Isaac Babel's Selected Writings* (W. W. Norton, 2009). He is the co-translator, with Strobe Talbot, of *Khrushchev Remembers: The Last Testament* (Little, Brown, 1984) and the translator into Russian of *The Federalist* (American *Amerikanskie Federalisty* [Chalidze Publications, 1990]). He has written on Russian culture, society, and politics for *The New Criterion, The New Republic, Los Angeles Times, Nezavisimaia gazeta, Neprikosnovenny zapas, Novoe literaturnoe obozrenie*, and *The Russian Review*. Since 1981, he has published extensively on Isaac Babel, including a long biographical essay in *European Writers (1990)*; he is completing his critical biography of Isaac Babel, *A Jew on Horseback*, for Stanford University Press.

**MICHAEL S. GORHAM** is an Associate Professor of Russian Studies at the University of Florida. His book, *Speaking in Soviet Tongues: Language, Culture and the Politics of Voice in Revolutionary Russia* (Northern Illinois University Press, 2003), was selected as an Outstanding Academic Book by *Choice Magazine* and won the 2004 award for Best Book in Literary and Cultural Studies from the American Association of Teachers of Slavic and East European Languages (AATSEEL). His current research explores the interdependence of language, culture, politics, and national identity in late- and post-Soviet Russia and has appeared in article and chapter form in publications in the United States, Russia, Holland, and Norway.

**ZSUZSA HETÉNYI** is Professor at the Institute for Slavic Studies at the University ELTE, Budapest, and an award-winning translator (Award by Academy of Sciences, 2002). In addition to her 180 scholarly articles in six languages, she is author of a monographic study about Biblical and messianic motifs in I. Babel's *Red Cavalry* (1991), and the editor and co-author of the *History of the Russian Literature* (vols. 1 and 2, 1997–2002). Her *In the Maelstrom: The History of the Russian-Jewish Literature* (in Hungarian, 2000, extended and revised English version 2007), the result of fifteen years of research, was produced thanks to grants given by the Swiss Confederation (Geneva University, 1993–1994, 2005) and the Soros Foundation (Florida International University, 1996–1997). Her main field of interest is Russian prose of the 20th century. Hetényi has lectured and given conference papers in Austria, Croatia, France, Germany, Great Britain, Italy, Israel, Lithuania, Russia, Slovenia, Spain, Sweden, Switzerland, and the United States.

**EFRAIM SICHER** is Professor of English and Comparative Literature at Ben-Gurion University of the Negev. His publications on Isaac Babel include two Russian editions and one in English, as well as his monograph, *Style and Structure in the Prose of Isaak Babel* (Slavica, 1986). He has also published a number of books and essays on Russian and comparative literature and on modern Jewish culture.

**CARL WEBER**, Professor Emeritus of the Stanford Drama Department, is a former collaborator of Bertolt Brecht, an internationally known stage director, and the translator/editor of the anthology *DramaContemporary: Germany: Plays* (Baltimore: Johns Hopkins University Press, 1996) as well as four editions of Heiner Müller's writings, most recently, *A Heiner Müller Reader: Plays, Poetry, Prose* (Baltimore: Johns Hopkins University Press, 2001).

**ALEXANDER ZHOLKOVSKY** is a Professor of Slavic Languages and Literatures and Comparative Literature at the University of Southern California, Los Angeles. He graduated from the Moscow Lomonosov University (MGU) in 1959, holds a Ph.D. in African linguistics from the Moscow Institute of Oriental Languages (1970), and has published extensively in English and Russian on linguistic theory and Russian literature. He immigrated to the United States in 1980. His two major English-language monographs of literary theory and criticism are *Themes and Texts* (Ithaca and London: Cornell University Press, 1984) and *Text counter Text* (Stanford: Stanford University Press, 1994 cloth, 1995 paper). He is also the author of several books of literary scholarship in Russian, of which the latest are: *Selected Essays on Russian Poetry: Invariants, Structures, Strategies, Intertexts* (Moscow: RGGU, 2005); *Isaak Babel's A Story and a Half: "Guy de Maupassant" and "Answer to Inquiry/First Fee": Structure, Meaning, Background* (Moscow: Komkniga, 2006); and *Mihail Zoshchenko: A Poetics of Mistrust* (Moscow: LKI, 2007). Alexander Zholkovsky lives in Santa Monica, California.

The Enigma of Isaac Babel

Part One
## Attempting a Biography

# 1

## Researching Babel's Biography
### Adventures and Misadventures

PATRICIA BLAKE

**SEARCHING OUT THE LIFE STORY** of Isaac Babel is the despair of the biographer. I have been at it, on and off, since 1962. The principal difficulty lies, of course, in the one stark fact that following Babel's arrest in 1939 he was expunged from Russian literature. His writings vanished from libraries, bookstores, and, often enough, from bookshelves in the homes of frightened readers. His unpublished manuscripts and other papers were seized and have not been recovered. His letters to people in the Soviet Union, numbering in the thousands, were often destroyed by his worried correspondents, or, if they themselves were arrested, taken by the NKVD. The biographies, appreciations, and reminiscences that in other countries would naturally follow the death of a great and celebrated author have remained unwritten. As the decades passed, Babel's contemporaries—those who knew him well and who had survived Stalin's terror—were dying off, many leaving little trace of their relationship.

In George Orwell's indispensable formulation, Babel had been dropped down the memory hole.

Of course he was not alone down there. As many as 2,000 writers were arrested during the Stalin years, 1,000 or so of whom were put to death.[1] Others, uncounted, died in the Gulag.

In addition there are some special features about Babel that have hindered the reconstruction of his life and work. One is that he failed, unaccountably, to take precautions to preserve his unpublished work—even during the Great Terror.

In contrast, in post-Stalin times a number of such works by suppressed writers have been recovered from their hiding places or from courageous friends who had agreed to secrete them. For example: a novel, *The Salt Barn*, that Boris Pilnyak buried, page by page, in his backyard at Peredelkino, and the poetry rescued from the lips of a widow who committed much of Osip Mandelshtam's work to memory.

True, Babel gave copies of five of his unpublished stories to Olga Brodskaya and Maya Ovrutskaya, but, as I understand it, not to safeguard the stories, but as gifts. (They include two crucial stories: the autobiographical "Detstvo. U babushki" and the superb "Kolyvushka.") His *1920 Diary*, written during the Soviet-Polish war, which served as the fundament of *Red Cavalry*, was also preserved by Ovrutskaya. But most of Babel's papers—original manuscripts, drafts, and letters—were in his Moscow apartment and his dacha in Peredelkino when the NKVD marauders arrived. Even the available texts of his writings, as originally published, were often unreliable, having been corrupted by censorship.

There was also the problem of Babel's penchant for mystifications. Some were meant to enhance his Bolshevik credentials—however dubious those might have been. Such as his claim to have fought in the defense of Petrograd against General Yudenich's army in 1919—unverifiable—or his preposterous assertion in 1930 that he had been working continuously for the Soviet Secret Police since October 1917, that is, two months before it was founded.[2] Pertinent records have thus far proved inaccessible to present-day researchers. The truth seems to be that Babel worked as a translator in the Petrograd Cheka for a few weeks some time in 1918.[3]

In addition, there were the mystifications calculated to put off his editors and creditors, his assurances that he was writing this and that piece of work (some of which he had really begun), which ultimately failed to materialize, including a novel about collectivization, another about a con man in the Donbas, and an evanescent novel (or was it a play?) about the Cheka.

Finally there are his myriad bits of mischief: lies about what he was doing when, where, and with whom. I prized one bit out of Clara Malraux, the former wife of the writer André Malraux, when I interviewed her in Paris. In Moscow in 1934 during the First Writers Congress, Babel drew her aside and whispered that he would like to have a long, quiet, unsupervised walk with her. During the walk he confided this to her: "Because I am a friend of Gorky I spend evenings, nearly once a week, together with him and Stalin. The Kremlin phones Gorky and announces Stalin's arrival.

Then the three of us stretch out before the fireplace and chat, relaxed."
Clara liked this cozy picture so much she repeated it in a later memoir.[4]

Actually I believe Babel never met with Stalin. Even when meetings
were scheduled for Stalin to talk with groups of writers, Babel avoided
attending—one of his rare acts of prudence.

These, then, are the intrinsic problems of Babel's biography. In addition, I personally encountered some dismaying difficulties when I first
undertook to seek the facts of Babel's life. What follows is an informal
account of my adventures—and misadventures—as I began gathering
materials about Babel in Moscow, Zagreb, and Brussels in 1962–1963,
and then, later, in Paris.

When I started out in Moscow in July 1962 I was a fairly experienced
journalist, speaking horrible-sounding but serviceable Russian. I had been
to the Soviet Union before, as a reporter for *Life* and *Time*, covering various political and cultural events. Since then, however, a passion for contemporary Russian literature had overtaken me.

On the trip in 1962 I was on my own, and foolhardy enough to
think I might gather enough materials for a biography of Isaac Babel—a
writer whose work held me spellbound, then, and for the rest of my life.

It seemed like a pretty good time to go, for my purposes. Babel
had been "posthumously rehabilitated" in 1954, a selection of his stories
(though many in their censored versions) had been published in 1957, and
the 22nd Party Congress in 1961 had lightened the general atmosphere.
Stalin had been removed from the Lenin mausoleum. The Cuban missile
crisis had not yet erupted.

At that time very little was known for certain about Babel's fate, save
for the date of his arrest: May 15, 1939. Antonina Nikolaevna Pirozhkova,
Babel's companion for more than six years before his arrest, had been a
witness to that. The rest was mostly rumor, abundant as ever in the Soviet
Union. People were looking for a *reason* for Babel's arrest, such as his relations
with accused Trotskyites, or with purged Civil War officers, his visits abroad,
Budenny's vendetta against him for *Red Cavalry*, and so forth. More to the
point was Anna Akhmatova's indignant response when anyone asked "What
was so and so arrested for?" She would cry out, "What do you mean *what for*?
It's time you understood that people are being arrested *for nothing*."[5]

Actually there is an explanation for the *timing* of Babel's arrest,
which took place singularly "late," in 1939, that is, after the Great Terror
had begun to subside. But that would not come clear for many years.

**I DIDN'T GO TO MOSCOW COLD.** I had found Babel's daughter Nathalie when she lived in Paris and we had become friends there, and also later in New York City, where she began teaching at Barnard College. She gave me an introduction to Antonina Nikolaevna Pirozhkova, which was to make all the difference.

When I called on Antonina Nikolaevna, she was still living in the apartment on Bolshoi Nikolo-Vorobinskii Pereulok that she had shared with Babel. I was inexpressibly moved to be there. The writer's workroom seemed to me too small to have contained so great a writer. I made a little sketch of it and its furnishings. Antonina assured me that hardly anything had changed there in the twenty-three years that had passed since Babel had been taken away.

She sat beside the only window, and as she talked with me she would occasionally lightly stroke the large chest by her side, where, she said, Babel had kept some of the papers that had been seized by the NKVD. She told me about his working routine, the morning tea that he had to brew a certain way, the writing paper he would cut to a particular size, his indispensable gold-trimmed fountain pen that had belonged to Antonina's father, how he composed cross-legged on the sofa or while pacing up and down, rolling a piece of string between his fingers like worry beads—that and a great deal more.

Antonina offered me a fine sense of what sort of person Babel had been to live with, as a man and as a writer. But the final years they had shared, during the Great Terror, had been dreadful ones, and I was hesitant to try to lead her into reliving much of them that day. Would there be another occasion? I was overjoyed when she said she would see me again before I left Russia.

Unfortunately, thanks to the intervention of the KGB, as I will shortly explain, I was not able to keep our appointment in Moscow until 1990.

Antonina sent me to see Babel's oldest and probably his dearest friend, Isaac Livshits. The two men had been brought up together in Odessa where Livshits was known as Izia and Babel as Isia, and that's what they called each other as grown-ups. Izia and Isia had gone to the Nicholas I Commercial School. They had learned to swim together in Odessa harbor—Babel hit his head on a stone when he first dived in. They had even endured violin lessons by Stoliarsky, commemorated as Zagursky in Babel's "The Awakening" ("Probuzhdenie").

Izia, then, and his wife Liudmila, known as Liusia, were a delightful couple, very small in size, very friendly, very voluble. Close as Livshits had been to Babel, he had not written anything about him, and now, at the age of seventy, he was overflowing with reminiscences. He told me that he had been something like Babel's business manager, acting for him with editors when Babel was away—surely a forlorn enterprise for poor Izia.

The couple told me stories about Babel's youth, his early enthusiasms, his favorite foreign authors, some of which I found surprising—Ibsen, Strindberg, and, especially, Céline. But as they talked on I had a growing sense that there was something important that they wanted me to record in my biography.

Livshits came out with it. "You know," he said, "Babel was arrested the same day as Ezhov's wife. She was the reason he was taken." He was reluctant to elaborate. I was bewildered. Ezhov? The executor of Stalin's Great Terror? I had never heard of the wife of Ezhov, let alone that she had some connection with Babel.

It is a measure of how little information was available when I began my research that even so close a friend of Babel's as Livshits had his facts wrong. As I would later learn, Evgenia Ezhova, Ezhov's wife, was not arrested. She died under murky circumstances in a sanatorium on November 21, 1938, six months before Babel's arrest. Nonetheless, it appears that Livshits had grasped the mortal danger to his friend that lay in Ezhova's death, the presage to Ezhov's own and the purge of everyone officially or personally connected with the couple.

**ALSO IN 1962**, in Zagreb, I talked with Ervin Sinkó, Babel's Hungarian friend and his lodger for eighteen months until April 1937. A year before our meeting he had published memoirs in Hungarian that dealt with his relationship with Babel.[6] Now, in his interview with me he had a great deal to say about Ezhov's wife, the ineffable Evgeniia Solomonovna—how she phoned Babel three or four times a day during the Great Terror—or, more pertinently, during the *Ezhovshchina*—and waited for him outside his apartment in her chauffeured limousine. Sinkó was convinced that she and Babel had then resumed an affair that had begun in 1927 before her marriage to Ezhov. I doubt that. But I do believe that Babel had come under Ezhova's protection, with all the advantages—and perils—that that involved.

One person I could not fail to interview was Ilya Ehrenburg. In his case I had no need of an introduction; he had recently published in a Soviet newspaper a ferocious attack on an essay I had written on Mayakovsky, as the preface to my first book, a selection in English of the poet's plays and his lyric verse. When I phoned Ehrenburg he told me to come right over, and he received me warmly as if nothing had happened. His living room was uninviting, polluted by the black French tobacco he chain-smoked, the walls decorated with several enormous abstract paintings by the French Communist artist Fernand Léger, starkly industrial-looking and somehow menacing. Ehrenburg gave me a long and lively interview about Babel, elements of which he would later repeat in his memoirs.

He imparted one startling new thing. As a member of the Writers Union rehabilitation commission in 1954, he was present when the purported dossier of Babel's criminal case was opened. There was nothing in it, Ehrenburg told me, save for one document, Babel's death certificate. This gave no cause or place of death, only a death date: March 17, 1941.

This was not encouraging. If only one document in Babel's case file had been made available to the official rehabilitation commission, it seemed that prospects of ever recovering any further information about Babel's fate were nil.

Even that lonely certificate was to prove worthless. There, the date of Babel's death had been falsified, set forward fourteen months from the actual date of his execution: January 27, 1940. Many years later I learned that after 1956 death dates were routinely advanced in the records of people executed during the Terror whenever inquiries were made about their fate. The purpose was to make it appear that the deaths had taken place over ten years' time in the Gulag—presumably from natural causes—and not as the result of the killing of almost a million people in a short span of time during the Terror of 1937–1938.[7]

I called on the eighty-six-year-old Ekaterina Pavlovna Peshkova, Gorky's wife, long separated from him but still his good friend and a frequent guest at Gorky's houses abroad and later, in the Soviet Union. She had known Babel there, and she obviously liked reminiscing about the goings-on at Gorky's mansion in Moscow and at his dacha in the suburbs where Babel visited, sometimes every day, until the NKVD barred visitors in early 1936.

She was a most impressive old lady. She told me in some detail about the so-called Political Red Cross she had founded, with Dzerzhinsky's permission, which had succeeded for almost twenty years in sending parcels of food and clothing to many thousands of political prisoners. In addition, relatives were often able to get from her Red Cross precious information about where prisoners were being held, what the latest charges and sentences were, when visits might be made—until Ezhov shut the organization down during the Terror and had the entire staff, and the relatives of prisoners currently being assisted, arrested and shot. "Only Peshkova was left alive, to suffer and die a free person," as Lev Razgon wrote in his memoirs.[8] I was amazed and moved when Ekaterina Pavlovna told me that even after her life's work was shattered and her colleagues dead, when Babel was arrested she went to NKVD headquarters in Lubyanka Prison to try to intervene for him with Beria himself.

When it came time for me to leave she said she wanted to give me something to remember her by. She presented me with one of those brightly painted Russian serving spoons, which I stuffed in my pocket.

**EKATERINA PAVLOVNA** lived in a small apartment house with an elevator. As I walked out her front door I saw men, a lot of men, immobile and silent, crowded into the stairwell. They were dressed in the dark ill-fitting suits and the black clodhoppers typical of the KGB. Once I got out into the street I reckoned there were about twenty of these thugs walking behind me. I stopped to make a phone call from one of the old glass-enclosed booths that displayed the number of each kiosk high up one wall. One of the men ran up to the booth and under my nose held up a notebook, penciled in the kiosk number, and ran off to a car, unmistakably signaling that my call would be immediately monitored. It was ludicrous—a Keystone Kops cartoon with the balloon reading "Gotcha!" Still, there was no ignoring the threat behind it, to me and to others. When I got into my car—I had rented a small sedan and a driver—the men scattered to their limousines, three ZIMS, and proceeded to follow me.

I had been invited to lunch that day by the French chargé d'affaires, Jacques de Beaumarchais, and his wife. I was shaken and I considered canceling, but, I thought, no, this is just the day I need their company. They had been extremely welcoming—we had acquaintances in common in France. The couple were both charming, cultivated, and elegant—he a direct descendant of the great eighteenth-century playwright Beaumarchais, author of *The Marriage of Figaro*. When I arrived Madame de Beaumarchais gave me a present she had brought from Ukraine—it was my day for gifts—a green ceramic pitcher in the shape of a ram, which is still on display, together with Peshkova's spoon, in my kitchen.

I told Beaumarchais what was happening and he went to look out a ground-floor window. Sure enough there it was, stretched out along the front of France's ambassadorial residence, my mini-motorcade, the KGB men stuffed like clowns into the three ZIMs. Beaumarchais became enraged, all pink and trembling. He ran outside with me behind him, stood at the lead car and pointed. He hardly spoke Russian but his meaning was irresistible. "*Ya frantsuzskii posol!* I am the French ambassador! *Fichez le camp!* Get out of here!" he shouted. And they did.

That was highly satisfactory.

But when I left after lunch they were waiting for me down the street.

I returned to my hotel and found the staff in a tizzy. There were an unusual number of people in the lobby, whispering among themselves and staring at me. One of the Intourist women approached me with a big empty smile and said, "Two men are looking for you." They materialized from behind the inevitable concrete columns, showed me their KGB credentials, grasped me by my arms and walked me through the lobby past the buzzing little crowd and into the street. I daresay it was my most impressive showing in Russia—my perp walk, as we call this sort of thing in America.

Here I must stress that I am exquisitely aware that, compared to what these types of thugs did to many millions of Soviet citizens, what happened to me was a triviality. For that reason I have never written about it. Nevertheless, in the story I am telling, it was a decisive event.

The two men drove me to an unmarked office building in central Moscow; I later learned at the American Embassy that it was a so-called KGB safe house. I was put in a room with three chairs and a desk and was kept there for eighteen hours. The first man who questioned me was a stylish fellow dressed in foreign-made clothes—a Harris tweed jacket, buttoned-down shirt, and what looked like a British regimental tie.

He began by saying that I had come to the Soviet Union on a tourist visa, but that I was not behaving like a tourist, but as a journalist. "You have been falsely representing yourself as a tourist to force yourself on important Soviet citizens," he said. He never named these people, save for Gorky's widow.

I was relieved. If that was all they were accusing me of, I thought, the worst they would do to me would be to expel me from the country and declare me persona non grata.

I found my retort right away. "Please tell me what law I have broken. If I have broken any law I will stop," I said.

He had no answer to that. He simply carried on about my not acting like a tourist. And I stuck to my question about whether I had broken any law, from time to time producing some variations which annoyed and possibly mystified the KGB officer. Having a not-too-precise recollection of Harold Berman's book *The RSFSR Criminal Code and Procedure*, which I had recently received from a practical-minded friend in America, I began tossing out some numbers at random. Had I broken the law under Article 33 (crimes by foreigners in the RSFSR)? or maybe 83 (illegal entry)? or 190 (circulation of defamatory fabrications)? This game between me and the KGB man went on for much of the night and then with another officer who spelled him toward morning.

At one point Harris Tweed came out with this: "You are not a tourist. You want to write about the Soviet nationalities question." I figured he meant about Soviet anti-Semitism, and I was not surprised. On my last trip, I had written a series for *Life* on religion in the Soviet Union that included a piece on the troubles of Orthodox Jews—the scarcity of synagogues, the unavailability of religious articles, like prayer shawls and matzos at Passover. This time, however, I felt sure that the authorities were aware that although I was doing research on a Jewish writer, now long dead, I was not focusing my efforts on interviewing Jews per se. On this visit I was not talking with old women on the balconies of synagogues in Moscow and Kiev. During this whole trip I had had occasion to interview only three Jews, Ehrenburg and Izia and Liusia Livshits.

As the night went on I became quite pleased with myself, standing up to the KGB officer the way I was doing. I was making him furious and I was rather enjoying it.

Then he did something that completely shattered my self-possession.

In the midst of one his diatribes he suddenly began quoting verbatim from my interview with Antonina Pirozhkova, a question I had asked and her lengthy reply. The content was of no consequence and I have forgotten it. But I was truly spooked.

I thought: "Here's this woman who has been through so much and now because of me they've bugged her apartment. The bastard has even memorized parts of what we said. Maybe they've been to see her and harassed her for talking to me."

I didn't respond, but I vowed to myself that henceforth I would stay away from the woman Babel had loved.

This was how the KGB won its contest with me.

**THEY RELEASED ME** in the early morning and another of their thugs drove me back to my hotel. I was not told I would be expelled from the country, or declared persona non grata, though in the end it amounted to that.[9]

When I got to my room I was wiped out. I could hardly take off my clothes. When a zipper stuck at the back of my dress I rang for the maid. She had been one of the staff who had witnessed my perp walk in the lobby. We already knew each other; we had talked a bit, about her family back in her village in Central Russia.

She came up behind me, folded her arms around me, and held me. I cried then for the first and last time over what had happened to me. I have not forgotten that dear woman's consoling gesture. It is one of the experiences that still bind me indissolubly to Russia.

That same day I went to the American Embassy, where the political officer took me to a supposedly debugged room and listened to my story. "Are you going to let yourself be intimidated?" he asked in a strong, confident voice.

Well, there's only one ready answer to that question: no. Nevertheless, I could not entertain the idea of calling on more good people, bringing along a KGB motorcade at my back. I reckoned that if I remained in the Soviet Union as long as my visa allowed the authorities would give me no respite, considering how many resources they had already invested to intimidate someone who had just been asking about Isaac Babel.

I lost heart and left Russia the next day, not to return for many years.

After a brief stay in Brussels, where I had a touching talk with Babel's sister Meri—who looked just like her brother, only prettier—I went to Paris, then and several times thereafter, where I interviewed several friends of Babel's, including the artist Iurii Annenkov, the writer André Malraux, and the historian Boris Souvarine. I had been crushed by the interruption of my work in Russia, but I reckoned that Babel—who had been in France three times, in 1927–1928, 1932–1933, and 1935—had probably talked more openly with his friends abroad than he had at home.

That turned out to be true. In the air of freedom and the company of people he trusted, the famously close-mouthed Babel became an irrepressible talker, teeming with news, gossip, jokes, speculations, rumors, predictions, and myriad personal opinions—all fresh from Stalinist Russia. I offer one example, his talks with Souvarine.[10]

As a would-be biographer I was confounded to learn from Souvarine that Babel loved to brag about having inside information concerning the

Soviet leadership, which, he intimated, he had gathered from his high-level connections in Moscow—all delivered with a mystifying air of omniscience and certitude.

Now, Souvarine was a founder of the French Communist Party, and a former executive of the Comintern, who had become a fierce anti-Stalinist. When he met with Babel, he was arguably the European with the most highly developed understanding of the power structure in the Kremlin. In 1935 he would publish his magisterial biography of Stalin.

For Babel, associating with such a man as Souvarine was risky, but fear had deserted Babel in Paris. The two men often met in 1932–1933 and talked nonstop in French and Russian, in each other's apartments, in cafés, on the streets, and even in the metro. They made a striking pair, two ebullient, opinionated Jews, both in their late thirties, both unusually short, the one a brilliant political intellectual, the other a writer of genius, talking their days away in the city of light.

During their walks a disconcerted Souvarine listened to Babel make pronouncements about any number of Soviet leaders, some of whom Souvarine had known personally in Moscow. It would be difficult to recount within the space of this essay everything Babel had to say about the doings of the political, military, and state security leaders whom he declared were Stalin's favorites with brilliant careers ahead of them. Of course Babel did not anticipate the forthcoming Great Terror—who could? Still, even without hindsight it is remarkable how mistaken he could be in his assessments of the Soviet leaders he mentioned, virtually all of whom would perish in Stalin's purges. An exception was Babel's old enemy, Semen Budenny, whom Babel declared had already "ceased to exist" in Stalin's eyes, adding the piquant detail that Budenny had murdered his wife and married a bourgeois woman. However irregular Budenny's marital life may have been, rapid advancement would in fact be a constant in his career. Medal after medal, including seven Orders of Lenin, would be festooned across his breast and in 1935 he became one of the first five Marshals of the Soviet Union.

Most of Babel's pronouncements, arising as they did from a miasma of rumor, suggest that where Kremlin politics were concerned he was an innocent, a veritable babe in the taiga.

Babel told several Stalin jokes to Souvarine, among them, this: "Do you know what people were whispering when Stalin went away to stay for three months in the Caucasus, leaving behind all the affairs of state, and especially the economy, in dreadful condition. They whisper '*nasral i uekhal.*'" Souvarine was puzzled by the first word, which was not in his Russian dictionaries, though it is by no means obscure. Babel offered a French translation: "*Il a chié partout et il est parti.*" In English that's "he shat all over the place and then he took off."

Why was Babel driven to tell dangerous jokes and make misguided political pronouncements to Souvarine—a man who was patently more informed and possessed of far better political judgment than he? There was a cocksureness about Babel's behavior in Paris that I found unsettling when, in the mid-1960s, Souvarine unfolded his account to me. Later I came to believe that Babel was marked by the arrogance of his own genius. He was in the grip of a desire to penetrate the purviews of absolute power and—failing that—to pass as an insider, privy to the happenings in an increasingly murderous secret world. When he talked with Souvarine in 1933, before the darkness of the Terror closed upon his country, the purported doings of the Soviet leaders seem to have provided him with something like an entertainment. Certainly he dared not, indeed could not, make use of such material in his art. Not for Babel, the short story writer, were the great leaders, the sweeps of history; he was the miniaturist, the master of the telling detail. Yet he was unrelenting in his attempts to draw near to power, and this would be his undoing.

**AFTER MY PARIS INTERVIEWS** I had to take stock. What I had learned about Babel left too many lacunae. I had to put what I had aside and go on to other things.

Gradually, however, information about Babel became accessible. His daughter Nathalie published many of Babel's letters to his mother and sister, written after they had emigrated to Belgium in the mid-1920s. Antonina Pirozhkova and her assistants collected more than 200 letters Babel had written to people within the Soviet Union. They also managed to locate some unpublished work, mostly sketches, as well as reportage that had appeared in ephemeral journals, all of which was published in two volumes in Moscow in 1990. As it turned out over the years, some Russian scholars, notably the dedicated Usher Spektor, had been quietly collecting materials about Babel. In Moscow two Russian researchers, Sergei Povartsov and Vitalii Shentalinskii, acting separately but with equal pertinacity, sought and ultimately procured an archive containing a key part of Babel's criminal case file. This revealed at last the terrible story of what Babel endured during the eight and a half months that passed from the time of his arrest until his execution in the basement of Lubyanka Prison on January 27, 1940.[11]

The Israeli scholar Efraim Sicher, one of our most devoted Babel specialists, has done the vital, painstaking work of establishing a credible bibliography,[12] as well as publishing two volumes of Babel's stories and early reportage in uncensored or otherwise uncorrupted form. Some of Babel's surviving relations—notably Pirozhkova—gradually came forward with reminiscences. In America, Western Europe, and Russia specialists continue to produce important critical studies of his work.

My imagination has thrived on all this. I resumed my own research and writing in 2000, and I am now completing my biography.

In closing, however, I am obliged to say that much of Babel's life story continues to elude me. I still despair that a biography of this great writer can ever be rendered in the amplitude it deserves.

# 2

## Two Babels—Two Aphrodites
### Autobiography in *Maria* and Babel's Petersburg Myth

GREGORY FREIDIN

### A Merciless Night

"A merciless night" is how Babel opened his story "Chinaman."[1] Datelined "Petrograd 1918" and barely three pages long, it packed all the necessary characters of Babel's central casting: a prostitute combining business and affection; her consort, a debased aristocrat, an emblem of civilization in decline; and completing the trio, a "Chinaman," the girl's customer, whose Russian vocabulary extends no further than the simplest terms of street trade.

In a telegraphic staccato, Babel shows just how unforgiving—and spectacular—all of it was:

A merciless night. Piercing wind. A dead man's fingers sort through Petersburg's frozen guts. Crimson pharmacies freeze on street corners. A pharmacist's well-combed little head droops to the side. The frost seized the pharmacy by its purple heart. And the pharmacy's heart conked out.

On Nevsky, there is not a soul. Ink bubbles pop in the sky. It is two past midnight. A merciless night.[2]

No matter. Soon enough Babel's trio are inside the rooming house where they are treated to homebrew, the Chinese man sates his appetite for sex, the prostitute earns her pound of bread, and the old aristocrat gets to enjoy added value, as he climbs into the girl's bed, vacated by her Chinese customer with whom he had struck a fleeting friendship. Harsh as the night was, the three have survived—and profited in the process. Its pathos deflated—popped like so many "ink bubbles" in the night sky—the story ends with a fitting telegraphic éclat: "Full stop" (*tochka*).

Do not look for a metaphysical truth here, Babel is saying. Rather, just take it for what it is: a terse report on the resilience of the human condition tapped in a modernist Morse code from a leaking but still seaworthy ship.

Babel was at the beginning of his journey.

## A Little Sunshine and a Little Levity: A Long Detour

As late as 1922, Babel planned a collection of such dispatches under the title *Petersburg 1918*,[3] but the project was abandoned in favor of *Red Cavalry* and *The Odessa Stories*. The two cycles made him famous as well as typecast him in the image of their narrator: a Jew, and intellectual, one "with spectacles on his nose and autumn in his heart," for the rest of his life. In these stories, written in 1921–1925, he celebrated humanity in its Rabelaisian aspect, his characters enjoying a colorful, if dangerous, life of excess and abandon. A Southern sensibility, it seemed, had finally vanquished the gloom and doom associated with the northern capital, St. Petersburg. Those aware of his debut in 1916 could have concluded that Babel was making good on the promise he publicized in his short essay "Odessa," part of a regular column he contributed to the Petrograd weekly, *Zhurnal zhurnalov*, in 1916–1917.[4]

Not unlike the young Petersburg poets, the Acmeists, who respectfully rebelled against the Symbolist mentors earlier in the decade,[5] and anticipating the Serapion Brothers of 1922–1923 with their slogan "Go West!,"[6] Babel set himself up in a polite opposition to the revered native elders. In his opinion, Russian literature had overindulged in the "stifling mists" of the Gogolian and Dostoevskian Petersburg—at the expense of the life-affirming sunshine of Gogol's early Ukrainian tales. Babel elaborated his point with youthful gusto and a lapidary precision: "The Overcoat"'s little victim "Akaky Akakievich, in his little modest way but on a frightening scale, cast his shadow over Gritsko," the devil-may-care heartthrob of every lass in Dikanka.

Naturally (pace Harold Bloom), this tussle with the dead founding fathers was a mere prelude. The ultimate target was the living classic himself, Maxim Gorky, at the time Russia's premier author and Babel's generous patron.[7] The author of "Chelkash" and "Twenty Six and One," Gorky championed brute vitality, clarity, and force—Babel allowed as much—and yet, he fell short of what the times demanded. Gorky, according to Babel, was too self-conscious, too tendentious, to be able to reform Russian letters: "Gorky knows why he loves the sun, why it ought to be loved." "It is because of this consciousness," Babel went on, tipping his arrow with Oedipal poison, "that Gorky is but a precursor, often magnificent and mighty, but a precursor nonetheless."

Fashioning himself with unreflective panache as the "literary Messiah from Odessa," the future author of "The King" wished to supersede the "precursor," to reach the world where art—free of any tendency—could reign supreme and be unqualifiedly true. Russian literature, he insisted, needed more light, pure and unalloyed, and there was plenty of it in the "steppes by the Black Sea" (read: where I, Babel, come from) as well as further west (read: Maupassant, my true inspiration).

The sunshine he had in mind, however, had less to do with the comfort and warmth of hospitable Odessa and more to do with the city's bourgeois character and the unblinking stare of Maupassant's prose, much better adapted for peering into the human condition through the appearances and subterfuges of the bourgeoisie, than anything hitherto produced by Russian writers. *Le soleil de midi tombe en large pluie sur les champs*, began Maupassant's "L'aveu," the story that obsessed Babel for years,[8] and, as he spelled it out in his "Odessa," it was this merciless noon sunshine "falling in a generous rain on the fields" that was fated to revitalize—re-fertilize—Russian letters. In case anybody was looking for such a rainmaker, they did not need to look any further: the messiah from Odessa was standing by.

Gorky would no longer suffice, as Babel showed by a mere juxtaposition of the pure artist Maupassant with the politically engagé Gorky. Unable to resist a French syntactical flourish, Babel averred on: "Maupassant, on the other hand—he is, perhaps, not *conscious* of anything, and yet—*perhaps, he knows it all*" [my italics, GF]. Art, Babel declared with the self-confidence of a Nietzschean modernist,[9] was a sufficient and autonomous form and did not require the writer to borrow ideas or values—*consciousness*—from elsewhere. It was art, indeed *ART*, not socialism or ideology, or religious metaphysics, that was the source of heavenly light raining down onto the earth and bringing about its renewal. This was the true religion for a writer; and Babel, along with other big names of his generation, was committing himself to a lifetime of worship in its temple.[10] Pure belles-lettres had their own way of illuminating life whether in Paris or the South of France, as in Maupassant, or in provincial wartime Saratov or Moscow, or even the cold and dark civil-war Petrograd.[11] Babel's early stories, his 1916 debut in *Letopis*, are in keeping with this reading of "L'aveu." Indeed, his entire oeuvre answers to this description.[12]

Inimical to metaphysical bombast, Babel pitched his voice low and, rather than fashioning himself as a Zeus raining down in a golden shower of sunshine on Danae-Russia, presented himself as a Russian Jew from Odessa who visits the blond female residents of Dostoevskian Petersburg (read: Russia) and romances them by offering, not some apocalyptic revelation, but "a little sunshine and a little levity," along with "a lot of sardines in their original tin can" ("Odessa"). He was a bourgeois *homo novus*—in *Odessa Stories*, he would be transformed into the gangster Benya Krik—who was barging in on the declining Russian gentry culture, ready, as he put it in "Odessa," to "refresh her blood."[13]

That was in December 1916. A few months later, the revolution came and wiped the slate clean. In 1918, the road to Russia's future swung to the east and from then on ran through the new Red capital, Moscow. Babel's experience of the Polish campaign of 1920, which put an end to Bolshevism's westward march, and the early years of the New Economic Policy (NEP), a "respite," reshaped both his art and image. His youthful plan to redeem contemporary Russian letters from their quotidian ethnographic realism as well as their excessive Dostoevsky-ism (*Dostoevshchina*) became inconsequential. What took its place was an exploration of the new age in which the earthy pragmatism and skepticism of the NEP combined with the exuberance, violence, and utopian hopes of the world's first socialist revolution. In his *Odessa Stories* and *Red Cavalry*, Babel was still offering the noon sunshine promised in his 1916 manifesto, but now it was blended liberally, and ironically, with the rosy-fingered (or was it bloody-fingered?) dawn of Russia's communist age.

Not everyone was equally impressed with Babel's ideological credentials. Many critics, however, foremost among them Alexander Voronsky, treated Babel's new writings as an acceptance, indeed a celebration, if qualified, of the Bolshevik revolution.[14] Babel did not protest. His 1924 "Autobiography," his sole public statement on the subject, was meant to lend support to such a reading and confirm his pro-Soviet stance.[15] But the 1920s was a dynamic time, and Babel was not standing still. As he continued to evolve, the old Petersburg motifs he was exorcising in his "Odessa" began to surface in his own writings. They did so even before the last traces of the NEP vanished and the Stalin Revolution seized the day.

### Akaky Akakievich Redux

An early sign of this sea change was recorded on June 25, 1925. Babel, at the time perhaps the most talked about author in Soviet Russia, wrote to Gorky that he was having doubts about the worth of his accomplishments to date, that he "had failed to live up to his [Gorky's] expectations," and that he now wished to strike out in a new direction.[16]

Albeit in a private letter, Babel was disowning *Red Cavalry* (the work whose success he had earlier attributed to Gorky's wise guidance) almost a year before it came out as a separate edition! The Oedipal entanglements aside, the *Odessa Stories* did not fare any better. The sun was dimmed for the first time in his movie script *Benya Krik*, and it was nearly turned off in his play *Sunset* (both dating to 1926). Before long, the *Petersburg* malaise began to haunt him with its familiar settings and memories dating back to the twilight years of the old regime, the revolution, and the civil war. His literary exemplars were reshuffled accordingly: the early Gogol was now trumped by the Gogol of the *Petersburg Tales*. In his memoirs, Ilya Ehrenburg recorded Babel's announcement of his change of landmarks.[17] The idea of revising some of the earlier Petersburg sketches in 1929–1932 may have stemmed from this shift, reinforced by the increasing pressure to publish new work that the cultural establishment, charged with organizing production of literary masterpieces, exerted on him in the early 1930s. When in the spring of 1933, Babel found himself at long last enjoying actual sunshine at the Sorrento villa of Maxim Gorky (the erstwhile "precursor"), it was the civil-war Petrograd, freezing and moribund, that he conjured up as a setting for his new come-back in the dramatic genre.

### *Maria*

Briefly, *Maria* is a play in eight scenes (or tableaux, *kartiny*) telling a story about the break-up and demise of an enlightened noble Petersburg family, the Mukovnins. The play begins, however, in a seedy hotel suite belonging to a black-market speculator, Isaac Dymshits, who employs as his salesmen and couriers a team of cripples masquerading as war veterans. In Scene 2, we are told that one of General Mukovnin's two daughters, Maria, has gone over to the Bolsheviks and joined the Budenny Cavalry in time to participate in the Polish campaign (her prototype, to be discussed later in this piece, was Maria Denisova, the original Giaconda of Mayakovsky's *Cloud in Pants* and a propaganda officer in Budenny's Cavalry Army). We learn about her experiences there from her long letter from Poland, written with a Babelian flourish, when it is read out loud in Scene 5 of the play.

The younger daughter, Ludmila, also tries to keep up with the times. She is introduced to Isaac Dymshits by a former Cavalry Guard officer, Viskovsky, an associate of Dymshits and his procurer. Ludmila schemes to have Dymshits abandon his family and marry her; instead, she is raped by Viskovsky who infects her with VD. Soon a gunfight erupts between Viskovsky and his friend Kravchenko, belatedly outraged at Viskovsky for the rape, and the hotel is raided by the police. Ludmila is arrested, and ends up in jail. The General, a Chekhovian bumbling father type, suffers a fatal heart attack when he realizes that Maria, the family's last hope, is not coming back to rescue him and Ludmila from their Petrograd hell.

What comes to Petrograd in the final scene is not Maria but springtime. Now empty of its owners and flooded by sunlight, the Mukovnin apartment receives new tenants: Safonov, "a bony, young, taciturn worker," and his pregnant wife, Elena, a "tall woman and with a small bright face." As part of spring cleaning, a gigantic peasant girl, Nyushka, is washing the windows. As the curtain falls, we hear her singing a few lines from a well-known Cossack ballad dating back to the Russo-Japanese war. The play ends, but Maria Mukovnin, anticipating Godot by a decade and a half, never shows up on stage.[18]

Babel's second and last known play, and the last major new work published in his lifetime, *Maria* has nevertheless attracted little interest from Russian or American scholars.[19] Following the revival of interest in Babel in the late 1950s and 1960s, *Maria* appeared to be a freak—a sop to the Soviet establishment—and it seemed to have no place in the picture of Babel's legacy as it was then imagined by his readers and scholars. My own interest in this play was kindled when I collaborated on a production with my Stanford colleague, Carl Weber, who had for decades dreamed of bringing it to the stage. In the course of this collaboration, it became clear that *Maria* was not only deeply rooted in Babel's oeuvre, but held a key to understanding the last and virtually "silent" decade of his life and career. When approached as an autobiographical allegory, the play begins to radiate its own very special light, illuminating the author's tormented soul, his fears for his future, as well as his misgivings about the course of the Revolution.

I therefore propose to approach *Maria* as an instance of Babel's "autobiographical fiction," as he once referred to his childhood stories,[20] a strategy justified by the deeply autobiographical character of Babel's entire oeuvre.[21] Hence in my discussion here I will treat *Maria* as (1) a play based on Babel's experiences during the civil war, (2) a product of Babel's evolution as an author in the late 1920s and early 1930s, and (3) as an autobiographical *cri de coeur* of an author, citizen, and man facing irreconcilable artistic, political, and personal dilemmas and contradictions.

## Life's Traces: Revolution and Civil War

Like many of Babel's works, *Maria* has powerful autobiographical overtones, including echoes of his most famous adventure during the Polish offensive of April–October 1920. But the background to the play's setting may be traced directly to Babel's sojourn in Petrograd from late February or early March 1918 to the early spring of 1919, when he resided at number 86 on the Prospekt of October 25 (as Nevsky Avenue was rechristened by the Bolsheviks in November 1918 to honor the day they seized power in Petrograd).[22] A good half of *Maria*'s action takes place at that particular venue, one of the grand Yusupov palaces transformed into a seedy residential hotel (today, the building houses the Theater Actors Club). This address was mentioned pointedly by Victor Shklovsky in a sharp critical appreciation of Babel's writings, his 1924 "Isaac Babel: A Critical Romance."[23] Apparently, the exact location of his civil war Petrograd residence mattered a lot to Babel, as he referred to it repeatedly throughout the play. He was making sure, it seems, that whatever else his *Maria* conveyed, it sent a distinct autobiographical message—one that his friends in the early 1930s could hear and one that his readers in posterity would be able to appreciate.

During his residency at Nevsky 86, beginning in late February–early March 1918, Babel seems to have successfully, if oddly, combined two careers: as a translator for the Petrograd Cheka and as a staff writer for the newspaper *Novaya zhizn* (New Life). Just as with the grain-fed leg of pork in the play *Maria*, which Dymshits doubts was actually grain-fed because he was not there to see it, nobody is really sure whether Babel did in fact work for the Cheka or merely claimed to have done so in order to use it as a flag of convenience. But as a reporter for Gorky's *Novaya zhizn*, he had plenty of opportunity to observe the life of civil war Petrograd in all of its aspects—his journalism of those days testifies to that. Unlike the Cheka, *Novaya zhizn* maintained a pointed anti-Bolshevik stance—despite its self-identification as "Social-Democratic" and the exhortation on its masthead for the proletarians of all countries to unite. Babel's first story in it appeared on March 9, 1918; his last, on the July 2 of the same year, right before the paper was shut down by the Bolsheviks, intolerant of a even loyal opposition.[24] Traces of the newspaper's attitude toward the Bolshevik regime, collected in Maxim Gorky's *Untimely Thoughts: Notes on the Revolution and Culture, 1917–1918* and evident in some of Babel's *Novaya zhizn* pieces, can be discerned just below the surface of the play.

In August or September, as we know from his 1918 sketch "Concert at Katerinenstadt,"[25] Babel traveled (either voluntarily or as a draftee) to the Volga region with a food provisioning detachment, which included a team of destitute veteran-amputees. These grotesque invalids would resurface in *Maria* in the form of Dymshits's jolly cripples parleying in Babel's choicest Russian *argot*. After returning to Petrograd in October, Babel fell ill, recovered, worked for the People's Commissariat of Enlightenment,[26] and continued to publish his pieces in the Petrograd paper *Zhizn iskusstva* (Life of Art). He stayed in the city through spring 1919 before leaving in May for Odessa, while it was still under the control of the Reds.[27] He remained in Odessa, working for the local Soviet publishing outfit, Gubizdat, through the summer,[28] or at least until August 9, the day when, according to the family lore, he married Evgeniia Gronfain.[29] Ten days later, the Denikin forces began their six-month-long occupation of Odessa. It is not known whether Babel stayed in Odessa or left it along with the retreating Reds. But he resurfaced in his native city after it was recaptured for good by the Soviets in February 1920.

By then, as Babel stated in his "Autobiography," he had also "served in the Northern Army against Yudenich" (*Sochineniia* 1, 32). The claim appears problematic since there is no other trace of this or any other soldiering experience (he claimed in "Autobiography" to have served on the Rumanian Front in 1917) anywhere in his extant work, except, of course, for his well-known stint with Budenny's Cavalry Army in 1920. Assuming, however, that the claim was authentic, he may have participated in early actions against Yudenich in May (a state of siege was declared in Petrograd on May 1). A more likely story, whether real or made up, is that Babel volunteered for the Northern Army during Yudenich's most famous second and last assault on the city, which began on September 28 and lasted till the final victory of the Reds on November 4, 1919. To have fought against Yudenich in the fall, however, Babel would have had to leave Odessa soon after the date of his marriage to Evgeniia Gronfain, a rather improbable eventuality by the standards of ordinary life but not altogether impossible, given the vicissitudes of the civil war and Babel's association with the Reds before Denikin took over Odessa. In *Maria*, these absences, sudden departures, disappearances, and periods of waiting—"the science of parting" as Mandelstam referred to it in his civil-war poem "Tristia" (1918)—account for much of the play's dramatic tension.

The winter and early spring of 1920 found Babel in Odessa working for the Soviet State Publishing House. It was during these months that Babel and Mikhail Koltsov collaborated on saving Pyotr Pilsky from the Odessa Cheka.[30] A popular journalist and critic, Pilsky knew Babel from the Petrograd days and recalled his encounters with the young "pink-cheeked Russian Maupassant" in his 1929 book of reminiscences and essays.[31]

In April 1920, Babel made his boldest move: with the papers made out in the name of Kirill Vasilyevich Lyutov he began his assignment as a reporter (a propagandist and at times a staff headquarters clerk) for Semyon Budenny's First Cavalry Army. Exempt from the draft in World War I and apparently without any military service or, at least, none worth writing about,[32] Babel, it seems, could not miss his "last chance" for sharing in the defining experience of his generation.

His family had no idea about his plans; afraid that they might prevent him from going, he left home without saying goodbye and returned some six months later after his father had been officially informed of his death and while his wife was looking for him among the wounded.[33] In his *Maria*, Babel recapitulated this leap from the bosom of his family into the world of war and revolution, assigning it, along with his own distinct literary style, to the character of Maria Mukovnin. Her letter from the Polish frontier, read out loud by Maria's cousin, takes up the entire length of Scene 5 and sounds ostensibly just like another story from Babel's own *Red Cavalry* cycle.

## Life's Traces: The First Five-Year Plan

The most piquant aspect of *Maria* is that the eponymous character—much as she is talked about by the other characters in the play, much as they await her imminent arrival in Petrograd—never appears on stage. The weight of her non-presence is so palpable that to some *Maria* appeared as merely a "pre-quel" to what was to be the ultimate *Maria II*.[34] But another explanation for this enigma is also possible. The key dramatic paradox did not only resonate with the tensions of the revolutionary years, with their unpredictable comings and goings. In the late 1920s and the 1930s, Babel was equally famous for his vanishing acts, disappearing from Moscow where he had taken up residence in 1925, and of course, his alleged disappearance from print, his vaunted "silence." Indeed, while *Maria* drew on Babel's experience in and his writings about the Civil War, it was equally, if not more so, implicated in Babel's works and days of the late 1920s and early 1930s.

Many have written about Babel's difficulties with the Soviet cultural and political establishment and its pressures both to conform to the party line in the arts and, more specifically, not to contradict the Cavalry Army myth being constructed at the time by Budenny, Voroshilov, and, indirectly, Stalin. No doubt, Babel chafed under the collar of Soviet censorship and political correctness, made worse by Budenny's attacks on him. Epistolary evidence and contemporary testimony document some of his ordeals.[35] However, he was also subject to stresses of a different sort.

Babel's personal life was becoming increasingly complicated and now demanded great logistical ingenuity as well as access to substantial amounts of money. From 1925 to 1932, he had to maintain his commitments to his mother and sister, who settled in Brussels; closer to home, in Moscow and Leningrad, he had to support, appease, mollify, and somehow manage the tempestuous Tamara Kashirina, who was simultaneously his friend, lover, and the mother of his first child (Emmanuil, renamed Mikhail, born in 1926), and who remained his literary and business agent long after they broke up as a couple.[36] He had to remain loyal, despite his gross infidelity, to his wife, Evgeniya, who left for Paris in 1925. Babel contritely rejoined her in 1927[37] and she bore him his daughter Nathalie in July 1929, a little short of nine months after he returned to Russia. Further, as of the summer of 1932, he had to juggle obligations to his kin in Brussels and Paris with yet another commitment: a budding romance with Antonina Pirozhkova, who later became his de facto wife and bore him his last child, daughter Lydia, early in 1937.

To keep his relationships going with the members of this "extended family" required a lot of energy, ingenuity, and imagination. Then there were the pressures generated by Babel's unrealistic and unrealized commitments to publishers and film studios as well as the impossible financial schemes he resorted to in order to discharge his obligations—real or imagined—to his mother in Brussels, to Tamara Kashirina and their son in Moscow, and to his wife and daughter in Paris. Perhaps no other Soviet author equaled Babel in the art of generating advances on unwritten stories, novels, plays, and film scripts. But sooner or later the time came to pay up, and for Babel, with his literary perfectionism and compulsion to polish a single story for months, the weight of these obligations was hard to tolerate. More than once, he had to face creditors and writs from the court to have his personal property confiscated.[38] At times the pressure was crushing, and Babel would disappear into his hideout in provincial Russia or his Molodenovo collective farm outside Moscow for months at a time. His passion for horses, stud farms (Molodenovo had one), and the world of the races offered, if not escape, then relief from "economic rationality," from his life as a literary moneymaking machine.

## Two Babels

This shuttling between the world of responsibility and the world of spontaneity makes more comprehensible the inner conflict tearing at Babel's personal and professional life. It elucidates one of the polarities of the play: the black-market dealer Isaac Dymshits, a married paterfamilias with a taste for Russian noblewomen at one extreme, and at the other, the idealistic Maria Mukovnin, a fiancée of a Red cavalry commissar. There was not one, there were two Isaac Babels.

One was a writer, a bohemian author of genius who romanced Russian women (Babel's two significant "other women" were not Jewish), who was bound to nothing but his Muse, and who needed to live the life of a vagabond à la Gorky, all in order to gather material and gain inspiration for his writings. His letters to his family and friends abound in his pleas for freedom, for his need to crisscross the country in order to be able to go on with his writing.[39]

But these same family letters point to the other Babel: a responsible, if grossly overtaxed, Jewish *paterfamilias*—husband to his Jewish wife, father to his daughter, devoted son and brother to his mother and sister, and a committed lover to his Russian women, Kashirina and later Pirozhkova, with ideas about constancy and loyalty that were rather old-fashioned for his times and that he, to his great chagrin, often failed to live by. This other Babel had to calculate and plan ahead, to meet deadlines and sign binding contracts. In short, he had to be a proper bourgeois Jew, a faithful offspring of a "tradesman-Jew" (*torgovets-evrei*), as he referred to his father with ostensible infelicity in his brief "Autobiography." For Babel, as for many of his coreligionists, there was, of course, a natural affinity between these two terms, a tradesman and a Jew, as there was for Karl Marx and Babel's older contemporaries Georg Simmel and Werner Sombart.[40] For this Babel, his literary gift, the only possible form of divine grace in the secular age, was nothing but a métier, a trade, namely a way of maintaining—in order of importance—his family, his status, and paying his bills on time.

As the 1920s drew to a close, the writer's mood darkened, and allegories of the inner conflict between the two Babels began to shape his art. The first intimations surfaced in his film script *Benya Krik*, in which he turned his own comical stand-in into a repulsive and greedy gangster receiving his just deserts when a Red Army soldier executes him with a shot to the back of his head. This shift in attitude was elaborated in Babel's first known play, *Sunset* (1926–1927), which dramatized the struggle between Babel's two alter egos: one was the old teamster Mendel Krik, scheming to run away with his young Russian consort, Marusya (*ma Russie*), and to take with him the family cashbox; the other, his gangster son, Benya Krik, now bent on bourgeois propriety and anxious to turn the old-fashioned horse-and-cart outfit into a modern, rationally run concern. Unlike his earlier incarnation in *The Odessa Stories*, the Benya Krik of *Sunset* had all of his Odessa *joie de vivre* leached out of him by a burning passion for respectability and cash. In *Sunset*, Babel was *sunsetting* his colorful, larger-than-life Odessa—the site, as he now saw it, of his illusory dreams.

Because in its style, setting, and cast of characters, *Sunset* is closely tied to *The Odessa Stories* and in a way completes them, the central theme of the play—the morphing of Babel's invented mythical Odessa into the traditionally mythical St. Petersburg—may have been blurred. Now, in his *Maria*, a play set in Petersburg proper, Babel made sure that this other, somber *Petersburg* come out monochromatic and unambiguously sharp. Several autobiographical stories of the early 1930s chart Babel's progress toward this new vision, signaling along the way the taming of *Red Cavalry* spirit and the demise of Babel's carnivalesque Odessa myth.

## The Flinty Road to *Maria*:
## Babel's Petersburg Mythologies

Three autobiographical stories are of particular relevance to *Maria*: "The Road," "The Ivan-and-Maria," and "Guy de Maupassant." All take Petrograd as either their setting, destination, or point of departure; all were published in quick succession (March, April, and June 1932) in a popular illustrated monthly, *30 dnei*, edited by Babel's journalist friend from the Petrograd days, Vasilii Aleksandrovich Reginin (Rapoport). All three bear the authorial date linking them to Babel's sojourn in wartime and revolutionary Petrograd. Two of them, in fact, have clear antecedents in Babel's publications of the early period. Whether intentionally or intuitively, Babel was laying the foundation for a Petersburg myth of his own. Without these pieces, his *Maria* would be as incomprehensible as *Sunset* would have been without the *Tales of Odessa*.

The first of these, "The Road," shares elements of the setting with the sketch "Evening at the Empress's (From the Petersburg Diary)" in which Babel recounted his visit to the Anichkov Palace in Petrograd some time in the spring of 1918, but without the agonistic tension and complexity of its later counterpart.[41] In its magazine publication, Babel dated "The Road" "1920–1930," referring to the time of composition since the story itself is set in 1917–1918. The second of the three stories, "The Ivan-and-Maria," recalled "Concert at Katerinenstadt," a report on a Petrograd food procurement expedition to the upper Volga, published in *Zhizn iskusstva* in November 1919; it, too, was signed with the dates indicating the beginning and the end of its revisions: "1920–1928." The action of the third story unfolded in Petrograd in the winter of 1916, when Babel wrote his essay "Odessa," an appreciation, among other things, of his French idol, Guy de Maupassant. Like the other two pieces, "Guy de Maupassant" was dated "1920–1922," clearly pointing to the time of its composition, though it is hard to believe that Babel was all of a sudden publishing a decade-old story (no earlier versions have survived). Possibly, some earlier idea for this story was revived when Babel worked as editor and translator on the three-volume edition of Maupassant in 1926–1927. Be that as it may, Babel did not always sign his stories with dates, and the fact that he did in this case indicates a deliberate strategy. The dates emphasize a continuity between Babel's "Petersburg" period, roughly 1916–1919, and the newly "revised" Babel of the late 1920s and early 1930s. Wearied of his association with Odessa, it seems, Babel wished to appear as the author of several new *Petersburg* stories. *Maria*, in turn, was supposed to flow naturally out of Babel's newly updated *Petersburg* oeuvre, just as *Sunset* had issued out of *The Odessa Stories.*

"The Road" is framed as a memoir about the author's arrival in Petrograd in 1918—controversial in 1931 because of Babel's work for *Novaia zhizn*—and articulates his *current* apprehensions about his future as a writer. The story is told in the first person and belongs to what Babel defined oxymoronically as "autobiographical prose fiction." Following the "disintegration of the front" (the Rumanian Front, as it would appear from his "Autobiography"[42]), the young author travels from his native Odessa to Petrograd through the unforgiving landscape of the Russian civil war, narrowly escapes death at the hands of a roving band of Jew-hating marauders, miraculously avoids amputation from frostbite, and finally reaches his appointed destination. Some of the details of his arrival in Petrograd, including a strip search of the vodka smugglers (*Sochineniia* 2:233), are transposed to Scene 1 of *Maria* to be voiced by Dymshits's invalid "mules" (*meshochniki* or bagmen). Once in Petrograd, the exhausted narrator of "The Road" nearly freezes to death but is ultimately rescued by an old army friend now working for the Cheka, the organization where the narrator finds "life-long friends" and employment as a translator.

Read by someone unaware of Babel's reputation as a writer, the story may be taken for just another heroic Soviet tale about a Jewish lad from Odessa who finally fulfills his destiny by joining the Cheka. But Babel was a famous author, and what implicitly propels the narrator toward Petrograd in "The Road" is his desire to realize his vocation as a writer, "to conquer Petersburg." Lest we miss his point, Babel had the narrator, in a semi-delirium from cold and exhaustion, compare himself to a mediaeval Jewish poet who perished within the sight of Zion:

"So goes the imperative of conquering St. Petersburg," I thought and strained to recall the name of the man, who was crushed by the hooves of Arab horses at the very end of his journey. It was Yehuda Halevi. (*Sochineniia* 2:204)

The editor-in-chief of *30 dnei*, Babel's old friend, Vasilii Reginin, must have winced at the implied analogy between Halevi's fate and that of the author, who was under attack by General Budenny, the Soviet cavalryman-in-chief. But a new story by the parsimonious Babel was a real coup, and Reginin, well aware of Babel's work for *Novaya zhizn*, let it pass. He had weathered worse. Once, he even allowed himself to be locked up in a cage with tigers in order to increase his magazine circulation,[43] and now he was riding the wave, with a sensational publication of a story by the "silent" Babel, not to mention the serialization of *The Golden Calf* by the Odessans Ilya Ilf and Evegeny Petrov. Thus Babel was able to cover up his work for Gorky's newspaper and at the same time stress his loyalty to the new regime, even as he conveyed, through ingenious circumlocution and allegory, the sense of danger he now associated with his career as a Soviet writer.

Budenny's latest attack on him, published in *Pravda* on October 26, 1928, took issue with Gorky's praise of the author of *Red Cavalry* as a Soviet Gogol. Coming at a time when Gorky was becoming a state cult figure in the Soviet Union, it had to have the highest sanction, namely that of Stalin himself. And it would have been typical of Stalin first to unleash Budenny and then come to the defense of his friend Gorky, thereby creating a good impression among the intelligentsia and indebting Gorky to himself.[44] Initially merely amused by Budenny's vituperation,[45] Babel soon took a more somber view of this assault. Perhaps, as he came to understand Stalin's machinery better, he realized that he had every reason to be concerned for his future in Soviet Russia.[46]

That Gorky's specter hovered over the story, not only by his glaring absence, becomes apparent if "The Road" is juxtaposed with Babel's mini-memoir, "Commencement" (*Nachalo*), published in 1938, in which Babel recalled his first encounter with his future patron and protector in the fall of 1916, after Gorky had accepted his stories for publication in *Letopis*.

"Nails can be small," he said, "and they can be big—as big as my finger." And he raised his slender finger, sculpted so powerfully and gently, to my eyes. "A writer's path, my dear *pistol*" (he stressed the "o"), "is strewn with nails, for the most part, large ones. You'll have to walk on them barefoot, and there will be a lot of blood; with every year the flow of it will increase."[47]

In 1932, Babel had every reason to appreciate Gorky's foresight. Having barely survived Budenny's threats, Babel had to withstand another attack on him in July 1930 for allegedly giving an anti-Soviet interview on the French Riviera. It was then that he asserted his loyalty by invoking his service in the Cheka beginning as early as October 1917—an intentional exaggeration or perhaps a Freudian slip uttered by a man whose whereabouts at the time of the Bolshevik coup d'état are to this day shrouded in mystery.[48] Although the interview turned out to be fabricated and Babel managed to clear his name formally, the air of political scandal continued to cling to him requiring further action. The nails that Gorky had warned Babel about were getting bigger and sharper, too.

"The Road" develops this theme—authorship as martyrdom in the cause of truth—by using analogies and substitutes, and transposing them to the allegorical plane. Addressing those who have ears, Babel touches the familiar chords of the Russian mythology of literary authorship with a subtle allusion to Mikhail Lermontov's famous reworking of Hamlet's "sleep" soliloquy: "Alone, I step out onto the road/Before me sparkles the flinty way" (Выхожу один я на дорогу, / Предо мной кремнистый путь блестит). Osip Mandelstam did the same in his 1924 "Ode on Slate" (Грифельная ода). He re-articulated Lermontov's lines—"the flinty way from the old song"—picking up the poetic relay as one who has lived through the ordeal of the civil war and borne witness to the Russian Revolution, albeit the way Doubting Thomas bore witness to the resurrection of Christ: "And I, too, wish to thrust my hand/Into the flinty way from the old song . . ." (И я хочу вложить персты / В кремнистый путь из старой песни).[49] Babel joined this conversation, offering his own version of Lermontov's "flinty way."

Unlike Mandelstam in his lofty exaltation atop a mountain peak, Babel characteristically took the low road—one running under the oppressively low skies and strewn with disemboweled, frozen carcasses of horses:

The Milky Way of the Nevsky Avenue flowed into the distance. The corpses of dead horses marked it like milestones. Their raised legs held up the sky that had dropped low. Picked clean, their bellies sparkled.

Lermontov's distant stars were now flickering in the gaping empty bellies of frozen nags.[50] Such was the road that led Babel's alter ego to the Anichkov Palace on Nevsky, where Ivan Kalugin, his old army friend and now a Cheka officer, let him rest and treated him to a warm bath (a baptism of sorts[51]), plenty of horse meat, and fabulous Turkish cigarettes. The latter were a gift from the last absolute ruler of the Ottoman empire (deposed in 1910) to Alexander III of Russia, a physical giant, whose enormous gown was now wrapped around the diminutive narrator, a native of the area once ruled by the Ottomans. Babel was choosing his luminous details well.

Now, again only obliquely, Babel begins to draw an extended analogy between himself and another traveler, this time not Yehuda Halevi, but the previous owner of the palace, the Danish princess Dagmar. Like the story's narrator, she too had come from afar—a proverbial "stranger," in Georg Simmel's striking phrase, "who came yesterday and stayed tomorrow."[52] Princess Dagmar sailed from her warm and cozy Copenhagen to the unforgiving city of Peter to become the wife of Alexander III, Empress of Russia Maria Fedorovna, the mother of Russia's next and, as it turned out, last tsar. She lived long enough to learn that her issue, her "birthing blood," as Babel referred to the royal family, "fell on the merciless granite of St. Petersburg."

The story was meant for publication in Stalin's Russia of 1932, and for obvious reasons Babel chose not to spell out the horrors of the murder of the royal family, but any reader his age or older would have picked up the chilling clue at once. Hounded by Budenny, pressed by his editors, threatened with evisceration by the censors, and barely able to clear his name from the accusations of betrayal, the "wise rabbi" Babel, as Ilya Eherenburg once called him, was still able to wonder in his published story whether his own "children"—the literary legacy of the stranger who came yesterday and stayed tomorrow—were destined to share the fate of Maria Fedorovna's murdered sons.

At the same time, Babel had other fish to fry. The story was meant to reaffirm—in as forward a manner as possible—Babel's credentials as a writer loyal to the regime. The ending, which has rubbed so many readers the wrong way, is where Babel trumpets his message. With Moisei Uritsky's personal approval, the narrator, Babel's alter ego, is hired as a "translator attached to the Foreign Department" (*Inostrannyi otdel*) of the Cheka with the assignment to "translate testimony given by diplomats, arsonists [*podzhigateli*, GF], and spies" (*Sochineniia* 2:206). Arsonists? The presence of these arsonists who, for some reason, chose to give their testimony in a foreign language lends the sentence the air of unreality. What makes it even more suspect is that there was no "Foreign Department" in the Cheka until December 1920.[53] These two gratuitous details cast the whole "recollection" under suspicion. Neither Babel nor his editor seem to have been interested in fact-checking, which was par for the course, given Babel's statement in 1930 that he started working for the Cheka in October 1917—two months *before* the Cheka was decreed into existence.[54]

Of course, the story ends with a happy Babel.[55] The narrator finds employment as a Cheka translator, gets a uniform, food ration cards, a job, and—Babel's enemies, beware!—"comrades, loyal in friendship and death, comrades like no other comrades anywhere in the world except in our country."[56] He did indeed have powerful friends, some in the Cheka. God forbid anyone should bring up the issue of Babel's writing for his friend Gorky's *Novaia zhizn*!

But it is the next (and last) sentence of the story that sounds utterly preposterous, a summing up of Babel's career since 1918: "Thus, began my life, full of thought and merriment." "Thought," not writing, should already put one on guard. "Merriment" is the last thing that comes through in Babel's private correspondence, filled with whining and moaning, even when he tried to put up a brave face.[57] Those aware of Babel's vicissitudes must have taken this coda for one of Babel's jocular, sarcastic mystifications. Clearly, the ending was tacked-on and only amplified two tragic analogies that the narrator drew to his own, by then increasingly torturous career as a Soviet writer—a stranger from the sunny bourgeois Odessa, who came yesterday to the old-regime St. Petersburg, soon turned into the revolutionary Petrograd, and stayed tomorrow in what had become Stalin's Moscow. The Anichkov Palace "baptism" created strange affinities but the writer's otherness was neither redeemed nor washed off: Hired as a "translator," he remained a mediator, a go-between.

IN THE SECOND STORY of this "Petersburg" cycle, "The Ivan-and-Maria" (based on "Concert at Katerinenstadt," 1918), Babel recalls his encounter with a larger-than-life Russian character who seems to have stepped out of Gorky's catalogue of colorful provincial types (the steamboat cook M. A. Smury from *My Apprenticeship* comes to mind).[58] In the story, Babel travels with a food procurement expedition to the German colony in the Volga region. The expedition includes a team of cripples, who enjoy sharing in the relative prosperity and peace of the region and whom Babel would soon transplant into *Maria* as Isaac Dymshits's cripples smuggling foodstuffs and other valuables through the civil-war checkpoints.

In the story, the narrator, Babel's alter ego, meets a remarkable steamboat captain who ferried ammunition for the Red Army detachments. An expansive Russian type, this captain is on a drinking binge and uses up the boat's precious fuel for a dangerous nighttime run for more spirits. He succeeds but ends up paying for his transcendent binge. His brains splatter the wheels of a peasant cart as he is shot by a Red commander for wasting army fuel. Having set the sun on his own high-spirited Jewish bandit Benya Krik, Babel was now drawing the curtain on Gorky's eccentric Russian misfits.

Back in 1915, Gorky made a big splash with his essay "Two Souls," contrasting the *yin* of Russian culture, its two souls—that of a dreamy Oriental and a volatile anarchic Slav—with the "Occidental" *yang*, with its cult of reason and purposeful action.[59] Babel's "The Ivan-and-Maria," in Russian *Ivan-da-Mari'a* (a field plant that combines violet and yellow flowers), echoes Gorky's thought and transposes it, allegorically, onto the Stalinist drive for industrialization meant to wrench Soviet Russia out of its traditional ways and transform it into a modern productive economy on a par with the urban and industrial West. Only those who are rational and disciplined—the story's "Germanic" Lett Larson and the Red merchant Sergei Malyshev—would be allowed to survive in Soviet Russia. The juxtaposition of the brain-splattered wheel (no doubt, the wheel of history) and a cheerful report on the success of grain procurement offered much food for thought (without too much merriment) for the Soviet reader in 1932. And the very idea of decoupling, better, purging, "Ivan" from "Maria," of eliminating one color of the flower from the plant that naturally sprouts two, would be developed further in the play *Maria*.

**THE FINAL STORY OF THE CYCLE**, "Guy de Maupassant" (1932), is set in the Petrograd winter of 1916 when the budding author is hired to help an amateur translator of Maupassant—a rich young Jewess married to a financial magnate, Bendersky[60]—to edit her translations for publication. Babel, of course, was involved in editing and translating Maupassant's collected works in 1926–1927, but the job as a shadow editor that his narrator contracts for also resembles Babel's main moonlighting trade as a script doctor and, since the emergence of sound, a writer of film dialogue for movies throughout the 1930s.[61] The regular editorial sessions of the two over Maupassant's volumes culminate one night in what readings of this sort have often culminated in since Paolo and Francesca—a mutual seduction. In the dead of winter, the two admirers of Maupassant became intoxicated by the lusty sunshine of his story "L'aveu." United in their passion for literature, and aided by a good, very good, wine (bottled sunshine, as the saying goes) from the banker's cellars, the translator and the editor collapse into each other's arms.

Maupassant's "L'aveu," it may be recalled, is about the simple, if greedy, peasant girl Céleste's regular trips to market for which she dutifully pays her coachman until one day the coachman allows her to keep her fare in exchange for a little sex. More trips lead to more savings until

Céleste gets pregnant, and is disgraced and ruined for life. Quite the opposite, it seems, happens to Babel's autobiographical narrator: he receives good money for his editorial magic and on top of that gets to make love, magically without consequences, to an attractive married woman. But as Babel's story draws to a close, the narrator learns that the invigorating sunshine of "L'aveu" did in fact exact a toll on the commercially and in every other way successful French author. After Maupassant's many trips to the literary marketplace, and many yachts and houses later, he died, as the narrator learns from his biography, a raving syphilitic. "I felt touched by a presage of initiation into a mystery," Babel concludes the story gravely, leaving us guessing what this mystery is all about.

The answer to the puzzle is, of course, simple enough: for a writer, as for the poor and quite earthly Céleste, there is no free ride. Publishing this story ten years after the putative date of its composition was a symbolic announcement by the "Russian Maupassant" that it was time for *him* to pay up. The bills were coming due for Babel.

## Extending Credit:
## Revising *The Odessa Stories* and *Red Cavalry*

Other stories written and published around the same time, even though unconnected to St. Petersburg, sounded a similar note. Set in Odessa, "Karl-Yankel" (1931) is the thinly veiled story of Babel's bereavement over the loss of his son, who had been adopted by Kashirina's new husband, the writer Vsevolod Ivanov. As Kashirina confirmed in her memoirs, the son Mikhail was forbidden by Ivanov to have any contact with his father.[62] The story came out in July 1931, the month of Babel's and Mikhail's birthdays (they were born on the same day, thirty-two years apart), and should be read as an ironic and melancholy farewell to Babel's sole male progeny. Suffice it to say that the serendipitous appearance in the story of a Kirghiz woman, who volunteers enthusiastically to nurse the baby Karl-Yankel at her own breast, referred the knowing reader to Ivanov's "Dityo" ("Babe," 1921), a story emblematic of the debut of this other protégé and friend of Maxim Gorky. An unabashed Soviet activist, the story's Kirghiz woman takes over the baby after the real mother faints from the stress of the absurd trial. What the Kirghiz woman says indicates that the child will be taken away from his mother: "With us, he will become an airman, he will fly under the skies . . ." Ivanov, who had adopted Babel's son Mikhail, could not have missed Babel's ironic dig. The Red soldiers from Ivanov's story who adopt the child of a couple they have just slain use the same utopian language: "With us, he'll grow up, and he'll fly to the moon . . ." As in the case of "The Road," the optimistic ending Babel tacks onto "Karl-Yankel" sounds hollow—too hollow to drown out the absurdities and cruelties of Soviet life that are the subject of this story about a wrenching discontinuity between the present and the past.[63]

In the 1932 story "The End of the Alms House," the old men feeding off the tips and bribes at Odessa's Jewish cemetery, the same characters who once provided Babel with the colorful material for his gangster tales, are packed away and taken from their familiar haunts to a Soviet retirement home. As the title suggests, neither the old shammes Arye-Leib (both words mean "lion"), nor the writer who made a career out of rendering his oral tales into published stories, can any longer make a living off the city's past glories and its myths. The jolly old Odessa that Babel had invented was now being mothballed and sent into retirement.

A similar theme of grudging accommodation and genuine grief over loss sounds in "Froim Grach" (1933), a new story, which, like "The End of the Alms House," was linked to the Odessa cycle but remained unpublished in Babel's lifetime. In "Froim Grach," Babel returned to the spring–summer of 1919, when he himself was probably back in Odessa, to tell a story about the demise of the second most exotic figure of his Jewish gangster tales. In the earlier *Odessa Stories*, in which Benya Krik functioned as Babel's alter ego, the allegorical prototype for Grach was none other than Maxim Gorky himself, which links this story to "The Ivan-and-Maria" (discussed above).[64] "Froim Grach" may have belonged or been related to Babel's unrealized or lost Cheka cycle.[65] Written in the third person, rare for Babel, and exuding the chill of distance from what was his signature in *Tales of Odessa*, "Froim Grach" demystifies none other than Babel's Benya Krik, exposing him as a sham. Apparently, his reputation as the king of Odessa gangsters was just a show for the uninitiated: "Borovoi [an Odessan working for the Cheka, *GF*] told them that it was the one-eyed Froim Grach, not Benya Krik, who was the true leader of the forty thousand Odessa thieves. He concealed his game from the outside eyes but everything played out according to the old man's schemes." While Borovoi (possibly one of Babel's Odessa Cheka friends from 1919—the story is written in the third person) revels in his own tales of Odessa gangsters, his new boss dispatched from Moscow, Vladislav Siemen (Simen), arranges for Froim Grach, unarmed and unsuspecting, to be *liquidated* in the back yard of the Odessa Cheka. Borovoi discovers Froim's body next to a "wall covered in ivy" after he had been shot by two Red soldiers, peasants with no idea of whom they had executed, one of them still in awe of Froim's physical strength.

Like Malyshev, Larson, and Makeyev in "The Ivan-and-Maria" Siemen is the new unsentimental, rational type, sent to introduce systematic recordkeeping in the Odessa Cheka and put an end to its "romantic" attitude toward executions, for which it was notorious,[66] as well as any romanticizing of Odessa's notorious criminal class. Bowing to the tradition that went back to, at least, Ivan Goncharov's *Oblomov* with his *Stolz*, in which a Russian of German blood stands, to borrow a phrase, for a "Protestant ethic and spirit of capitalism," Babel's Siemen sees no place in the Soviet future for the mythic figures of Odessa's history, nor does he think that it is wise for others to be curious about such things. Babel concurred—reluctantly—in the third person, a voice untypical of his writing.

*Red Cavalry*, too, was brought into line. The 1932 novella "Argamak," not "The Rabbi's Son," now concluded the civil war cycle and radically altered the book's trajectory. In "Argamak," the familiar bespectacled narrator, Babel's alter ego Lyutov, comes by chance into possession of a prize steed. But he is an unskilled rider, causing horrible sores on the animal's back and practically destroying it; worse, he begins to draw to himself the angry stares of Cossacks sensing in him a stranger. Feeling ashamed, tormented by guilt, and frightened, he gives up Argamak; in return he gets a docile mare that he soon learns to ride well; at long last, he blends in with the Cossacks. The author, it appears, was trading the Pegasus of his *Red Cavalry* inspiration for a tame mount—all for the sake of what sociologists call passing!

In a way, Babel was closing his books, and at the same time, paradoxically, thematizing his retreat from his ideals in his own new writings. The setting had to be old: by 1932, he surely must have despaired of ever seeing his collectivization stories in print (Stalin preferred Sholokhov to "our slippery Babel"[67]), but his lyric voice as well as the story's allegorical plane stayed current. Even somewhat fragmented and fragmentary, his Petersburg oeuvre became a vehicle for his ambivalent attitude toward the times, and *Maria* appears to be the summation and culmination of this cycle. This was a dangerous strategy, as it went against the "social command" or, better, orders issued from on high to depict the Five-Year Plan.

But in the frantic world of the Stalin revolution, output counted for a lot: the stories bought time and extended credit.

## *Maria*: Topography and Character in Babel's Petersburg

From the very opening of *Maria*, Babel cranks up the tension between his two autobiographical extremes by giving each a different street address. Economic rationality, with its Jewish "accent"—Isaac Dymshits—resides at the hotel at Nevsky 86 and traffics in all manner of commodities through his team of grotesque invalids. The all-too-Russian unrealistic, romantic dreamers—the members of General Mukovnin's family—inhabit an old-fashioned apartment on Millionnaya, across the street from the great Hermitage and the Winter Palace.

For a reader sensitive to Babel's lifelong, quasi-autobiographical project, it is not hard to recognize in *Isaac* Dymshits a distillation of *Isaac* Babel's own authorial persona—a writer who became a commercial success through his stories about all manner of twisted and debased humanity. Babel's 1918 sketch, "Concert in Katerinenstadt," and his more elaborate 1932 version of it, "The Ivan-and-Maria," lend support to this reading. "Two weeks ago," he wrote in November 1918,

I arrived in Katerinenstadt with unusual people, I arrived with some cripples. We organized them in Petersburg into a food procurement detachment and departed in search of bread from the Volga [German] colonies.[68]

The scheme, though not predatory, was akin to that devised by the character of *Isaac* Dymshits, who shared with Babel both a first name and a place of residence at Nevsky 86. The similarities do not end there. Dymshits's family situation (his wife and children live elsewhere, out of harm's way) and his attraction to gentile women have striking parallels with Babel's own life.

At the other end of Petrograd's main artery, on Millionnaya street—opposite the Hermitage (the world of high art) and the Winter Palace (the old regime), Babel placed the Mukovnins, an old-style, noble intelligentsia Russian family, and their entourage: General Mukovnin, his daughters Ludmila and the now-absent Maria, their cousin Katya Veltsen, the old nanny, and Maria's old lover manqué, Prince Golitsyn. Crushed by the Revolution and now in rapid decline, the Mukovnins and their circle still cling to aspects of Dostoevskian spirituality (Golitsyn and Katya), Russian

Populist penitence before the people, Russian nationalism of the Change-of-Landmarks type (the General is happy to collaborate with the Bolsheviks for the sake of the country), cultural refinement (a taste for ballet at the Mariinsky), and of course book culture and learning (Mukovnin, like his prototype, General Aleksei Ignatiev, is writing a history of the abuses against the lower ranks in the imperial army).[69] Underneath it all, there is the Mukovnins' fervent desire not just to survive but to find a worthy place in the new world.

The two Mukovnin daughters, Ludmila and Maria, choose different strategies for moving with the times. Here Babel employs a familiar Greek dichotomy. Ludmila is a twentieth-century version of Aphrodite Pandemos (Ludmila, that is, to people's liking, popular), takes the low road, and is willing to sell herself to a rich and unsavory Jew. The other is her heavenly counterpart, Aphrodite Urania, who prefers the high road and, like Babel, joins Budenny's Red Cavalry. An approximate Christian equivalent of the Greek Aphrodite Urania is the New Testament Mary of Martha and Mary, hence the title of the play. The fact that Maria Mukovnin never shows up in the play serves only to emphasize her identification with the celestial Aphrodite Urania. The nomenclature of Babel's play seems to echo Maupassant's ironically bestowing the heavenly name Céleste upon the all-too materialist milkmaid of "L'aveu."

The Mukovnin family name, derived from *muki*, the Russian for "torment," confirms their socio-historical type as members of the intelligentsia with its cult of martyrdom and amplifies the torments they experience in the crucible of the revolution. By settling on this name, Babel, it seems, wished his audience to associate the play with Aleksey Tolstoy's famous civil-war trilogy, *Khozhdenie po mukam* (somewhat misleadingly translated as *Road to Calvary*). It, too, revolves around the fate of two sisters; and its first installment, *Sisters* (1921), like Babel's *Maria*, was written abroad. *Sisters* served as proof of Tolstoy's loyalty to the new regime when he returned to Soviet Russia from emigration in 1923. The title of Tolstoy's trilogy as well as the Mukovnin name in Babel's play strongly echo the popular apocryphal "Descent of the Mother of God to Hell" (literally, "walking through torments"). In the "Descent," Maria Mother of God comforts the sinners and pleads successfully before her Son to grant the sinners some respite. In a subtle allusion to this tale, the entire Mukovnin household is condemned to the living hell of the 1920 Petrograd. Their only hope is to be saved by the family's favorite child, Maria, a strong, de-

cent, beautiful woman who incarnates the Russian intelligentsia's pure romance of the Revolution. But they wait for her in vain. The divine Maria
never appears and only sends an emissary with a spare pair of boots—a
signal to the family to get packing and go, most likely, into emigration.

This scene, along with the death of General Mukovnin, who expires
realizing that he would never see his beloved Maria, has strong autobiographical overtones. Babel was in Moscow in May 1924 when he heard the
news of his father's illness, and he returned to Odessa too late to say goodbye or even participate in the funeral. This experience apparently haunted
him, and he had tried to assimilate it into his art, although unsuccessfully,
in his unfinished novel *The Jewess* (Evreika). *Maria* offered another opportunity, and Babel made use of it, interweaving several personal motifs:
his abandoning his family in 1920 to join Budenny's forces in the manner
of Maria Mukovnin, an homage to his late father, who, like the General,
never adjusted to the new world,[70] and finally his own conviction (at least
in 1933) that his family was better off outside Soviet Russia, notwithstanding all of his letters to the contrary.[71]

The people of Babel's milieu, whether they were aware of his personal
circumstances or not, had no trouble recognizing in the character of Maria
a version of Babel's own authorial persona—an old-world intellectual redeemed by the Revolution—an image that Babel assiduously cultivated
with the appearance of *Red Cavalry*. Dymshits and Maria, then, define the
play's opposite poles, embodying two conflicting and/or complementary
aspects of what it meant for Babel to be a writer—a person called upon to
combine transcendence with commerce. This was not dissimilar to Babel's
other favorite professional type—the prostitute—who combined romance
and profit. The play was a melancholy meditation of a desperate man. In
1933, approaching forty and still unable to make a choice in his personal
life, Babel was haunted by the thought of never repeating his coup of the
mid-1920s, when *Red Cavalry* and *The Odessa Stories* brought him to the
apex of fortune and fame.

### *Maria*: Paying Off Old Debts

Rooted as *Maria* is in Babel's anecdotes of civil-war Petrograd,[72]
there are strong indications that Babel may have conceived the play late
in 1929, prompted by Vladimir Mayakovsky, in anticipation of the tenth
anniversary of Budenny's First Cavalry Army (more on this below). If so,

he was soon preempted by Vsevolod Vishnevsky, who fulfilled his "social command" by producing the play *The First Cavalry Army* in time for the anniversary and in accordance with the script of Budenny and his coterie. Babel, however, did not give up the idea. According to Babel's letter to Solomon Mikhoels, his good friend and the head of the State Jewish Theater, Babel had received an advance on the play, produced some unsatisfactory drafts, and was postponing further work until he could finish a cycle of stories.[73] Another letter (hitherto unpublished), addressed to actor and director Vasily Vasilyevich Kuza, the deputy chair of the Vakhtangov Theater Artistic Council, speaks directly of Babel's continued attempts to finish the play in January 1932:

Dear V. V., if I do not arrive at your theater at the end of February with a finished play, then it means nothing has worked out. I simply won't have enough strength to continue working on it any further. Let's give it one last try. Yours, I. B.[74]

Nothing came of it, it seems, until Babel's arrival at Gorky's villa in Sorrento in April 1933. There, away from his family and enjoying Gorky's hospitality, he wrote the first full draft of *Maria* in the space of two weeks (something similar happened to him with his other play, *Sunset*, in 1926).

What ten years earlier Alexey Tolstoy's novel *Sisters* did for Tolstoy, *Maria* was to do for Babel—serve as his "return ticket" to the USSR. In September 1932, he finally wrested from the Politburo permission to travel to France for two months, ostensibly in order to collect his wife and daughter and bring them back to the USSR.[75] He had now overstayed his allotted two months by another five, lending credence to the rumors then rife in Moscow that he was planning to settle abroad for good, perhaps in the manner of a "loyal émigré" like Evgeny Zamyatin, who had been granted this dispensation by Stalin himself. Whether or not he entertained such plans seriously, by the time Babel arrived in Sorrento, he had decided to go back to the Soviet Union and felt it in his interest to have something new and substantive to show for his overextended stay abroad. His generous host Gorky must have thought so, too.

In the spring and summer 1932, Gorky repeatedly interceded on Babel's behalf before Kaganovich and Stalin[76] when Babel's request for permission to go to France was being blocked. We now know that the culprit was Stalin, then enjoying his long vacation in the South. It was only after Stalin's arrival in Moscow, at the end of August 1932, that Babel was miraculously waved through, receiving his permission to travel on

September 3, 1933. Stalin liked to play the role of the intelligentsia's bene-factor, and the timing was meant to put Babel and Gorky on notice that the author of the miracle was none other than Stalin himself. Eight months later, long after the deadline of the allowed two months,[77] it was payback time. Babel, of course, had more than one outstanding item on his Soviet account books. *Maria* was supposed to cancel some of these debts and, in a manner of speaking, to extend his credit as a bona fide Soviet writer.

Babel's biggest liability was his diminished literary output at a time when the whole country, including members of the literary and artistic elite, was mobilized for the First Five-Year Plan. A play, especially a suc-cessful play, could help discharge his writerly obligation. Another weighty debt was owed to the Red Cavalry Commander, Semyon Budenny. *Maria* was supposed to convey a long overdue conciliatory gesture to a powerful critic as well as his superior, Kliment Voroshilov, Stalin's trusted civil war comrade-in-arms and since 1925 People's Commissar of Defense. Both Budenny and Voroshilov had high ambitions to lead the armed forces of the new state and ever since the end of the civil war—especially since the ouster of their former nemesis, Leon Trotsky, in 1927—both had been concocting a heroic legend and linking it to Stalin's progressively inflated civil war record. They could not forgive Babel for presenting them in his *Red Cavalry* for who they were—brave and inspiring leaders of a ragtag Cossack army, but also, like their men, uneducated and crude. It mattered little that Babel never intended to diminish their valor—nothing short of a legend would do. With its runaway success at home and abroad, Babel's *Red Cavalry* was for them a public relations disaster.

Worse still, *Red Cavalry*, which began with a victory and ended in retreat, told the story of one of the biggest fiascos of the war, the Soviet defeat in the Polish campaign, in which Stalin may have played an invidi-ous role when he disobeyed orders to have Budenny's army link forces with Mikhail Tukhachevsky's outside Warsaw. This episode threatened to undermine Stalin's military credentials and irked him enough for him to order the evidence destroyed.[78] Babel had to be aware of the controversy, but in 1925–1926, when he was putting the finishing touches on *Red Cavalry*, the artistic integrity of the cycle must have overridden other considerations. He concluded the story "The Rabbi's Son" with the ugly rout of Soviet forces as its setting. In the late 1920s and 1930s, when Sta-lin and his supporters were trumpeting the myth of his martial prowess, Babel's *Red Cavalry* was bound to rub the wrong way. Indeed, they would have crushed Babel despite his international acclaim and forced him into emigration had it not been for Gorky's powerful protection. For his part, Babel, who had little interest in joining the fray, and even less in adjudicating military appointments, tried to mend fences—but never in such an elaborate fashion as he did in *Maria*.

### *Maria*—Denisova

Well-placed veterans of the Polish campaign of 1920 (and there were many) would have easily guessed that Maria Mukovnin, the eponymous protagonist of the play, was, in part, modeled on her namesake Maria Denisova—a famous Odessa beauty and the original inspiration (the "Giaconda") for Mayakovsky's great love epic, *Cloud in Pants*.[79] A modern, independent woman with strong leftist convictions and, apparently, a young illegitimate daughter, Denisova studied sculpture and art in Switzerland during World War I until the Swiss expelled her as a political undesirable in 1919. Back in Russia, she joined what was to become Budenny's First Cavalry Army. Like Babel, she worked for the army's Political Department, designing posters and conducting political education classes among the ranks during the Polish campaign.

More important for Babel's rehabilitation scheme, during this time Denisova met and soon afterward married Efrem Afanasyevich Shchadenko ("Akim Ivanych" in the play). Shchadenko was the Red Cavalry's number-three man, after Voroshilov and Budenny, and like them, he would climb to the highest ranks of the Soviet armed forces, his career accelerating tremendously during Stalin's infamous Red Army purge.[80] Although Denisova's marriage was unhappy,[81] she shared her husband's (and Budenny's) passion for the official legend of the Polish campaign— not as a defeat but as a feat of superhuman heroism—and would have had no trouble recognizing herself in the character of Babel's Maria. In her letter to Mayakovsky, she even confessed to liking Babel as a writer. What she objected to was, as she put it, Babel's "looking under the skirts of the revolution"; judging by her sculpture, she herself preferred the Revolution in a more dignified, heroic, and essentially phallic posture.[82]

In *Maria*, Babel made her wish come true. The touchingly naïve pathos of Maria's description of the Red Cossacks in her letter home—she compares them to Italian peasants—provides a temporary relief from the somber and stifling atmosphere of the play. Maria's letter functioned also as an olive branch that Babel was offering—without fawning—to the power-ful Red Cavalry trio and their patron on high. We can only guess if Babel's conciliatory message reached its intended addressees; perhaps, it helped to thin some of the clouds that were gathering around him in the mid-1930s.

### *Maria*: A Balancing Act

The romantic élan of the Polish campaign, muted by its distance from the play's setting, is counterpoint to the play's other dominant motifs of helplessness, cynicism, and darkness. These two poles—the detached, naïve pathos and the all-too-palpable despair—account for the play's over-all message. Even in the sunny, springtime final scene, there is enough ambivalence to amplify the other side of this polarity.

A working-class couple is moving up from their basement to the Mukovnins' luxurious digs. Elena, the worker's wife, is pregnant, about to give birth, as it were, to the child of the Revolution. But Babel has her worried that her hips might be too narrow for a healthy birth, leaving open the question whether the new world would actually issue from the loins of the Russian proletariat.

Uncertainty over the future of the revolution is further compounded by the giant peasant girl Nyushka. She resembles both the Céleste of "L'Aveu" and Vera Mukhina's famous sculpture of the peasant baba, *Kres-tianka* (1927).[83] Like Céleste, she enters the scene bathed in sunshine. And it is her histrionics that bring the play to an end. Babel introduces her into the play as a peasant antipodal to the Hermitage Caryatids, known as the Atlantes, that are supposed to be visible from the windows of the Muk-ovnins' flat. Likewise, she presents a great contrast to the taciturn Elena, the bony worker's wife:

Her belly sticking out, the woman [Elena] steps cautiously keeping close to the walls, touches them, looks into adjoining rooms, turns on the chandelier, turns it off. Enter Nyushka, an immense ruddy peasant wench (*devka*), holding a bucket and a rag—to wash windows. She climbs up on the windowsill, tucks her skirt up baring her knees; rays of sunlight pour over her. *Like a statue supporting a vaulted ceiling,* she stands against the background of the spring sky [emphasis added—G. F.]. (*Sochineniia* 2:355)

As the curtain falls, we hear Nyushka belting out in her "basso"—male—voice a popular Cossack ballad. Far from being heroic, as might be fitting for the scene awash in spring sunlight, the ballad tells a story of a romance tragically destroyed by vile pecuniary treachery.[84] The curtain cuts the ballad short at its bright introductory part, and the audience does not hear the rest of it, but the ballad was popular enough in Babel's day for, at least, some in the audience to be able to complete it in their heads. Those who knew it by heart would have wondered what the author had in mind, ending his play on a note of such foreboding: the Cossack tricked into committing suicide, his young bride still expecting him to return, the culprit evil witch who had been "bribed with money" to destroy the young lovers. True, the play leaves little doubt about the death of the old world, but there is no such certainty about what has come to replace it. Dead lovers leave no progeny.

Indeed, the last scene, if viewed as an allegory for the Revolution, presents a picture of a disoriented working class unsure of its future and overshadowed by the giant peasant *baba*, the embodiment of the "uncivilized" but fecund, not to say, virile and powerful Russian peasantry, still a vast majority in Soviet Russia even at the end of the First Five-Year Plan.

Apparently Babel shared Gorky's apprehensions about the Revolution and his fear that Russia's miniscule intelligentsia elite might disappear "like a pinch of salt thrown into the bland swamp of the Russian village." As Gorky elaborated in his obituary of Lenin in 1924, "All my life I have felt oppressed by the fact that our illiterate village, with its zoological selfishness and almost complete absence of social conscience, dominates the city." Gorky may have expressed his regret for having written these words earlier, but he left them in the second edition of his Lenin essay, published in 1931,[85] adding, not without a trace of irony, a Russian saying: "What has been written with a pen cannot be hacked out with an axe." Babel's giant Nyushka, who overshadows and overwhelms with her voice the other characters on stage, resonates with Gorky's apprehensions. What is more, her singing the ballad about love destroyed by treachery, as the play fades out, suggests a concatenation of ideas that go, as Babel put it in his letter to his mother, "against the General Line."[86]

Babel could be subtle, even cryptic, he could withhold inconvenient facts and cover his tracks, but in his writing, by and large, he bowed to the gods of art, observed their rules, and, as the ending of *Maria* shows, he managed to speak his mind. The spring sunshine at the end of *Maria* owed much, as it turns out, to the merciless sun of Maupassant's "L'Aveu." In *Maria*, even more so than he did in his private interviews with Boris Souvarine and Boris Nikolaevsky in France in 1932–1933,[87] Babel remained himself, knowing he was playing with fire.

## The Precursor Strikes Back

Gorky, the patron of the erstwhile "Messiah from Odessa," had a mixed reaction to the play. He was not discouraging when Babel recited *Maria* to him in Sorrento, but he reversed himself when he read the manuscript later on, apparently, after leaving his villa for the Soviet Union. A carbon copy of his undated letter to Babel about the play records his impressions.[88] Gorky found the play's message "elusive," its action excessively grotesque, some of the dialogue easy fodder for anti-Semitism, and most important, the happy ending artificially tacked on. Clearly, Gorky had trouble getting used to this new—*Petersburg*—Babel, whom he saw as indulging in "Baudelaire-like passion for spoiled meat." He did not notice or remained indifferent to Babel's formal innovations, in which Chekhovian depth combined with expressionist satire in the manner of Mayakovsky and Brecht, all of it shaped into a new cinematic structure.[89] Instead of trying to probe the bases for the play's dark mood, he prodded his old protégé to revive his earlier sunny or, as Gorky put it, "romantic" disposition, having in mind, no doubt, *The Odessa Stories* and *Red Cavalry*. We can only wonder if Gorky appreciated the irony of the situation: the "precursor" asking the "Messiah from Odessa" for more sunshine. Curiously, he either failed to or chose not to notice the play's apparent autobiographical subtext. His wondering if it was the late Zinovy Grzhebin who served Babel as the prototype for his Isaac Dymshits may be seen as Gorky's way of signaling his unwillingness to engage with Babel at the personal or political level.

Babel could not ignore this criticism and although no drafts of *Maria* have survived, the published version suggests that he may have tried to meet Gorky halfway, at least. One may imagine that in the earlier draft, the last scene was as unabashedly cheerful as the crude happy end of "The Road"—one way for Babel to emphasize the extra-literary character of a stock Soviet closure. In the known, later, version of the play, the ending—because of its ambivalent and contradictory signals—resonates better with the previous seven scenes—dissolving, to quote Gorky, without a trace that "pinch of salt" of the Russian intelligentsia and enlightened working class in the "swamp of the Russian village."

## Marketing and Reception

While Gorky's cool reaction could not have improved the play's chances, Babel did not view his objections as insurmountable. In 1933–1934, with the worst horrors of collectivization receding into the past, the country was going through a selective liberalization: greater tolerance in the cultural sphere and limited rapproachment with the West. Babel had great hopes for *Maria* as a stage success and, more important, as a work inaugurating a new era in his career as a writer: he now felt drawn to the dramatic form as never before.[90] This new creative spurt after a dry spell of some seven years would put an end to the rumors—Stalin kept tabs—that his "silence" was an expression of opposition to the General Line, namely, Stalin's policy, and an act of resistance against the country's total mobilization.

In some superficial ways, *Maria* was a play after the fashions of the late 1920s and early 1930s. Several civil-war dramas had been produced that enjoyed both critical acclaim and box office success, and Babel had every reason to hope that *Maria* might follow suit.[91] His earlier play, *Sunset* (1928), had a mixed reception and premiered in Moscow in his absence. Babel learned his lesson. This time, he took great care in orchestrating his comeback in order to maximize both visibility and income from advances. Parts of the play were published early in 1934 in Moscow and Leningrad. The play was translated into Yiddish and was supposed to be playing simultaneously at both the Vakhtangov Theater and the State Jewish Theater of Solomon Mikhoels. Babel gave public readings at various venues, feeding the excitement and paving the way for what he hoped would be the play's triumph on stage. For a while, everything proceeded according to plan. In his letters to Brussels, Babel mentions rehearsals at the Vakhtangov and the State Jewish Theater as well as some negotiations to have the play staged in Leningrad.

On December 1, 1934 the world changed and all of the plans collapsed. The assassination of Kirov, the Leningrad Party Secretary and a rising member of the Politburo—the crime of the century, as Robert Conquest qualified it—abolished the rules of the game and signaled the beginning of a new round of repression and purges.[92] Staging a new play, one that was ideologically suspect, perhaps even dangerous, by an author as controversial as Babel, became too risky an enterprise for anyone to undertake. Having at first resisted the publication of the play (he wanted the public to be surprised by it onstage), Babel now hoped that once vetted by the censor and published, *Maria* would appear less dangerous to the theater establishment. Indeed, it was published in the journal *Teatr i dramaturgiya* in April, 1935, although not under the circumstances of Babel's own choosing.

Running parallel with the text of the play was a patronizing and discouraging review by the influential arts editor of *Pravda*, Isai Lezhnev.

The reader's eye could conveniently skip from the play's dialogue, printed on the upper part of the page, to Lezhnev's droning critique below, where the reader could learn quickly whether Babel had overdone it on sex or underdone it on the class approach (both, according to Lezhnev). More ominous, Lezhnev was wise to Babel's code and although he did not elaborate, it was clear enough that he had cracked Babel's code when he wondered how Babel could have written a play about the Revolution and neglect to show the leading role of the working class in it. *Maria* seemed doomed but for a glimmer of hope. Citing the author's private communication suggesting that *Maria* was intended as the second play in a trilogy, the authoritative reviewer advised Babel to tone down the sex scenes and to rectify his ideological stance in the other parts of the trilogy, if he ever wished to see the play staged.[93]

Babel attempted—or merely pretended—to heed Lezhnev's advice, though apparently without much success or enthusiasm. References to some version of *Maria II* crop up from time to time in Babel's correspondence in 1934 and 1935 but they soon trail off, suggesting that the project was abandoned. It had the same fate as Babel's earlier planned peacetime sequel to *Red Cavalry* (his unfinished novel *The Jewess*). Busy with his assignments for the Soviet film industry (for Babel, lucrative hackwork), he now focused his efforts on preserving his literary legacy—negotiating new editions of his writings, justifying republication by adding a few new or unpublished stories. The fullest edition of Babel's work during his lifetime came out in 50,000 copies in September 1936, a rare privilege he probably owed to his friendship with Maxim Gorky, who two months earlier had passed away.

## Full Stop

We shall never know the direction Maria Mukovnin's life would have taken in the planned sequel, but the actual play *Maria* seems to have scripted the remainder of Babel's life.

Halfway through the play, in Scene 4, Babel introduces two episodic characters: Yashka Kravchenko, a former lieutenant in the imperial army and "now a Red artillery man," and "Madame Dora, a citizen of the French Republic," who has her French passport and is madly in love with Kravchenko. This French connection, altogether gratuitous in the play, becomes meaningful if one takes into account *Maria*'s autobiographical subtext, especially

Babel's loyal and forgiving Parisian wife, Evgeniia, who pleaded with him to remain in affluent France (hence Dora, *d'or*) even as he was working on the play's first draft. Like the iconic young Babel, bespectacled, plump, short, and pink-cheeked, Kravchenko, then, is supposed to represent an aspect of the play's author. Neither he nor Madame Dora ever reappear in the play but they figure in it at the crucial moment when the Mukovnins' fragile equilibrium is shattered by Viskovsky's rape of Ludmila.

In a play about the revolution, one can read the scene as an allegory of the abuse that Russia suffered in the hands of those whose duty it was to offer her protection. After all, the officer of the guard Viskovsky, a man of the Mukovnins' milieu who had once courted Maria Mukovnin, transgressed both the fundamental rules of his class and basic human decency by violating a young woman who was a guest in his apartment. Babel used a similar allegorical formula in his 1923 story, "The Sin of Jesus," though the target in the latter was, on the whole, the Russian intelligentsia. Here, Babel is not shedding any tears for the old regime or the Whites in casting Viskovsky, a stand-in for both, as the play's sole character who is unambiguously odious. But precisely because Viskovsky is the most unlikely to serve as the author's mouthpiece, Babel chooses him for a monologue that would have placed the play totally out of bounds, had it been spoken by any other character. Viskovsky addresses his tirade to Yashka Kravchenko, a fellow officer who had once pledged allegiance to the Tsar but who is now quite content, like many former officers, in his new role as a Red Army specialist (*spets*).

Using terms that were anachronistic for the civil war but apt for the 1930s, Viskovsky warns Kravchenko of what might happen to him next, outlining the stages of creeping Soviet totalitarianism with chilling precision. First comes the bribe: "You will do [as they say] as long as they let you be and strum your guitar, sleep with slender women: you are plump and you like slender women. . . ." Then, once the *spets* or, for that matter, a non-party fellow traveler like Babel, gets hooked on the good life, he will be forced to compromise his conscience: "You will do anything, and if they say to you: thrice renounce your mother—you will renounce her." After the *spets* has betrayed his own principles and is filled with self-loathing, the Bolsheviks take away from him his good life:

Yashka, the point is that they will go further: they won't let you drink vodka in the company of the people you like, they will force you to read boring books, and the songs they will force you to learn will also be boring. . . ."

These new restrictions are too confining and the person, who has once happily cooperated with the regime, begins to look for ways to escape the trap: "And then you will get angry, my Red artillery man, you will go mad, your eyes will start darting this way and that. . . ." But by then, it is all hopeless. Once the Bolsheviks learn that the *spets* is trying to slip out of their clutches, they simply dispose of him:

Two gentlemen will pay you a visit. . . . "Let's go, Comrade Kravchenko . . ." "Should I," you will ask, "take any things with me?" "Oh no, you need not take anything, Comrade Kravchenko, it won't take but a minute, just an interrogation, trifles. . . ." And they will put a full stop for you, my Red artillery man, and it will cost them four kopeks. It's been calculated a revolver bullet costs four kopeks and not a *centime* more.

With Mayakovsky's suicide—his decision "to put the bullet's full stop at life's end"—still fresh in everybody's memory, the passage had all the urgency of the present moment. It would have sent chills down more than one spine, had it sounded from the stage of one of the theaters in Stalin's Moscow. Mayakovsky's suicide, of course, had a lot to do with his no longer being allowed to keep the company he liked (Babel surely knew that Mayakovsky had been blocked from rejoining his fiancée in Paris) and his being forced to "learn boring new songs" (his joining the RAPP was a surrender and a sensation). Now Mayakovsky may have seemed lucky to be out of the game. In 1933–1935, many in Moscow's theater audience—members of the intelligentsia, officials of the Party and the NKVD—could have identified with either Yashka Kravchenko or those who forced him "thrice to renounce his mother," or indeed, with both at the same time—a phenomenon Nikita Mikhalkov explored in his *Burned by the Sun* some sixty years later.

Notwithstanding such foresight, Babel persevered. He continued to cultivate his career as a Soviet writer, albeit a "silent" one, as he confessed self-mockingly at the First Congress of Soviet Writers in 1934. He had little choice. For a while, he remained an important cultural figure, and friends abroad, associated with the anti-fascist Popular Front, made him a valuable asset for the Soviet regime. After André Gide and André Malraux threatened to walk out of the Congress of Writers in Defense of Culture and Peace in Paris, Babel and Pasternak were retroactively included in the Soviet delegation and rushed to France in June 1935.[94] This was Babel's last chance for an escape. His role in the Soviet anti-fascist charm offensive in the West, with his friends Ilya Ehrenburg and Mikhail

Koltsov as Stalin's point men, must have influenced his decision to return to Russia in 1935. Other factors were Gorky's continued patronage and friendship, not to speak of the work for the Soviet film studios, which by then must have accounted for the lion's share of Babel's income. Most important, Babel knew from his experiences in 1932–1933, when he tried unsuccessfully to break into the film business in France, that he would not be able to provide support for his family—his mother and sister in Brussels, his wife and daughter in Paris, not to mention himself—unless he could maintain his position as an important Soviet writer and international celebrity. Despite the considerable space for maneuver that only very few cultural figures could then enjoy, Babel was trapped. It was his own predicament he transposed into the script that *Maria*'s Viskovsky outlined for Kravchenko.

The wisdom of his decision to return in the fall of 1935 was severely tested at the beginning of 1936, when a new campaign of cultural repression was inaugurated by an abusive editorial in *Pravda* against the composer Dmitry Shostakovich. In retrospect, the *Maria* debacle—it was, after all, no less raunchy than Shostakovich's *Lady Macbeth of Mtzensk*—must have felt like a stroke of good fortune. Having stuck his neck out with *Maria*, Babel now had to thank Soviet censorship for dodging this bullet and restoring to him, in a manner of speaking, the reputation of the great "master of the genre of literary silence" (*Sochineniia* 2:381). "Babel is a clever tactician," declared Leonid Leonov at the Writers Union meeting on March 10, 1936, where writers were supposed to hash out their response to *Pravda*'s attack on Shostakovich. "Just keep reprinting the same work that has passed the test," Leonov went on, "but do not publish anything new."[95] Babel himself was very lucid about this tactic, as he explained it around this time to his friend Ervin Sinkó.[96] Thanks to Gorky's protection, Babel was able—perhaps, even had to—nurse some illusions, and for a while he treated the campaign as a mere trifle. "You're making too much ado about nothing," a secret informer reported him saying. "Nobody has taken this seriously. The people are silent but deep inside they are laughing quietly. Budenny used to castigate me in worse terms, and nothing came of it. I am sure the same will be true of Shostakovich."[97]

Whether his instincts were good or because he was well informed, Babel turned out to be right about the Formalism campaign, if not the larger picture. Following Gorky's meeting with André Malraux in March 1936, with both Babel and Koltsov in attendance, Gorky intervened and, it seemed, convinced Stalin to reverse gears lest the anti-Formalism campaign alienate Soviet friends in the West.[98] "Babel has known Malraux for years," Gorky wrote to Stalin to give him the measure of Malraux's outrage at the campaign, "and while in Paris, he has been following the growth of Malraux's reputation in France. Babel says that Malraux's opinion is valued by government ministers and that among the intelligentsia of the Romance countries, this man is the most prominent, talented and influential figure, who, in addition, possesses a talent for organization." As Gorky's emissary and now, apparently, a foreign-policy go-between, Babel was happy to carry the message to the panicked Soviet writers and reassure them that Gorky was going to put an end to their travails.[99] We shall never know if Babel himself appreciated the melancholy irony of his mission. Gorky's patronage was at its lowest ebb.

Gorky's death in June 1936 was a deep personal loss for Babel, and it also made him exceedingly vulnerable to attack. According to a secret police report filed on July 5, 1936, Babel told Antonina Pirozhkova that he had felt invincible as long as Gorky was alive but now he could no longer be sure.[100] A. N. Pirozhkova, who was a friend of this secret informer, remembers Babel saying something considerably stronger: "Now I am done in for."

Danger was everywhere. For a while, the film industry afforded him a safe haven because of the option not to have his name listed in credits even when he was the primary author of a script.[101] This, too, changed after he agreed to Sergei Eisenstein's entreaties to collaborate with him on the new version of the film *Bezhin Meadow*. Babel yielded with great reluctance—he sensed danger.[102] His instinct did not deceive him. The film was denounced in February 1937, with Babel and Eisenstein accused, among other things, of using their leftist friends in the West as leverage to expand the range of the permissible in the Soviet Union (they dared to show the yet uncensored reel to Leon Feuchtwanger then visiting Moscow).[103] Both Babel and Eisenstein were lucky to get out of it alive.[104] The Great Terror had commenced, and every member of the Soviet elite went to bed expecting, as Babel's Viskovsky put it, "two gentlemen to pay them a visit."

Babel had plenty of opportunities to recall Viskovsky's monologue from *Maria*. He must have thought of it when he heard the news of the execution of his friend Efim Dreitser, along with Kamenev and Zinoviev, in August 1936, and then again at the end of January 1937 when he had to write and sign a denunciation of the old Bolsheviks (he knew some of them personally), who had been convicted at the show trial of the Parallel Anti-Soviet Trotskyite Center.[105]

The theme of treachery and betrayal on his mind, he completed and published in July 1937 a story thematically linked to *Red Cavalry*. As A. N. Pirozhkova maintains, the story was meant to serve as the closure in the new edition of the cycle. Thematically, it was a variation on the analogous episode that happened in the Garden of Gethsemane and was accordingly entitled "The Kiss."[106]

As mass repressions gathered force, Babel grew desperate and began looking for a way out. A new story, "Di Grasso," published in June 1937, shows what was on his mind: it revolves around the themes of betrayal, indebtedness, entrapment, escape into emigration, and the magical redemption through true and popular art, the endeavor in which he knew he had succeeded beyond measure.[107] But miracles, Babel knew, happened only in stories or with a stroke of Stalin's pen. Hoping for the latter, he decided to reach out to his foreign friends. In late summer or fall 1937, using intermediaries, he pleaded with André Malraux to write to Stalin and ask him, as he had done successfully once before, to allow Babel to travel to Paris. For whatever reason—the Frenchman may have been apprehensive that Babel would defect—Malraux never complied. He was now deeply involved in supporting the Republican cause in Spain and, which seems likely, did not wish to find himself on the wrong side of Stalin, whom he thought to be the last hope of the Republican Spain.[108]

The times were such that one had to choose between saving a friend and saving a country from fascism. In his letters to the family, Babel at times made a pun on Malraux's name, intentionally spelling it as *mal-heureux*. Now "this most prominent member of the intelligentsia of the Romance countries" appeared to be validating Babel's word play. Babel's loved ones abroad were aware of Babel's efforts to obtain a visa and, perhaps, to wait out the wave of terror abroad. As Babel wrote to his mother and sister in Brussels on November 1, 1937, Malraux's brother Roland, Babel's friend, had brought back with him from France instead of the gift Babel hoped for—an invitation to journey to Paris—"a *stylo*, which, alas, writes horribly, and a Canadian fur jacket which will serve me very nicely . . ." The sentence trails off in suspension points: Babel may have had in mind an unscheduled journey to Siberia. "He saw Ehrenburg," Babel concluded the letter, "but almost never saw his brother, who is mostly in Spain, though he has found time to write a small novel, *L'Espoir.*"[109] Malraux's *Hope* was Babel's despair. Babel's sarcasm could not have been more bitter.

As Babel's important friends and fellow writers were disappearing one after another (Elena Sokolovskaia, director of Mosfilm and Babel's old Odessa friend and patron was arrested on October 12; Boris Pilnyak, on October 28), his own chances of survival were growing bleaker by the day. At times, he tried to remain cheerful when communicating with his mother, but as we know from the recollections of his friends and his letter to his Moscow friend Anna Slonim, with whom he could be forthright, he had been, by and large, deeply depressed. A new story, "The Trial," published in June 1938, is a wistful account of a Russian émigré being given ten years—a familiar sentence in the Great Terror—for stealing from his girlfriend, a rich middle-aged French widow. The name of the Russian was *Nedachin*, no doubt a pun on the Russian *dacha* and *neudacha* (misfortune, *malheureux*), with a lot of resonance for Babel, who was spending as much time as he could at his dacha in Peredelkino and hoping for an intercession from Malraux. His debts to publishers were piling up, his institutional creditors were losing patience; he was threatened with confiscation of his personal property if he did not return his advances.[110]

Pirozhkova recalled in her memoirs that Babel was working on the manuscript of a collection called *New Stories*, which he planned to submit to the publisher in the fall of 1939, hoping the publication would, among other things, restore his finances.[111] This "sacred work" (*zavetnyi trud*), as he called the book manuscript in his last letter to the family (May 10, 1939), needed one "final polishing" to which Babel would devote himself as soon as he was done with his responsibilities for the film version of Gorky's autobiographical trilogy.

Babel's letters of the 1930s, whether to his family, editors, or friends, are full of variations on this formula. We do not know what stories constituted his "sacred work"—only five new stories had been published since the 1936 edition. But even if he had as many in his desk drawer (we shall probably never know for certain), he could hardly have expected to be embraced by the Soviet publishing establishment circa 1939. Even in 1932–1936, when Babel was close to Gorky and enjoyed the munificence of his patronage, his publication record, when it came to new work, remained woefuly small.

As 1938 was drawing to a close, Babel's association with the leaders of anti-fascist causes in the West was losing its value to the regime. The André Gide debacle, his clear-eyed portrait of life in Stalin's USSR (*Retour de l' U.R.S.S.*), what he saw as a betrayal of the Revolution; the failure to reverse the course of the Spanish civil war; the arrest of Mikhail Koltsov, implicated in both, in December 1938—all signaled the end of the interlude when Stalin relied on his cultural entrepreneurs for swaying public opinion in the West in favor of Soviet proposals for collective security. No longer willing to "pull the chestnuts out of the fire" for England and France, as he put it memorably in his speech to the Nineteenth Party Congress on March 10, 1939, Stalin was now turning toward an alliance with Nazi Germany.[112] Hitler echoed the "chestnut" phrase in his April 1 speech, and the courtship dance of the two dictators commenced in earnest. On May 3, 1939, Stalin sent a new and unambiguous signal to Hitler by sacking Maxim Litvinov, the People's Commissar for Foreign Affairs, known for his pro-Western orientation.[113]

Babel was arrested twelve days later, perhaps as an afterthought following the arrest and interrogation of Nikolay Ezhov; perhaps as a follow-up to the sacking of Litvinov; or perhaps for no other reason than that his number came up at last, as it had for millions of other people. When the "two gentlemen paid him a visit," in a memorable phrase from *Maria*, he could no longer count on his "immunity" as a protégé of Gorky, a good friend of Nikolay Ezhov's wife, or a writer and international anti-fascist celebrity and a good friend of André Malraux.

We know from the publications of Arkady Vaksberg, Vitaly Shentalinsky, and Sergey Povartsov[114] that the charges were standard issue for the Great Terror and altogether baseless: spying for France (Babel's association with Malraux) and Austria (Babel once shared an apartment with an Austrian engineer) as well as conspiring to assassinate the leaders of the Soviet party and state. Beaten and tortured for days by his interrogators, Babel complied with their demands and "confessed"—only to renounce his testimony against himself and the others later. Perhaps like the accused who followed a similar trajectory, first submitting under torture to the interrogator's will and later renouncing their false confession (for example, Mikhail Koltsov), he hoped that the fantastic nature of the charges would open the court's eyes to the sheer absurdity of the indictment against him. But this strategy, if indeed it was a strategy, had no effect unless one counts the dropped charges for conspiring to assassinate members of the Soviet leadership.

Babel was number 12 in the alphabetical list of 346 men and women designated for execution, which was signed by Stalin on January 17, 1940. Nine days later and seven months after his arrest, Babel stood before the rubber-stamp court, which took twenty minutes to examine his case and to pronounce him guilty of most charges. He was shot in the Lefortovo Prison basement a few hours later and buried in the same unmarked grave at the Donskoy Monastery in Moscow as were his friends, executed around the same time. Among them were the writer and editor Mikhail Koltsov, an old Petrograd friend, who had helped him to join Budenny's Cavalry; an old friend from the Polish campaign, the Chekist Efim Evdokimov; the former party boss of Kabardino-Balkaria, Betal Kalmykov, the subject of a never completed biography; the theater director Vsevolod Meyerhold; and paradoxically, the former head of the NKVD, Nikolay Ezhov, whose wife, Evgeniya Solomonovna, had been a close, sometimes intimate, friend of Babel's (she had committed suicide in November 1938).

Different as they all were, all had identified with the promise of the Revolution and all fell victim to Stalin's treachery—like the young Cossack and his bride from the folk ballad that Nyushka belts out as the curtain falls on the final scene of *Maria*.

Aphrodite Urania never came back.

The night had no mercy for Isaac Babel.

FIGURE 1. The Babel family apartment in Odessa (the top floor above the billboard) at the corner of Rishelievskaya and Zhukovskogo, where Babel resided in 1906–1911 and, on and off, in 1919–1924. Photo © by Gregory Freidin.

FIGURE 2. The building on the left is 9 Bolshaia Monetnaia Street in St. Petersburg that housed the apartment of Lev and Anna Slonim where Babel rented a room in 1916–1917. Gorky's apartment and the offices of *Letopis*, where Babel's stories were published in 1916, was at 23 Bolshaia Monetnaia. Photo © by Gregory Freidin.

FIGURE 3. Kliment Voroshilov, Semyon Budenny, and Efim Shchadenko, the three top leaders of the First Cavalry Army, circa 1920. The photo appeared in A. Rodchenko and V. Stepnova, designers, *Pervaia konnaia* (Moscow: Ogiz-Izogiz, 1938). Irwin T. and Shirley Holtzman Collection, The Hoover Institution Archives.

FIGURE 4. Joseph Stalin (center) on vacation in the Caucasus in the summer 1932; Nestor Lakoba (left), the party boss of Abkhazia; Lavrenty Beria (with a hatchet stuck in his belt), then the party boss of Georgia. During this summer, Stalin was blocking Babel's request for permission to go abroad and did not relent until he returned to Moscow at the end of August 1932. The Hoover Institution Archives.

FIGURE 5. Isaac Babel and his wife, Evgeniya (née Gronfain), on a beach in Ostende, Belgium, during the summer of 1928. Photograph from the private archive of Christine Galitzine.

FIGURE 6. Isaac Babel (circa 1935?). Photograph by Moisei Nappelbaum.

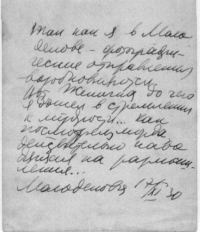

FIGURE 7. Isaac Babel's self-portrait. The note on the reverse, addressed to his wife Evgeniya, reads: "Since I am in Molodenovo, the photographic postings have resumed. This is what I have come to, Zhenechka, in my striving for wisdom. . . . I just took one look: there's a mug that really gives one pause . . . Molodenovo, 11.17.1930." The Hoover Institution Archives.

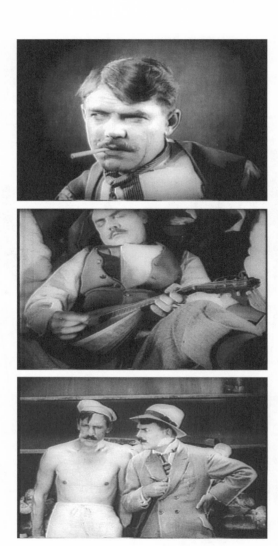

**FIGURE 8.** The film *Benya Krik* (1926), along with Babel's film script, grew out of his collaboration with Sergei Eisenstein in 1925, but a series of financial scandals at the Moscow film studios forced Babel, strapped for cash, to sell his script to the Ukrainian VUFKU, where it was shot and directed by Vladimir Vilner. In the script, as in the play *Sunset*, Babel chooses to renounce his former carnivalesque alter ego by presenting Krik as a sinister and trivial thief. The three frames exemplify Babel's about-face: Krik (played by Yuri Shumsky) is a wily schemer, a hedonist sexpot, and a treacherous ally of the Bolsheviks. Authenticity, the character's attribute in *The Odessa Stories*, has been transferred to the bare-chested Russian baker Sobkov (bottom), who orders Benya's execution later in the film. The mustachioed baker, the film's good guy, also suggests a biographical subtext: Babel's mentor Maxim Gorky was once a baker himself and tried raising the consciousness of the proletariat in a small basement bakery. The film was released early in 1927 (in January, Babel was still writing intertitles for it), was briefly banned by Lazar Kaganovich, then the party boss of Ukraine, and was back in theaters in February. *Ed.*

**FIGURE 9.** Boris Shchukin as the flying school director and Evgeniya Melnikova as a flight school cadet in the 1935 film *Lyotchiki* (U.S. title, *Men with Wings*), dir. Yuli Raizman and Grigory Levkoyev, script by Alexander Macharet and, apparently, Isaac Babel. In a letter to his mother (March 31, 1935), Babel claimed to be the actual author of the film script, not just the dialogues, and blamed himself for refusing to have his name listed in the credits. He worried *Lyotchiki* would fail; instead, it turned out to be a hit. The film tells a story of a romance between a middle-aged pilot and his very young female flight school cadet before each is assigned to duty at opposite ends of the USSR. The motifs of separation and a September-May romance echo Babel's own life at the time. Boris Shchukin went on to play Lenin in *Lenin in October* and *Lenin in 1918*; and Melnikova starred as Rayechka in *The Circus* (dir. G. Aleksandrov), for which Babel wrote the dialogues, and *The Fall of Berlin*, along with another dozen or so movies. *Ed.*

**FIGURE 10.** Cover of Maria Denisova (Shchadenko) exhibition held at the State Museum of Vladimir Mayakovsky in Moscow in 2000. The text on the cover: *Maria Denisova-Shchadenko, Sculptor.*

Part Two
**Babel in the Context of Russian History**

# 3

## The Reds and the Jews, or the Comrades in Arms of the Military Reporter Liutov

OLEG BUDNITSKII

THIS CHAPTER is about the treatment of the Jews by the soldiers, peasants, and workers who propped up the Bolsheviks, and whose sentiments the Bolsheviks had to take into consideration at least to some extent.[1]

The Bolsheviks' internationalism was present merely at the highest levels of the hierarchy (which included the Jews), whereas the masses that they relied on were pervaded with anti-Semitic, pogrom-hungry attitudes. There was, of course, no directive for the persecution of the Jews. The "president" of the Don republic, cavalry-sergeant (*vakhmistr*) Fedor Podtelkov, when asked in Novocherkassk, "What to do about the Jews," explained, "Soviet principles state that even a Kike counts as a human being."[2]

Let us remember that the Cavalry Army, which hosted the reporter of the *Krasnyi kavalerist* (*The Red Cavalryman*) newspaper, Kirill Vasil'evich Liutov, drew its ancestry from the river Don region in the south of Russia, which was predominantly populated by Cossacks.

The picturesque and terrifying scenes of Rostov's Bolshevik period were captured by contemporary authors. The liberal pro-Kadet journalist and the "first pen" of the Don region's most popular newspaper *Priazovskii krai*, Petr Gertso-Vinogradskii, recalled the first Bolshevik search in his apartment building:

> The machine-gunner comrades showed up. The first question they asked the concierge was "Do any Kikes live here?"

Translated by Eugene Budnitsky

Gods of the socialist Olympus, dead or alive, do you hear this?

Our building was already robbed quite thoroughly during the first search and, getting into the hang of it, any distinction between Hellenes and Judeans was quickly forgotten. Though robbery will always remain just robbery, I have nothing against the principle of equality of nationalities in this process. If you're robbing, then rob everybody!

Nevertheless, that famous "socialist" phrase "Do any Kikes live here?" cannot ever vanish from my non-socialist memory.[3]

In his memoirs, Prince Grigorii N. Trubetskoi, the former special envoy to Serbia, described a typical scene. Soon after the Volunteer Army left Rostov, Trubetskoi departed for Moscow in the middle of February 1918 with Petr Struve, his son, and Nikolai Arsen'ev, a philosopher, scholar of literature, and theologian. They made a loop through Cossack villages (*khutora* and *stanitsy*) to get to the railway. When the coachman, whom they had hired in Novocherkassk, delivered them to his home village (*khutor*), peculiarly named Trekhiarusnyi ("three-leveled"), it turned out that a revolutionary military committee had already been organized there, whose members subjected the travelers, who carried fake identification, to a search and an interrogation.

"They were most suspicious of Arseniev," Trubetskoi recalled. "For some reason they mistook him for a Kike. Our efforts to communicate to them that he was from a most Orthodox family, and that two of his uncles were priests were in vain. Our coachman tried to defend him by saying that throughout the journey Arseniev told him stories of the lives of various angels and saints. "That they know how to do," the committee chairman noted. He was the most malicious of the interrogators. It was typical that they picked on Arseniev as an alleged kike. This crowd would show equal, if not stronger, vigor under the *Black Hundred*. These were truly rebellious slaves," concluded the prince.[4]

"Judophobia is an organic element in Communists," Mikhail Mikhailovich Prishvin wrote in his diary in September 1919. Prishvin was a writer and a sympathizer with the Socialist-Revolutionary Party, who spent almost all of the Civil War years "under the Reds" in the provincial city of Yelets, and who, judging by his personal notes, did not harbor any warm feelings towards Moses' people.[5]

Another literary figure, but of a much lower caliber than Prishvin, a future *OSVAG* (Information and Propaganda Agency of the Volunteer

Army) employee by the name of Vladimir Amfiteatrov-Kadashev, wrote the following in a diary entry on November 23, 1918:

There's a peasant uprising in Pavlograd. They gathered round a red flag, held a public prayer for Lenin's good health, raided the Jews and went on to fight under the flag of the International "for land and freedom!" "Oh Russia! Oh Russia!" Oh the "responsible voting citizen!"[6]

The Kiev branch of the *Azbuka* intelligence organization, which regularly kept the White leadership informed of the developments in the *Sovdepia* (that is, territory under Soviets' control, or Soviet Russia), reported the escalation of anti-Semitic sentiments among the Red Army men. An anonymous informer claimed, "The slowness of evolution of this phenomenon into its external forms [read: pogroms—*OB*] is evidently explained merely by the technical difficulty of unification and finding common ground on the issue." This anonymous informer circulated a leaflet among the draftees that urged them not to serve the Jew Trotsky. The leaflet ended with the slogan: "Down with Trotsky and horsemeat, long live Nicholas and pork."[7]

According to intelligence of the Military Forces of the South of Russia (a report from the Don region dated June 10, 1919), "The Reds treat the Jews with great hatred, for they don't see them among the ranks of the army. There is a conjecture that the Jewish pogroms in Sovdepia are several days in the making. The Jews take positions only in the communist cells. The Soviets are overflowing with Jews."[8]

A review of the Soviet press prepared for internal use by the Denikin's propaganda department had a whole section devoted to the "growth of the anti-Semitic movement" in Soviet Russia. Referring to publications in the central and local Soviet newspapers, the compilers of the review asserted that "the Soviet officials are extremely concerned with the strong anti-Semitic movement, which threatens a pogrom wave all over Russia and a physical extermination of the Judaic tribe." Albeit the prospect of "extermination of the Judaic tribe" was not a concern to the Bolsheviks in itself but rather in the context of their struggle against the enemies of the Soviet power. *Pravda*, in an article entitled "Against the Jew—for the Czar" (May 14, 1919), pointed out that "struggle against the Jewry is being inseparably tied to struggle against the power of the Soviets and against the party of Communists," and that "the intensified propaganda against the Jews is in essence propaganda for czarism, for clergy, for serf-owners. Anti-Semitism warrants the same struggle as the one the revolution wields against monarchism."[9]

**THE ANXIETY WAS NOT GROUNDLESS.** Prishvin wrote of rumors circulating about the Red Army regiment stationed nearby: "They say that Makhno's 'teaching' is quite popular among the soldiers of our Forty-Second Division, 'Down with the kikes and Communists, long live the Soviet power!' The 'teaching' is to the benefit of the peasants."[10]

A "special" attitude toward the Jews was, however, not present solely among semiliterate peasants. Speaking at a Sovdep meeting in Kharkov, Iurii V. Sablin, a former Tsarist army officer and one of the first Red military leaders, read Makhno's call to "slaughter masters, ministers and kikes," and declared that, "While disagreeing with comrade Makhno on some issues, I entirely agree with his solution to the Jewish issue." Sablin was arrested but soon released, as the Red Army could not do without his services. Of course, this story, written down by Amfiteatrov-Kadashev, sounds like a joke, but the *OSVAG* employee knew "Iurochka" Sablin quite well and talked to him once in a while when the latter was "Red," and, it seems, let his attitude toward the Jews show.[11]

Amfiteatrov-Kadashev's diary is a bottomless pit of such stories. The author scrupulously took note of both what he saw and what he heard from others. Perhaps the most colorful and, in many ways, funny story in which the Jewish question was mentioned, the author heard from a well-known man of letters from the Don, Veniamin Alexeevich Krasnushkin, better known under the pen name of Viktor Sevskii, the editor of the *Donskaia Volna* weekly. Sevskii, of course, somewhat enhanced his story, but it was based undoubtedly on true and telling facts. Telling not just because they show the attitude of a certain Red commander toward a Jewish commissar, but also the general level of cultural awareness among the fighters for the "bright future."

The story told by Sevskii took place during the Reds' takeover of the Konstantinovskaia *stanitsa* (village). Sevskii was actually a native of the *stanitsa*, and his mother spent the entire period of the Red rule there. The Red military was headed by Konstantin (Kost'ka) Pulatkin, "a rowdy teenager who got expelled from the secondary school," a local of non-Cossack origin.

Having entered the *stanitsa* at the head of an undefeatable peasant-worker armada, this twenty-three-year-old commander sent a local girl, by whom he was earlier rejected, the following "love note": "Dear Lelia! I offer you my hand and heart. In case of rejection, you will be shot." The girl obviously agreed, but demanded that they wed in church. Kost'ka agreed, claiming that he "won't tolerate any animal custom." The wedding turned out quite Homeric: Kost'ka arrived in his former headmaster's carriage (the very one that expelled him from secondary school) drawn by three white horses and covered with carpets. Next to him sat a gramophone, which he constantly wound up, and it roared, "Glory, oh glory to the Russian Czar!" The wedding was followed by heavy drinking that ended scandalously. The groom ended his revolutionary toast with a pompous "Down with the kikes!" and immediately set an example by dragging a nearby Jewish commissar by the ear. A gunfight erupted, in which two were seriously wounded and the newly made Madame Pulatkin variously scarred. Her present sense of regret about her husband was hardly surprising: "Oh, how I wish the Whites catch Kost'ka! They'd hang him now and I'd be a widow. As it is, it's awkward for me; I'm married to a Bolshevik, and I can't divorce the damn guy!"[12]

INFORMATION ORIGINATING from the White camp and contemporaries' accounts of anti-Semitic attitudes in the Red Army are confirmed by documents from the highest levels of the Bolshevik party hierarchy. A recent study by V. L. Genis and S. A. Pavliuchenkov, based on the party's Central Committee archive, perhaps for the first time showed how deeply the Red Army was infested with anti-Semitism, the army being a mirror image of the rest of the population.

Upon his return from the Ukraine in the spring of 1919, a Jewish member of the VChK (All-Russian Extraordinary Commission, or Cheka) Collegium, Grigorii S. Moroz, wrote a brief report to the Central Committee of the Russian Communist Party (Bolshevik) (CC RCP), in which he described the present pre-pogromist atmosphere: "In trains, at train stations, diners, markets and even clubs, you constantly hear, 'The kikes are everywhere,' 'The kikes are ruining Russia,' 'The Soviet rule wouldn't be so bad if it wasn't for the Jews,' etc." Moroz suggested that, within the former Pale of Settlement, Jews holding important posts be replaced with Russians and Communist Jews be recruited into the Red Army.[13]

The Main Committee of Poalei-Zion, the Jewish Socialist Party, sent a letter on April 25, 1919 to Lenin, suggesting that Jewish regiments be formed within the Red Army. In terms of fighting against anti-Semitism, this would have been probably the worst possible move. However, Poalei-Zion's proposal was approved by the Political Bureau of the Bolshevik Party. But this initiative was faced with severe resistance from the local military authorities and Evsektsiia (Jewish Section of the Communist Party). In any case, as Pavliuchenkov writes, "in the midst of the Civil War, the Central Committee of the Russian Communist Party refused to recruit the Jews into the Red Army like the rest of the population," and "on August 6, 1919, the Organizational Bureau expressed its wish to the Central Committee for the Jews in the Red Army to form separate regiments, 'due to the ever-present anti-Semitism in the army.'"[14]

The question of recruiting the Jews into the Red Army was raised in the Central Committee several times and always had the same results: it was shelved. As that same researcher writes, one of the reasons was "the natural reluctance of the recruits to be drafted into the gray ranks of the army," especially because "in the primarily peasant-based Red Army, anti-Semitism crossed the line and often surpassed that of the rebels and White armies whom it fought."[15]

PERHAPS THE MOST EXPLICIT anti-Semitism was displayed in the First Cavalry Army, one of the most legendary armies of the Civil War. Essentially, one doesn't have to talk about attitude, but rather pogroms, which hardly differed from those of Denikin.[16] The Red cavalrymen "distinguished themselves" during the Soviet-Polish War of 1920, and the pogroms generally took place during the period of defeat and retreat, but the "symptoms" were present much earlier. A political report based on the information from the Political Council of the First Cavalry Army on June 30, 1920, and signed by the deputy chief of the Political Department, S. N. Zhilinskii, spoke of the growing decomposition of the army, banditry, looting, and heavy drinking.[17]

Zhilinskii provided an analysis of the condition of various divisions that the army was composed of, which included the following information about the Fourth Division:

There is widespread brigandage, POWs are stripped of their clothing, anti-Semitic agitation is displayed almost openly. The commanders and *politrabotniki* [political commissars and other representatives of the Communist Party—*OB*] generally lack qualification and make only feeble attempts to deal with the above-mentioned problems.[18]

The Sixth Division, to which Babel was assigned, was described in similar terms: "The division has been plagued by a harmful element under whose agitation there has been increasing persecution of Jews, the growth of brigandage and abuse of civilians." It was also noted that the Eleventh and Fourteenth Divisions, which were composed primarily of Denikin's deserters and POWs who had been enlisted into the Red Army, were involved in marauding, robbery, and heavy drinking. The commanders and *politrabotniki* were either not capable of taming their subordinates or were actively involved in the looting.

This report resulted in the firing of Zhilinskii. The Army Commander Semen Mikhailovich Budenny, along with members of the Military Council of the Army Klement Efremovich Voroshilov, Sergei Konstantinovich Minin, and the chief of the political department I. V. Vardin (Mgeladze)—the high military and political command of the First Cavalry Army—issued a statement in which they protested against the "portrait" of the First Cavalry Army painted in the report. "They admitted," V. L. Genis writes, "that the First Cavalry Army was often referred to as 'brigands,' 'hooligans' and 'anti-Semites,'" and that "a near-majority of our comrades honestly believe that it is impossible for a Jew to ever show up at the First Cavalry; that Communists and their commissars would be killed there; that they, in their time away from combat, always loot, rape and torture."

Nevertheless, the members of the Revolutionary Military Council explained that "such wild views" as these were a reflection of the hatred harbored by the "bourgeois, petty bourgeois, and intelligentsia elements" toward the army, "the most prominent embodiment of Soviet Russia's strength."

From the point of view of Budenny and others, the Cavalry Army embodied "the peasant element that had risen up against Russian landlords and the rich Cossacks of the Don and Kuban'," and if it indeed looted in order to supply itself, then who would do otherwise? No army could otherwise survive.[19]

The last remark wasn't entirely baseless, because, in the almost total absence of regular procurement services, the implementation of the so-called Wallenstein model of supplying the army, namely requisitioning of food and other goods from the local population, as Albrecht Wallenstein did in the Thirty-Year War, was a common occurrence, regardless of whether the army was Red or White.

They were also correct in citing the largely peasant composition of the First Cavalry Army. At different points, peasants accounted for 71 to 77 percent of the army, while industrial workers and members of the intelligentsia accounted for 20 to 25 percent and 3 to 4 percent, respectively.[20] The Cossacks were evidently counted by them as peasants.

Actually, during the Soviet-Polish War of 1920, the Whites and Reds somewhat blended within one army. Many members of the White movement, as well as a number of officers who were captured by the Reds after the catastrophe at Novorossiisk, were conscripted into the Red Army. Those selected after the "purging" of the ranks were, in theory, the ones who "had not marred their reputation with crimes against the peasant-worker rule." There were as many as twelve thousand former White officers in the Red Army before January 1, 1920. These were obviously not all part of Denikin's army, but undoubtedly most of these officers were enlisted from its ranks in 1920.[21]

Former servicemen from the White Army under the command of General *Denikin* could easily be spotted in the First Cavalry Army. A contemporary by the name of Vladimir Fischer, a man of letters from St. Petersburg, who spent the Civil War years in the Ukrainian town of Dashev in the Kiev province (*guberniia*), recorded his impression of yet another coming of the Reds in the summer of 1920:

> The Bolsheviks moved in a never-ending line, and it was frightening to think what would happen to the places where they will be quartered. We heard rumors that they looted the homes where the Poles had stayed earlier.
>
> There were old friends among these *Budenovtsy*—former Cossacks from Denikin's army who had ravaged Dashev last November. They were immediately recognized, but they didn't loot this time around, because they were in a hurry. An overly happy Jew was telling me, nearly choking with excitement:
>
> "Look, Comrade (he immediately started referring to me as Comrade), what the Soviet power means! These same people were despicable brigands under Denikin, you and I both know that! But they went over to the Red side and now they're heroes!"[22]

These heroes would soon return.

In the brochure issued by the Political Department of the First Cavalry Army entitled "The Political Condition of the First Red Cavalry Army (June 15–August 15, 1920)," the department's chief, I. V. Vardin, wrote, "There is no active anti-Semitism in the Army. There is anti-Semitic prejudice; there is the purely peasant, subliminal and passive dislike towards the Jew, but nothing more. There is hardly any malicious, pogromist, or hooligan action towards the Jews."

A part of Babel's diary written around this time offers a good description of this stage of "passive dislike" of the Jews by the Red cavalrymen.[23] On June 6, 1920 in Rovno the military reporter Liutov remained with a Jewish family until the *Budenovtsy* left in order to foil their plan to rape the lady of the house. On July 11 in Belev, he recorded a conversation with a local Jew: "Same old thing, the Jews are looted, confusion, they were waiting for the Soviet authority as liberators, and instead there are screams, whips, kikes."[24]

The Jews, having suffered under the Polish rule,[25] awaited the Red Army as a real liberator. The secretary of the revolutionary military council of the First Cavalry testified to "an unusually attentive" attitude of the almost entirely Jewish population of Novograd-Volynsk towards the *Budenovtsy*.[26] But the illusions were quickly dispelled: "A cobbler awaited the Soviet power," recorded Babel, "and he sees the kike-beaters and robbers, and there won't be any earnings, he is shocked and looks suspiciously. . . . The same hatred, the same Cossacks, the same cruelty, different armies, what a nonsense. The life of the shtetl. There is no salvation."[27]

The old Jewish cemetery outside Malin prompted the war reporter Liutov to indulge in historiosophical reflections. The cemetery, he records in his diary, "witnessed Khmelnitsky, now Budenny, the miserable Jewish populace, everything is repeating, now this history—the Poles—the Cossacks—the Jews—is repeating with amazing precision, the new thing is Communism."[28]

On July 21 Babel recorded a conversation with the chief of staff of the Sixth Division, K. K. Zholnarkevich: "What is our Cossack? The layers: plundering, boldness, professionalism, revolutionary spirit, animal cruelty. We are the avant garde, but of what? The population is waiting for liberators, the Jews—for freedom—and then these Kuban Cossacks arrive. . . ."[29] Another commander is also quite realistic—the commander of the artillery division, Maximov: "Our army marches for the sake of gain, it is not a revolution but rather an uprising of the roaming outlaws. It is just a means which the party does not shy away from using."[30]

On August 3, a Red Army soldier, who correctly appraised the national identity of the military reporter Liutov, refused to give him any bread, citing his rule: "I have no business with the Jews." On August 8, another cavalryman, Ilchenko, who probably belonged to that 3 to 4 percent segment of the army consisting of the intelligentsia, discoursed on the economic policies and summed up: "the Jews are to blame for everything." "A dumb, Slavic creature," wrote Babel without consideration for political correctness, "who stuffed his pockets during the looting of Rostov."[31]

In Komarov the Budenny men threw the Torah scrolls out of a synagogue and took the velvet scroll coverings for their saddles. "By night *our troops* were looting . . . ," recorded Babel.[32]

So much for the passive stage in the "dislike of the Jews." Soon it evolved into an active form among the cavalrymen. In late September–early October 1920, the *Budenovtsy*, primarily those of the Sixth Cavalry Division, engaged in pogroms as they were retreating from the front line. These pogroms were no different from (and, according to some contemporaries, even surpassed) the one perpetrated by the Whites in cruelty and the number of victims. In any case, the dispatches from the Revolutionary Military Council of the First Cavalry called the pogroms that the Red troops staged in *mestechko* (shtetl) Berezovo and in the vicinity of Mlynov "horrible." Attempts at restoration of the order with the own forces of the command of the division were futile: the pogromists, arrested as of September 24, were freed by their own comrades, who also dispersed the Revolutionary Military Tribunal of the division along the way. The Sixth Division was no exception: a pogrom in the *mestechko* Rogachev was perpetrated by the troops of the Fourteenth Division.[33]

The commander of the Eighth Cavalry Division of the *Chervonnoe Kazachestvo* (Ukrainian Red Cossacks), Vitalii Markovich Primakov, who incidentally was a friend of Babel in the 1920s, reported the following to the headquarters of the South-Western front on October 2, 1920:

Today and yesterday the Sixth Division of the First Cavalry Army passed through my entrusted territory. Along its way, the Army engages in mass robberies, killings and pogroms. Yesterday over 30 people were killed in the *mestechko* Salnitsa, including the chairman of the Revolutionary Committee and his family; in the *mestechko* Lubar, over 50 people were killed. The Commanders and commissars are not taking any measures to stop this. In the meantime, a pogrom is under way in the *mestechko* Ulanov. . . . Taking into account that the officers are taking part in the pogrom, the struggle against pogroms might turn into an armed conflict between the Cossacks and *Budenovtsy* [who, in fact, also consisted of Cossacks from the Don—*OB*]. Yesterday, I talked to the chief of the Sixth Division (Apanasenko). He informed me that members of the Military Committee and several Communists were killed a few days ago by their own soldiers for shooting a group of brigands. The soldiers no longer obey their superiors including himself, their division commander. . . . The Sixth Division is moving towards the home front under the slogan, "kill the kikes, Communists and commissars, and save Russia." The soldiers talk of Makhno as the leader who provided this slogan.[34]

Primakov's information was entirely confirmed by the Emergency Investigation Committee headed by the Party and Trade Union activist Grigorii N. Melnichanskii, who visited the First Cavalry Army to assign political representatives and organize Party work.

According to Melnichanskii's committee report, cited below, the Sixth Cavalry Division unleashed a pogrom that lasted several days in the shtetl Samgorodok. On the first day of the pogrom, according to witness accounts, the pogromists stormed the shtetl "with slogans such as "Kill the kikes, Communists and Commissars," "Anarchy is the Mother of Order," and started slaughtering the Jewish population meeting no resistance, as the civilians were powerless and the administrative bodies, such as the Local Military Committee and the Militia, had fled the city the day before." The usually drunk *Budenovtsy* who settled in neighboring villages continued to raid the shtetl in groups of ten to fifteen men who "looted, raped women and burned down houses." On the eve of October 5, 1920 during yet another raid followed by the burning down of a building, the report went on, "they took four girls to the nearest village where they held them for entertainment purposes for two days. Neither were they merciful with old women: according to credible sources, over 50 of them were raped. They also killed 2 women. During their 15-day 'party,' all Jewish homes were robbed and many parents with infants hid in the fields and trenches in the cold autumn nights."

According to the Melnichanskii Committee's information, slogans like "kill the kikes—Commissars and Communists," "Let's go rid the home front of Jews," and "Let's go unite with Batka ["Father"] Makhno," were popular among the Red cavalrymen. G. G. Shepelev, a political commissar who was assigned to work with the Sixth Cavalry Division and went to the shtetl of Polonnoe to stop a pogrom that started there, was killed under the following circumstances (Melnichanskii's report):

On his way from the *mestechko* Polonnoe to Novoe Mesto, which is an exclusively Jewish settlement, screams were heard coming from almost every house. When comrade Shepelev entered one of the houses at the request of a female victim, he witnessed a horrifying sight: on the floor lay an old man of about 60, an old woman and their son, disfigured by broadswords, on the bed was a wounded man. In that same apartment, a Red Army soldier, the medical attendant of the Third Squadron of the Third Cavalry regiment by the name of Rudykh, and a nurse of that regiment were loading their bags with stolen items. Seeing the military commissar, the Red Army soldier rushed out of the building and wanted to flee. Shepelev followed him and after he refused to stop when prompted, the military commissar shot him.

The Commander arrested the nurse, but she managed to tell the soldiers that Shepelev had shot one of their comrades. According to the investigation materials, the cavalrymen were especially infuriated by the fact that the commissar was "defending the kikes." Ultimately, the angry crowd delivered swift "justice" to the commissar: he was first shot in the shoulder and later killed. The names of both cavalrymen who raised their weapons against their political supervisor were established by the investigation.

However, "neither the brigade commander nor any of the other commanders," Melnichanskii reported,

took any measures to find the instigators and the murderer. As the division moved along, there was a classic pogrom organized in the *mestechko* Lubar and, rumors have it, 60 Jews were killed, but, once again, the commanders took no measures to stop the pogrom and arrest the pogromists. When we were visiting the Sixth Cavalry Division in the towns Priluki and Vakhnovka, wine factories were raided and pogroms organized. 21 civilians were killed in Priluki, 12 were wounded, and many women and children were raped. According to locals, women were raped in the street in front of everyone. Many of the prettier girls were taken along. In Vakhnovka, 20 were killed, we don't know how many were raped or wounded, but 18 houses were burned down.

During the Priluki pogrom, the whole committee witnessed the decomposition of the Sixth Cavalry Division and the complete inactivity and connivance of its commanders. The pogrom was started by the billeting officers of the Second Brigade in the presence of the patrolling squadron of the Staff of the Sixth Cavalry Division, which didn't guard anything because its members were either standing aside idly, or also looting. The Military Commissar of the squadron personally tried to persuade the crowd to calm down, but in vain. The committee rushed to the scene and made the brigands flee, having taken two of them prisoner and handed them over to the Military Commissar, from whom they were reportedly rescued by their comrades. The pogrom itself was fully under way by nighttime. When we arrived at the site where the division headquarters were stationed, we sent an offer to the Sixth Division Commander to assume responsibility to stop the pogrom and although the latter ordered the commandant to dispatch forces, a witness survey showed that the order remained on paper. After interrogating the Seventh Division Commander who stayed in the *mestechko* of Priluki, we found out that the Sixth Division Commander visited him to forewarn that if his Cavalry starts "fooling around," the Seventh Cavalry shouldn't do anything "as to avoid conflicts."[35]

A Dashev resident, cited earlier, recalled:

"In autumn [of 1920] we had to, yet again, experience true horror when the *Budenovtsy* came. We immediately found out that they had killed the kikes. Let's be fair though, they were devoid of this bias. It turned out that they were able to rise above national stereotypes and paid equal attention to Christians. . . .

They killed a lot of Jews too. When, on the second day, there was a funeral for the murdered Jews, the *Budenovtsy* attacked the funeral procession, dispersed it and killed the attendees."[36]

The situation turned completely intolerable, and on October 9, 1920, the Revolutionary Military Council of the First Cavalry issued an order for dispersal of all the regiments that had been engaged in pogroms, and trying "all the murderers, pogromists, provocateurs and their accomplices." This implied the Sixth Division. It was not easy to disarm it. The secretary of the Revolutionary Military Council and the faithful "sword-bearer" of Voroshilov, S. N. Orlovskii, described in his rather credible diary the heroic and sentimental scene of the disarmament: the division succumbed to the demands of Budenny and Voroshilov who arrived at the camp, while "the commanders and the troops were crying loudly as they surrendered their weapons and banners."[37] But the matter was decided not by the unquestionable authority of the senior commanders. Initially the division refused to disarm, and only after being encircled near the town of Belaia Tserkov by the special brigade under the command of K. Stepnoi-Spizharnii,[38] artillery and armored trains, did they surrender their weapons.[39]

Curiously enough, the rumor had it that Budenny was preparing to lead their campaign against the rear area. According to other rumors, the commander was arrested by "Jewish commissars."[40]

The regiments gave up 107 "active participants of the banditry"; 300 more dispersed in the forests to avoid the worst. However, sixty of them were soon captured. The disarmament of the Sixth Division did not preclude anti-Semitic rhetoric even at the army party conference that took place three days later. The presidium received notes from the voting member participants with a demand to have the issue of "why there are no Jews in the Cavalry Army" included in the agenda. This demand, needless to say, was not met but as a result, ten voting delegates were excluded from participating in the conference.[41]

In the meantime, the pogroms continued; Jews were not only victimized, but they were clearly given a "preferential treatment."

V. L. Genis cites telegrams reporting misconduct by the *Budenovtsy*, such as this one, sent by the administration of the Kiev province (*guberniia*) to the head of the Ukrainian Council of Peoples Commissars (Ukrainian Soviet Government), Khristian Georgevich Rakovskii, on October 14:

> In recent weeks, there has been an incessant rain of complaints about misconduct by the passing divisions of the First Cavalry Army. In Taraschansk . . . all citizens, Soviet officials and even Soviet institutions [were] robbed. The total [number] of casualties is 150. On October 10, there was a Jewish pogrom, Communists were beaten, the penitentiary was opened, 4 houses were burned, 30 were killed, 4 were wounded. . . . There are reports from Skvir' saying that after the First Cavalry divisions passed through, only five of the sixteen local Military Commanders remained in place, the others have been reported missing. The Khodorovskii Metalwork Factory was looted, and many civilians killed. Telegrams came from Berdichev saying that "the passing divisions of the First Cavalry Army are robbing Jews, we fear an upcoming pogrom." The Kiev Provincial Military Committee reports that "the passing divisions of the First Cavalry Army have shot seven Red Army soldiers and the members of the horse purchasing committee."

Similar information was coming from Kremenchug:

> Divisions of the Cavalry Army passing through the Cherkasskii *uezd* [district] are "terrorizing the administration," looting and executing civilians and even the families of Red Army soldiers, and taking the farm animals with them. "With screams of 'Kill the kikes and Communists,'" read a telegram from the Provincial superintendent of the rear, "they are running around villages and boroughs. There are some killed and many wounded, among them many Soviet officials. Families of Red Army soldiers, Soviet officials, local Military Commanders and Revolutionary Committee chairmen are looted and beaten nearly to death. Soviet Jewish officials are also being killed. The civilians and administration are fleeing in panic, hiding in forests and fields. The results of the misconduct are already showing: those villages that were pro-Soviet and far from participating in brigandage now intensely hate the Soviet power and the Red Army."[42]

The moral decay of the Cavalry Army was of special concern to the high command, because, upon repletion of its thinning ranks, it was to be dispatched from the Polish front to the Black Sea—to fight against Wrangel's forces. It was decided that surgical measures were called for. On October 18 the Revolutionary Military Council proposed that the Revolutionary Military Tribunal, in examination of the cases of soldiers and commanders of the Sixth Division, "be guided not so much by the formal side as by the revolutionary consciousness and the importance of the moment for the fate of the First Cavalry." The "revolutionary justice" was given the task of reviving "all the healthy, conscious elements" and raising the combat preparedness of the army "to the appropriate height."[43] Evidently, it was assumed that the revival of the healthy forces would require the elimination of a certain number of the erstwhile heroes.

If we use the Sixth Division, which Babel accompanied in the Polish campaign, as an example, we see that the "militant" anti-Semitism was far from being the prerogative of the Don Cossacks. Initially about a half of the Sixth Division fighters were enlisted in the Stavropol region; the other half was recruited in the regions of Astrakhan and Smolensk.[44]

In the Sixth Division, 387 men were put under arrest; their cases were reviewed by the extraordinary session of the tribunal of the First Cavalry Army. The tribunal held open hearings in Elizavetgrad on October 21–23, 1920. On the first day, according to different sources, the tribunal tried 141 to 182 men accused of participating in the pogroms, including 19 officers; 110 were sentenced to death and immediately executed; 31 had the death penalty replaced by varying terms of incarceration. Among the remaining men, 57 persons were sentenced to death and executed. The tribunal, it seems, continued its proceedings against the men of the Sixth Division, albeit in closed session, until October 30, bringing to completion their "educational assignment" in early November. It is possible that the total number of those executed reached four hundred.[45]

The tribunal also tried a group of officers. To keep up the good appearances, a number of Red commanders, too, were sentenced to death. However, taking into consideration that some of the sentenced joined the Red Army voluntarily at the early stages of its formation, and in commemoration of the third anniversary of the October revolution, the sentences were suspended and the officers placed under the authority of the staff of the Southern front to be dispatched to cavalry regiments "with a considerable reduction in rank."[46] The latter policy was identical to the practices employed by the Whites, who also sent those sentenced for participation in the pogroms to the front lines, where they would have ended in any case. The tribunal sentenced the commander of the Sixth Division I. R. Apanasenko and the commander of the brigade V. I. Kniga to death with the forfeiture of their Orders of the Red Banner. Later, the death sentence was commuted to a suspended sentence of fifteen years of forced labor, further suspended with the understanding that the accused resume their active military service, except in the First Cavalry Army, with the right to serve as commanders of a lower rank (the former division commander could now at best be in charge of a regiment, and the former brigade commander, of a squadron).[47]

Although it almost ended sadly for Apanasenko (Babel's Pavlichenko), the episode had little effect on Apanasenko's subsequent career. Like other former Cavalrymen, he became "untouchable," however many purges he passed through. Apanasenko served as commander of various regiments, and was twice awarded with the Order of the Red Banner. In February 1941 he was elected to the Central Committee of VKP(b) as a candidate member and promoted to general. On August 5, 1943, Apanasenko, then deputy commander of the Voronezh front, was mortally wounded and died soon thereafter. Delirious as he was dying, he was imagining that it was August 3, 1920 and he was crossing the river of Styr; he was yelling orders that were incomprehensible to his aide. The last words of the former commander of the Sixth Division were, purportedly, "Sons of the revolution. . . ."[48] Babel would have appreciated this scene.

The cruel measures were somewhat instrumental in reinforcing the discipline, but overall the Cavalry Army bore little resemblance to a regular military unit. Curiously, while engaged in action on the Southern front, the cavalrymen found themselves in the famous nature preserve Askania-Nova. There, they immediately began hunting rare animals, while one of the soldiers even tried to ride an ostrich. However, the ostrich managed to hold his own and kicked the unfortunate rider.[49] The troops could refuse to accept a new commander if they disliked him from the start, especially if he was "a Jew by the look of him,"[50] as was the case in one of the regiments. Timoshenko, then in charge of the Division, could do nothing but reinstate the previous commander.[51]

Philosemitism failed to take root. However, it was not that easy to root out the anti-Semitic sentiment, which often intertwined with an anti-Communist one. In December 1920, an employee of the Political Inspection of the Southwestern front, P. Y. Vitolin, reported, "The divisions' attitude is," as one (Communist) Party official put it, "militant: kill

Jews and Communists and save Russia. And, indeed, these two elements are intertwined . . . and it is not that pogroms and brigandage come to an end, rather, they merge with the military operations and as a result, become less evident." In April 1921, the chairman of the Central Executive Committee of the Ukraine, Grigorii Ivanovich Petrovskii, reported to Moscow that the First Cavalry Army raided the provision distribution teams in Lubny (Poltavskaia *guberniia*) and Elizavetgrad (Nikolaevskaia *guberniia*). He said, "they did not allow for bread to be prepared; they took everything, saying that Kikes and Communists should not be fed," and that the slogan, "kill kikes and commissars and save Russia," was still popular among Red Cavalrymen.[52]

THE TOTAL "SHARE" OF POGROMS that the Red Army is "credited" with during the Civil War years in the Ukraine is, according to N. Gergel, 106, or 8.6 percent of the total number of pogroms. The Red Army soldiers killed 725 Jews.[53] Although the Red Army organized half as many pogroms as did the White forces under Denikin, their Jewish victims numbered one-seventh of those killed by the Whites.

The Soviet government, unlike the White leadership, actually wished to stop the pogroms and had no intention of using anti-Semitism as its ideological banner. In general, unlike the Whites, the Reds had many other appealing slogans. The mercilessness with which they eventually treated the pogromists proved effective. The Bolsheviks demonstrated that, if necessary, they would not hesitate to carry out mass executions. Most Jews did not have any reason to like the Bolsheviks, who proclaimed trade and business to be crimes, thereby destroying the very basis of Jewish economic existence. But the choice between the Reds and the Whites became a matter of life and death for Jews. It is not surprising that they chose life.

# 4

## Isaac Babel and the
## Jewish Experience of Revolution

CAROL J. AVINS

THE DECEMBER 1931 ISSUE of *30 dnei*, a popular journal published by the Union of Soviet Writers, must have passed through many hands: in addition to such regular features as literary news, profiles of Five-Year-Plan successes, and a glossary of the latest neologisms, it included the final installment of one of the most widely read novels of the day, Ilf and Petrov's *The Golden Calf.* This sequel to the authors' satire *The Twelve Chairs* continues the adventures of a rogue bound for a life of wealth and ease, preferably far away from the land of the Soviets in sunny Rio de Janeiro. Readers eager to learn whether the dénouement did indeed fulfill the hero's fantasy may have noticed (after the inevitable letdown) that the same issue's contents page promised another tale of travel as well: a story by Isaac Babel entitled "The Journey." Those who turned to the designated page, however, were disappointed—or perhaps rewarded, depending on their inclinations. Where Babel's story was meant to be, one finds instead a four-page rallying cry to heed the lessons taught by comrade Stalin in a recent pronouncement concerning Lenin's role—and that of the traitorous Trotsky—in Bolshevik history.[1]

Why the replacement of Babel's story with Stalinist polemics? Though Babel was habitually behind schedule in delivering manuscripts, correspondence shows that he submitted the manuscript in October, presumably in time for December publication.[2] That October, however, saw the publication elsewhere in the press of a lengthy open letter by Stalin entitled "On Some Questions Concerning the History of Bolshevism," a response to an article by historian A. G. Slutsky that had appeared in the journal *Proletarskaia revoliutsiia*. Stalin, incensed by Slutsky's depiction of pre-revolutionary factionalism, lambastes what he calls "archive rats" and other falsifiers of history who spread dangerous errors in their efforts to reconstruct the past.[3]

Slutsky's article led to his arrest and exile; its consequence for Babel was the bumping of his story to a later issue of *30 dnei*. Soviet historical journals were instructed to rush into print Stalin's response along with editorials explaining its significance; other periodicals evidently received such instructions as well.[4] The article in *30 dnei* included excerpts from Stalin's letter along with paraphrase and praise of the leader and the following warning: because our enemies understand the enormous significance of Party history for the waging of world revolution, it is precisely on the front of history that we must take up arms.[5]

The depiction of recent history, as it happens, was a matter on Babel's mind at this time as well. Though the editorial slip that kept his story on the contents page while replacing it with commentary on Stalin is in itself of no significance, the juxtaposition between the prose of the political and literary masters is suggestive. The commonalities between the two authors' publications—Stalin's letter and Babel's story—are more intriguing than their differences. In their preoccupation with the representation of the past, and in their chosen themes, the two find common ground. Stalin warns of the need for even the most loyal historians to exercise vigilance in the face of counterrevolution; "The Journey," set in the period immediately following the Bolshevik takeover, ends with the narrator joining the ranks of those countering foreign and domestic subversion. Stalin insists upon the proper mapping of the route traversed by Lenin in his struggles with ideological enemies; Babel traces an embattled journey to join the revolution in which some are cut down and others survive to become transformed by their experience. Stalin allies himself with a Lenin of his own making; Babel also creates his own version of a predecessor, an earlier self whose path leads to a historically correct destination.

Babel's tale of an alter ego's path to participation in the revolutionary enterprise is one of several stories he published in the early 1930s that look back at the revolution's aftermath with an eye for the transformations that history requires of those who live through turbulent times. The protagonists of these stories are Jews, and they are marked by this fact of their identity; thus these stories involve not simply the individual's encounter with the revolutionary era, but what could be called the Jewish experience of revolution. Exploring "The Journey" in the context of Babel's contemporary publications, and in the context of what surrounded them on the page, yields new perspectives on how he problematizes both the contingencies of life in a time of upheaval and the forms of Jewish identity compatible with the post-revolutionary age.

To speak of a Jewish experience of revolution—of how Jews viewed, participated in, and were affected by the Bolshevik Revolution and consequent remaking of society—is not a simple matter. There were Jews in the Russian and then Soviet state at many points on the political and economic spectrum; their situations and stances were conditioned by multiple variables from age to education to geography. Even to generalize about the depiction in Babel's writing of Jews in the revolution's aftermath entails dealing with a wide range of types from makers to victims of revolution (and those who can be seen as both).

In the diary Babel kept during his service in the 1920 war between the fledgling Soviet state and Poland, we find him denigrating Communist Party members in the army's political section as "incredibly feeble Jewish men and women from the underground"(4 July); describing with horror and empathy a young Jewish woman who worked in the Revolutionary Committee and was drawn to a seductive Cossack (24 July); encountering Jews who were Zionists and Hasidim, dentists, millhands, and shopkeepers.[6] He reassured civilians fearful that Bolshevism would mean the end of private enterprise and the destruction of their livelihood, telling what he himself cynically called "fairy tales" about the utopian future ahead under Soviet rule. Intermittently concealing his own Jewishness behind an assumed name, he sometimes, among Jews he found kindred, tried to have it both ways, claiming that his mother was Jewish but his father Russian.[7]

In the *Red Cavalry* stories, which came out of those wartime experiences, the range of Jewish types is narrower, curbed to serve Babel's design. More striking in that design than the types themselves are the tensions between them. These tensions go beyond the central opposition between the exhausted spiritual leader and his ambivalently revolutionary son, inspired but ultimately wasted by ideological struggle ("The Rebbe"; "The Rebbe's Son"). There are other telling oppositions: between the old Jew whose throat is slit by a Cossack and the young Jew in uniform—the narrator—who silently watches ("Berestechko"); between the narrator and the warring factions of impassioned Hasidim whom he briefly joins in vociferous debate on a public square in an effort to vent, if not reconcile, the warring parts of himself ("Squadron Commander Trunov"). Beyond *Red Cavalry*, in other works set in the early post-revolutionary years, we find Babel's folkloric Jewish gangsters blasted by the Bolsheviks (Froim Grach in the story of that name, Benya Krik in the eponymous screenplay), as well as Jews divided by their orientation toward both religious tradition and the new secular authority. We shall return to two stories about such conflicts after examining the complex landscape of "The Journey."

"The Journey" is distinctive among Babel's stories in several respects. It is the only story set after the revolution in which the narrator is a victim of anti-Semitic violence. Of all his works, it is set closest in time and place to the Bolshevik takeover—in early 1918 in Petrograd, birthplace of the revolution and still the capital. Like the stories Babel designated as belonging to the cycle he called *The Story of My Dovecote*, it is a pseudo-autobiographical story about origins—in this case, not his origins as a child of Jewish Odessa but as a deracinated charter member of a newly formed order. Because "The Journey" builds on an earlier story, it enables one to see the writer at work, expanding a sketch by adding significant elements. Among these elements is an ending unlike any other in Babel, one that marks his most conspicuous failure to heed his own advice in "Guy de Maupassant" (published in *30 dnei* three issues after "The Journey"). The narrator of that story warns against the fatal error some make in turning the lever of a phrase not once, but twice, and counsels the proper understanding of verbal art as an arsenal of powerful weapons, chief among them a period deployed in the nick of time.[8]

Let us proceed with a brief look at "The Journey"'s antecedent, a piece Babel published in 1922 called "An Evening at the Empress's."[9] In that sketch the narrator, who characterizes himself as a homeless poet at large in frigid 1918 Petrograd, finds temporary refuge in Anichkov Palace, former residence of Alexander III and his consort Maria Feodorovona. A search yields sustenance for both body and soul: in addition to food, a collection of books brought by the young future empress from her native Denmark. The narrator is captivated by what the books reveal of her beginnings in that tranquil kingdom far away and long ago; finally, after midnight, he emerges from a fairy-tale past into reality, heading for the train station to bed down for the night.

This narrator is a man en route to nowhere in particular, without any evident destination beyond whatever warm spot can keep him off the streets. His experience of playing interloper in the lap of tsarist luxury remains when Babel revisits the scene ten years later in "The Journey," but now this vignette acquires a frame. The narrator is given an ethnic identity as well as a life before and after his sojourn at the palace—a path toward revolutionary Petrograd and a path onward from there.

"The Journey" reveals nothing of his life before the revolution, however: that event sets the story in motion. "I left the shattered front in November of 1917," begins the narration.[10] The line that follows describes in seven dry words a stop at home to get outfitted by mother; then the protagonist sets off to make his way toward the capital. After this very brief scene-setting comes the central episode of the journey: on the train, the narrator witnesses the murder and mutilation of a fellow Jew and narrowly escapes the same fate. Arriving after many travails in Petrograd, he looks up his former commander Kalugin, now working for the newly organized All-Russian Extraordinary Commission for Combatting Counter-revolution, Speculation, Sabotage, and Misuse of Authority (known as the Cheka) and spends the night with Kalugin in the royal digs at Anichkov Palace recovering from the rigors of the trip. (Cleansing himself of the grime of the past, he engages in a kind of parodic carnivalistic reversal, donning not the tsar's royal robes but the tsar's ragged bathrobe—a combination of self-crowning and self-mockery.) The rejuvenation he experiences after bathing and dressing in imperial garb, and the perspective he gains from communing with the Romanovs' possessions, are, in this story, not simply hedonistic pleasures but means to an end. In the morning he is ready for service and is welcomed into the new ruling class, approved for work as a translator by the head of the Petrograd Cheka, Moisei Solomonovich Uritsky.

"The Journey" can be seen as, among other things, a tale of the post-revolutionary Jewish path from victimization in the provinces to centrality in the capital. The moment of initiation into the new order is depicted as a kind of rebirth. In this respect the story conforms to the conventions of the period, which is full of works involving the post-revolutionary transformation of self. One need look no further than other issues of the same journal, where a story about a young Jewish man's encounter with the new order in which one is defined by class rather than religion is entitled "Katznelson's First Memory"—as if his previous existence had been canceled out.[11] The title character, believing that as a Jew he is condemned to suffer, is led to cast aside that crippling notion and reconceive himself as a proud proletarian and Red Army soldier. Another young Jewish man who leaves town with the conquering Red Army can be found in a story by David Bergelson that neatly illustrates the Marxist maxim that the places of the high and the lowly shall be reversed.[12]

Such experiences of reincarnation are of course not limited to Jews, and they are also commonly recounted in another genre to which "The Journey" belongs, the reminiscence about one's role in the historic early days of the new regime. The line between memoir and fiction in such works can be blurred. "How We Took the Winter Palace," one such piece that appeared in *30 dnei*, is a typical example. The author's account of routing the Provisional Government from the palace includes a description of working-class soldiers stirred to realize that the lavish possessions filling the halls now belong to the people—and that they are thus the new proprietors. Babel's narrator in "The Journey" waxes both lyrical and ironic in detailing his encounter with the imperial family's books and baubles; the tone in this more typical flashback to revolutionary days is purely triumphalist. "How We Took the Winter Palace" concludes with a recitation of the Military Revolutionary Committee's proclamation announcing their takeover, part of which declares: "The cause for which the people struggled: the immediate proposal of a democratic peace, abolition of landowners' rights to land, workers' control of production, the creation of a soviet government—this cause is assured."[13]

While Babel's story is of a different type, the closing section of the "The Journey" is in this triumphalist mode, complete with catalogue of all that the protagonist has achieved. The above-quoted passage about the revolution's goals is a good starting point for an examination of the story's ending, the part of "The Journey" that has attracted the most critical attention. Several paragraphs follow the moment when the narrator crosses the threshold of the Cheka headquarters; they are punctuated by two final lines that sum up the narrator's status and bring the reader forward in time to the present. This two-part coda reads as follows:

> Not a day had passed, and I had everything: clothing, food, work, and comrades faithful in friendship and death, comrades the likes of whom can be found nowhere in the world except in our land.
>
> Thus began thirteen years ago my superlative life, filled with thought and gaiety. (43)

The first journey—the pre-revolutionary life—completed, a second has been embarked upon, marked not by tribulations but by intellectual and emotional fulfillment.

The closing lines appear tacked-on, improbably sanguine—a Stalinist-era ending in the testimonial style. They are "the oddest thing" in the story, writes one scholar who regards them as written tongue in cheek.[14] The "cliché ending," writes another, raises doubt "that the new Jew who enjoys some of the power stripped from his former oppressors will be truly happy."[15] Though many readers cannot help but read irony into Babel's words, he apparently hoped that the readers he cared about most at the time of publication would not. Vadim Kovskii argues quite persuasively that the design of the story's ending is dictated by pragmatic considerations. Babel had recently weathered an accusation that he had given a virulently anti-Soviet interview when last in France; now he was trying to gain permission once again to return to Paris to see his family, particularly the daughter born in his absence.[16] (Such an effort to curry favor with the authorities is at odds, though, with other stories he published in 1931–1932 such as "Gapa Guzhva" and "The End of the Almshouse," which were more likely to have the opposite effect.)

Rather than dismiss the closing as an artificial appendage, let us take a closer look, first stepping back to examine the paragraphs that precede it. These depict two scenes: the narrator's inspection by Uritsky and his assimilation into the culture of his new workplace. The encounter with Uritsky is theatrically staged. The narrator, who has stayed up until dawn unable to tear himself away from the diaries, letters, and aura of the dowager empress, is taken that morning to Cheka headquarters and enters another realm of mystery. Told to wait while his mentor Kalugin speaks to Uritsky, he listens in the wings to the presentation of his case:

> I stood behind a drapery that fell to the floor in waves of cloth. Fragments of words floated through to me.
>
> "He's one of us" [*paren' svoi*], said Kalugin. "His father's a shopkeeper, a tradesman, but he's broken with them. . . . He knows languages . . ."
>
> The Commissar of Internal Affairs for the Communes of the Northern Region walked out of his office with his swaying gait. Behind the lenses of his pince-nez hung his loosened, swollen eyelids, scorched by insomnia. (43, ellipsis in original)

The narrator's identity as a Jew has been a near-fatal impediment en route to the capital; the ranks of the Cheka include a disproportionate percentage of Jews, however (Uritsky among them), and here it is not his religion but his class origin that places him in jeopardy.[17] The nature of the enterprise he seeks to join is implied by the condition of its leader, the arbiter of his fate as of that of so many others. In the portrait of Uritsky, consumed by his task, Babel implies that such work may ravage the narrator as well. The grotesque figure of the seemingly sightless, wordless Uritsky casts a long shadow over the remaining lines of the story, dimming the happy-ever-after light of the coda.

The scene invites comparison with another scene in Babel of reporting to serve the revolutionary cause: the appearance of *Red Cavalry*'s narrator before the Cossack commander Savitsky in "My First Goose." Uritsky, with his inflamed, exhausted eyes and shaky gait, is an opposite to the hyperbolically vigorous, dazzling giant, merriment dancing in his eyes. Uritsky's frightening gaze aside, acceptance in the Cheka office proves far easier to win than acceptance among Cossacks in the field: the narrator of "My First Goose" is rewarded with words like Kalugin's ("the lad'll suit us," *paren' nam podkhodiashchii*) only after he has performed an act of sacrifice.[18]

Will service in the Cheka entail analogous violations of conscience? There is no such indication, unless we read it in Uritsky's face. The narrator's description at the end of "The Journey" of the work he embarks upon is neutral and brief:

They made me a translator in the Foreign Division. I was issued a military uniform and dinner coupons. In the corner allotted to me in a room of the former Petersburg City Hall I set about translating depositions given by diplomats, arsonists, and spies. (43)

Babel had himself for a short period in early 1918 apparently served as a translator for the Cheka, after which he began writing reportage for the anti-Bolshevik newspaper *Novaia zhizn'*, which railed against it.[19] Had he ended the story here, with a venerable hall adapted to a new purpose and the task of combating subversion before us, these lines would have borne some resemblance to what he was writing back in 1918 about struggling new institutions and the gulf between their ideals and realities. His reportage covered a wide range of problems and locales, from the care of juvenile delinquents to that of blind veterans, from morgues to maternity homes (where, he observes, one is grateful not to hear the conversations about arrests that have become so common).[20] Babel did not write directly about the Cheka at that time, but his fellow contributors to *Novaia zhizn'* reveal much about attitudes in 1918 toward the goings-on behind the doors of Gorokhovaia Street number 2, Cheka headquarters. One open letter to Comrade Uritsky in April bitterly challenges him to reconcile evidence of unjust arrests and sentences with his "communist conscience."[21] Another article, on the same page as one of Babel's pieces, expresses outrage at the order, signed by Uritsky, that any persons seeking an explanation of a search or arrest will be arrested themselves.[22]

Writing in 1931, Babel could assume that his readers' memories were long enough to recall the Cheka's methods of protecting the revolution from subversion. The reference toward the end of "The Journey" to the depositions of foreign agents and spies would also have evoked more contemporary associations—particularly the 1931 trial of former Mensheviks, who were accused of participation in a conspiracy involving Mensheviks in exile as well as English and French agents planning to sabotage the Soviet economy and launch a war of intervention.[23] Babel's description of the documents he translated, however, hinting of ideological struggles ahead, is canceled out by the line that follows, a list not of threats to revolution but of the fruits of revolution—what I have called the first line in a two-part coda. To quote this line once again: "Not a day had passed, and I had everything—clothing, food, work, and comrades faithful in friendship and death, comrades the likes of whom can be found nowhere in the world except in our land."

This description of the revolution's bounty, as indicated above, appears so utopic as to imply an ironic reading. The language conforms not only to the rhetoric of reminiscence about glorious revolutionary days past but also to the 1930s rhetoric of gratitude to the state for its beneficence.[24] The narrator's assessment of his acquisitions is not, however, as simple as it seems. The passage is complicated by the sense in which it serves as an inverted echo of the horrific episode early in the story involving a young Jewish schoolmaster, traveling to Petrograd with his new wife to work in Lunacharsky's Commissariat of Enlightenment, who is murdered by anti-Bolshevik and anti-Semitic partisans on the train.

The narrator, seated next to the newlyweds on this train headed northward from Kiev, notes the schoolmaster's devotion to his cause and to his bride: all through the journey they whisper about new pedagogical methods; when they fall asleep, their hands remain clasped together. Yehuda Veinberg is the man's name, and when the train is boarded by partisans his documents are inspected, he is shot in the face, his trousers are unbuttoned, and his genitals cut off and stuffed in his wife's mouth (with a taunt about trying something kosher). The narrator, also recognized as a Jew, is thrown off the train but allowed to escape, apparently in exchange for the gold coins torn from his underwear.

Think once again about the story's closing description of the pleni-tude achieved by the narrator after he finally makes it to his destination. "Clothing, food, work, and comrades faithful in friendship and death"— each of the terms in that catalogue of what the narrator has acquired has a point of resonance with the lurid story of Veinberg's violation, of what he has lost: the trousers; the gruesome genitals; his educational mission; the young wife as comrade, tested in death.

That the narrator rather than his fellow passenger makes it to the promised land is purely arbitrary, but he and the schoolmaster, who both journey from the former Pale to enlist in building a new order, are not interchangeable. The narrator is unencumbered, free to find kinship in comrades, the mother mentioned in the second line of the story as having packed him food and clothing now superfluous. Veinberg, traveling with his wife in a microcosm of loving domesticity, intent on changing the world by peaceful means, is not a double of the narrator but an alternative type. True, the narrator (though he is straight from fighting on the World War I front) is something of a bookish type himself: he knows languages, he gets a desk job. But he seeks his share of thrills through proximity to men of action.

In "An Evening at the Empress's," the story's early version, the excuse the narrator concocts to explain his presence in the palace is that he is waiting to see Lunacharsky (whose commissariat controlled not only the former Ministry of Public Education and other institutions but the royal palaces as well).[25] In "The Journey" Lunacharsky, littérateur and orator as well as revolutionary politician, is the prospective mentor of the mild-mannered Veinberg; the narrator is headed for a job in a different sort of agency. Lest one make too much of this contrast, however, one should note that Lunacharsky was as determined to silence counterrevolutionaries as any of his fellow Bolsheviks, and that his view of words as weapons was more than metaphorical. Justifying in a 1925 lecture the continuing need for censorship, he responds to those concerned about artistic freedom that "we are living in a period of fierce class warfare," describing Soviet writ-ers as warriors in combat with an enemy whom they must disarm or be destroyed themselves.[26]

By creating Yehuda Veinberg, Babel marks the memory of those fallen at the hands of anti-Semites and counterrevolutionaries, suggest-ing that the path to Jewish transformation in the post-revolutionary era— which involves the transcendence of Jewish victimhood—is not as smooth as the closing of "The Journey" implies. Though the story's ending turns the attentive reader back to the martyred Veinberg, the narrator, like the men of action he admires, wastes no energy on looking back at the victim. When, struggling up the frozen Nevsky weeks after setting out, he tries to recall the name of the historical figure who was trampled by Arab steeds at the very end of a journey, it is himself he is comparing to the medieval poet Yehuda Halevi at the gates of Jerusalem, not that other Yehuda who perished before arriving in the promised land.

Babel's character sees in his experience an echo of legend; for the reader, there are also echoes of earlier Babel. One thinks of his treatment of Jewish victimization in a different revolutionary year, 1905, "The Story of My Dovecote": another protagonist (a boy) assaulted on a journey to assimilation and fulfillment; another victim (the great-uncle) murdered and mutilated in front of his family (castrated symbolically if not literally, a fish shoved in his fly). "The Story of My Dovecote" emphasizes the burden of being marked as a Jew and the impossibility of liberation from that fate, no matter what one's attributes. In "The Journey," a post-revolutionary pogrom story, escape is possible, identity redefinable, and fulfillment, however unconvincingly described, awaits.

Another story of Babel's about a Jewish revolutionary's death on a train is relevant here as well. Ilya Bratslavsky the rebbe's son, Hasidic sage by destiny but Bolshevik by conviction, dies at the end of *Red Cavalry* not by violent means but of typhus—and of trying to carry too much baggage. (Recall the often-quoted catalogue of his incongruous belongings—Hebrew verse and Party resolutions, a lock of a woman's hair alongside portraits of Lenin and Maimonides.) Bratslavsky is not mutilated, but he is rendered incapable of perpetuating his line nonetheless; Babel depicts him laid out on the floor of the train, missing his trousers, the "stunted, curly manhood of a wasted Semite" exposed.[27] The narrator buries and mourns Bratslavsky at a minor station on the line, reflecting elegiacally on their kinship and exuding survivor's guilt. No hint of the elegiac mode enters into the account of Veinberg's death in "The Journey," and it is worth noting that the narrator is unmarked by any possessions: by the time he reaches Petrograd, he has twice been stripped of his luggage.

Free of belongings, he is ready to belong—and what this empty vessel comes to be filled with, the story's last line tells us, is satisfaction both of mind and of spirit. Babel's final flourish, seemingly designed to ensure that the story is understood as autobiographical and recently completed, declares: "Thus began thirteen years ago my superlative life, filled with thought and gaiety (*polnaia mysli i vesel'ia*)" (43). However facile the line may seem, this pair of abstractions warrants some attention.

On one level the division of the narrator's condition into realms of "thought" and "gaiety" signifies that he has been made complete, one with the realms of both mind and heart, reason and feeling. These are the milk and honey awaiting the wanderer, offering not simply sustenance but satisfaction. One might also usefully see Babel's *mysl'* and *vesel'e* as markers for the two terms that, in Leninist theory, are engaged in a dialectical struggle driving historical development: consciousness (*soznatel'nost'*)and spontaneity (*stikhiinost'*).[28] How to foster the resolution of that opposition and thus smooth the path of progress toward communism was one of the theoretical problems acted out in the plot of the socialist realist novel, which resolves itself in the hero's arrival at the end of a road to maturation. Babel's hero struggles to get to his geographic destination but finds a shortcut to completeness once there (the story's ending comes from a related genre, the fairy tale).

The achievement of "thought" and "gaiety" are presented as unproblematic, but if we focus on the second term we may find further meaning in what might seem flippant or ironic. Babel took his *vesel'e* seriously—and this, one is tempted to point out, is another matter on which he and Stalin would agree. It was not until several years later (in November 1935) that Stalin was to give fun a secure status in the hierarchy of values by proclaiming that "life has become better, comrades. Life has become merrier [*veselei*]."[29] But the idea of joyousness as a criterion of well-being and an end worth seeking was of course not new—nor was it new to Babel's work. He had featured it in his fiction long before—most prominently in the *Red Cavalry* story called "The Rebbe," set in Zhitomir.

When the narrator, Liutov, comes to the Rebbe's with the old shopkeeper Gedali, he is asked four questions: where are you from; what do you do; what have you studied; and what do you seek. "What seeks the Jew?" (*Chego ishchet evrei?*), inquires the Rebbe; the narrator answers in one word: "*Vesel'ia.*"[30] It has been noted that Liutov's answer is consonant with the teachings of the Hasidic masters who elevated the attainment of joy to a sacred level, seeing it as integral to the experience of oneness with God.[31] There is irony here in that joy seems impossible to experience in this war-ravaged environment, in this room likened to a morgue. But one should also understand Liutov's declaration as conveying a genuine wish of the anxious narrator, a wish for a kind of completeness, a oneness with the world, that eludes him. He confesses here and elsewhere in *Red Cavalry* his desire not for understanding—for more words, theories, intellectualizing—but for the ability to suspend understanding and take refuge in comfort and affirmation.

Liutov's choice of words in "The Rebbe" may be influenced by his earlier visit to the philosophizing Gedali, in whose view the revolution has no justification if it is not to be a source of pleasure. In the diary entry where Babel notes his conversation with Gedali's prototype, the man's wish for a "kind government" is an individual dream.[32] But the fictional character's cry of longing for a "sweet revolution" is not his alone: he describes it as the cry of all thinking people, all the learned men of Zhitomir.[33] In Gedali's telling, those who seek understanding seek also an order that is not only just but brings the kind of justice they can revel in.

The tension between a younger and older generation of Jews that constitutes part of the drama of *Red Cavalry* is developed in two other Babel stories published within a year of "The Journey": "Karl-Yankel" and "The End of the Almshouse." In both stories—one of birth and initiation, the other of death and burial—Babel probes the legitimacy of ancient tradition and the legitimacy of its present abandonment. The conflicts that drive the plots of these stories—over whether, in this new age, an infant should be circumcised and whether a body should be buried in accordance with Jewish law—are not clearly resolved in favor of one side or another, though Babel satirizes the young Soviet secularizers more severely than the guardians of tradition. But the stories do make clear that the stakes are high. At issue (as in "The Journey") is where the post-revolutionary road will lead. Both stories end with an image of the road ahead that conveys an ambivalence about the forces that shape the characters' destiny.

"The End of the Almshouse," which presents the more pessimistic path, appeared in *30 dnei* just two issues before "The Journey," and thus readers who followed the journal might have viewed the two stories in relation to each other. Consider, in comparison with the closing of "The Journey," the final lines of "Almshouse," which describe the expulsion from Odessa's Second Jewish Cemetery of the indigent elderly men and women who had sustained themselves by working there. Ordered to report to a city office to register for a new work assignment, the old folks set out along the road to town. Babel's hyperbolic description of the route could hardly be more expressive of the barrenness of their exile: the land-scape is stony, devastated, a wilderness. The concluding line sums up the scene: "An inexpressibly sad road led once upon a time in Odessa from the city to the cemetery."[34]

Those en route to the dust heap include Arye-Leib, the repository of tales whom Babel's readers had met first in that other story involving the same cemetery, "How It Was Done in Odessa." That the destination of the old should be the grave (rather than an earthly paradise of the sort sketched at the end of "The Journey") is of course natural; that the younger generation pushes out the old is part of the order of things, revolutions or no. But the cost of the older generation's demise is presented here as unnaturally high.

Their end is hastened not by a faceless Soviet order but by younger Jews ready to ally themselves with new institutions and create new identities. In "Karl-Yankel," the identity at issue is that of this generation's children. The trial at the heart of the story, which charges a grandmother and a mohel with circumcising an infant against the father's wishes, is still underway at the story's end, though it is clear that the plaintiff will win. Whether that constitutes a victory for the child is another question—the question implicitly raised in the story's closing, which focuses not on the legal conflict but on the conflicts yet to be confronted by the child as he makes his way in the world. The narrator, an observer at the trial, shifts his gaze from the proceedings to the city out the window—to the straight streets of Odessa stretching into the distance, streets on which he had marked the trajectory of his own childhood. Where will they take the next generation? In the scene just before this, other characters discuss what the baby might be when he grows up; the narrator's concern, how-ever, is not the boy's future status but his state of mind. This narrator, the hero of Babel's childhood stories grown to anxious maturity, whispers to himself: "It's not possible . . . that you won't be happy, Karl-Yankel. . . . It's not possible that you won't be happier than I. . . ."[35]

The double negative of his wish—for his statement is the traditional wish for a child's good fortune twisted by equivocation—implies that the odds against happiness are high. The narrator's own misery is intimated to have been great: thus to be happier than he may be no cause for rejoic-ing. Nonetheless, here as at the end of "The Journey," it is on the matter of the post-revolutionary era's potential to satisfy a new generation's need for happiness that Babel concludes his plot.

One must turn to a work unpublished in Babel's lifetime for a view of a path beyond revolution that leads to fulfillment not because it entails a break with one's origins but at least in part because it does not entail such a break. "The Jewess," a fragment of a novel that Babel apparently worked on in the late 1920s and early 1930s, can be seen in some sense as a sequel to "The Journey." Set in the early twenties, it involves a former Red Army commissar, now a student at the Military Academy, who travels home to Kremenets after his father's death. He comes only to get his mother and sister and bring them with him back to Moscow—where, the mother has heard, people were "happy, cheerful, spirited" (*"schastlivy, vesely, bodry"*).[36]

This train journey north is on an express train, first class. (One thinks of those tall tales of such wonders as express trains that Babel describes himself, in his 1920 diary, telling Jews apprehensive about what occupation by the Red Army might bring; here he brings such visions to his fiction.) The residence that awaits them in the capital is not literally in a palace (as in "The Journey") but it is in a formerly unattainable space: part of an apartment previously occupied by a deputy governor general of Moscow. The mother, overwhelmed by its magnificence, settles in, and inter-generational harmony seems to reign—at least as far as the story goes.

Is fulfillment available to those whose Jewish mothers mingle with their comrades? The point at which the manuscript breaks off suggests that trouble may lie ahead. The final lines describe how the neighbors begin to object vocally to the reek of mama's garlicky cooking, objections that one imagines go beyond the culinary. Babel stops here, as if uncertain whether to use garlic and onion as the catalyst of conflict or to search for some other plot device. The question of whether freedom from Jewish customs and constraints is a necessary condition for happiness in the new Soviet context remains unresolved.

On the typescript of "The Jewess," which is full of parenthetical variants and question marks, Babel wrote at the top of the first page several interrogative notes to himself about what style he was aiming for— notes like "More dialogue . . . ?" "Strengthen the factual side . . . ?"[37] The very first question is of a different sort, concerning not style but substance: "The Wandering Jew?" (*"Vechnyi evrei"*—"Eternal Jew," in Russian). What he might have meant is unclear, but presumably it is not related directly to the legend of the Jew condemned by Jesus to eternal life. Perhaps Babel had in mind the title character, who has left one world behind and transplanted herself into another; perhaps his note alludes to the incongruity between the outcast Jew of legend and the title character's son, whose generation, having found a home in the capital of internationalism, need wander no more.

A return to our starting point, the Ilf and Petrov novel serialized in *30 dnei* just before the publication of "The Journey," provides an additional—and satirical—perspective, implying that the Wandering Jew is a thing of the past not because he has been assimilated, but because anti-Semitism during the Civil War era is so virulent that even the "eternal Jew" could not be immortal. Toward the end of *The Golden Calf,* the schemer Ostap Bender tells the story of the Wandering Jew's demise. Yes, he was supposed to live forever, says Bender, but now the Wandering Jew is no more, because the old man took it into his head to make his way in the year 1919 to Russia. As he crossed the Dnepr he was recognized as a Jew by the notoriously anti-Semitic followers of the Ukrainian nationalist leader Petliura, who shot and killed him, his protestations of immortality notwithstanding.[38]

The joke takes us back to those idealistic young Jews en route to revolutionary Petrograd in "The Journey," who were assaulted by partisans of similar convictions. One is killed, his wife violated; the third, Babel's narrator, is allowed to escape, with a parting insult from the peasant who fleeces him and tells him, in Yiddish, "Beat it, Chaim" (41). Sent packing as the archetypal Jew, he becomes by the end of the story the archetypal new Soviet man, citizen of a new nation of comrades.

We cannot leave "The Journey" without noting the presence of one other traveler redefined upon arrival in a new land, and of one other body left bloody on history's path. The former is Maria Feodorovna, Danish princess turned Russian empress; the latter is her son, Tsar Nicholas II, executed in a cellar in Ekaterinburg in July of 1918. In "An Evening at the Empress's," Babel had waxed poetic in imagining the dewy gardens, dear companions, and weeping mother whom the Princess Dagmar left behind in her "small and chaste country" when she set off for "ferocious Russia."[39] In "The Journey" his description of her foreign past is less sentimental, but he adds to his portrait an emotionally charged reference to what, from the vantage point of winter 1918, would be her progeny's tragic future. "Bearing the last of the sovereigns," he writes, "the small woman with the malice of a fox rushed about in the palisades of the

Preobrazhensky grenadiers, but her birthing blood spilled out onto the implacable, vengeful granite earth . . ." (43). Babel's ellipsis leaves a moment for the reader to envision the tsar murdered in a distant city, and to recall how the granite of the imperial city (a literary image since the time of Pushkin) had figured in the story a page or so before. The narrator describes himself struggling up the Nevsky and finally reaching the granite base of one of the equestrian statues on Anichkov Bridge. Exhausted, he stretches out on the frigid pediment, but only momentarily: "the granite singed me, shot me out like a bullet, struck me and propelled me forward, toward the palace" (42). The harsh elements align to bring his journey to a charmed end; in the case of the sovereign, however, the revolver shot is not figurative.

"The Journey" thus is a tale not only about the Jewish experience of revolution but about the Romanovs' experience of revolution as well. As Babel's reader would have known, at the time the narrator was in Anichkov Palace going through Nicholas's childhood possessions and his mother's diaries and letters, the tsar and the dowager empress were still alive—he under arrest in the city of Tobolsk, she confined in one of the imperial villas in the Crimea. In the last extant letter she wrote to him, dated November 21, 1917, she laments their separation and Russia's condition, writing: "I live only in my memories of the happy past and try as much as possible to forget the present nightmare."[40] Nicholas had evidently confessed to her his own preference for retreating into the past. His mother commiserates: "I well understand how you must enjoy re-reading your old letters and diaries, although these memories of a happy past rouse deep sorrow in the heart. I have not even got that consolation, for mine were all taken away from me in the spring when they searched the house. . . ."[41] The papers confiscated were apparently from her life as a Romanov, not those from her foreign youth that remained in Petrograd to be pored over by an anti-tsarist Jewish parvenu.

Babel's stories set in the early post-revolutionary years include many figures, Jews and non-Jews, who find their paths blocked or redirected— by force, by the sovietization of mores and institutions, by the competing conceptions of their compatriots, and by the changing shape of their own convictions. There are few straight paths in Babel's fiction—a truth illustrated in the design of *Red Cavalry* itself, which begins with the narrator marching down a road built by Nikolaevan peasants to participate in the epic of Russian history and ends (in the original edition, at least) with the narrator in retreat and invoking his tie to a Jewish lineage stretching back to ancient times. The writer's own path took him in the end to charges of Trotskyism ideologically consonant with the article that had preempted his story about a young Jewish man hired by Petrograd Cheka chief Uritsky in that 1931 journal issue.

As fate would have it, an Uritsky was among those prisoners of the Cheka's successor agency, the NKVD, to allege Babel's Trotskyite ties. This was Semyon Borisovich Uritsky, an editor Babel knew who had been arrested a year earlier than he, in 1938. In the course of his interrogation Babel was shown Uritsky's accusations; the latter's file holds documents with his incriminating testimony bearing these words in his fellow prisoner's hand: "Read by Isaac Babel."[42] Our view of Babel's alter ego reading the depositions of political prisoners at the end of "The Journey" is thus colored by our knowledge that he became a subject of this genre, not just a reader, and that the course his own life took was far darker and more complex than that of his fictionalized self. But we know, too, that the path he extended to his readers leads to what the protagonist of that story regarded as the height of fulfillment: a realm filled with pleasures of both mind and spirit.

# 5

## Writers at the Front
### Language of State in the Civil War Narratives of Isaac Babel and Dmitrii Furmanov

MICHAEL S. GORHAM

In the life of the word, an heroic era has arrived. The word is bread and flesh. It shares the fate of bread and flesh: suffering. People are hungry. Still hungrier is the state. But there is something even more hungry: time. Time wants to devour the state. He who lifts up the word and shows it to time, as a priest lifting up the Eucharist, shall be the second Joshua. There is nothing hungrier than the modern state, and a hungry state is more terrifying than a hungry man.

—Osip Mandelshtam, "The Word and Culture" (1921)

In the tempest of civil battles you write about the particularities of Greek vases. . . . They are beautiful and worthy, but still, you're a son of a bitch—either due to idiocy or class.

You have to write that which serves, either directly or indirectly, movement forward. For porcelain vases there is a porcelain time, not a steel one.

—Dmitrii Furmanov, *From the Writer's Diary* (1934)

IN HIS BOOK *Nation-Building and Citizenship*, Reinhardt Bendix discusses how modernizing states—especially those that are lagging economically—depend for their survival on the effective verbalization of their ideas for social and political change.[1] The language used to express these ideas has been referred to in literature on nationalism as "language of state," a term that goes beyond the linguistic material of official state

---

Portions of this article appeared in Michael Gorham, *Speaking in Soviet Tongues: Language Culture and the Politics of Voice in Revolutionary Russia* (DeKalb, IL: Northern Illinois University Press, 2003) and are used here with permission.

documents to refer to an entire mode of expression, a discourse employed by and within a state to represent verbally (and symbolically) its visions for social, political, and cultural order. If a modernizing state in the midst of chaotic change depends heavily on public discourse for the dissemination of its ideas, then it follows, as Geertz, Shils, and others have suggested, that artists (and, for my purposes here, writers), given their primary focus on verbal and symbolic representation, play a formidable role in generating and legitimating the central value system of that state.[2] Writers of narrative fiction, as professional storytellers, have a special capacity through their verbal constructs to make sense out of reality, to make experience comprehensible, or, in the more poetic imagery of Mandelshtam, to save the state from the jaws of time.

My goals in this chapter are twofold: first, to map out the cultural dimensions of the early Soviet state's dependence on, and preoccupation with, the reconstruction of public discourse; and, second, to look at how the public language of the revolutionary epoch received expression in two influential works of fiction from the period—Isaac Babel's *Red Cavalry* (1926) and Dmitrii Furmanov's *Chapaev* (1923). By combining these perspectives, I hope not only to demonstrate the degree to which public discourse and its source institutions helped generate authority and legitimacy for the emerging state; I want also to suggest the unique place of narrative fiction within the context of state-building in early Soviet Russia.

## Language and Revolution

When the Bolsheviks seized power in October 1917, they sought to create a "dictatorship of the proletariat" in a country dominated by semi-literate peasants. The violence and famine resulting from a divisive civil war dramatically reduced by 1921 an already insignificant working-class population, exacerbating the Bolsheviks' already precarious position as "a superstructure in need of a base." The violence and famine resulting from the war years sharply reduced by 1921 the small working-class population, and sent the nation into even deeper economic chaos.[3] Lacking the material and social bases, the new Bolshevik leadership was forced to depend primarily on *ideas* about the proletarian state and revolutionary world order to legitimate its power symbolically. Just two weeks after assuming power, Vladimir Lenin, recognizing the ideological clout of the printed word, issued decrees authorizing government control of all newspapers.[4]

The country's high illiteracy rate in many respects eased the Bolsheviks' task of molding both language and citizens to shape their ideas. Under the direction of the "Commissariat of Popular Enlightenment," or *Narkompros* (the Bolshevik reinvention of the Ministry of Education), the state intensified its literacy campaign "with the aim of providing the entire population of the Republic the opportunity of conscious participation in the political life of the country," as a 1919 decree signed by Lenin openly declared.[5] Party directives made no attempt to conceal the specifically ideological goals of press and education policy. The resolution on press and propaganda from the Eleventh Party Congress in 1922 stated outright: "The press is one of the mightiest weapons in the Party's struggle for influence over the masses, for their Communist enlightenment and organization."[6] In that same year, the Soviet censorship apparatus was institutionalized in the form of "Glavlit."

The emphasis on "conscious political participation" suggests that it was not good enough simply to be able to read and understand the decrees that dominated the pages of the daily news: citizens bore the responsibility of propagating and putting to action those verbal declarations. The period thus witnessed the mass proliferation of agitators, orators, and activists, and a wide-scale effort to instill newspapers, public speaking, fiction, and other language media with new life, or the "living word" (*zhivoe slovo*), as it came to be called. Special agitational trains canvassed the cities and countryside, supplying populations with an arsenal of verbal ammunition—banners, slogans, songs, theater productions, and the "living newspaper"—all geared to transmit in a comprehensible way the ideas and symbols of the central state, and the envisioned place of its would-be citizens.[7] School curricula encouraged literature and language teachers to orient their assignments toward fulfilling the demands of the new Soviet society. Grigorii Vinokur, one of the more prominent members of the Moscow Linguistics Circle and the catalyst for the study of "language culture" (*kul'tura iazyka*), went so far as to deem it the obligation of the members of a given community to construct their own modes of speech.[8] As in many aspects of early Soviet culture, then, the domain of language was subjected to broad-based and self-conscious attempts at reconstruction—or even reinvention—steeped in a utopian mentality that viewed discourse as one of the major tools for implementing radical social change.[9]

There was plenty of new linguistic material in the discourse of the day to lend credibility to this vision of language reconstruction. When the Bolsheviks assumed power, the language of revolution that had been active for over a decade in unofficial circles quickly invaded the public sphere. The Russian language experienced an increase in both the influx and productivity of neologisms, acronyms, stump-compounds, foreign terms, old words subjected to semantic shifts, and an odd stylistic mix of substandard slang, bureaucratese, and high Marxist rhetoric. Serious linguists of the day stopped short of calling these changes "revolutionary."[10] But it was more than enough to perplex those who were the main targets of the campaigns for literacy and political enlightenment. By 1923 there was well-documented evidence, in fact, that the emerging discourse was either incomprehensible to, or—even worse—misinterpreted by large portions of the peasantry and urban working class, the supposed heirs of the socialist state. Studies of language reception among peasants, factory workers, urban schoolchildren, and Red Army soldiers all revealed confusion, suspicion, and alienation as a result of the onslaught of new public discourse.[11] Instead of adopting the language as their own, they expressed mistrust toward what they called the "language of power" or "authority" (*iazyk vlasti*) and turned away in great numbers from newspapers, agitators, and the party itself.[12]

It is precisely due to this communication gap between the center and the periphery, at a time when language and symbols were the primary instruments for establishing the legitimacy and defining the contours of the emerging state, that narrative fiction can be seen as an important organizing force. Given their special adeptness at verbal representation, writers played a critical role in making symbolic sense (or nonsense) out of the often chaotic, conflicting, and incoherent values and ideas cluttering the post-revolutionary landscape. Or as Victoria Bonnell and Lynn Hunt put it, narrative's power lies in its ability to "provide a link between culture as system and culture as practice," as "an arena in which meaning takes form, in which individuals connect to the public and social world, and in which change therefore becomes possible."[13] Russian literature of the 1920s, in particular, exhibited wide and conscious experimentation in language and voice, and was charged with a sense of urgency and import that stemmed from Russia's traditionally high regard for the writer and the power of the word (as expressed in the Mandelshtam quote serving as an epigraph to this chapter), compounded by the "hunger of the modern state" and its race against time.[14] As a method of bringing order to symbolic confusion, then, fiction carried the potential of transmitting, through narratives, viable models for writing and speaking in the new Soviet order. And while a broad range of authors chose to employ the emerging state discourse, their modes of appropriation and representation gave rise to quite different portraits of power and authority.

## Language and Authority in Civil War Narratives

Isaac Babel's *Red Cavalry* and Dmitrii Furmanov's *Chapaev* share at least two important features for my purposes here. First, they are both set at the military front—Babel's with the Cossack troops of General Semen Budenny's First Cavalry Division during its campaign against Poland, Furmanov's with the partisan regiments of the legendary peasant Divisional Commander Vasilii Chapaev. Beyond its military significance, the civil war provided symbolic import for the Bolshevik Party by strengthening its legitimacy to the controls of power not only over internal and neighboring enemies but also over the less organized peripheries of the new state. As Sheila Fitzpatrick has pointed out, the Red Army soldier played the important symbolic role of a "surrogate proletariat" in a class struggle that was otherwise largely fictitious. For most of the predominantly peasant soldiers, service in the Red Army marked the first direct encounter with the new "Soviet" ideology.[15] In a similar vein, Stephen Kotkin argues that "the Civil War not only gave the daring, opportunistic Bolsheviks a modus operandi and helped solidify their still amorphous identity as the consummate builders of a socially oriented, powerful state; it also furthered the process whereby the Bolsheviks' being in power came to be identified with the cause of 'the revolution.'"[16] No less significantly for most of the predominantly peasant soldiers, service in the Red Army marked the first direct encounter with the new Soviet ideology, and the civil war provided one of the most fertile grounds for establishing a common language between the state and its citizens.[17]

Both stories are also told from the perspective of educated and trained representatives of the central state. Babel's narrator, Kirill Vasil'evich Liutov, works as a party-appointed journalist and activist; Furmanov's Fedor Klychkov is a political commissar sent to coordinate the "enlightenment" campaign among Chapaev's spirited, though somewhat anarchistic, regiments.[18] But while each narrative describes an encounter between the politically "organized" center and the "elemental" chaos of the periphery, their focus is quite different: Furmanov's emphasizes the mobilizing force and didactic clarity of political enlightenment; Babel's highlights the unintended consequences of its verbal distortion. The deployment of language of state on at least three levels of narrative construction—plot, narrative voice, and direct speech—proves instrumental in realizing each of these perspectives.

## Organization of Plot

Though both authors set their stories at the military front, they organize them using different temporal and spatial segments. Furmanov depends on the military struggle to structure and develop his story, on movement across spaces that are usually restricted to the official public sphere—the train depot, the public rally, the battlefield. The novel's first chapter demonstrates each of these organizing segments. It opens at a public rally at the Ivanovo train station, where local textile workers have gathered to bid farewell to their comrades who have volunteered to fight against Kolchak and the White Army in the Volga-Urals region. In ideologically charged speeches, Communist Party activists spell out for the crowd (and the implied reader) the tasks of the mobilization effort. This theme carries the story forward, following the newly transformed worker-soldiers on their journey to the front. At local train depots along the way, agitators from the geographical and ideological center organize instructional meetings for the unenlightened masses of the periphery: "No matter the stop, the echelon had new work. The entire route was filled with numerous meetings, gatherings, conferences, lectures, a variety of separate discussions in circles of enthusiast-participants."[19]

Condensed here into a pair of sentences, this "poetics of mobilization" structures the bulk of the book's space and time. The defining events fall into two kinds of conflicts—between the Red Army and its enemy, and between the politically enlightened representatives of the central state and the peasant masses of the outlying regions. The spheres in which these conflicts are played out—the battlefield, the demonstration, the meeting of military and political strategists—define the central space of the novel. They are for the most part *public* spheres, constituting the legitimate domain of the party-state. The author limits interactions between private individuals to those that involve the main hero, Fedor Klychkov, and the popular peasant commander Chapaev—a relationship that addresses metonymically the broader issue of statehood and citizenship.

In contrast to this "poetics of mobilization," Babel's narrative vignettes highlight the margins of battle, often entirely ignoring the spatial and temporal frame of the state. The opening lines of the first story, "Crossing the River Zbrucz," offers a case in point. What begins as a military narrative ("The commander of the Sixth Division reported that Novograd-Volynsk was taken at dawn today. . . .") quickly transforms into a lyrical description of the natural surroundings ("Fields of purple poppies are blossoming around us, a noon breeze is frolicking in the yellowing rye, virginal buckwheat is standing on the horizon like the wall of a faraway monastery").[20] Babel employs a highly self-conscious language which, though it may reek of war ("The orange sun is rolling across the sky like a severed head, gentle light glimmers in the ravines among the clouds, the banners of the sunset are fluttering above our heads. The stench of yesterday's blood and slaughtered horses drips into the evening chill" [203]), nevertheless removes the reader from the mobilizing army to a still-life portrait of an environment and characters largely disconnected from the war effort:

> Late at night we arrived in Novograd. In the quarters to which I am assigned I find a pregnant woman and two red-haired Jews with thin necks, and a third Jew who is sleeping with his face to the wall and a blanket pulled over his head. In my room I find ransacked closets, torn pieces of women's fur coats on the floor, human excrement, and fragments of the holy Seder plate that the Jews use once a year for Passover. (203–4)

In fact, here as in many of the stories it is impossible to speak of a "plot" in the traditional sense of an engagement, a series of reversals, capitulation, and denouement. The stories that make up the collection are "miniatures," still-life portraits of the private world of war-torn communities, static snippets that shed light on a single personage, a single dwelling, a single experience of the narrator, oftentimes highlighting the idiosyncratic intersection of two or more very different worlds. If the language and images of state enter the scene, they do so most often as one component in a bizarre juxtaposition of symbols. "The Rabbi," for example, contrasts the world of two elderly Jews with the modern chimera of the Soviet agitational train by inundating the reader with the sights, sounds, values, and rituals of the Hasidim, and then, in the final paragraph, following the narrator to his wholly modern, Soviet place of work:

> I gave the old man some money and went out into the street. Gedali and I parted, and I went back to the railroad station. There at the station, on the propa-

ganda train of the First Cavalry, I was greeted by the sparkle of hundreds of lights, the enchanted glitter of the radio transmitter, the stubborn rolling of the printing presses, and my unfinished article for the *Krasnyi kavalerist*. (236)

Many of the stories altogether ignore issues and personages of import to the newly emerging state. They describe instead the likes of the bandit-hero Afon'ka Bida, the vengeful Red Army soldier Pavlichenko, and the saintly artist Apolek; they reproduce conflicts more often featuring horses and houses of worship than the courageous war efforts of Budenny's First Cavalry. In such portraits the language and imagery of state remains outside the frame, creating an impression (among some contemporary critics) of either disregard for the Bolshevik cause or misguided praise.[21]

## Narrative Voice

The contrast extends into the voice of the two narrators. *Chapaev's* storyteller writes in the language of a seasoned party activist who employs the language of state masterfully and transparently, thereby reinforcing the legitimacy of the activist's work and the need to organize the masses politically:

These volunteer regiments performed truly heroic deeds. . . . They held on for a long time, fought steadfastly and bravely, frequently and successfully beat the Ural Cossacks who rose up against Soviet power. In fighting terms, they stood invariably high from start to finish; in political terms, they did not mature immediately and did not immediately grasp and clarify the reasons for and the dimensions of the unfolding social struggle; weak discipline, a peculiar conception of "freedom," an extended struggle for the appointment of the communist staff, an unclear and imprecise understanding of the tasks and directives emanating from the center—all these features long distinguished these spirited, volunteer, utterly peasant regiments from the regiments of central Russia. (38)

The naturalized use of terms such as "heroic deeds," "Soviet power," "social struggle," "weak discipline," and "utterly peasant" ascribes legitimacy to the language of the party-state and the order it presumes. Questioning its authority would require the reader to actively resist the language and narrative persona behind it. The narrator's occasional "slip" from the third-person to first-person voice ("The forces were almost even—we put up an army slightly smaller than Kolchak's" [103]) further encourages the reader to share the storyteller's historical and ideological perspective.

The narrator's allegiance to the party-state also shows in Furmanov's liberal use of quasi-direct discourse when relating the experiences and impressions of his main hero Klychkov. The vocal blending occurs most frequently in passages expounding on issues of political organization and control—as when the narrator outlines Klychkov's plan of action upon first arriving at the front:

> With the feel of an organizer, Klychkov understood what he needed to do.
>
> In the first place, he decided to familiarize himself factually, through documents and reports, with the work in the brigade. . . . In the second place, he decided to insist on the convocation of small meeting—conferences of the party cells, cultural commissions (*kul'tkomissii*), committees for economic control (*kontrkhozkomissii*), meetings of the military commanders (*voenkomy*), etc. That would help him immediately see and understand a great amount.
>
> Next he planned to travel around to the units and observe the actual status of the political work there; and finally he wanted to participate personally in the upcoming battles in the capacity of a rank-and-file fighter, and in so doing earn the name of a good comrade and brave man. This condition could influence the successes or failures of his future political work.
>
> Over the next several days, right up to the offensive, Fedor persistently carried out the tasks set before him. (43)

The passage not only reflects a mastery of language of state—from the numerous stump-compounds to the employment of such classic Soviet turns-of-phrase as *faktischeski, riadovoi boets*, and the bureaucratic *osushchestvlial nastoichivo postavlennye pered soboiu zadachi*—it also shows a manner of thinking characteristic of the model activist of the day: ideologically conscious (*chutiem organizatora*), organized (in both life and language), and oriented toward overachievement (*srazu mnogoe uvidet' i poniat'*). This narrative authority was in all likelihood compounded by the common knowledge of contemporary readers that Furmanov had actually served as political commissar in Chapaev's division.[22] Neither the legitimacy of the activist's work nor the need to organize the masses through such work is questioned by the "insider"-narrator: they are a given. And so they are meant to be understood by the implied readers of the novel. The question posed by the narrative on agitation and propaganda is not *whether or not* to organize and control, but by *which* means to *do* so.

In Babel's Liutov, rather than a linguistic confidant of central authorities we find a Jewish intellectual distanced almost equally from the state as he is from the coarse Cossack soldiers.[23] The frequency of language of state is sharply diminished and the references that do appear are often curiously transformed—or even deformed—in the process. Such is the case in the story "My First Goose" when Liutov reads to a group of Cossacks an agitational speech by Lenin from the central party newspaper *Pravda*. The speech, already refracted by its appearance in newsprint, undergoes a second transformation through the narrator's almost mystical representation of the discourse, then, finally, a third, through the Cossack Surovkov's reaction to it:

> And in a loud voice, like a triumphant deaf man, I read Lenin's speech to the Cossacks.
>
> The evening wrapped me in the soothing dampness of her twilight sheets, the evening placed her motherly palms on my burning brow.
>
> I read, and rejoiced, waiting for the effect, rejoicing in the mysterious curve of Lenin's straight line.
>
> "Truth tickles all and sundry in the nose," said Surovkov, when I had finished. "It isn't all that easy to wheedle it out of the pile of rubbish, but Lenin picks it up right away, like a hen pecks up a grain of corn." (233)

In "The Rabbi's Son" (the final story in the first edition of *Red Cavalry*), the narrator juxtaposes the symbols of state with those of the local Hasidic culture by cataloging the worldly possessions recovered from a recently killed Red Army soldier and Rabbi's son:

> I threw everything together in a jumble, the mandates of the political agitator and the mementos of a Jewish poet. Portraits of Lenin and Maimonides lay side by side—the gnarled steel of Lenin's skull and the listless silk of the Maimonides portrait. A lock of woman's hair lay in a book of the resolutions of the Sixth Party Congress, and crooked lines of Ancient Hebrew verse huddled in the margins of Communist pamphlets. Pages of *The Song of Songs* and revolver cartridges drizzled on me in a sad, sparse rain. (332)

While not necessarily questioning the legitimacy of the state language and symbols, contrasts such as these do *qualify* that language's absolute authority by bringing to light the transmutations it undergoes when rearticulated by peripheral citizens. The state can distribute as many iron busts, pamphlets, and slogans as it likes, but there is no telling what company they will eventually come to share, nor what symbolic power they will come to hold.

## Direct Speech

On the level of direct speech, Furmanov simply stifles the voices of the periphery. Aside from Chapaev himself, none of the peasants, Cossacks, or other non-party, non-official characters is given a direct voice. Instead, they assume the collective portrait of a "faceless, utterly dark mass," a "black workers' crowd," and "black darkness" (11, 5, 9). Although Chapaev provides an exception to this gag rule, his speeches to the soldiers are reduced to isolated phrases and sentences, the rest being filtered through a combination of indirect discourse and critical commentary from the storyteller. In recalling one of the commander's speeches, for example, the narrator writes:

> He began without any introduction or explanation of the reason for which he summoned the fighters. . . . He then proceeded to latch on incidentally to many other things, he kept on latching to anything that accidentally came to mind, that could in some way arrive at the deed at hand. His speech lacked all signs of order, unity, or the emergence of any one general idea in Chapaev's speech: he said what ever came to mind. (74)

The contrast between "accidental" and "orderly" language is clearly intended as a metaphor for political chaos and cohesion. The possibility of there being alternative ideological views and forms for expressing them is ostensibly denied by the tag of "accidental" to all that fails to conform to the "order" as defined by the language of state. Furmanov's narrator underscores this denial of content when he later refers to Chapaev's "speeches" (the narrator uses this word in quotations) as "contentless," "meaningless," and, in the spirit of Karl Marx and (after him) Maxim Gorky, "stupid."[24]

Unsurprisingly, it is the narrator's alter-ego Klychkov who provides the conscious, content-latent positive model of Bolshevik rhetoric, best exemplified in his address to the throng of textile workers of Ivanovo before the volunteers' departure:

> Comrades! Minutes remain, the final bells will sound and we will leave. On behalf of the red soldiers of the detachment I say to you "Farewell!" Remember us, your comrades, remember where we went and what awaits us, and be prepared to follow after us yourselves the moment you are called. Do not cut ties with us, send us news, send what you can, help us. There is hunger at the front, it is hard—harder than here. Do not forget this. Also don't forget that many of us leave behind or-

phaned, uncared for families, children doomed for hunger. Do not leave them. It will be hard to sit in the trenches, suffer through the campaigns, perish in battle; but it will be a hundred times harder if we know that at the same time our families are dying, helpless, abandoned, forgotten. . . . Also—work! You are weavers and know that the more you weave in Ivanovo, the warmer it will be in the snowy steppes of Uralsk, Orenburg, and everywhere your goods should wind up. Work and remember that victory is not only in our bayonets, but in your labor as well. Will we see one another again? We shall trust that we will. But if there is no meeting, why grieve? The revolution does not count individual victims. Farewell, dear comrades, on behalf of the red soldiers of the entire detachment, farewell. . . . (10)

His address bears the markers of politically conscious party-state rhetoric. It begins and ends with proper forms of address, with the caveat of his speaking "on behalf of red soldiers," and with statements concerning the courage and unity of those departing from the front to fight for the revolutionary cause. It creates a direct link between the human trials and sacrifices awaiting them at the front and the general need for self-sacrifice, perseverance, and productivity in the home and at the factory (using contrast and hyperbole to remind those staying behind of the relative fortune (*trudno . . . trudnee, tiazhko . . . stokrat tiazhelei*). And it frames the potential suffering faced by individuals from both groups in a vision of the greater, collective victory of revolution. All this becomes neatly organized through the regular repetition of key words and phrases, most of them imperatives (remember . . . *remember . . . do not forget*); trebling (*sit . . . suffer . . . perish; helpless, abandoned, forgotten*); and a mixture of lofty or poetic forms, on the one hand (*zov, stokrat, vestniki, obrechennyi, razluka*), with colloquial speech (*shlite, tiazhko, tuzhit'*), on the other—a feature characteristic of Bolshevik oratory and that of Lenin in particular.[25]

In contrast to Chapaev's "empty," "childlike," and elemental speech, Klychkov's represents the substantive, mature, conscious language of the Soviet state. This second language stands without commentary, truly authoritative speech, in addition to being direct; it is the language of power, and the language to be modeled by all those aspiring to become citizens and spokespersons themselves.

The language of the official state representatives in *Red Cavalry*, in contrast, is regularly subjected to authorial intrusion, deformation, and defamiliarization. One of the more glaring examples appears in the closing paragraphs of the story "Berestechko," not surprisingly in the context of a public meeting. As in the general orientation of plot, the narrator is located at the periphery of the public scene, walking along the war-torn walls of an ancient Polish castle perched atop a hill overlooking the town square:

> A rally was gathering on the square below. Peasant, Jews, and tanners from the outlying areas had come together. Above them flared Vinogradov's ecstatic voice and the clanking of his spurs. He gave a speech about the Second Congress of the Comintern, and I roamed along the walls where nymphs with gouged eyes danced their ancient round dance. Then on the trampled floor, in a corner, I found the torn fragment of a yellowed letter. On it was written in faded ink:
>
> *Berestechko, 1820, my beloved Paul, I hear that Emperor Napoleon is dead. Is it true? I feel well; it was an easy birth, our little hero is already seven weeks old.*
>
> Below me, the voice of the divisional military commissar is droning on. He is passionately haranguing the bewildered townspeople and the plundered Jews: "You are the power. Everything here belongs to you. There are no masters. I shall now conduct an election for the Revolutionary Committee." (272)

As in several other scenes of public speaking depicted in the stories, Babel deflates the solemnity of the occasion through a series of defamiliarizations. First, he reduces the content of the agitator's speech to a series of laconic quips about power and ownership, privileging, instead, its exaggerated rhetorical form ("ecstatic voice flared," "*droning on*," "*passionately haranguing*"). Second, he draws ironic contrasts between the Second Comintern and the round dance of nymphs with gouged-out eyes, and between the nineteenth-century letter inquiring into the death of the great French emperor and the commissar's passionate ravings about empowerment. Finally, he adds to the irony by portraying the addressee of the agitational harangue as a ragtag collection of perplexed petit-bourgeois craftsmen and plundered Jews.[26]

Far more profound consequences come from speech acts at the margins of war and party-sponsored events. And while the voice of politically marginal citizens exhibits many of the features characteristic of the language of state, it does so in forms and contexts either unintended or unanticipated by that language's central producers. One Red Army soldier invokes the language of state to justify murdering a peasant woman stowaway ("'And I took the loyal rifle from the wall and wiped that blot off the face of the working land and the republic'" [276]). Another of peasant stock gets revenge on his former master for stealing and raping his wife by conjuring up a fictitious decree from Lenin: "'In the name of the people . . . for the establishment of a future radiant life, I order Pavli-chenko, Matvei Rodionovich—to deprive, at his discretion, various persons of their lives'" (257). And two aging war heroes employ the language of state to settle a dispute over the ownership of a much sought-after stallion, one writing in a letter to the other: "'To you, Comrade Savitskii, as an international hero, the working masses of Vitebsk, where I am the chairman of the District Revolutionary Committee, send the proletarian cry: 'Give us world revolution!' And we hope that that white stallion will trot beneath you on soft paths for many a year to come in aid of Freedom so beloved by all, and the fraternal Republics in which we must keep a sharp eye out for the provincial authorities and the district units in an administrative respect'" (304).

Of course, the authority of all these uses of language of state is not only checked by the incongruity between language and context—the use of the essentially public language of state for the legitimizing of personal actions or claims—but also brought into question by the faulty use of that language by the speaker or writer. Collectively, the voices reveal speakers cognizant of the power of the language, but as yet unable to master it. In several cases, Babel' promotes these tongue-tied citizens to the position of storyteller in the form of a *skaz* narrative, which in its more useful formulation is oriented not only toward oral speech but also (and more importantly) to the "discourse of the other" (what Bakhtin calls *chuzhaia rech'*).[27] Quite frequently, the voice bears the markings of a particular class or social group and, particularly in modern literature, becomes the object of an ironic chuckle between the implied author and implied reader—behind the back, as it were, of the narrator himself. In Babel', the *skaz* narrators are members of the rural peasantry or Cossack soldiers in the midst of a kind of "linguistic sovietization" through their involvement in the Red Army. They appear in a number of the stories when the regular narrator, Liutov, retreats to the margins of the text giving way to a letter or a story he obtained in the course of his duty at the front.[28] The story "A Letter," for instance, reproduces a letter from a young Red Army soldier to his mother, dictated to Liutov and written down "without embellishing it . . . word for word," in which he informs her of the death of his brother (her son) at the hand of his father (her husband). Though a personal letter about a family tragedy, the document is peppered with language of state. The second paragraph begins:

"Dearest Mama, Evdokiia Fedorovna Kurdiukova, I hasten to inform you that I am in Comrade Budenny's Red Cavalry Regiment, and that my godfather Nikon

Vasilich is also here and is at the present time a Red Hero. He took me and put me in his special detachment of the Polit-otdel in which we hand out books and newspapers to the various positions: the Moscow TsIK *Izvestiia*, the Moscow *Pravda*, and our own merciless newspaper the *Krasnyi kavalerist*, which every fighter on the front wants to read and then go and heroically hack the damn Poles to pieces, and I am living real marvelous at Nikon Vasilich's." (208–9)

The markers of language of state here—from bureaucratic cliché to revolutionary terms and turns—enter the text seemingly unbeknownst to the letter writer. They mix with the colloquial language of his peasant background to form a kind of narrative "hybrid"—a mix not only of two different languages, but of two different belief systems as well.[29] And it is precisely in the context of this hybrid, promoted to the level of narrator and set apart from the voice of the author, where the language of state becomes a tool for parody. The *skaz* narrative, I would argue, makes two different statements about the emerging language of state: first, that it is a language of power and authority (citizens feel compelled to employ it) and, secondly, like any public discourse, it is susceptible to "twists" entirely unanticipated by the producers of that language when reappropriated by peripheral consumers.[30]

In the broader context of the narrative fiction of the 1920s, this second "consumer" orientation was not at all uncommon. Some scholars have gone so far as to link its prevalence to a general "crisis in authorship." They cite most frequently Mikhail Zoshchenko's defense of his own *skaz* narrators as parodies of "the contemporary intellectual writer who may not exist now, but who ought to exist, if he were to fulfill precisely the social demand . . . of that sphere and that society which has now been thrust into the spotlight."[31] In the context of my own work on the language culture of this state-building period, the narratives of these authors all echo, with varying degrees of refraction, a set of voices that, in the society-wide debates over public discourse, called for either the "popularization" of public language or, along similar lines, for its "proletarianization." Particularly in the first half of the decade, a large and vocal body of critics and cultural leaders demanded that public discourse be reshaped to model the everyday language of the factory, or the "simple," "fresh," even "succulent" language of "the people." In the domain of the central party newspapers and official state documents, implementing such a language may have been simply untenable (though there were some prominent attempts). In narrative fiction, while entirely possible, implementing it proved in most cases too threatening to the official and authoritative visions of citizenship. Indeed, by the beginning of the "Great Break" in the late 1920s, it was not enough simply to acknowledge the power of the language of state; increasing pressure was placed on the writer to depict in narrative form positive models of public speaking and writing, heroes who had already successfully "mastered" it and who used it in appropriate contexts toward appropriate ends. Although this voice often came from a member of the working class or even the peasantry, it was first and foremost the voice of a loyal communist, a "conscious" and "enlightened" activist, who both spoke with and commanded authority. Recognition as a discourse of power was only the first step in the emerging single-party state's establishment of legitimacy and control; once it had done this, it needed also to require the appropriate use of that language, legitimating not only the power of the central value system, but its authority as well. With increasingly active and restrictive policies toward institutions of literature and publishing, the mobilizing discourse of the heroes of Socialist Realism eclipsed the imperfect and faintly mangled language of the struggling, "unconscious" citizens of Babel as the object of narrative representation. By the latter part of the decade, and more common to published narrative fiction, was an implied author who depicted, with authority, articulate heroes; less common was the author who chose instead to chuckle or sob behind the backs of "unenlightened" narrators and their verbal reappropriations.

# 6

## Thinned and Diluted
### Babel in Published Russian Literature of the Soviet Period

MARIETTA CHUDAKOVA

The guards are making jokes through the peep hole
The cons are yelling listlessly outside:
"Stepan, lend us your spouse for a minute,
We'll get her diluted thin for everyone."

—Yuz Aleshkovskii, "Family Visit" (1963)

## I.

Paradoxically, during the first years of Soviet power, Russian prose authors moved away from politically tendentious literature toward literature as such. They were reacting as much to the pull of the grand ideological novels of the second half of the nineteenth century as to inflated Symbolist prose (so effectively criticized by Osip Mandelshtam in his 1922 essay "Sturm und Drang"[1]). Instead, they oriented themselves toward the example of Pushkin's prose, which was unburdened by psychological and ideological baggage but could serve as a vehicle for a good, well-told story, sparing in its details and descriptions.

And yet there was, perhaps, nothing paradoxical in this. The energy of literary evolution (in Yurii Tynianov's sense) had not yet been spent. By the end of the nineteenth century, largely thanks to Anton Chekhov, the conventional, outworn nature of the grand novelistic style had become all

---

Translated by Gregory Freidin

too apparent. For a while, it seemed that its lease on life could be extended by the Symbolist novel. But, like its classical predecessor, the Symbolist novel soon began to yield the stage to the small genres: the stories of Mikhail Zoshchenko and, a little later, those of Isaac Babel. However, if the writers of the 1920s were reacting to the Symbolist novel, they were doing so not directly but via the writings of Ivan Bunin. He was the first to cultivate the "Pushkinian" prose style, and his successes resonated powerfully with the emerging mainstream of Russian literature.

"The aesthetic value of a work of art is not the same as its content value," wrote P. Bitsilli in 1931.

Tolstoy and Dostoevsky are greater and more valuable than Pushkin. But, since Pushkin and Gogol, Russian literature has not had an author more perfect than Ivan Bunin. . . . In this sense, the period of Russian literature that commenced with Pushkin . . . terminates in Bunin.[2]

Bunin's influence on Russian literature of the Soviet period is so intertwined with that of Babel that I must pause here to examine the phenomenon of Bunin before turning to my main subject.

Early in the twentieth century, Russian literature faced a number of challenges. To begin with, there was a need to replace the old workhorse protagonist—the *superfluous man*—who had inhabited Russian fiction for some seventy years. This task was dictated as much by the very nature of modern literature, by its demand for renewal, as by the new social forces that were taking Russia by storm. Indeed, during the revolution of 1905–1907, the role played by the "people" (*narod*) was so powerful that it shook Russia to the core. This was true especially in the countryside, where it entailed the wholesale destruction of gentry estates and the brutal murders of their owners. The people had now entered the political stage—to the considerable surprise of educated Russian society. As before, writers were called upon to solve the "puzzle of the people"—in part, by creating a new protagonist, one whose origins were rooted in the life of the lower social classes.

The challenge of creating a new literary language, of renovating *speech*, loomed even larger than the need for a new protagonist. The de facto democratization of Russian society in the twilight of the old regime suddenly filled public spaces with the speech of the "plain folk." In order to begin to solve the "people puzzle," writers needed not only to imagine a new protagonist but also to have this protagonist discourse, and be discoursed about, in a radically new way.

Finally, a new set of expressive techniques was required, in addition to the old tools of the trade, if Russian authors were to do justice to the literary representation of these emerging social forces.

Later, in 1928, addressing the crisis of Russian literary prose, Georgii Adamovich suggested that Russian writers should take their cue from the French who, "on average," write "better than we do," and have learned that "the use of external descriptions in literature had reached its limit by the end of the nineteenth century."[3] In Russian literature, however, the saturation point that Adamovich had in mind was reached considerably later.

In the 1910s, the peak of this expressive style was reached in Bunin's writings, which impressed the Russian reader by, among other things, their unusual attention to color—first in poetry, then in prose.[4]

Writing in 1915, Kornei Chukovskii emphasized this aspect of Bunin's achievement: "Before him, we did not know that white horses are green in the moonlight, their eyes, lilac, . . . and black earth is blue!" Bunin's verbs "express not the action of things but their colors—to glow crimson, blue, pink [*alet', sinet', rozovet'*]."[5] In Bunin, any object that "fell under his gaze is recalled so vividly . . . with all of its minute qualities, colors, smells, that it seems the object was literally before Bunin's eyes as he was working on its description."

Along with his striking visual palette, Chukovskii continued, Bunin began developing an "astonishingly sensitive ear—colors recede—and his attention shifts . . . to the speech of his petty bourgeois and peasant characters."

What Chukovskii is talking about is not just an abstract auditory capacity, not even Bunin's prodigious memory for overheard speech. Rather,—he refers to Bunin's attempt to transform his narrative, to make it memorable by the inclusion of aurality ("the peculiarities of this speech, its hues, its twists and turns"). In looking for precedents, Chukovskii correctly refers to Nikolai Uspenskii and Vasilii Sleptsov— especially the latter's story "Pitomka" (1861). Notably, Chukovskii does not refer to Turgenev or Tolstoy. It is not the famous two, but the other writers of the 1860s who produced this new quality (bracketing out Gogol for the moment). This new narrative quality can be defined as follows: the character dialogue became *memorable,* like the dialogue in Griboedov's *Woe from Wit* (anyone who has read Uspenskii's "Oboz" could not help remembering and quoting the phrase: "Let's take, for example, you be a dime, and I be a quarter: this way, it's easier to figure things out").

Notwithstanding his few successful attempts at this new *speech*-oriented genre, Bunin barely touched it. His distinctive contribution remained for the most part on the plane of the Russian literary, *written* language, which is so different from speech.

His other distinctive trait was his ability to convey the image of the visible world, as if he were competing with a painter. It is in this way that Bunin met the challenge of developing new expressive technique which confronted Russian literature at the turn of the twentieth century. In employing his bright and sophisticated palette, he was moving away from Chekhov, in a direction that would later be taken by Isaac Babel.

Chekhov, in other words, became the point of departure for the next stage of literary evolution.

N. Ia. Berkovskii, a thoughtful, subtle critic, if stifled by the confines of Soviet aesthetics, commented about a passage in Chekhov's "Muzhiki": "Olga, all lit up, short of breath, looking with horror at the red sheep and the pink doves flying about in the smoke, kept running up and down." Berkovskii wrote: "Yes, the red sheep look striking and so do pink doves in the smoke—if you concentrate on the palette alone, but Chekhov paints here a picture of a great misfortune, and that is the most important thing here, one that the reader is not allowed to forget." Here color does not live a separate life—it "shares the fate of objects and actions that convey it."[6]

Babel, by contrast, removes the one who does the looking, along with the narrator's horror—and what is left are the red sheep and pink doves seen by who knows whom amid a great misfortune.

Or take a juxtaposition of the descriptions of the sunset in Chekhov and in Babel.

In Chekhov's "Krasavitsy" (1883):

There are times when clouds gathering without any order at the edge of the horizon, and the sun, hiding behind them, paint the sky in all kinds of colors. . . . The fire covers a third of the sky, shines in the cross above the church and the window panes of the master's mansion, reflects in the river and in the puddles, trembles on the trees; far, far away, a gaggle of wild geese are flying against this sky somewhere to settle for the night. . . . And the little shepherd's helper, and the masters taking a walk—all stare at the sunset, and all like one find it beautiful, but none of them can explain what this beauty consists of."[7]

This and many other Chekhovian descriptions are *absorbed* by Babel, but are transformed by his distinct voice, such as in *Red Cavalry*'s "The Road to Brody":

And we moved towards the sunset. Its seething rivers were flowing down the embroidered towels of peasant pastures. Silence was beginning to glow pink.[8]

Babel reads like a song. After the first sentence, there is a musical phrase without words that can be rendered verbally approximately as follows: "Now try and recall everything you know about the sunset and all of its past descriptions." Then he resumes: "Its seething rivers . . ."

Georgii Adamovich wrote in 1928 that Bunin's later works, after his "Gentleman from San Francisco," are perfectly expressive and complete, and yet appear as it were thrust forward, as if "*they could not bear the weight of their own perfection. . . .*"[9] Indeed, Bunin's later prose, in many respects, reached its *limit*; it peaked as an expression of a certain type and in that sense marked the point of the beginning of its own decline.[10] But in some of his stories, those of a new kind, Bunin managed to touch on the "people puzzle" with a memorable force. As one contemporary critic wrote with enthusiasm: "'The Night-Time Conversation' made a deep impression on the reader," bitterly mocking "the Populists' illusions about the ideal, kindly people." He continued: "The gentleman Populist suddenly realizes that those same peasants, with whom he had ardently dreamed of merging, are practically all murderers, 'butchers,' monsters—to the very core, though still kindly looking."[11]

In Bunin's novella "Village" (1910), one of the characters tells a story within a story:

"There are so many prostitutes there—without count. And they are hungry, damned beasts, so hungry—you give her half a loaf for her work, and she'd just gobble it up right under you. . . . We were all in stitches!"

"Note," Kuzma cried out with severity and stopped, "They were all in stitches!"[12]

In this passage, one can almost sense the characters from Babel's *Red Cavalry.*

In other words, Bunin prepared the soil for Babel, pioneering a style and a subject matter that would, ten years later, reappear, condensed within the tight frame of a Babel story.

## II.

In the early 1920s, pre-revolutionary Russian literature became "untranslatable" for the sensibility of the new Russian reader, while "the Ivanovs and Petrovs of today" (B. Eikhenbaum) were yet unable to become material for literature, as they fitted into the old mold too easily. The hardest challenge was the creation of a new pattern, a new mold, so to speak, for new Russian literature. Until this was done, Formalist critics believed, the Russian literary market would continue to be flooded by translations.

Writing along similar lines, Osip Mandelshtam proposed in 1922 a "project," to use today's terminology, for Russian literary prose: it must distance itself from the Russian tradition of belles-lettres, which had degenerated by the turn of the twentieth century into the psychological, ethnographic prose of "Andreev, Gorky, Shmelev, Sergeev-Tsenskii, Zamiatin."[13] In 1924, Shklovsky echoed Mandelshtam when he recalled Babel's debut in Gorky's journal *Letopis* in 1916:

The journal was full of soft, lumpy prose fiction that was even less fresh than old straw. Authors who wrote for it differed one from another only by surname.[14]

Both Mandelshtam and Shklovsky write about the burden of the tradition of the nineteenth-century novel and Symbolist prose. Needless to say, the epigones of the classical Russian novel modeled themselves not on Tolstoy or Dostoevsky, but on Turgenev.

Mandelshtam saw the challenges as follows:

Rejection of description of quotidian existence (*bytopisanie*)
Rejection of psychological analysis (Mandelshtam's famous quip calling the character's *psychology* a wheelbarrow to which a convict is chained)[15]

An Acmeist, optimistic attention directed *outward*—as opposed to the Symbolists' interiority and, curiously, detailed descriptions of daily life (*bytopisanie*) that produced only boredom. In 1922, Mikhail Bulgakov had a similar reaction to this venerable tradition. Mandelshtam was calling for an attitude bringing forth a bright world, one full of sunlight, not the gloomy and gray "Petersburg" universe of Dostoevsky and the Symbolists.

Any form of dynamic expressiveness, whether produced by the tension in the plot (Mandelshtam preferred the adventures of Bret Harte's heroes, even in a poor translation, to the *psychology* of all the literature of the 1900s and 1910s, from Leonid Andreev and Gorky to Zamiatin), or by the intense luminosity of a depicted detail. This was a stance Mandelshtam shared with the Formalists.[16]

That Mandelshtam would prefer a bad translation of adventure fiction meant that the plot and the ability to isolate luminous details were far superior to the vaunted narrative description and the clichéd third-person Russian narrative prose (the standard Turgenev novel). Hence the vigorous emergence of *skaz* prose in the 1920s.

Mandelshtam brought into the foreground *new material*, a focus on the unusual and the exotic that contrasted favorably with the outworn descriptions of everyday life that had long been the hallmark of Russian literature. These nineteenth-century conventions had become automatized and, according to Mandelshtam, had to be replaced with *folklore*, as he defined the new "linguistic and ethnographic material" that literature was supposed to collect and record for posterity.

Babel accepted Mandelshtam's "project" as a subcontractor (Mikhail Zoshchenko's *vzial podrid*). Needless to say, demand for the changes outlined by Mandelshtam had predated Mandelshtam's program.[17] Using less striking examples, a contemporary critic observed:

> Pre-revolutionary Russian literature was static, plotless, burdened with psychological analysis, philosophical reflection. By contrast, the new literature, which emerged in the years of the revolution, is highly dynamic, with muscular plot construction, and practically devoid of psychological analysis.[18]

Let us go back to Mandelshtam's "sub-contract" for the uses of contemporary speech folklore in literature. What he had in mind was the anecdote, a line from an urban chanson, street talk, or slang (*razgovorchiki* in Mandelshtam). All of this was what has always surrounded a writer, but this folklore had rarely been recorded before,[19] and it tended to disappear without a trace (compare Tynianov's thought that speech was a verbal order that was the closest to imaginative literature).

The Jews of Odessa represented for Babel this sort of ethnographic material, with one important proviso: its constructive, organizing principle was minimalism. Just one phrase in a dialogue, one carefully "overheard" line, became the equivalent of an entire plot. Babel employed this device all the way into the 1930s. In the story "Di Grasso," just one such phrase belonging to Madame Shvarts is worth volumes: "And what do I have from him . . . animal things today, animal things tomorrow. . . ."[20]

This one phrase from a lopsided dialogue can compete with the whole tradition of lengthy philosophical digressions that were supposed to be so edifying to the reader. Here minimalism became a new and important quality undermining the venerable novelistic tradition.

In his prose Babel is free of any ideological dependency, ignoring the Russian novelistic tradition.[21] But significantly, he gains this freedom from what Mandelshtam called "the dropsy of grand themes without an elaborate plot construction [*fabula*]—contrary to the recipe proposed by Lev Lunts in the Serapion Brotherhood manifesto 'To the West!'"

> Retelling Babel's stories is very difficult and sometimes impossible.
> *His compact plot* [fabula] *is contained in a single phrase:*
> The old man fell, stretched his legs, and out of his mouth there poured forth a foaming coral stream. . . .
> The night, pierced by the flashes of cannon fire, arched over the dying man. . . .
> The commander winked at the peasant; the peasant placed the lantern on the floor, unbuttoned the dead man, cut off his genitals with a little knife, and started shoving them into the mouth of the wife.

The utterly quotidian "with a little knife" (*nozhikom*) and the imperfect of the predicate "began shoving" (*stal sovat'*) are equivalent to entire chapters, while their semantic density requires no deciphering or further elaboration.

These are examples of a new genre—a phrase that packs both a tight plot (*fabula*) and a complex story (*siuzhet*). The density of the phrase, its enormously dense mass, became one of the main qualities of Babel's prose. This is a phrase that deserves to be reread, closely looked at, studied.

This is why Babel's prose easily competed with novels, the generic workhorse of Russian classical literature.

## III.

The trend of the 1920s points away from the tradition of a large psychological novel: having played its role in literary evolution in the 1910s, Andrey Bely's *Petersburg* is perceived in the 1920s not as an experimental work, but as a classic Russian novel in Symbolist disguise. Literature at that time was evolving along the lines reminiscent of early nineteenth-century prose, with its two distinctive characteristics: Pushkin's *un-psychological* prose, relying on a short phrase and minimalist in terms of the description of details; versus Gogol's prose, with its hyperbolic, sometimes grotesquely enlarged detail, bright colors, pictorial clarity, and beauty. Gogol's grotesque, of course, was later stifled by the "naturalist school," of which Gogol was one of the founders, and which substituted his grotesque "Physiology of Petersburg" with the same old description of everyday life.

Sviatopolk-Mirskii singled out three stories by Babel that appeared in 1923: "King," "Letter," and "Salt." For him they embodied "perfection," because, among other things, of the "complexity of their final effect in which heroic *pathos*, crude *realism*, and lofty *irony* are fused into a unity of a new kind."[22]

Shklovsky, recalling the Babel of 1918–1919, wrote in a similar vein: "He alone preserved in the revolution a stylistic *sang-froid*. . . . He turned out to be a man with a voice marked by curiosity, never shrill, but fond of pathos."[23]

Pathos—understood as an Acmeist thrill before the objectivity of the bright visible world—is perhaps the key feature of Babel's poetics. Babel's stories, notwithstanding the horrors depicted in them, possess a life-affirming narrative energy, derived in part from the author's sense of freedom, his emancipation from the fetters of the Russian literary tradition and its naïveté.

Boris Vladimirskii, who produced subtle interpretations of Babel's stories, perceptively chose the phrase "rejoice and shudder," from a parody of Babel by A. Arkhangelskii, as a key to understanding Babel, and used it as the title of his collection of articles on Babel.[24]

In order to begin employing contemporary material, literature needed a writer of a special kind, one not associated—ideologically, stylistically, thematically—with the mainstream of Russian pre-revolutionary culture. "Babel has the wherewithal to find aesthetic expression for our new age," wrote P. S. Kogan. Echoing Shklovsky's well-known formulation of Babel's style as that of a Frenchman observing Russian exoticism ("Kriticheskii romans"), but ridiculously simplifying it, Kogan went on to elaborate on Babel's "strangeness" in a manner less fitting for the 1920s than the 1940s and the campaign against "rootless cosmopolitanism":

He is a Jew. And, perhaps, this is the main source of those peculiarities of his art that made him so interesting for the critics and the reading public. He does not know any traditions, he is not fettered [*sic*] to the rustling groves and green pastures, like Esenin; his roots are not intertwined with the age-old traditions of and customs of our peasantry, as in Leonov, he does not recall pre-Petrine Russia that holds Pilnyak spellbound. . . . He looks at the picture of life unfolding before him with a fresh look. It takes no effort on his part to jettison the burden of the past. He pursues his literary career without inner tragedies and contradictions that wracked the mind of Blok, Esenin, Briusov and other poets in whose breast clashed the whirlwinds of two worlds—one that is dying and the one that is dawning.[25]

Be that as it may, Babel was freeing Russian prose, first, from its *psychologism* and reflexivity (both of the protagonist and the author) and, second, from its dependence on the tradition of Russian narrative. Paradoxically, the "native material," which was so hard to integrate into contemporary literature (as was noted by the OPOYAZ members[26]), was presented through the prism of a narrator who confronted it, as it were, for the first time. Third, Babel introduced into twentieth-century Russian literature a spoken phrase (by contrast with characters' monologues in Bunin, which are closer to the style of the 1860s)—a phrase that not only carries the entire story but is also calculated to stick in the reader's memory.

## IV.

Before long—indeed, almost immediately after the publication of his first *Red Cavalry* and *Odessa* stories—Babel's manner began to be copied by his contemporaries.

In April 1925, Vladimir Lidin, an enterprising and impressionable writer, wrote a story called "Salazga," in which he—only a year after the ascent of Babel's star—plagiarizes his style, and does so with such arrogance and enthusiasm that his syntax even begins to break down. Here is a passage describing a hero who lost his life on the battlefield:

With Fedia's hand that knew the chilling cruelty of a rifle and the immortal softness of a woman's breast, a woman [there goes the syntax—*M. Ch*] made a sign of a cross over him and kissed him on his high, voluminous [*mnogorechivyi*] brow [pure Babel!—*M. Ch.*], and the two of us carried him on a sackcloth to the monastery cemetery; for the last time, I kneeled before Fedia, kissed his hand, disfigured by rats, his brow of astonishing whiteness, and said goodbye to him. . . . [27]

Here there are plenty of the oxymoronic epithets and "Avvakum-like" syntax.

But the widespread utilization of Babel took the form of small but necessary doses.

All his life Ivan Semionovich Pronin has been tormented by thieves. They pursued him everywhere—these seekers of unearned affluence. The crawled at him like infantry resembling an army of hungry wingless locusts. They penetrated through the factory gate, with him they entered the new shop, and they stood next to him.[28]

This opening shows how Babel was grafted onto the tree of Soviet Russian literature. The author continues:

> Slowly circling around the machine parts strewn on the floor, Grishka stepped with his right toe facing inward like a skater taking a corner. A black beret was floated [*reial, as in a bird floating in mid-air*] over his white face.
>
> It has been three months since they began installing the new flywheel.
>
> The roofs dripping in the first thaw marked black lines on the pavement still covered with snow. The sun was barely shining into the shop; its rays were glowing blue and whirled in a haze of smoke from the burning oil.
>
> A man in an open military top coat was walking on the iron board of the shop floor towards him. The folds of the long cavalry top coat were moving like a banner at half-staff and blowing in the wind. The man was smiling, his eyeglasses glistening.[29]

Needless to say, this writer, who left no trace in Russian literature, seasons descriptions à la Babel with a lot of psychology.

N. Atarov produced several stories and novellas in the 1930s (in the 1950s, he came to occupy an important place in the literary establishment). One of the stories dealt with the 1919 Petrograd that the author, born in 1907, could hardly have remembered.

Let us first recall Babel's story "The Road" (1932). The year is 1918; the setting is a train originating in Kiev.

> At night the train jolted and came to a stop. The door of the cattle car was rolled away, and the green glow of snow opened up before our eyes. A railroad telegraph operator came in. He wore a sheepskin coat tied with a little belt and soft Caucasus-style boots. The telegraph operator stretched out his hand and pointed his finger to the open hand.
>
> "Your papers here . . ."
>
> . . . . Next to me there sat dozing a teacher Yehuda Weinberg and his wife. The teacher got married a few days ago and was taking his wife to Petersburg. The whole trip they were discussing in a whisper the new method of complex instruction, then they dozed off. As they slept, their arms were intertwined, hands linked.
>
> The telegraph operator read their papers, signed by Lunacharsky, pulled out of his sheepskin coat a Mauser pistol with a narrow, dirty muzzle and shot the teacher in the face. Behind the telegraph operator stood a big peasant with hunch back and a fur hat with untied flaps. The commander winked at the peasant; the peasant placed

the lantern on the floor, unbuttoned the dead man, cut off his genitals with a little knife, and started shoving them into the mouth of the wife.

"You disdained the treif," said the telegraph operator, "now eat the kosher stuff."

Compare it to Atarov's story:

At night, there came the report that the Red Army had seized Ekaterinoslav. In the morning the communists were mobilized to hold rallies . . . editor Langovoy was assigned the suburban Okhtensky Factory. . . . Copyeditor Rachkov, who doubled as a driver, egged on his underfed horse with a whip. . . .

"Look: there is one that hasn't been finished off yet [*nedobityi*]," said Rachkov pointing into the thick of the forest.

A tall old man wearing a city top coat and a soft down cap stood under the pines in the virgin forest, looking through a pair of binoculars at rowan trees clustered at the edge of the forest.

Langovoy opened his holster, jumped out of the cab, and approached the suspiciously absurd figure of a city man. The old man did not even turn, absorbed as he was with his odd observation.

"Hey, citizen, come here," said Langovoy.

"And what would you like?" asked the old man politely and with a smile. . . .

"Do you know what territory you've wandered into?"

"I am in the territory where the rowan tree thrush do their wintering," the old man responded promptly. "Would you like to see my permit?"

It was clear that this was not the first time he had been pestered with questions. . . . The old man promptly pulled out his permit with a quick gesture as if he were pulling a spent cartridge out of a gun. But all of a sudden his face darkened, the tender ironic smile was extinguished; what was left were his cold ears, fatigue in his eyes, red lines of an old age flush in his cheeks; and this combination of a hunter's agility and a helpless expression somehow convinced the editor that the old man was telling the truth. He barely glanced at the permit issued by the Forestry Institute.[30]

Here, we have Babel's "The Road" in reverse.

One of the fiction writers of the 1930s–1950s, A. Pismennyi, recalled with admiration the impression that Ivan Kataev's sketch, "The Third Span," made on him and his friends. He quoted from it:

What we saw at first was not even a bridge but an idea of one, a thinnest, lightest outline suspended in glow of air and water. The morning was not bright, there was an even cloud cover, but the expanse was such that it did not need any more light;

the white river glistened with its Baltic silver. An hour later, the outlines of the bridge gradually thicken, it begins to materialize. One can already discern the low arches of all six spans, the thin (from the distance) supports and, lowered into the water, black lines of their reflections.

Pismennyi remarked: "A writer could give a lot for these 'lowered into the water black lines of reflections' and 'Baltic silver'"[31] Why use the subjunctive—"a writer *could*"? Writers *did* give a lot, quite a lot, for the opportunity to learn to draw these "thin lines" and, more importantly, for the right to display the results of these lessons in print, the fruits of their literary mastery. They tried, with the help of such "thin lines," to convey human emotions and feelings that somehow had to be retained and passed on to the next generation. This is what Konstantin Paustovskii did in his seminar at the Moscow Literary Institute in the post-WWI years: he focused on these very same "thin lines" that delineated these same emotions, ever suspended over our sinful earth, and he became canonized as a classic in his lifetime just for that—only to dissolve later on into nothing, along with the thin lines.[32]

This idea of learning writing technique from the master was prompted largely by Babel's prose, which was read, reread, studied, indeed, copied.

## V.

In the 1930s, writers began adding a little Babel into their largely Bunin-seasoned brew. The question is why Bunin alone did not suffice. The answer is apparent to those who are immersed in the history of the official literary production of the 1930s, a complex process that resists a simple explanation.

First of all, the density of Bunin's descriptive prose was practically impossible to imitate at that time, because the conditions of literary production were such that one simply could not go so deeply into anything. Nor did these conditions—the rules, so to speak—permit the other type of "analytic description," the psychology of Tolstoy. Both styles required depth that was not available in the shallow waters of the official literature (Alexander Fadeev tried practicing deep Tolstoyan psychology, but his *The Last of the Udegueh*, just as Shklovsky predicted, was never finished). Besides, a truly Tolstoyan psychological analysis was taboo, because self-analysis and reflexivity were seen under Soviet conditions as markers of a double life.[33]

Bunin's exhaustive descriptions became impossible under the conditions of Soviet life. Victorious Marxist materialism could not tolerate literature's close look at the conditions of life. In the early 1930s, the time of the avant-garde "naturalism," daring representation of everyday experience was coming to an end. Only recently, a Soviet critic could define Babel as a "master of clear prose in the 'French style.'" This so-called French style was the entire toolkit that writers used as means of distancing themselves from the classic novelistic tradition.

But in the 1930s, literature began to lose its "French" license and with it the ability to deal freely with all kinds of material. As Babel's "French prose" was being pushed into the background, it was being replaced by the powerful, traditional style of Russian literature, except that now the old canon had been polished to a sheen (the easier to use as the "mirror of the Russian revolution") and prepackaged into "classics," and could not abide anything like the recent innovations. There was no place for the lofty irony intertwined with the "non-Russian" pathos of Isaac Babel. Muted colors, which Babel so recently had expelled from Russian literature, were coming back; allusion and allegory, albeit without much depth, were also back in fashion. Babel was increasingly out of place now.

And yet, he had already been assimilated by Russian narrative prose; in a few short years, his blood had been absorbed into the Russian soil and changed its composition. The well-known, diffuse, lyrical-universal narrative style acquired its final shape in the early 1930s (for example, in the works of Konstantin Paustovskii). For years it served as a safe haven for those who tried to steer clear of the mainstream of the official Soviet literature. This other style of Soviet literature was that of Babel's prose, albeit highly diminished in intensity and very much flattened out.

Confused billboards and towns of different hues—that is what constituted our country that year. Winter was full of snow. Closer to spring, the weather turned freezing. Postmen rode around in long sheepskin coats. Peasants held meetings close to hot stoves. . . .

This is a fragment from the prose of Evgeny Gabrilovich.[34] But it could just as well have been written by Konstantin Paustovskii, Semyon Gekht, S. Bondarin, R. Fraerman,[35] N. Atarov, or V. Kozhevnikov.[36] Indeed, it could have been written by Roskin himself, for example, his biographical novella about Chekhov, "Antosha Chekhonte" (1939): "New mining sites appeared in the steppes. Next to the ancient burial mounds, mountains of violet slag kept growing. Hawks perched on telegraph wires and looked on the passing trains with new indifference."[37]

The same novella contains an observation worth citing here at length:

As he was studying his brother's drawings, it occurred to Anton that ugly things are no more real than things that are beautiful.

He believed there was truth in this simple thought, a truth important for anyone who wished to create something new in art.

However, when he himself tried to write beautifully, what came out was something odd resembling an illiterate translation of a foreign novel.[38]

One would look in vain for such thoughts in Chekhov's own writings—neither about the ugly nor the beautiful, nor about the similarity between a beautiful and a bad translation. As one of those Soviet writers who practiced "diluting Babel," Roskin was giving expression anachronistically to the taste of a later time—his own stylistic preferences and those of his milieu.

This phenomenon of the "diluted Babel," typical of the 1930s, was in sharp contrast with Babel's impact on Russian prose in the second half of the 1920s, when his style became the thread holding together the prose of such writers as Yurii Olesha, Ilia Il'f, Evgenii Petrov, and Valentin Kataev. Kataev's *Embezzlers* shows a distinct influence: "Iron beat on iron. Magnificent windmills, stations flew by on their electric wings." Babel's "school" emerged even earlier, in 1923, when he named several young Odessa writers in a preface to a planned collection: Semyon Gekht, Lev Slavin, Konstantin Paustovskii, Ilia Il'f. But stylistic dilutions were not on the agenda then.

Babel's stylistic origins and those of later Soviet Russian prose may be traced to the Pushkinian narrative model wherein, in Yuri Tynianov's words, "actions and events are not elaborated but enumerated." Pushkin's own style could be traced, as one scholar has recently written, to travelogues, historical chronicles, reports, and the old Russian chronicles (letopis')."[39] In the 1920s, prose was oriented toward the same genres, and Babel found and sealed its form. Sviatopolk-Mirskii wrote in 1925 that "the true epic core" was "the most surprising feature and, perhaps, the most precious trait of Babel's prose."[40] This epic quality is what was absorbed by the writers of the "foreshortened line."

Babel himself, while he was giving the impetus to the new prose, was probably unaware of the power of his own example. For example, the oft-commented on ending of "The Road"—*the superb life of mine* [prevoskhodnaia moia zhizn'], full of thought and merriment"—is significant not only because of its sudden turn toward an ideological tone but also because of its semi-inverted word order. Such inversions later became the hallmark of "lyrical prose." Five years later, in "Di Grasso," Babel, whose influence had been absorbed by the younger generation, seems to be writing under their influence, in particular that of Paustovskii:

... and suddenly, *with a clarity I had never before experienced* [Babel had never previously *elaborated* that much—M. Ch.], I saw the towering columns of the Duma ... and saw for the first time my surroundings as they really were—becalmed and ineffably beautiful. (emphasis added)[41]

The last phrase reminds one of Arkady Gaidar: "And life, comrades, . . . was quite wonderful!" Here, one can discern the first outlines of an emerging Soviet idyll, prompted perhaps—if we follow Anna Akhmatova's observation on the endings of Pushkin's *Tales of Belkin*—by the apotropaic impulse to cast a spell against the impending doom.

Indeed, Babel's stories of the late 1930s merge in some instances with the stylistic manner of Konstantin Paustovskii, who had long ago absorbed Babel's own style, along with a secret dose of the émigré Ivan Bunin. Seen especially through the prism of the later Soviet literature, Babel of the late 1930s begins to read like an epigone of Paustovskii. Babel's 1937 story "The Kiss" is a good example.

The cast of characters, the props, the setting—the nobly paralyzed old father, his daughter, a widow of "an officer killed in the German war," her five-year-old son, the entire "family of a school teacher, a family of kind and helpless people"—all resemble the formula of Paustovskii's stories from the 1930s through the 1950s. Here are a few characteristic passages from Babel's story:

Frozen, she stood there, arms dangling, in her old-fashioned cape that clung tightly to her slender figure. Unblinking, looking straight at me were her blue eyes, widening and shining with tears.

. . . Never have I seen a creature more impulsive, free, and easily scared.

. . . Once, I drew to myself the head of Elizaveta Alekseevna and kissed her. She slowly pulled away from me, straightened herself out and, clutching the wall, leaned against it.

. . . Awakened by me, the old man was anxiously watching me from under the foliage of the lemon tree.

"Say that you will come back," he said repeatedly, his head trembling.

Elizaveta Alekseyevna, a fur jacket over her batiste nightdress, accompanied us out onto the street.

. . . Autumn came, along with the silently drizzling Galician rain.

. . . Wearing the same batiste nightdress with its hanging lace, Tomilina came rushing out onto the porch. She took my hand in her hot hand and led me into the house.

. . . Tomilina gave me her chilled hand. As always, she held her head high.

These Paustovskii-like passages, directly associated with the narrator, are stitched through with a rough thread: the narrator's orderly Surovtsev. The character of the latter is woven from two strands: the crudeness of unadorned reality (from sex to death), and his speech of a commoner. It is this speech that conveys the specifically Babelian moments in the plot:

"Where do you take your rest? . . . You lie down closer to us, we are fun folk [liudi zhivye]."

. . . "She's agreeable," he said, settling down, "She just don't say it in words."

. . . "The main thing is the horses are wiped out," he said merrily, "Otherwise, we'd go for a ride."

. . . I went into the house to say goodbye to the old man.

"The main thing is we don't have the time," Surovtsev said, blocking my passage, "saddle up—we're leaving . . ."

He pushed me out into the street and gave me the reins. . . .

. . . I turned my horse toward the clearing and turning yelled to Surovtsev:

"Wish I could stay longer. You spooked us too early."

"Not too early," he replied. . . . "If it wasn't for the old man, I'd have come for you even earlier. . . . But I couldn't. The old man got to talking to me, got excited, started squawking, leaned to the side, and keeled over. I rush to him, I look, he's dead, it's all over for him!"

Leonid Rzhevskii shows many examples of Babel's influence on Paustovskii.[42] Babel's short phrases, his technique of concatenation of heterogeneous details[43] saved Paustovskii from banality:

A bright night was glowing outside. Water glistened like foil. Sunset barely shone in northern darkness. The odor of the grass and wet boulders outside seeped into the room along with the twitter of the birds. (*Northern Tale*, 1939)

Avoiding high drama, Paustovskii habitually joins the melodramatic expressiveness of the old French novel (Dumas) with that of the Russian prose of the late nineteenth and early twentieth centuries.

"What? Taube cried out in a *thin voice* and his *cheeks began to tremble*, "Perhaps I misheard you?" He turned to Kisilev his *pale puffy face*. "You have no right to order me around. You have no right to say anything. You are a murderer, and for this you will pay by losing your epolets." (*Northern Tale*, 1939, emphasis added)

This passage is precisely what I mean by "a diluted Babel." This modifier here is completely value-neutral. If it had not been for Babel's horrible end, and the unimaginable torments of months-long waiting, the whole picture might have looked different. As Tynianov wrote of Esenin's poetry after the poet's untimely death, Babel's demise in the Great Terror, his martyrdom, endowed his legacy with a special meaning.

Those authors who practiced diluting Babel, though they did so constrained by the officially imposed set of rules, subtracted from his legacy the very core—his complete freedom in the choice of subject.

There are occasional traces of the way these authors consciously rejected Babelian themes. Emil Mindlin recalled how, after being discharged from the hospital, he told Paustovskii the story of his neighbor in the hospital ward. He was a gravedigger who, as he was dying, "kept complaining for days about his bad luck":

"Bad luck, such bad luck! . . . That it should happen to me now—in the golden season! You wait for this time to come the entire year! And now it's here but I am sick and lying in the hospital, while good money there is going to waste. Oh Lord, forgive me for my sins!"

According to the grave digger, during the summer, children die like flies. You bury them one after another. A child's grave is much easier to dig up than an adult one. You just give it a couple of shovels, and it's done! But "when it comes to paying up, there ain't no difference if it's adult size or for a child." And tips are much better. "There is more profit from a child's funeral than any other."

"What a wonderful subject for a story!" Paustovskii cried out.

"Here, take it and write!"

"And you?"

I said that I was not going to use it. And I kept pressing him to "use" this theme. Paustovskii thought for awhile, and refused. It was not *his* kind of a theme. He did not know how to write about the ugly and immoral. He cannot even write about spiritual defects. For him life manifests itself only in its beautiful aspect.[44]

Paustovskii could "hypnotize one with his landscapes with their obliga-
tory black line of autumnal rivers, the smell of the fallen leaves and rain-
soaked fences." So writes I. Goff in her memoirs, citing Paustovskii's letter
of 1960 about one of her stories:

I was reading and feeling joy for you, for your true mastery, your *laconic style*, precisely and subtly sketched objects, especially where it tends to be *psychological* and
*allusive*. The melancholy of this story is as beautiful as the melancholy of Chekhov's
"Lady with a Dog."[45]

Babel's "rejoicing and shuddering" are replaced by melancholy, his pathos,
by lyricism, and behold—diluted Babel fuses with diluted Chekhov. Babel was keen on Maxim Gorky's device of juxtaposing the heroic and the
lyric that Gorky wrote about in his "Notes on the Petty Bourgeois Culture" (1905). According to Gorky, a petty bourgeois

likes a good life, but his emotions are not deep, the *tragic character of social existence* is
inaccessible to him; only the horror of his own death can be deeply felt by him, and
on occasion it is expressed brilliantly and with real force. A petty bourgeois is ever a
lyricist; *pathos* is absolutely inaccessible to the petty bourgeois; in this instance, they
are truly cursed with the *curse of impotence*. . . . (emphasis added)[46]

In the 1920s, after the "mists of Symbolism" had dissipated, critics began
to see something "new and surprising" in the attention that objects received in Osip Mandelshtam's writings. The same may be said of Babel's
narrative style. By the early 1950s, thanks to the capable leadership of
Konstantin Paustovskii, Russian literature returned to the Symbolist
mists; however, unlike actual Russian Symbolism, which was part of an
international movement committed to some metaphysical exploration of
the world, this latter Symbolism did not stray further than the little rivers
with their black water and the smell of a rain-soaked fence.

Even Nikolai Gribachev, perhaps the most hardcore of the officially
sanctioned writers, and a true believer to boot, could begin his "Story
about First Love" (1953) with a phrase full of cool Babelian pathos: "The
river was aflame in moonlight."[47]

When Shimon Markish wrote that Babel's death was not accidental,
in the sense that "there was no place for him in the literature of the 1940s
and 1950s,"[48] he was absolutely right. But in another sense, one can say
with certainty that there was, in fact, plenty of space for him, too much

in fact—as long as Babel remained nameless and shorn of his most crucial qualities. To resort to the vodka analogy, if true Babel was 100 proof (the result arrived at after much trial and error), the printed literature of the 1930s through the 1950s was a beverage in which Babel's dose was so weak that it could no longer be tasted.

# Part Three

# Babel in the World of Letters and On Stage

# 7

## Babel, Flaubert, and the Rapture of Perception

ROBERT ALTER

BECAUSE FLAUBERT, more than any other European novelist, turned the practice of fiction into an exacting form of exquisite art, he became a model that was often and variously imitated in the next three generations of writers. Tolstoy brilliantly assimilated the narrative technique of *le style indirect libre* that Flaubert had brought to a high order of perfection. That technique is abundantly deployed in the first three episodes of Joyce's *Ulysses*, gradually segueing into stream of consciousness, and Joyce also carries forward Flaubert's iconoclastic enterprise of extending the aesthetic to the realm of the sordid and the mundane. Kafka, like his Central European Hebrew contemporary, S. Y. Agnon, seems above all to have been riveted by the ideal of the novelist fanatically devoted to a demanding art that was embodied by Flaubert, though he also adopted a deadpan version of *le style indirect libre* to convey an experience of constant epistemological anxiety, while Agnon, informed by Freud, used the same technique to expose the tensions between consciousness and what it repressed. And all of these writers, it should be said, assumed a posture of self-containment or restraint in their fiction that was first strikingly exhibited by Flaubert.

Babel was clearly an attentive reader of Flaubert,[1] though there are patent differences in aim and sensibility between the two writers. There is a manifest element of exuberance in Babel, sometimes, paradoxically, even when he is representing horrors, whereas Flaubert kept a certain clinical distance between himself and the world, observing it with wonderful precision but from a vantage point of emotional estrangement from it.

To cite a symptomatic case, political events for him are pure spectacle, instances of the eternal cycle of human futility and self-deception, as one sees in his representation of the Revolution of 1848 in *The Sentimental Education*. Babel, writing in a different post-revolutionary era under the censor's watchful eye, could scarcely permit himself the luxury of transparently detached cynicism, nor does he by and large seem inclined to indulge that luxury. Babel also evinces none of Flaubert's interest in the consciousness of his characters: the only consciousness that much engages him is that of his first-person narrators, and the very use of the first-person form precludes Flaubert's signature technique of *le style indirect libre*.

And yet, there are affinities between the craft of fiction deployed by each of these two writers. One can detect certain Flaubertian practices in Babel, reworked according to the bent of his own very different vision of the world. Because the historical landscape that confronted Babel, from the pogroms of 1905 to the Revolution and its bloody aftermath, was repeatedly grim and violent, Flaubert's aestheticization of the ugly proved to be a valuable precedent for him. I am thinking of such elements in Flaubert as the lingeringly precise description of the hideous blind beggar in *Madame Bovary*, of the disastrously bungled operation on Hippolyte's club foot in the same novel, of Emma's arsenic-induced death throes, of the wholesale killings in the streets in *The Sentimental Education*. Here is a more mundane instance of Flaubert's procedure. Charles Bovary, early in his acquaintance with Emma, comes to visit her at her father's farmhouse at three o'clock on a warm afternoon. The shutters have been drawn against the sun.

Through the cracks of wood, the sun laid down great thin stripes over the flagstones that shattered at the angle of the furniture and trembled on the ceiling. Flies, on the table, climbed the sides of glasses that had been used and buzzed as they drowned at the bottom of the lees of cider. The light that came down through the chimney, turning the soot on the hearth into velvet, gave a blue tinge to the cold ashes. Between the window and the fireplace, Emma was sewing: she wore no kerchief; on her bare shoulders one could see little drops of sweat.[2]

All this, we can infer, is observed from Charles's point of view, culminating in the drops of sweat on the exposed shoulders, which remind us that the young woman at the center of this painterly rustic genre scene is an object of sexual interest for him. What is more pertinent to Babel is that the concrete details, through the very precision of observation, are made to transcend their banality and are transformed into a beautiful aesthetic object: the sunlight filtering into the shuttered room, exerting an alchemy on the objects within it, the beads of sweat on female flesh, and, above all, those flies drowning in the lees of cider. Let me match this representation of the quotidian with a more extreme moment in Babel, the depiction of the officer's bullet-ridden body at the beginning of "Squadron Commander Trunov": "The coffin was open, the clean midday sun lit the lanky corpse, lit his mouth filled with smashed teeth and his carefully polished boots, their heels placed together as at a drill."[3] Flaubert's interest in using the perspective of the observer to convey the emotional and psychological location of the character is absent here (the viewpoint is the first-person narrator's, and he speaks on behalf of the "we" who constitute the unit of soldiers); but the impassivity of observation, the rigorous selection of details—pairing smashed teeth with carefully polished boots—even the visual tracking of the image through the sunlight that illuminates it, are eminently Flaubertian. Sudden death, which occurs often in Babel's stories, is bound to be horrific, but the narrator, exercising scrupulous restraint, gives no explicit expression to the horror, letting the observed details speak for themselves. Indeed, together with the horror there may even be an element of grotesque comedy here in the corpse's elegant heels "placed together as at a drill." Flaubert had shown Babel how one might write about what was most disturbing in the world without pathos, without a hint of the histrionic, conveying a sense of things violently awry all the more powerfully through the stance of impassivity.

Flaubert's impulse to aestheticize the world he represents, which I think Babel picked up and developed with a rather different effect, is worth emphasizing. Here, for example, is a brief moment from *The Sentimental Education* when the protagonist, Frédéric Moreau, is coming back from an outing to the Bois de Boulogne with his mistress Rosanette. The two are seated in a small carriage: "Finally, they returned through the Arc of Triumph and the great avenue, breathing in the air, with the stars over their heads, and, to the very end of the perspective, all the gas lights linked up in a double row of luminous pearls."[4] What is distinctively Flaubertian about this is the meticulous attention to visual sight-lines—he even uses the painterly term "perspective"—which are presumably those of the couple riding along the boulevard in their carriage. The metaphor of the luminous pearls is of course what turns this moment of experience into an aesthetic object. There are many counterparts in the figurative language of Babel's stories, though his aestheticizing metaphors tend to be less verisimilarly grounded in the process of perception of the characters and more flamboyant or even deliberately fantastic.

Let me offer one final example of an aestheticized scene in Flaubert, again from *The Sentimental Education*. It involves a panoramic view—urban panoramas of course abound in Babel's Odessa and Petersburg stories—and, somewhat atypically, the perspective seems to be that of an overviewing narrator rather than of one of the characters. A traffic jam during a rain shower after the races at the Champ de Mars has just been described. Now the congestion breaks up:

. . . everything resumed movement: the coachmen loosened the reins, lowered their long whips; the horses, animated, shook their harness chains, tossed foam around them, and the hindquarters and the damp harnesses smoked in the water vapor intersected by the setting sun. Passing under the Arc of Triumph, it cast a reddish light at a man's height that made the wheel hubs sparkle, the door knobs, the tips of the team shafts, the saddle rings; and, on both sides of the great avenue—resembling a river in which manes, clothing, human heads undulated—the trees all glistening with rain loomed, like two green walls. The blue sky above came out again in patches, soft as satin. (271–72)

The elegant precision of observation scarcely needs comment. As elsewhere in Flaubert, painterly attention to the effect of light plays an important role in defining the scene. The figurative language at the end—the undulating river of traffic, the green walls of the trees, the satin softness of the sky—is not obtrusive but contributes strategically to the aestheticizing of the urban scene. What is most notable about this moment is how beautifully *composed* it is. One can detect here the beginnings of a literary genealogy that will lead to a recurrent feature of modernist fiction. Joyce famously developed a doctrine of epiphany, the enrapturing moment of aesthetic revelation. The privileged moment in Proust, usually involving memory, is a cousin of Joycean epiphany. Later writers as different from each other as Nabokov and Bellow would continue to sustain interest in the epiphany, and I believe something quite like it can be seen in many of Babel's stories. The aestheticized moment in Flaubert is not yet epiphany even if sometimes, as here, it rather looks like it. The difference is that the term given currency by Joyce has a theological background and implies an experience of revelation: the writer, open to the world, is suddenly flooded by it, vouchsafed a lovely constellation of beautiful elements that exalts him, moves him to register it in artful language. Flaubert is too much the conscious artificer to open himself to such a quasi-theological experience of revelation from the world. He is more like a lapidary shaping the rough gem of the observed world into an exquisite jewel with the fine tools of his craft. But his ability to use the medium of fiction to bring forth such luminous moments as this sunset Parisian panorama created a precedent for the modernists, who learned from him but were more emotionally responsive to the pulsing energies of experience.

Let us now consider some of the distinctive features of the exalted moment in Babel. I shall begin with a brief instance from one of the Odessa stories, "Liubka the Cossack." It occurs in the midst of a description of the motley assemblage of guests at Liubka's inn: "The sun hung from the sky like the pink tongue of a thirsty dog, the immense sea rolled far away to Peresip, and the masts of distant ships swayed on the emerald water of Odessa Bay. The day sat in an ornate boat, the day sailed toward evening . . ." (157). The extruded simile of the sun as the pink tongue of a thirsty dog is of course quite unlike anything in Flaubert, and it is worth noting that Babel uses some of his most fantastic images to represent the sun, the moon, and the stars. There is, however, a sense of underlying unity here, a unity both "revealed," as in Joyce, and manifestly composed, as in Flaubert. One sees a kind of painterly composition in these lines, the pink of the sky against the emerald sea, though the simile of the thirsty dog's tongue might suggest a painter more like Chagall than the sort of nineteenth-century French realist that Flaubert often had in mind. The unity is also kinetic: rolling sea and swaying ships turn the day itself, through metonymy, into an ornate boat sailing toward evening. The Flaubertian precedent of aestheticizing the urban panorama is on the way to becoming epiphany because the prose registers a sense of excitement about the enlivening spectacle that the narrator beholds. The Odessa stories are of course memorable for their vivid characters—the Jewish gangsters, the con men, the procuresses, the Rabelaisian women—but what equally seizes the imagination are these repeated artful apprehensions of an exalting sense of unity in the teeming heterogeneity of urban experience.

The peculiar magnetism that Babel's fiction exerts is often associated with its celebration of the world's sheer multifariousness. Babel is so committed to this way of seeing that it even sometimes asserts itself in landscapes wracked by violence. Here, for example, is a view of Petersburg's main avenue in the winter of 1918 in "The Road":

The Nevsky Prospekt flowed into the distance like the Milky Way. Dead horses lay along it like milestones. Their legs, pointing upward, supported the descending sky.

Their bare bellies were clean and shiny. An old man who resembled an Imperial guardsman trudged past me, dragging a wooden toy sledge behind him, driving his boots with difficulty into the ice. A Tyrolean hat was perched on his head, and he had tied his beard with a piece of string and stuck it into his shawl. (662)

The one distinctly Flaubertian note here is the careful, impassive precision with which the spectacle of the dead horses is represented, with the focus on an unexpected detail—the clean and shiny bare bellies of the equine carcasses. This is not, strictly speaking, an effect of defamiliarization but rather of hyper-lucid and somewhat unconventional perception, a procedure often cultivated by Flaubert. One should note how the sky is drawn into the scene—again and again in Babel's moments of integrated perception, the sky, or the sun, or the moon, or the stars are made part of the picture, as if the terrestrial scene could not be complete without its celestial backdrop, as if what the experience demanded were some sort of cosmic frame of reference. Thus the Nevsky Prospekt is likened to the Milky Way,[5] and the supine dead horses, resembling figures in a grotesque mythology, are said to support the descending sky with their stiffly up-thrust legs. The figure of the bedraggled old man pulling the toy sledge then crystallizes the baffling incongruity of the whole scene. One doesn't know what to make of the bizarre elements of his appearance that are singled out—the Tyrolean hat (in revolutionary Petersburg!), the beard tied with string, the toy sledge—but the oddest thing is that everything here seems uncannily to fit together: the old man, the dead horses, and the great avenue turned into the Milky Way. Man and beast perish in the pitiless cold of winter and in the violence of war and revolution, but the great spectacle of the world—sky and earth, old age and youth (the narrator), human accoutrement and animal nakedness—continues to arrest the imagination, inducing here nothing like euphoria, as in some of the other stories, but nevertheless a sense of wonder and bemusement.

Babel's explicitly celebratory panoramas, however, are the more typical ones. Here is a scene outside a tavern in Tiflis in "My First Fee":

Georgian princes in blue Circassian jackets and soft leather boots sauntered past in casual parade. They picked their teeth with silver toothpicks and eyed the carmine-painted Georgian women with large feet and slim hips. There was a shimmer of turquoise in the twilight. The blossoming acacias howled along the streets in their petal-shedding bass voices. Waves of officials in white coats rolled along the boulevard. Balsamic steams of air came flowing toward them from the Karzbek Mountains. (710)

The heterogeneity of the represented details is pulled together by the painterly composition, the blue of the jackets set off against the silver of the toothpicks, the carmine of the women, the shimmer of turquoise light, and the white jackets of the officials. The play between variety and unity helps impart to the observed scene the sense of a splendid parade, exciting the observer. In this instance, the overarching sky is not explicitly introduced though it is implied in the invocation of the quality of twilight illumination. One modernist touch is the bold use of synesthesia in the acacia trees howling with bass voices. Another image that is nearly synesthetic is the balsamic air coming down from the surrounding mountains, either redolent with fragrance or tangy in taste. Eyes, ears, nostrils, and palate are all stimulated by the scene, and this involvement of the senses makes it an apt prelude to the young narrator's meeting (in the very next paragraph) with the good-spirited Georgian whore who will initiate him into sex, in the end accepting the stories he tells her as payment. The Flaubertian precedent of beautifully composed visual representation of a scene with no strictly narrative function has been embraced and also, as one would expect when one original writer encounters the achievement of another, entirely transformed. The exotic panorama here intoxicates the observer in its gorgeousness, its abundance, its sensuous variety, a mood that often seizes Babel's narrators, even when they are not getting ready to lose their virginity.

After the narrator's night of love—it is he who chooses that word to characterize his experience—he and the woman breakfast on tea and rolls in an outdoor market. The great parade of the previous evening has not ended, only changed in the colors and sounds it displays:

We drank tea in the bazaar of the old quarters. A placid Turk carrying a samovar wrapped in a towel poured tea, crimson as a brick, steaming like blood freshly spilled to earth. The smoking fire of the sun blazed on the walls of our glasses. The drawn-out braying of donkeys mingled with the hammering of blacksmiths. Copper pots were lined up under canopies, on faded carpets. Dogs were burrowing their muzzles into ox entrails. A caravan of dust flew toward Tiflis, the town of roses and mutton fat. The dust carried off the crimson fire of the sun. (716)

Babel exhibits a certain affinity with Flaubert in his attention to the source of light as a means of realizing and unifying the visual scene. But because he is using a first-person narrator rather than a dispassionate third-person narrator who both filters and carefully orders the consciousness of the character, there is a sense of intimate, experiential connection between the speaker and the solar source of light: the "smoking fire of the sun," which a few lines down becomes a "crimson fire," is not merely a painterly property that helps turn the scene into visually integrated artifice, as in Flaubert, but is felt as a torrid presence that envelops the speaker as he and his lover drink their tea. The crimson of the tea and the crimson of the sun constitute more than a compositional link because the figurative language registers this morning moment in the Georgian setting— an unabashedly "Orientalized" moment—as a kind of archaic ritual, the red tea calling up an association of sacrificial blood poured to the earth, with the smoking crimson fire of the sun, perhaps like the fire that consumes the sacrifice on the altar, taking part in the ritual. If there is some latent sense of the archaic here, what is emphatically manifest in the passage is the celebration of heterogeneity in which Babel so often takes delight. The braying of the donkeys joins in raucous concert with the percussion section of the blacksmiths; the ceremony of tea poured from a carefully wrapped samovar is counterpointed by the dogs burrowing into ox entrails; and, in what amounts to a summarizing zeugma, Tiflis, in a grand flourish, is declared "the town of roses and mutton fat." In Flaubert, the world is often displayed as pictures at an exhibition, each scene exquisitely arranged within an invisible frame. In Babel, the enrapturing interconnected beauty of the observed scene is frequently asserted, but the artful observer is part of it, stirred by its multifaceted, contradictory beauty.

"Beauty" may not always be the most appropriate term for these moments of integrated perception that punctuate Babel's fiction. As we have seen, such moments can focus on dead horses or cadavers with smashed teeth as well as on Oriental bazaars. The concept of beauty might perhaps be rescued if we regard Babel's enterprise as an extension of Flaubert's aesthetic project of representing the ugly or the sordid with such elegant artistry that it is transformed into an object of art. Babel was keenly interested in human panoramas as well as in scenic ones, and he typically set them in a perspective that managed to be both appreciative and satiric. What may be the most telling evidence for Babel's deep attraction to unified vision is that it sometimes manifests itself even in his social scenes.

Consider, from "In the Basement," his description of a group of ostentatiously wealthy Jewish women playing cards on a late summer afternoon on the veranda of a dacha outside Odessa owned by a prosperous banker, the father of a schoolmate of the narrator's. The point of view is obviously satiric, but not just satiric:

The women—card-playing gourmands, sluttish coquettes, and furtive debauchees with large hips and perfumed undergarments—fluttered black fans and staked their gold. The sun pierced its way to them through the copse of wild vines. The fiery globe was immense. Copper sparks weighed down the women's black hair. Flashes of sunset pierced their diamonds—diamonds that hung everywhere: in the deep hollows of breasts pressed apart, from powdered ears, and on plump and bluish female fingers. (637)

As in all the other scenes we have considered, the disparate elements are pulled together into a visual composition: black fans and gold coins, the copper highlights (or could they be actual ornaments?) in the women's black hair brought out by the fiery sun, the dazzling points of diamonds everywhere. The narrator, a boy who comes from a much more modest Odessa Jewish milieu and is entering an unfamiliar world, is obviously put off by these flamboyantly vulgar-rich female card-players. At the same time, he is also fascinated by their flaunted sensuality: he duly notices the large hips and the displayed cleavage of the breasts, and, in one precious detail that is surely not direct observation but projection, he imagines their perfumed undergarments. The story will end painfully when the banker's son makes what proves to be a disastrous visit to the narrator's embarrassing family, but this scene on the veranda marks a moment of excitement and even exultation, the sort of moment in which the distinctive life of Babel's fiction pulses most strongly. The bediamonded women are at once objects of derision and of admiration. In their very vulgarity they manifest an extravagant vitality, an appetite for life, which is a quality Babel celebrates equally in his Odessa Jewish gangsters and his Cossack cavalrymen. At the same time that the young observer in the story is daunted, dumfounded, perhaps a little repulsed by these showy rich women at the card table, he is also attracted to them, and the language he uses to report this moment makes it, in all the sharpness of its satire, a sustained moment of enraptured perception: here is life in all its gaudy fullness, drawn together in a paradoxical epiphany—the fiery glow of the sun, the profusion of female plumpness, the black fans, and the diamonds.

To point to an affiliation between writers is not to claim an equation, as I hope I have made clear throughout this discussion. Babel, whose experience encompassed considerably more in the way of historical horrors than Flaubert's, remained ultimately an enthusiast, an enthralled observer of life's spectacle, and that enthusiasm vividly informs the celebratory moments of his fiction that we have considered. Enthusiasm is an attitude quite alien to Flaubert's profoundly disenchanted imagination of the world. What Flaubert was able to show Babel, as well as a number of other writers of the earlier twentieth century, was the possibility of breaking out of the limits of conventional aesthetic categories through a studied descriptive art of fiction. The impetus of realism increasingly manifested in fiction from the middle decades of the nineteenth century and on into the twentieth had moved many writers to engage with some of the gritty, even nasty aspects of physical, social, and political reality that by and large had not been represented in fiction earlier. Flaubert, bringing the novel to a new degree of consciously crafted formal perfection, set a precedent in fashioning indifferent or downright disagreeable materials from the real world into finely wrought aesthetic wholes. Babel's narrators, moving through milieus populated by gangsters, vulgarians, whores, pimps, bloody-minded pogromists, and ruthless combatants, manage to uncover treasures of beauty in this roiling world, and also to convey a sense of gratitude for the beauty that they find.

# 8

## Toward a Typology of "Debut" Narratives
### Babel, Nabokov, and Others

ALEXANDER ZHOLKOVSKY

THE RECURRENCE IN BABEL'S TITLES of the word *pervyi*, "first" ("First Aid," 1914; "My First Goose," 1924; "First Love," 1925; "My First Fee," 1922–28), catches the eye and prompts an inquiry into his involvement with the theme of initiation.[1] "Initiation" is discussed in *Бабель / Babel*,[2] which centers on "My First Fee" (*Moi pervyi gonorar*) / "Answer to Inquiry" (*Spravka*), without any reference, however, to an important pre-text: Sholom Aleichem's 1903 story entitled, punningly, "My First Romance" (*Moi pervyi roman*)—in a clear foreshadowing of Babel's title and, to a great extent, plot.[3] Sholom Aleichem was, of course, one of Babel's favorite authors and objects of professional attention (Babel translated his texts into Russian and turned his *Bluzhdaiushchie zvezdy (Wandering Stars)* into a movie script).

"My First Romance" goes, briefly, as follows: The narrator, an educated but famished Jewish young man, gets a position as home tutor for the son of a rich Jewish landlord. At first the mother of the pupil doesn't feed the narrator well, but then the tutor and pupil make a pact: they will pretend that they are engaged in lessons, but in fact will do nothing but gorge on food and have fun. The only unavoidable duty of the tutor is to conduct—on behalf and in the name of the pupil—a correspondence with his fiancée.

The narrator gets involved in the correspondence and gradually falls in love with the well-read and intelligent correspondent. He dreams of meeting her and nurtures plans of declaring his love on the day of the wedding, telling her the truth about his authorship and proposing she marry him rather than his lazy and ignorant pupil. But at the wedding he meets her tutor, a bespectacled Jewish young man like himself who has been writing the sophisticated metaliterary letters he fell in love with.

Even this short summary gives an idea of the role played by the theme of lying/inventing/writing that is so relevant to Babel's wedding of literary creativity with love and sex. These and many other links between the two stories, as well as more general affinities between the two writers, were analyzed in the corresponding chapter of my book "*Poltora Rasskaza Babelia*" (see note 3), without, however, broaching the issue of "debut" narratives as such. An unexpected parallel in the work of a closer contemporary, Vladislav Khodasevich, helped formulate the problem as a more general one.

Writing about the treatment of monkeys/apes in Vladislav Khodasevich's poem "A Monkey" ("*Obez'iana*," 1918) and a chapter in Mikhail Zoshchenko's *Youth Regained* (*Vozvrashchennaia molodost'*, 1933),[4] I wandered into Nabokov territory: Chapter 11 of his autobiographical *Conclusive Evidence* (1951) / *Speak, Memory* (1967), which originally appeared in the September 1949 issue of *Partisan Review* as a short story entitled "The First Poem."

As has been noted by Nabokov scholars,[5] this piece is not a strictly factual account of the author's creative debut; in fact, the very poem in question has not been identified among the Nabokov corpus. To this I added the issue of the text's arch interplay with several poetic pre-texts, including Bunin's and most notably Khodasevich's "monkey" poems, as well as some Fedor Tiutchev and Afanasii Fet lyrics, especially the latter's "*Na stoge sena noch' iu iuzhnoi ...*" (Upon a Haystack One Southern Night ...). The relationship with Khodasevich's poem was especially telling, as Nabokov borrowed from it not only the country house setting and the motif of a monkey and its owner, a Slav barrel-organ player (*sharmanshchik*), but also the momentous historical date of the encounter: the day of the beginning of World War I.

No wonder Nabokov wrote the piece only a decade after Khodasevich's death, in English, and never did include it in the Russian-language version of his autobiographical narrative *Other Shores* (*Drugie Berega*, 1954), which accounts for the discrepancy in chapter numbering between the two versions. (To make this real-life plot even thicker, the very first poem actually penned by Nabokov in English on his arrival on these shores seems to have been his translation of Khodasevich's "Monkey" [1941]—several years after the poet's death!) Ironically, half a century later, it was Nabokov's posthumous cult in post-Soviet Russia that resulted in a translation of the self-excised chapter into Russian—for all to see and deconstruct.[6]

Grouped together with Babel's "Answer to Inquiry / My First Fee" and Sholom Aleichem's "My First Romance," Nabokov's piece emerges as one more instance of a special metaliterary sub-genre of fictional(ized) initiation narrative.[7] This naturally suggests searching for more analogs, primarily those carrying in their titles words like "my first story" ("tale," "novel," "fee," "debut," "role," "premiere," "beginning," and so forth). In what follows, I look briefly at two more texts that can be seen as more or less immediate precursors of Babel's story.

Leonid Andreev's "A First Fee" (*Pervyi gonorar*, 1900) is not strictly metaliterary (the fee in question is for lawyering), but it clearly belongs in the "debut" cluster. It is told in the third person from the point of view of a young initiate.

An experienced defense lawyer has to leave for Petersburg and delegates a case to his idealistic young assistant, who is afraid of but also honored by the responsibility. On studying the case he concludes that the defendant, a general's wife, is, indeed, guilty of illegitimate sales of cigarettes. But then, proud of his first-time role as a defense attorney—*zashchitnik*, literally, a "defender"—he reviews the file, finds some openings, and, once in court, manages to sway the judges both by his handling of the case and his naive youthful enthusiasm. Especially successful is his line about the honorable gray-haired head of the distinguished lady, who is not present in the court, due to illness.

But soon after the verdict has been handed down, he realizes he defended the guilty party. Indeed, the general slips into his hand two gold coins (30 rubles). One of the witnesses offers him further services as a professional false witness; while another, a clerk at the general's shop, tells him that the defendant used to be a lowly cook who got the general to marry her, that she had already done time, and, finally, that she is red- rather than gray-haired! The salesman says, admiringly, "That was really smart of you, to slip in the one about her gray head!" The protagonist is in despair: his profession, his life, and the entire world seem sordid and pathetic to him.

When his boss the great lawyer returns, he goes to see him and tells him the entire story. The boss is amused and glad they won the case. He reprimands the young man for inventing the gray head, but even more for accepting the unfairly small bribe. He promises to get what is really owed by the general and pass it on to the young man. The protagonist can't help pointing out to his mentor that "in reality, she was guilty." The older lawyer says: "Reality? Who knows what happens in reality?... Reality! Oh, you funny man! [*Ah, chudak, chudak*]," as he looks at the young man and seems to recognize something nice, kind, long forgotten.

Despite the heavily realistic, somewhat muckraking, tenor of the story, the punch line about the dubiousness of "reality," crowning the leitmotif role of the invented "gray-haired head," makes Andreev's "First Fee" a precursor of Babel's story in terms not only of the title but also of a whole range of motifs. Note the trepidation of a young, timid, yet ambitious novice, his encounter with the grisly circumstances of real life; the presence of an older experienced mentor; the supplanting of "reality" with a felicitous verbal find; and even the money—two gold coins!—changing hands in recognition of the successful invention.

The other story, Anton Chekhov's "Moi pervyi debiut" (My First Debut, 1886), is also about lawyers. Although related to the "debut" topos by its title, it is somewhat less representative of it.

The story is told in an ironic third-person manner, sticking to the point-of-view of the protagonist, and it revolves around the miserable self-perception of a young defense lawyer when he loses his first case. He imagines that he was no good, that the public and the jury laughed at him, and that the claimant and his lawyer despised and humiliated him. He insults the two in the courthouse building and then, on his way home unexpectedly having to share a roadside room with them, behaves in a hysterically aggressive way, while they treat him with friendly care and try to console him, explaining that his is a typical first-case psychological syndrome.

Centered as it is on the sad first experience of a lawyer defending a wrong case, "My First Debut" may have served as an actual subtext of Andreev's story, and thus as a proto-subtext of Babel's "My First Fee."

We can now try sketching out a framework of invariant parameters that inform fictionalized treatments of "creative debuts," drawing primarily on Nabokov's "First Poem" and Babel's "My First Fee" / "Answer to Inquiry" with occasional reference to Chekhov's, Andreev's, and Sholom Aleichem's stories. Despite obvious differences (for example, the absence in Nabokov's text of the "sexual initiation" motif, so central to Babel's), the two stories share several constitutive topoi: semi-ironic first-person reminiscing mode; acknowledgement of juvenile imitativeness; role of parent figures; subversive Bloomian play with literary "fathers"; and some others.

Even the time frames seem to coincide: the year 1914. Both the affinities and differences help formulate a tentative definition of the "debut" genre of quasi-autobiographical prose.[8]

1. Both Babel and Nabokov wrote their pieces as parts of a larger, more or less fictionalized autobiographical project. In the case of Nabokov this is obvious; as for Babel, he wrote several stories about the maturation of a young boy-writer but never had a chance to complete the project. Both Nabokov and Babel write from the hallowed, ironically detached perspective of an older first-person narrator looking back on his naive younger self up for literary initiation. The distancing, of course, is already a first step toward fictionalizing the experience.

A similar first-person perspective is used by Sholom Aleichem. Both Andreev and Chekhov use a more realistic, objective, comic third-person narrative, perhaps because their protagonists are not writers, after all.

2. In a further fictionalizing move, in both Nabokov and Babel, the "realness" of the alleged "first work" is precarious. In Nabokov, as I said, the poem as such does not seem to exist or to ever have existed (and an aura of mystery is enhanced also by the obliqueness of references to the historical and literary bearings of the narrative). In Babel, the "text" is brazenly declared to have existed only as an oral performance. This results in a remarkable tension in the narrative: between the virtualness of this "first work" and the generous helpings of textual quotations from it.

In Sholom Aleichem, the "romance" means mostly "love affair," but to some extent the correspondence (crowned by the never-delivered final letter with a marriage proposal) does constitute a sort of "epistolary romance / novel," in part quoted, in part paraphrased in the narrative. In Andreev, fictionalization is represented by the quoted invention of the "gray head of hair" and the punch-line about the precariousness of "reality."

3. The metaliterary aspect of the genre involves the Bloomian problematic of discipleship, imitativeness, and rebellion vis-à-vis literary parents. The imitation of nineteenth-century poetic stereotypes is explicitly discussed by Nabokov (in a somewhat stentorious academic manner, which led to the rejection of the story by the *New Yorker* in 1948[9]). But Nabokov is much less open about his archly hidden borrowings, from Afanasii Fet and Fedor Tiutchev and above all from Vladislav Khodasevich's "Monkey." Babel, too makes fun of the clichés he is using, and is quite cynically playful about their efficacy. He is less open, but quite transparent, about the subversion of the tradition of narratives about the rehabilitation of

prostitutes (Gogol, Dostoevsky, Chernyshevsky, Gorky). But he is rather tongue-in-cheek about his ironic spoof of the entire "victimized child-hood" sensibility that underlies his literary mentor and protector Maxim Gorky's *Childhood* (*Detstvo*) and *In the World* (*V liudiakh*).[10]

As for Sholom Aleichem's story, it is heavily metatextual in the way the correspondence between the two intellectuals keeps returning to liter-ary issues and also, on a subtler level, the way it is a parody of Dostoevsky's very metaliterary, epistolary *Poor Folk*.

4. Plotwise, the Bloomian element usually takes the form of its Freudian basis: the Oedipal. In Babel's story, this is quite obvious: the orphaned narrator claims to have been victimized as a boy prostitute by a succession of negative father figures, whereas the loving prostitute herself is cast as a surrogate mother to the protagonist and other characters. In Nabokov, it is precisely to the mother that the adolescent poet brings his first poem, while the father is absent on business but still holds the full attention of the mother, so that a certain hidden Oedipal rivalry shows through, despite the idyllic atmosphere of the dacha.

In Sholom Aleichem, the protagonist is practically an orphan, and the most prominent parent figure is the father of the pupil: a colorful liar who fosters the entire atmosphere of "lying/creativity." In Andreev and Chekhov, the protagonists are similarly thrown at the mercy of the sur-rogate, somewhat ambiguous but eventually protective father figures—the older lawyers.

5. Cognate to the treatment of parent figures is the choice of the type of childhood that underlies the autobiographical, and hence debut, narrative. Of the two types analyzed by Andrew Wachtel,[11] the happy aris-tocratic and the unhappy plebeian, Nabokov clearly portrays the former (with all the accoutrements: a loving mother, a paradisiacal country house, the closeness of the capital), while Babel pointedly and with a parodic irony exploits the latter. Characteristically, in "Answer to Inquiry" Babel uses not so much his own real childhood/youth but rather draws on the archetypal "Gorky-style" wandering proletarian youth.

Interestingly, the adopted paradise of a country estate is also in evi-dence in Sholom Aleichem—only to have the poor protagonist banished from it in the end. Just like in Babel, the protagonists in Andreev and Chekhov are poor, practically orphaned, and behave in a childlike way (especially in Chekhov), although they are no longer children, but rather young adults on their first assignments.

6. Yet another archetypal parameter of the "debut" paradigm is "love/sex." In "Answer to Inquiry," Babel combines literary initiation with sexual. In Nabokov's piece, "love and sex" are practically absent— displaced as they are into a separate chapter of the autobiography (chapter 12 [English]/chapter 11 [Russian], about the narrator's romance with Tamara), although surreptitious references to them do appear in the first poem chapter. Instances of such separate treatment can also be found in Babel: "My First Goose" deals with male bonding almost to a complete exclusion of literature (which, to be sure, does surface at the end, as the narrator reads Lenin's "crookedly straightforward" text to his new mates), while "The Beginning" sticks to the issue of "literary debut" without indulging in sex.

The "sex-cum-writing" combination also underlies Sholom Aleichem's "Romance," with the amorous claims of the protagonist being comically frustrated. In Chekhov, the sexual dimension is completely absent; in Andreev, at the moment of an early elation over the first case, the protagonist at least writes to his girlfriend.

7. In terms of the setting of the action, Nabokov's paradise of a country house near the capital contrasts predictably with Babel's provincial inn/whorehouse. Yet, the two narratives do have certain aspects of the setting in common, namely, those representing the banality of the prosaic surroundings that serve as a contrasting backdrop to the creative act. In Nabokov, the "prose" is represented by the *sharmanshchik* with a monkey and the gypsy-style songs on the dacha's veranda; in Babel, by the entire ambience of the inn, but especially the routine behavior of the prostitute that depresses the protagonist and thus finally spurs him into an inspired improvisation. One unexpected and probably extraneous similarity concerns the time when the action takes place: in Nabokov it is the eve of the war; in Babel, it is approximately the same year 1914 (when the real author, Babel, was twenty years old—the age of his protagonist).

8. As far as the setting, or context, of the actual writing is concerned, Babel's story was written almost two decades before Nabokov's, in the early 1930s, after the peak of Babel's success, under Stalin; Nabokov's was written during the author's third emigration, in the United States, after the earlier successes of his Russian years, but prior to the success of *Lolita* in the second half of the 1950s. Babel doesn't appear in Boyd's 1991 index of names, and Nabokov's reception of his work remains largely unknown, but, attentive as he was to the work of Soviet authors, he did read Babel

and at some point considered him third best among them.[12] In fact, he could even have read "Answer to Inquiry," as its only lifetime publication was in English, in the export-oriented Soviet magazine *International Literature* (1937). As for Babel, he apparently read Nabokov's Russian-language books.

9. Related to the circumstances of writing are the central thematic concerns of the stories, mostly different. Babel's theme, along with literary and sexual initiation as such, is the conceit "literature = prostitution," involving a carnivalesque glorification of both and, at the same time, a subversion of Russian and Soviet literature's spiritual / official pieties. Nabokov's tenor is a nostalgic recreation of the golden time of his youth, not so much opposed to as ignoring the intervening Soviet reality.

To sum up, the stories as such are very different. Babel's is a deflating, almost avant-gardist brand of modernism, while Nabokov's is a variety of highbrow modernism. As a result, Nabokov conceals or displaces much of what Babel seeks to subvert by laying bare. Yet, despite the manifold differences, the common parameters of the "debut" narrative and even some common solutions show through.

# 9

## *Pan* Pisar'
## Clerkship in Babel's First-Person Narration

**ELIF BATUMAN**

IN *"PAN* APOLEK,"** arguably the pivotal story in Babel's *Red Cavalry* stories,[1] the title character imparts a secret gospel to Babel's narrator, Kirill Liutov: "There is something I have to tell you, *pan pisar',*" he whispers.[2] Throughout the story, Apolek addresses Liutov as *"pan pisar'"*: an appellation typically translated as *"Pan* Clerk" or "Mr. Clerk," in accordance with the Polish meaning of pan (sir or Mr.), and the Russian meaning of *pisar'* (clerk). On the other hand, *pisarz* in Polish means "writer"—suggesting that Apolek, a Polish painter, is trying to call Liutov "Mr. *Writer.*"[3]

The clerk is actually a writer, the writer is also a clerk. This slip between *pisar'* and *pisarz* furnishes the point of departure for my paper, which explores the doubling of clerk and writer in some of Babel's "metaliterary" stories. This project is informed in part by the work of Mikhail Iampolski and Alexander Zholkovsky, who treat economic transactions as both subject matter and structural principle in Babel's "Guy de Maupassant" and "My First Fee" / "Answer to Inquiry."[4] The *pisarz/pisar'* duality finds a counterpart in Iampolski's reading of "Answer" as a text that begins as a bureaucratic document ("In answer to your inquiry I inform you . . ."), and ends as "literature" ("I break off the story [*rasskaz*] here"). By writing a *rasskaz* and entitling it *spravka*, Iampolski suggests, Babel establishes a formal affinity between the bureaucratic and literary text (BB 174). My claim is that, by showing us a *pisarz* and labeling him *pisar',* Babel suggests a formal affinity between literary composition and bookkeeping.[5]

The doubling of the clerk and the writer corresponds to a credit and debit in artistic creation: a balance between the raw materials of lived experience and the finished products of preexisting art. This balance is evident in the artistic method of *"Pan* Apolek," which Liutov vows to imitate: Apolek inserts the features of his neighbors and acquaintances into paintings of religious subjects. Apolek charges 50 zloty for a *Last Supper* "portraying all the client's family." For an extra 10 zloty he will represent "the client's enemy . . . as Judas Iscariot" (TCB 219). This premise is likely borrowed from an anecdote about Leonardo da Vinci. During the painting of *The Last Supper*, the story goes, a church prior complained to the Duke of Milan that Leonardo was lagging behind schedule. Leonardo reassured the Duke that the *Supper* was, in fact, near completion; only the head of Judas was missing, for want of an appropriate model—and, in a pinch, "there was always the head of the prior, who was so insistent and indiscreet."[6]

Leonardo's joke hinges on the leveling of the hierarchy of evil, the equation of the officious supervisor with the greatest sinner of all humankind. The anecdote fuses the ontologically incommensurable discourses of Holy Scripture and the artist's daily life. This joke becomes, in *"Pan* Apolek," the source of a secret truth: namely, that art always *comes from somewhere*. The face of Judas does not appear in the mind of the artist as a magnificent abstraction; it is acquired through experiences, through human interactions with ordinary people. From this perspective, using the face of the prior to represent Judas is not really comic at all: where else should Judas's face come from?

A useful critical framework for considering the dialectic between Judas and "the client's enemy"—between the two ontological levels in Apolek's paintings—is provided by Michel Jeanneret's binary of *imitatio* versus mimesis. Jeanneret defines *imitatio* as the imitation of canonical discourses ("the operation of rewriting which legitimizes all classical literature"), and mimesis as the replication of nature: the creation of a duplicate world "realistic enough for the imagination to go along with it," recognizable as "a universe which is coextensive with the world of actual experience."[7] In terms of *"Pan* Apolek," the subject of the *Last Supper* is imitatio; the face of "the client's enemy" is mimesis.

As Jeanneret observes, imitatio and mimesis are mutually dependent. Without mimesis, imitatio is "mere formal acrobatics." Without imitatio, mimesis is meaningless, a shopping list: "the raw object taken from the world of phenomena has no meaning as such. . . . Just as mimesis must give the illusion of life to imitatio, so imitatio must give mimesis form and meaning" (Jeanneret 274–75). The subject of the *Last Supper* must be mimetically represented in order to solicit the viewer's belief. Conversely, the client's enemy's head has no intrinsic meaning or artistic value, until it is absorbed as material into a work of art.

Although all modern literature may, as Jeanneret suggests, involve both imitatio and mimesis, not all writers explicitly play the two modes against each other, as Babel does in his metaliterary stories. When Efim Nikitich, the athletic proofreader in "The Awakening," reads a "tragedy" penned by Babel's young narrator, he immediately diagnoses it as lacking in a "feel for nature": "your landscapes resemble descriptions of stage sets" (TCB 633). Babel's narrator suffers, in other words, from a lack of affinity for mimesis: an inability to convincingly replicate the outside world, which bristles at him with its "unknown shrubs and nameless trees" (TCB 634).

The lack of sense for mimesis corresponds to an exaggerated sense for imitatio, as we see in "My First Fee": "From my youth, I devoted all the strength of my being to the composition of novellas, plays, thousands of stories . . . I did not want to write them down too soon. It seemed to me a pointless exercise to write worse than Lev Tolstoy did" (SS 2002, 1:227). Babel represents writer's block as the paralysis of mimesis by imitatio: the narrator is prevented from writing by his desire to resemble Tolstoy. And yet, it is this imitatio that gives rise to writerly aspirations in the first place. In Babel's stories, the desire to be a writer is an impulse to reproduce, not the marvels of an outside world that, in fact, seems arbitrary and meaningless, but the works of Tolstoy and Maupassant.[8] The would-be writer is originally a *reader*, who wishes his own arbitrary and contingent life to resemble the meaningful narratives of his favorite books. The metaliterary plot in Babel thus takes the form of a journey through imitatio to mimesis and back.

This journey from imitatio to mimesis is typically associated less with the short story than with the novel, in which it plays a key role. As Georg Lukács puts it, each new novel must traverse anew the "unbridgeable chasm": the "opposition between essence (*Wesen*) and life," "between meaningfulness on the one hand and the events and raw materials of daily existence on the other."[9] Babel traverses, in an incredibly short space, this "chasm" that has provided the structure for so many very long books: for example, Marcel Proust's *In Search of Lost Time* (1913–1927).

I pause here for a moment to justify the comparison of Proust and the self-declared "master of silence," who in fact have much in common: for instance, an ornate, highly "written" prose style (Proust's endless subordinate clauses, Babel's icily precise "army of words"), and mastery of a distinctive semi-fictional, semi-serial autobiographic form:[10] once one looks beyond quantity, there is not such a large qualitative difference between Proust's *roman fleuve* and the Babelian "story cycle." Both authors related with some ambivalence to their Jewish backgrounds, both achieved greatness in the dominant literary culture,[11] and the Marcel-Swann relationship in Proust's *Recherche* is similar in various ways to the Liutov-Babel relationship in *Red Cavalry*.

Proust's *Recherche* describes the same kind of journey between imitatio and mimesis that is traveled by Babel's metaliterary narrators. Proust's Marcel is, from earliest childhood, plagued by writer's block, and obstructed by his favorite authors. So intensely does he wish to write a book resembling the *Arabian Nights* or Saint-Simon's *Memoirs*, that he cannot "imagine without horror [writing] any work which should be unlike them": much like the narrator of "My First Fee," who cannot bear to write worse than Tolstoy. Finally, in *Time Regained*, Marcel realizes that the single-minded pursuit of imitatio is a dead end, and that "one can remake what one loves, only by first renouncing it":

> When one is in love with a literary work, one would like . . . to write something just like it, but one must sacrifice this love . . . and think, not of one's taste, but of a truth which does not ask for our preferences, and prohibits us from thinking about them. And only if one faithfully follows this truth will one sometimes stumble again upon what one has renounced, finding that, in forgetting these works, one has written the *Arabian Nights* or the *Memoirs* of Saint-Simon of another age.[12]

Likewise, it is only by renouncing Tolstoy and following "the truth" that Babel's narrator can captivate his first reader. "Truth" in this context does not, of course, mean *literal* truth. Babel's "first story" is fabricated from start to finish—but it is fabricated from real materials and is faithful to what Babel elsewhere calls "the truth of [his] world" (TCB 638). It has an epistemological basis in the author's lived experience.

The epistemological "responsibility" of the novelist, the responsibility to the truth, originates in another important novelistic intertext: Cervantes's *Don Quijote*. Don Quijote, longing for his life to be as meaningful as that of Amadís of Gaul, embarks upon a full-scale *imitatio Amadís*. Quijote is a figure for the *writer* of *Don Quijote*: a fanatical *reader* of chivalric romances, who would like to write something similar—but who refrains from merely following his preferences, and rewriting his favorite books. From Cervantes onward, the writer cannot simply invent a giant from thin air; the giant must be reached through the raw materials of lived experience, for example, through the windmill. Quijote, a sick man, is unable to mimetically represent the world to himself; he looks at windmills and sees giants. Such is the "madness" of a writer who obstinately follows his literary "preferences," instead of the truth. The role of "clerk" is filled in *Don Quijote* by Sancho Panza, who follows Quijote through the world keeping the balance sheet of literary delusions versus their raw materials: "[Those] aren't giants, but windmills, and what seem to be arms are just their sails, that go around in the wind and turn the millstone."[13]

Babel knew and read Cervantes,[14] and there are important resonances between the two authors' biographies. Cervantes, too, began his adult life as a heroic participant in a large-scale military nationalist campaign (the Battle of Lepanto). He, too, ended up an outsider within the dominant culture.[15] (Cervantes's central-marginal social position has even led scholars to ascribe to him a secret *converso* ancestry.[16]) Both Cervantes and Babel were schooled in bookkeeping. Babel graduated the Kiev Commercial Institute with top marks in general accounting (Freidin, 1990).

Before writing *Don Quijote,* Cervantes worked for seven years as a commissary clerk, requisitioning wheat and olive oil in exchange for promissory notes (a bookkeeping task of monumental proportions), in order to fund the Armada's last, doomed campaign.[17] In 1918, Babel held an analogous job as a clerk in a "produce expedition," trading goods for wheat along the Volga (described in his "Autobiography" and "The *Ivan-and-Maria*").[18]

Both Cervantes and Babel suggest in their works a kind of credit-debit relationship between literary "romance" and agricultural "reality," represented by the figure of the windmill, which accounts for the giant. When Quijote is dubbed a knight, the innkeeper swears him in on an account-book "in which he recorded the straw and barley he supplied to the mule drivers" (Cervantes 20); I return to this theme in my discussion

TABLE 9.1. Debits and credits

| Debit | Credit |
| --- | --- |
| Writer | Clerk |
| Literariness | Documentary truth |
| The giant | The windmill |
| Lukács's *Wesen* (essence) | Lukács's "practice" (daily life) |
| The writer's favorite books | The writer's lived experience |
| *Imitatio* | Mimesis |

of "The *Ivan-and-Maria*," below. Mention may also be made of Babel's *Chinese Mill*, a screenplay about a provincial Komsomol secretary who aspires to liberate China from the yoke of imperialism. The Komsomols eventually abandon this "giant" project in favor of restoring the local mill, and the last shots are of "flour flowing from the millstones" (TCB 968).

HAVING SET OUT THE GENERAL IDEAS of this paper, I now turn to specific readings of five of Babel's "metaliterary" stories—"Guy de Maupassant," "The *Ivan-and-Maria*," "The Story of My Dovecote," "My First Fee," and "*Pan* Apolek"[19]—in which I examine the narrator's double identity as clerk and writer, and the epistemological accounting for literature through the materials of life.

I begin by presenting "Guy de Maupassant" and "The *Ivan-and-Maria*" as a diptych, based on the dualities mentioned above: clerk and writer; mimesis and imitatio; lived experience and preexisting literature. In "Guy de Maupassant," an unhappy story, the narrator is stymied by his imitatio of Maupassant; in "*Ivan-and-Maria*," imitatio and mimesis find a harmonious balance.

I turn next to another negative-positive pairing: "The Story of My Dovecote" and "My First Fee." In "The Story of My Dovecote," the narrator is punished for renouncing great-uncle Shoil's stories; in "My First Fee," the narrator is rewarded for overcoming his imitatio of Tolstoy and telling a story based on the truth of his lived experience. In "Dovecote," an unhappy childhood story, the narrator loses 10 rubles; in "Fee," a triumphant story, the narrator wins back those 10 rubles—by telling a story about an unhappy childhood.

I conclude this chapter by returning to the subject of *Pan* Apolek's artistic method, and to his apocryphal story about Christ and Deborah, which I discuss with reference to Proust's metaphor of the "two ways."

## Accounting for Literary Material: "Guy de Maupassant" and "The *Ivan-and-Maria*"

"Guy de Maupassant" and "The *Ivan-and-Maria*" present diametrically opposing stances toward the vocation of the clerk. In "The *Ivan-and-Maria*," set during a 1918 "produce expedition," the narrator "end[s] up a clerk" (TCB 667). In "Guy de Maupassant," set in 1916 Petrograd, the narrator vehemently "refuse[s] to become a clerk": "better to suffer hunger, prison, and homelessness than to sit at a clerk's desk ten hours a day" (TCB 679–80). The contradiction is very striking, especially given the implied continuity between the two stories, which suggest themselves, together with "The Road," as the productions of a single narrator.[20] In this section, I explain this discrepancy by treating "Maupassant" and "The *Ivan-and-Maria*" as before-after scenarios in the narrator's quest for fulfilling work. "Maupassant" is a story about the recognition of error: of error in the narrator's own vision, and of a general wrongness in the social order, which is naturally corrected by the Revolution.

The narrator of "Guy de Maupassant," like Goethe's Wilhelm Meister, rejects double-entry bookkeeping in favor of art. He turns down a clerkship at the Obukhovsky factory—"not a bad form of service [*nedurnaia sluzhba*], granting freedom from conscription" (SS 2002, 1:198)—implying that such work is mundane, prosaic, and cowardly. In 1916, the Obukhovsky factory was operating as a military steelworks—at a time when state support of military industries crippled civilian Petrograd with poverty and food shortages.[21] In order to keep his hands clean, the narrator falls in with Kazantsev, an absentminded Spanish translator, who has memorized every river, castle, and mountain in Spain. As Don Quijote relives *Amadís of Gaul* in la Mancha, so does Kazantsev live a kind of quixotic life in Peski. The narrator attempts to follow suit; Kazantsev finds him a job translating Maupassant, and he sets out to relive "L'Aveu" on Nevsky Prospect.

Babel's narrator introduces "L'Aveu" as a "joyful" tale, whose hero is "the sun, *le soleil de France*." But notwithstanding the sun-drenched setting, "L'Aveu," like many of Maupassant's stories, narrates a ruthless economic exchange. (Maupassant himself worked for eight years as a clerk for the French Ministry of the Navy.[22]) The eponymous "confession" is not, as Babel initially implies, a confession of love. It occurs when Céleste, helping her mother with farm work, collapses to the ground and announces that she is pregnant. Enraged, the mother beats Céleste, and instructs her to hide the pregnancy from Polyte, in order to get a few more months of free rides.[23]

The plot of "L'Aveu" is as follows. The coachman Polyte drives the milkmaid Céleste to the market twice a week, charging 10 sous (6 for Céleste, 4 for her bucket). One day, Céleste asks Polyte for a discount. Polyte offers to waive the fee altogether, in exchange for a "rigolade"; he repeats his offer, in vain, every week for two years. At the end of two years, Céleste calculates that she has paid Polyte a total of 48 francs: impressed by the enormity of the sum, she finally accedes to his bargain.

Although Babel's narrator does not mention Céleste's pregnancy,[24] his retelling of the "joyful" story acquires increasingly sinister overtones, particularly in the details which diverge from Maupassant's original.

Babel changes the color of Céleste's stockings from blue to red, and turns Polyte's carriage from black to reddish (*poryzhevshii*).[25] Babel's narrator begins reading "L'Aveu" in a rosy light, which becomes actually infernal. Babel effects a similar change in mood by translating the French "*ce diable de Polyte*" as "*etot d'iavol Polit.*" Although both *diable* and *d'iavol* mean *devil*, the French locution implies that Polit is "devilish," a rascal;[26] the Russian phrase implies rather that he is literally diabolical.

The "reddening" in Babel's retelling also represents the influence of Bendersky's 1883 Muscatel, which the translators have been drinking as they work, and which seems literally to seep into the text: "tears of mirth . . . the color of rust-red blood and wine" run down Polyte's face (684). "Guy de Maupassant" exhibits, in this respect, the frame-content structure observed by Iampolski in "My First Fee": a fictitious story (the story of "L'Aveu") borrows its material from the "factual" frame in which it is enclosed (the story of Babel's narrator). "The construction of the '[inset] story' is apparently guided by materials stolen from the 'frame'" (BB 181), by much the same process whereby a dream is "guided" by materials "stolen" from waking life. Babel's white nag, unlike Maupassant's, has "lips pink with age": this pinkness is borrowed, like a dream detail, from Raisa's "pink-rimmed eyes." The material of lived experience guides the narrator's imitatio of Maupassant.

The hellish coloration of Babel's "L'Aveu" reflects the narrator's sense of having made a deal with the devil. As we have seen, the narrator refused the clerkship at the beginning of the story in order to avoid the stigma of arms profits. But he is increasingly unable to ignore the fact that the translation is commissioned by Bendersky, a man who made his fortune in armaments: "The profits he had made from military supplies had given him the look of a madman" (683). The narrator has accepted blood money—as he is reminded by the obtrusion of Bendersky's expensive 1883 Muscatel into the story. Babel's narrator's sense of having been "paid off" represents another parallel between the frame and the inset story in "Guy de Maupassant." The narrator high-mindedly refuses the clerkship, much as Céleste high-mindedly refuses Polyte; but both end up selling out their principles.

The frame is closed, in the last scene of the story, by the narrator's reading of Maupassant's biography, apparently for the first time. For the first time, the narrator is seeking the answers to Maupassant's work in the "raw materials" of his life. After he finishes the book, Babel's narrator is "touched by a premonition of truth [*predvestie istiny kosnulos' menia*]" (TCB 686). This phrase harks back to the moment of insight into Apolek's *Death of John the Baptist*: "The face of the dead man seemed familiar. I was touched by a premonition of mystery [*predvestie tainy kosnulos' menia*]. The hacked-off head on the earthen platter was modeled after [the traitorous curate] *Pan* Romuald" (TCB 216; SS 2002, 1:300). The two realizations are linked by the recognition of "raw material" in the final product of art. The narrator recognizes *Pan* Romuald's head in the painting of John the Baptist, as he recognizes Maupassant's unhappiness in "L'Aveu"—and he recognizes his own fate in the life of Maupassant.

The capsule biography of Maupassant vividly echoes the biographies of the narrator's "luckless" male relations, mentioned in passing during the "childhood" stories. For example, Maupassant "struggled with passion," traveled frenetically, and died "in a madhouse"; Uncle Lev abducted the daughter of a Kiev quartermaster, abandoned her in Los Angeles, and "died in a whorehouse [*durnoi dom*] among Negroes and Malays" (SS 2002, 1:127). Maupassant went mad and "wrote unceasingly"; Grandfather Levi-Itskhok goes mad and works tirelessly on *The Headless Man*, a "novel" cataloguing "all [his] neighbors over a period of sixty years" ("Awakening," TCB 639). Maupassant reverts "to an animal condition"; both Levi-Itskhok and Simon-Wolf have animals inscribed in their names (lion, wolf); Simon-Wolf visits the Medved' (Bear) tavern, and buys furniture in the shape of antlers and lions' jaws ("In the Basement," TCB 640). These histories represent the truth that the narrator would prefer to ignore, and to replace with Pushkin and Shakespeare: the truth of his fate, his birth into particular circumstances and a particular history.

"Guy de Maupassant" is about the recognition of error. The narrator renounces clerkship in favor of literature—then recognizes that creating literature is itself a kind of bookkeeping. He recognizes that "L'Aveu" is not a "joyful" tale, and that real literature is never an escape from the sordid and awful materials of real life, because literature is itself made of the materials of life. The narrator realizes that he cannot and must not lose himself in Maupassant, as Kazantsev loses himself in Cervantes: an image illustrated in the last scene of the story, when Kazantsev has literally "fallen asleep by the stove, leaning over *Don Quixote* in a 1624 edition" (SS 2002, 1:204). Babel's narrator remains wakeful. He stays up all night to read Maynial, and in the last lines of the story, gets up from bed and looks out the window.

In "The Road," set in 1918, the Cheka actually redeems the task of the translator, by fusing it with the historical present: the narrator gets a job "translating the depositions of diplomats, arsonists, and spies," the incipit of "a splendid life filled with thought and joy" (SS 2002, 1:187).

What "The Road" does for the translator, "The *Ivan-and-Maria*" does for the clerk. In this story, Babel's narrator is a clerk on board the *Ivan Tupitsyn*: a tugboat hauling goods from Petersburg to be exchanged for wheat with the Volga German peasants. This "produce expedition" is directed by a real historical character, Sergei, known as "The Red Merchant." Within the world of the story, "Ivan Tupitsyn" is also a real person: "the Volga merchant who had been [the boat's] previous owner" (TCB 667). In Baronsk, the *Tupitsyn* is docked next to the *Ivan-and-Maria*, a steamship carrying weapons to the Red Army. The name of the boat refers to, not a historical character, but a wildflower, *ivan-da-mar'ia* (*Melampyrum nemorosum*), named in turn for the Ivans and Marias in Russian fairy tales. The *ivan-da-mar'ia* bears both yellow blossoms and violet blossom-like bracts, so that two flowers appear to be growing from a single plant; in Slavic folklore, the plant is associated with binary pairs: brother–sister, male–female, night–day. The double structure of Babel's story is thus mirrored in its title.[27] The captain of the *Ivan-and-Maria*, Korostelev—a jailbird, former monk, and vagabond—is not a historical but a literary character: a larger-than-life Gorky-style mariner.[28] The other crew members include such "types" as an affable red-haired muzhik and a scornful Germanized Latvian commissar.

The *Tupitsyn* and the *Ivan-and-Maria* represent the dialectics of mimesis and imitatio, life and literature, agriculture and romance. The *Tupitsyn* is loaded with the materials of Auerbachian mimesis, of everyday life: "bales of calico, scythes, nails, leather goods . . . concertinas and balalaikas" (TCB 667). The *Ivan-and-Maria* is loaded with the materials of adventure tales: rifles, shells, and "boxes with skulls stenciled on them, under which the word 'lethal' was written" (TCB 761). As the two "blossoms" in the *ivan-da-mar'ia* spring from the same plant, so does imitatio in this story spring, literally and organically, from mimesis.

One evening, Babel's narrator and another clerk, Seletskii, visit

Korostelev on the *Ivan-and-Maria*. Korostelev is out of vodka, and decides to sail forty versts to a town rumored to have *samogon* (home-distilled liquor). Unable to disembark in time, the clerks are dragged along. When they return to dock the next morning, Korostelev is shot for wasting fuel.

Although Korostelev's execution would be a logical end-point for the story, Babel brings us back to the *Ivan Tupitsyn*, where Malyshev draws up the accounts:

> "You can be the nicest fellow in the world, have locked yourself up in mon-asteries, sailed the White Sea, been a desperado—but please, whatever you do, don't waste fuel!" Malyshev and I went into the cabin. I laid out the financial records . . . and Malyshev started dictating to me a telegram to be sent to Ilyich. "Moscow. The Kremlin. To Comrade Lenin." In the telegram we reported the dispatching of . . . wheat to the proletariat of Petersburg and Moscow: two trainloads, each twenty thou-sand *poods* of grain. (TCB 678)

These, the last lines of the story, seem to require some explanation. Why end with Malyshev and the *Ivan Tupitsyn*? In fact, what are Malyshev and the *Tupitsyn* doing in the story, to begin with? Seletskii himself seems to perceive his own superfluity: "At least let us get off!" he shouts when the *Ivan-and-Maria* starts moving; "What do you need us along for?" (TCB 674).

The answer to Seletskii's question is that the *Tupitsyn* functions as a "realistic" frame, accounting for the "material" of the inset adven-ture story. This structure is borrowed from the traditional nineteenth-century double-plot novel, in which a romantic adventure is enclosed in an agricultural-autobiographical frame. Seletskii's query *"My-to pri chem?"* recalls, in this sense, the bewilderment of certain contemporary readers of *Anna Karenina*: why is half of Tolstoy's novel about some land-owner, Konstantin Levin, who barely even knows the title character?[29]

In *Anna Karenina*, as in "The *Ivan-and-Maria*," an already "literary" plot (the Anna plot, conceived through imitatio of the French adultery novel) is framed within an autobiographical-agricultural, mimetic plot (Levin on his estate, his book on the Russian laborer, and so forth). The bookkeeping scene at the end of "The *Ivan-and-Maria*" corresponds to the transition between Parts 7 and 8 of *Anna Karenina*, in which Tolstoy continues the novel past Anna's suicide, past the book of her life, to the estate where Levin sows the winter rye, reaps the oats, and feeds the seed corn into his new threshing machine.

If we zoom out still further, the turned page between romance and agriculture is an important metaphor in the novel. (It appears already in *Don Quijote* 1:26: a letter of exchange (*carta de pago*) for Sancho's donkey colts is written on the reverse of a love letter (*carta de amor*) from Quijote to Dulcinea.) The transition between Parts 7 and 8 in *Anna Karenina* recalls the turned page between Parts 2 and 3 of Balzac's *Lost Illusions*, which takes us from Lucien's rise and fall in Paris, back to Angoulême, where David Séchard is embroiled in a lawsuit concerning his invention of vegetable-based paper: Séchard literally lives inside a paper mill, surrounded by the detritus of credit-debit invoices. In similar fashion, one turns the page after Korostelev's death and finds oneself facing the "financial records" of the produce expedition.

In such works, it is only the "frame" character—Sancho, Séchard, Levin—who has the double consciousness necessary to understand both the hero's imitatio, *and* the mimesis that makes the world go round. This is in fact the double consciousness of the author.[30] Babel's clerk-narrator represents the double consciousness necessary to tell Korostelev's story: he sees and understands both the *Ivan Tupitsyn* and the *Ivan-and-Maria*. Curiously, the transition between the two halves of the story is marked by the quixotic image of the windmill: after Korostelev is executed outside the *Ivan-and-Maria*, as the settlers bring their wheat to the *Ivan Tupitsyn*, the narrator observes "windmills . . . turning on the colorless, metallic horizon" (TCB 677). Korostelev, the extinct giant, has been replaced by a mill.

**RETURNING TO** the socioeconomic "morals" of "The *Ivan-and-Maria*," the tidy, balanced double plot reflects both the harmony between the narrator's two vocations (literary writer, "apprentice" to the people), and the felicitous economy between the Volga German peasants and the Petrograd workers. In terms of social and poetic justice, the closing scene of "The *Ivan-and-Maria*" redeems Chekov's bleak final tally in the last scene of *Uncle Vania*, in which the Serebriakovs have just left for Moscow, and Sonia and Vania are left to balance the books ("Carry forward from the old debt two seventy-five. . . . On the second of February, twenty pounds of butter; on the sixteenth, twenty pounds of butter again").[31] This final scene of bookkeeping demonstrates that, for every romance lived by the Serebriakovs in Moscow, somebody in the provinces is adding up the accounts. Meanwhile, Chekhov's Vania and Sonia will be repaid for their labor only in the next life, when God will see how they suffered and show them "a sky all in diamonds [*nebo v almazakh*]."[32]Babel's "Red Merchant" substitutes Sonia's pie-in-the-sky promise with earthly rewards and earthly justice. When Korostelev lives wastefully, he is killed. The clerks are book-keeping, not for him, but for the people. Babel's "twenty thousand poods of grain" cancels out the debit of Vania's "twenty pounds of butter": Ivan Tupitsyn redeems Vania Voinitskii. The death of Korostelev (captain of the munitions boat) also, finally, balances out the unfair profits of the arms dealers, like Bendersky, in "Guy de Maupassant," and exonerates the narrator for once sharing in these profits.

## Balancing the Books: "The Story of My Dovecote" and "My First Fee"

In "The Story of My Dovecote," Babel draws our attention to numbers and numerical equivalencies by the frequent repetition of a single number: five. The story is set in 1905. The narrator must score two fives (*piaterki*) on the entrance exam for the Odessa Gymnasium, in order to break the 5 percent quota for Jewish students. The narrator duly impresses the examiners—particularly, a warden called Piatnitskii (whose name contains *piat-*, five)—with an impassioned recital of Pushkin's verses on Peter the Great. As a reward for his two fives, the narrator's father gives him one and a half rubles, to buy doves for his dovecote. The narrator buys two pairs of doves, for 55 kopecks each (mirroring the two *piaterki*).[33] Meanwhile, a pogrom erupts in the town, and the narrator's great-uncle Shoil is brutally murdered. (So are the doves.) The narrator is taken to see Shoil's corpse, and instructed to place two 5-kopek coins (*piataki*) on the dead man's eyes. The story that began with two *piaterki* ends with two *piataki*.

As Gregory Freidin has observed, the pogrom in "Dovecote" functions as a "hand of poetic justice," which "punishes Jewish boys for playing successfully by the rules of the hated empire" (Freidin, 1990). The narrator is punished for coveting the doves, for memorizing Putsikovich and Pushkin, for achieving the two fives. His punishment is the murder of great-uncle Shoil, and the link between crime and punishment lies in Shoil's defining feature: "his fabricated histories [*lzhivye istorii*] about the Polish uprising of 1861" (SS 2002, 1:128)). At the entrance exams, the narrator had to memorize Pushkin's history of Peter I—displacing (as it might seem to a child) Shoil's "histories" of Nicholas I, and relegating Shoil to the status of "an old ignoramus [*neuch*], a naïve fabulist [*lgun*]" (SS 2002, 1:128). This is the logic of Shoil's death: Here, take your *piaterki*—now they are *piataki*.

We find a similar crime and a similar punishment in "In the Basement": a story in which the narrator, having invited a much admired school-friend for tea, contrives to hide all his male relatives. Having dispatched Uncle Simon-Wolf to the tavern, and Grandfather Levi-Itskhok to the neighbors' house, the elated narrator recites to his friend the burial monologue from *Julius Caesar*. Levi-Itskhok and Simon-Wolf come home early. Scandal ensues. The narrator tries to drown himself in a rain-barrel. The only fruitful yield of the entire episode is that Levi-Itskhok has acquired a new page of material for his novel, *The Headless Man*: it is about the neighbors "at whose house, through my ministrations, he had spent the whole day" (TCB 642). In "In the Basement," the narrator's crime is his attempt to replace *The Headless Man* with *Julius Caesar*—for not realizing that the two poles can and must be synthesized. What are Apolek's Judases and Johns, if not "headless men," waiting to be endowed with the faces of Apolek's neighbors?[34] In "Dovecote" and "Basement," Babel's narrator learns that imitation of preexisting works must not preclude observation of the truth of his world.

IN "MY FIRST FEE," the narrator redeems the error of "The Story of My Dovecote": he earns back, with a hundred-fold interest, the two 5-kopek pieces that he had to place on the eyes of Shoil's corpse.

The narrator of "Fee," a twenty-year-old aspiring writer, falls in love with a prostitute called Vera. To win her favors, he must present her with either "words of love," or 10 rubles. Having no words to spare, the narrator scrounges up the 10 rubles. Vera agrees to go with him to a hotel, but the evening turns out to be unromantic, banal, a total disappointment. In the hotel, frustrated to tears, the narrator yells out his "first" story, a fictional autobiography, about prostituting himself to an Armenian man, who met fiscal ruin after entrusting his crooked friends with "bronze promissory notes."

The bronze promissory notes carry the day: "Vera believed everything I said, once she heard about bronze promissory notes" (714–15). What is so special about the bronze promissory notes? Literally, "bronze promissory notes" are worthless, fictitious; but the conceit of fictitious promissory notes ruining an old Armenian man echo the fate of Grandfather Levi-Itskhok: "a rabbi chased out of his shtetl for forging Count Branitskii's signature on promissory notes" (TCB 638). Babel's narrator redeems his grandfather's crime, transforming it into an act of artistic creation. His choice of *forging promissory notes* as a metaphor for storytelling serves to acknowledge a literary debt: it is Levi-Itskhok who taught him that even the most dull, unpromising, bronze-looking aspects of real life may be spun into a golden tale. By acknowledging this debt, moreover, the narrator expiates his own childhood crime: the shame he once felt of his own grandfather. The efficacy of the "bronze promissory notes" in the narrator's story rests upon their specificity and their derivation from the sphere of biography. Their success is contrasted with the narrator's failed mention of "a rich old man, a church warden . . . stolen from some other writer . . . the invention of a lazy heart that didn't feel like working towards the birth of a living character" (SS 2002, 1:231). Vera, who was so captivated by the bronze promissory notes, loses interest at the first mention of this church warden. As Jeanneret has observed, mimesis is essential to the "suspension of disbelief . . . without which the text, in spite of its virtuosity, would not come to life" (174). Only a bad, unconvincing writer will try to jump vertically to already-written literature, to Tolstoy or to a "church warden."[35] A good writer, deserving of the reader's trust, must reach his destination himself, using the materials around him. Realizing this, the narrator swiftly kills the church warden: "To regain my ground, I shoved asthma into the old man's yellow chest . . . a loud whistle of suffocation . . . the old man would jump up from bed at night . . . and, groaning, breathe in the kerosene night of Baku . . ." (SS 2002, 1:231).

Iampolski has observed that the whistling of the man's chest and the "kerosene night" are both "stolen" from the frame story, in which Vera boils water on a kerosene burner:[36] the narrator corrects his error of mindless imitatio with recourse to mimesis. In this way "Fee," like "Maupassant," presents the structure of a "realistic" frame that supplies the inset story with its material. In the frame story, Vera asks, jokingly, if the narrator is a thief; in the inset story, he *is* a thief ("At age ten I began stealing money from my father," SS 2002, 1:231). In the frame story, Vera is a prostitute; in the inset story, the narrator is a prostitute. The *dukhanshchiki* (tavern-keepers), to whom the narrator claims to have been prostituted, are borrowed from the *kabatchik* (tavern-keeper) in the frame story.

So successful is the narrator's story, that Vera teaches him all her secrets for free (a redemption of the failed love encounter in "Guy de Maupassant") and refunds him the 10 rubles in two gold 5-ruble coins (*piatirublevki*). These two gold 5-ruble coins are the restitution of the two 5-kopek coins the narrator placed on his grandfather's eyes in "Dovecote," proving the capacity of art to redeem suffering, and with interest. The boy who betrayed his great-uncle for Pushkin has now redeemed his counterfeiter grandfather and acknowledged his debt to his family, and receives commensurate payment.

## "*Pan* Apolek" and the Two "Ways"

I conclude this chapter by returning to "*Pan* Apolek," through Proust's metaphor of Swann's way and the Guermantes way, two walking-paths in Combray. The two "ways," I propose, correspond to the writerly paths of mimesis and imitatio. "Swann's way" is named after Marcel's next-door neighbor, the son of a Jewish banker, a man who belongs to a spatially contiguous, historical present. The "Guermantes way" designates neither a real living person nor a material place, but an artistic idea: "so abstract, so ideal," that Marcel can imagine the Guermantes only in a medieval tapestry or a stained-glass window, "invariably wrapped in the mystery of the Merovingian age."[37] The Guermantes way (imitatio), where Marcel first formulates his dream of becoming a writer, represents his desire to replicate his "favorite authors."[38] The very charm of the Guermantes way lies in its resemblance to "a fragment of that fluvial country which I had longed so much to know, since coming upon a description of it by one of my favorite authors" (SW 243).

In *Time Regained*, Marcel realizes that the material of his book is nothing else than the material of his life, and that Swann's way—always the less prestigious and less mysterious of the two ways—is actually the source of this material:

[T]he raw material of my experience, which would also be the raw material of my book, came to me from Swann. . . . even my presence at this very moment in the house of the Guermantes . . . came to me from Swann. . . . the "Guermantes way" too, on this interpretation, had emanated from "Swann's way." (TR 328–29)

Like Levi-Itskhok's *Headless Man*, Marcel's novel is bequeathed to him by his next-door neighbor; and it is this way of mimesis that brings him, in the end, back to imitatio: back to the fulfillment of the desire to "become a writer," to "write books," and back to the Guermantes way: "*On ne peut refaire ce qu'on aime qu'en le renonçant.*"

The unity of Swann's way and the Guermantes way is represented on multiple levels, including a literal, topographic connection: as it turns out, it was all along possible to reach the Guermantes way *from* Swann's way. More metaphorically, the same unity is represented in the person of Mlle. Saint-Loup: the progeny of Gilberte Swann and a Guermantes nephew, an incarnation of the "crossroads" of "the two great 'ways.'" Like an Apolek saint, Mlle. Saint-Loup represents a synthesis of mimesis and imitatio, and bears the traces of both in her appearance: her "beaklike" Guermantes nose is "cut off," like the Swann noses, by a "horizontal line at its base" (TR 502).

Mlle. Saint-Loup's "miraculous" parentage shares a certain vertiginous quality with the apocryphal story, the "hidden gospel" at the end of "*Pan* Apolek." In this story, Christ—the man-god who unites in his person the highest imitatio and the most earthly mimesis—is physically united with an ordinary woman, Deborah. This union takes place at a wedding which, in its material, mimetic detail, bears less resemblance to a Biblical parable than to the wedding of Dvoira Krik in the Odessa stories.[39] As Deborah's bridegroom, an Israelite ivory merchant, approaches the nuptial bed, Deborah is so terrified that hiccups rise in her throat, and she vomits everything she ate at the wedding banquet. Amid the subsequent domestic disorder, "Jesus, filled with pity [for] . . . the woman who was thirsting for her husband but also fearing him . . . united himself with Deborah as she lay in her vomit." Jesus then "left the banquet hall unnoticed, and went into the desert east of Judea, where John the Baptist awaited him" (TCB 222): an amazing sentence, beginning at the wedding scandal, and ending "east of Judea" with John the Baptist.

TABLE 9.2. The two ways

| *Debit (*Guermantes way*)* | *Credit (*Swann's way*)* |
| --- | --- |
| Guermantes, the stained-glass window | Swann: the next-door neighbor |
| Judas (in "*Pan* Apolek") | "The client's enemy" (in "*Pan* Apolek") |
| The *Ivan Tupitsyn* | The *Ivan-and-Maria* |
| *Julius Caesar* (in "In the Basement") | *The Headless Man* (in "In the Basement") |
| The church warden (in "My First Fee") | The bronze promissory notes (in "My First Fee") |
| Christ (in "*Pan* Apolek") | Deborah (in "*Pan* Apolek") |
| *Imitatio* | Mimesis |

The union of Deborah and Jesus is a union of two ontological poles, and is blessed by the birth of a son. When Liutov, greatly excited, asks what happened to this child, Apolek replies that "the priests have hidden him," and taps his own nose (TCB 222)—implying that perhaps he himself is a descendant of Christ and Deborah. Apolek's "family resemblance" to this strange marriage of Christ and Deborah expresses itself in his artistic method, which illustrates the sacred using the profane, bestowing upon the Virgin Mary the face of the priest's married housekeeper.

The moral of Apolek's apocryphal story is that imitatio by itself is sterile. For new art to come into being, imitatio must by some cognitive leap be wedded to mimesis—as Christ is wedded to Deborah. To quote Viktor Shklovsky: "If the line is not crossbred with the non-aesthetic fact, no new art can be created."[40] The hidden truth which Pan Apolek imparts to Liutov is the secret of the regeneration and remaking of literature.

# 10

## The Child's Eye
Isaac Babel's Innovations in Narration in
Russian-Jewish, American, and European
Literary Contexts

ZSUZSA HETÉNYI

RUSSIAN-JEWISH LITERATURE was the first in world literature to
develop forms for placing the problem of Jewish assimilation into a universal context, describing the characteristic experience of one's search for
identity and what we now refer to as multiculturalism. The narrative method of the child's eye, reflecting the dual identity of succeeding generations,
is a phenomenon that seems to be the most outstanding achievement of
the Jewish literature of assimilation.[1] I attempt to define the substance
of this innovation by focusing on the parallel motifs in works of Isaac
Babel—whose oeuvre I regard as the peak achievement of Russian-Jewish
literature—and those of Babel's Russian-Jewish literary predecessors as
well as Babel's successors or followers in world literature, sometimes moving back and forth in time in order to isolate these overlapping motifs of
different authors. These cross-national literary links, some of which can
be followed up to this day, are a living proof that Russian-Jewish literature
may be justly considered a particular tradition within world literature and
one that is important in its own right.

The irreconcilable conflict between loyalty and distance is the fundamental feature of Babel's oeuvre. The simultaneity of the external and
internal viewpoints combining his Jewish and Soviet identity, the ambiguity of deeply felt affection on the one hand and the viewpoint of the

---

Dedicated to Shimon Markish (1931–2003), to whom I spoke many times of these ideas,
and who insisted that one day I should write them down.
My English text was edited for style by János Boris.

reserved, critical outsider on the other—this tension is clearly evident in *Red Cavalry, The Tales of Odessa*, and many of his other short stories.

## Ambivalence and Narrow Perspective: "Childhood. With Grandmother"

In Babel's early short story "Childhood. With Grandmother" (1915), the antithetical commands of "flee from it and remain forever" are actually repeated three times by the young storyteller.[2] Babel found the ambivalent dual antitheses for his main message: "room" and "outside," "escape" and "freedom," "flee" or "remain," "hot-stuffy" and "fresh-cool."

This dualism is most successful when the author does not assume the role of "omnipotent" narrator but creates a distance[3] by using the narrow focus of a hero. Babel's very first short story, "Old Shloime," already "narrows down" the scope of vision of the narrative: Shloime is not only old, a condition limiting his field of interest and competence, but he is also physically confined to the town, and later to the house itself, that is, his scope of movement is also limited. In this way Babel presents the world as seen through a special filter: the mind of the old Jew. The reader is left to draw his own conclusions regarding the changes going on outside Shloime's world. The same "narrowing down" of the field of vision is employed in the childhood stories, but while the old man's perspective has already lost much of its scope, the child's perspective has not yet entirely opened up.

In "The Story of My Dovecote" and "First Love," the horrors of the pogrom are shown indirectly, only to the extent of their influence on the child's life. From the perspective of the child the pogrom appears as an event of secondary importance, and the nonobjective narrative approach, seemingly diminishing the pogrom, actually makes it psychologically more significant and tragic in the reader's eye. Babel handles historical events in the same way in *Red Cavalry*: the war, the actual battle, is not shown at all, except as a backdrop for the narrator's ambivalences and his problems.[4]

In Babel's short story "First Love," the boy witnesses his father humiliating himself before a Cossack officer. What fascinates him, though, is the new and interesting visual information: he admires the Cossack on horseback, his elegant uniform, his reserved indifference, his masculine beauty.[5] The same dissonant approach is present in the description of a young peasant smashing up the house of the boy's uncle, or in a "fine" woman (in Russian: "with beautiful face") carrying home things looted from a ruined Jewish shop.[6] The child's impartial look is not yet able to separate the enemies from the friends—the "objective" physical beauty existing in itself arouses his admiration.[7]

In the child's mind, objects and phenomena are transformed into images rather than into concepts or ideas. The child contemplates phenomena but does not understand them in the same way as grown-ups; that is why he finds unusual connections and relationships between them. Babel describes the details of his native town as follows: "I was firmly convinced that in them I could see the principal thing, the secret thing, what we grown-ups call the essence of the things" ("Childhood. With Grandmother," CS 21). The "essence" may mean the hidden secret that opens only to the artist's eye and can never be defined by words, only by an inner vision.[8]

The reason a child does not make logical connections between phenomena is not only that he or she lacks the necessary background knowledge or practical information, but also because his character is still unstable. His self-identification is not yet fully established, hence his impartiality; he does not have the adult's preferences and discriminations, and his hierarchy of values is not yet developed either. This unstable self-identification is an absolutely crucial feature of the child heroes in the Jewish literature of assimilation because the choices open to a child and leading toward a new self-determination or identity stand as a metaphor for all those confronted with the choice of identification. The child's malleability mirrors the adult's ambiguous self-identification.[9]

A different aspect of what may be called childish logic is employed in the story "Gedali" from *Red Cavalry* (1926). Gedali, an old shopkeeper, stubbornly sticks to a highly simplified, bipolar thinking of "yes" and "no," "good" and "bad" (see on Bettelheim's theory of the polarity of a child's thinking, below). The wise old man's Talmudic philosophy and the naive simplicity of the child overlap here to express a common yearning for order in the chaotic world of real life—*ordo ab chao*.[10] Babel integrates these contrasting qualities into his textual structures by the important semantic and linguistic technique of *parataxis*.

## Parataxis, Catalogue, Artistic Associations of Images

The child's-eye view allows the author to set things side by side that are otherwise irreconcilable. This psychological parataxis is the starting point for the ambiguous feelings of the assimilated Jewish boy—he wants to escape from his grandmother and to stay forever at the same time. He does not suppress his negative impressions of his grandmother, nor does he keep his admiration for the elegant power of the Cossack humiliating his father under control.

Later, in *Red Cavalry*, Babel lends the same ambiguity to his narrator, Liutov. He looks at the Cossack officers with a teenager's admiration ("My First Goose," "The *Konzapas* Commander"), and wishes to be one of them, yet at the same time he also fears them. This time Liutov's uncertainty is meant to mirror the corresponding attitude of the hesitant intelligentsia, "childish" in its inability to choose. This apparent indecision and childishness, however, are also seen as positive, associated with human tolerance and contrasting with the thoughtless, cruel decisiveness of the merciless Cossacks and their primitive value system.[11]

Duality is reflected visually in the description of the things belonging to the rabbi's son, an emblematic figure whose death symbolizes the impossibility of coexistence—instead of confrontation—of the Jewish tradition on the one side, and the revolution on the other.[12]

This kind of cataloguing is employed elsewhere in *Red Cavalry*, for instance, in the passage where the little shop of Gedali is described. There is a very similar catalogue also in one of Babel's early childhood stories, "The Story of My Dovecote." The device of the catalogue appears in "Childhood. With Grandmother," too, along with a mysterious or mythic atmosphere: a trunk, full of *bric-a-brac*, is left behind by an uncle.[13]

In the child's mind the connections are made by intuition, that is, by association, the most organic feature of the artistic language. Due to the child's perspective, a highly artistic text is created, one rich in images. These images are combined without any explanation—the discrete details merge into a single concise totality in the perception of the reader, amassing meanings by association. Children, Babel implies, embrace the world with their eyes, by gazing, marvelling, contemplating, and not by "inadequate" speech or by naming things.

The catalogue is also a basic poetic feature of the Bible, deeply rooted, first of all, in the paratactic structure of Biblical Hebrew language itself; it is also an ancient poetic device. Paratactic structures are usually elliptic, and the ultimate coherence is produced through association in the reader's mind. One of the secrets of Babel's text is its visual nature, things depicted side by side without any textual element of cause and effect, with a hidden logic to be decoded by the reader. This type of "and . . .

and . . . and" language is characteristic of the ancient structure of Hebrew (allowing multilevel explications of the Biblical text),[14] of poetic language in general (visual impressions, metaphoric imagery, parallels), and of the child's language as well.[15] The paratactic linguistic form of Hebrew also implies a special, open structure of time; not the simple chronological flow of past / present / future, and—due to the absence of different connective particles and relative pronouns—not a strict, linear sequence of cause and effect, of events past and still ahead. The same applies to children's language: time for the child is not strictly structured, and children basically use the multifunctional "and" as a connective particle between the clauses. The metaphorical / imaginative power of primitive[16] language and primitive thinking lies in open structures. By their use of these "traditional" elements—parataxis, cataloguing, Biblical allusions, parabolic images, elliptical and metaphorical associations—Jewish authors not only enriched modern prose but also found a place in the vanguard of 20th-century modernity in general.[17]

The paradoxical, childish admiration for a physically strong enemy, which is one of Babel's favorite narrative devices, established a paradigm not only in Russian-Jewish literature but for Jewish literature in other languages in the 20th century, when Jews were confronted with a strong army: in the literature of the Shoah.[18]

## "My Dovecote," but Whose Homeland or Prayer?

The very title of "The Story of My Dovecote" underlines the personal character of the first-person narrator in a direct way: *my* dovecote is what it is all about. The focus is not on the exams, or the pogrom, but his dovecote. Once again the most important element is the person of the child, while "History" (in the form of the pogrom) remains in the background. We will see a similar shift in the other short story dealing with the pogrom, "First Love," where the pogrom actually provides the opportunity for the boy to be together with his love, Galina. Of course, the dovecote itself becomes a symbol: a home for the bird symbolizing peace and reconciliation, antagonistic to the violence of the pogrom. In addition, pigeons, so precious for the boy, are completely "useless" when compared with the utilitarian objects stolen by the pogrom participants. The boy's hierarchy of values is starkly different from that of the others. Here one must think not only of the Biblical symbol of the dove, returning to Noah with an olive branch.

Pogroms were routinely staged to coincide with Christian holidays, such as Easter, and started from the procession carrying Church banners with images of Christ and the saints.[19] So here the reader is also meant to recall the Christian-Evangelical meaning of the dove, the symbol of the Holy Spirit, to become all the more shocked by the contrast between the Christian ideal of love and the horror of the pogrom. A similarly double-edged symbol is the fish (a typical Jewish dish and a symbol of Christ) at the end of the short story—fish are put in the mouth and trousers of the murdered great-uncle.

This paradoxical mix-up of different cultures, the Jewish and Christian meanings of the very same symbols, acts as a kind of powerful spotlight to reveal the real character of the pogrom, a tool that, I think, was first used by Semion Yushkevich in his "The Lord's Prayer" (1906). A Jewish boy cannot stop repeating the Christian prayer "Our Lord . . ." taught him by his parents who wanted to save him from the pogrom in this way. The striking paradox of the Jewish "Our Lord . . ." is meant to underline the even more paradoxical, or absurd, nature of the "Christian" massacre of the pogrom. (I shall come back to the issue of these dual Jewish and Christian symbols later on.)

In Aleksandr Kipen's "Who Art in Heaven . . ." (1910),[20] the entrance exam for school is the turning point for an assimilated family, whose children have never even heard of their Jewish origin until then. The little boy, confused about his identity, wants to begin praying on Friday evening at the same time as the other Jewish children who, up until then, he had despised and thought ridiculous. He repeats mechanically the only words of prayer he knows, which had been taught to him by his Russian nurse: "Our Father, who art in heaven. . . ." He has no idea what kind of Father / Lord he was addressing, and he utters the prayer in a garbled way, since he knows nothing about the difference between the two religions.

In "The Story of My Dovecote," this paradoxical scene becomes fundamental to Jewish literature as a whole, not only Russian-Jewish literature. The 10-year-old boy has to pass a difficult entrance exam to win one of the few places that Jews could compete for in a gymnasium. He is the best, but the rich father of another Jewish boy bribes the school and has his son admitted with the result that the protagonist of Babel's story has to wait another year. A year later, he is overprepared and very nervous:

". . . trembling, straightening up, in haste, I shouted Pushkin's stanzas with all my might. I shouted them for a long time, no one interrupted my crazy squealing, choking, muttering. Through a crimson blindness, through the violent freedom that had taken possession of me. . . ." (CS 29). He feels "convulsions of exhausted dreams," (CS 30) and he has to be shaken awake from his enthusiastic declamation.

The child in this scene has no understanding of the controversial character of the situation: Peter the Great and Pushkin's poem about him are the foundation stones, the very essence of the official Russian culture that discriminates against him. The Jewish boy depicted here is representative of the pattern of assimilation in Russia: from the 1860s on, entire generations of Russian-speaking Jews and Russian-writing Jewish authors were convinced that Russia would be their new homeland. Some of them dreamed of a dual cultural affiliation; others wished to abandon their roots altogether. The psychological pattern characteristic of the assimilationist Jews—common for many national minorities on the road to assimilation—is to want to be even more patriotic and more zealously devoted to the host culture than those born to it. The examination scene in Babel's story illustrates this phenomenon, highlighting the identity confusion. Some aspects of the scene are calculated to elicit a greater psychological response from readers. The boy is naive and not aware that his triumph at the exam does not signify his acceptance by the host culture—something he will learn in the course of the story. At this point, his personality is only moving toward identification. Babel makes us witness it being derailed, the boy's *égarement*.

Some of Babel's predecessors in Russian-Jewish literature had remarked on this phenomenon. In 1897, after enumerating anti-Semitic actions, Mikhail Ryvkin provided a survey of Jewish public schools, where pale, scrawny boys recited patriotic Russian poems.[21] Jewish boys may be found declaiming a patriotic poem in American-Jewish literature contemporary with Babel's writings (see below).

## Michael Gold and Isaac Babel

The father of an American-Jewish boy, an immigrant from Russia in New York, spends his time in a wine cellar. Proud of his son, he makes him stand on top of a table in a crowd of Jews, and tells him to recite loudly the patriotic rhyme: "I love the name of Washington / I love my country, too / I love the flag, the dear old flag / the red, white and blue."[22] This is a scene from Michael Gold's *Jews without Money* (1930), a novel of memoirs showing some astonishing parallels with, if not the direct influence of, Isaac Babel. (Gold actually read Soviet literature and visited Soviet Russia. He was fascinated by the mass meetings, "organized emotions," and "new rituals" of the revolution.[23])

Still, no matter how similar the two scenes are at first glance, they are quite different in their larger vision. Odessa was the most assimilated spot in Russia because it was a port city founded in 1804 when Catherine II invited several nationalities to boost business life there. The nine nationalities formed a melting pot (as Jabotinsky points out in his novel *The Five*, 1936), but a melting pot "*à la orientale*," not in the same way as in the United States and especially in New York. Jews were accepted here due to their leading role in trade, but they always remained a target of anti-Semitism. Gold's Jews are also forced to organize a self-defense team consisting of boys of all ages to protect themselves against the "murder-loving Christians" (Gold 37), the Ku Klux Klan, and other (Italian) gangs. The difference between Babel and Gold here lies mainly in the existence of legal discrimination against Jews in imperial Russia and its absence in the United States. Thus in the scene in which the Jewish boy declaims a patriotic poem, Gold is offering a critique not of anti-Semitism but of social and economic injustice as seen by an unemployed, working-class man. Babel's implied protest condemns the anti-Semitic legal system of the old-regime Russia, the institution of the Pale of Settlement, and the *numerus clausus* established for the Jews in education. However, there are some further important parallels between the two authors.

Like many stories in Babel's *Red Cavalry*, Gold's text is also *ornamental* (a term that, to the best of my knowledge, has never been applied in American literature), which means that the text is highly stylized with elements of poeticism. He uses a host of metaphors, alliterations ("peanut politicians, pugilists" [Gold 13]), enumerations ("Excitement, dirt, fighting, chaos"); alliterations ("Carnival and catastrophe" [Gold 14]), anaphors, puns, and poetic intensification ("Even in sleep, I could hear it, I can hear it now" [Gold 14]). Pathos is expressed by rhetoric triplets, too, and, just like with Babel, it is immediately combined with the negation of the pathos: the high and the low, the beautiful and the hideous or vulgar, are combined in a single, ambivalent binary contrast ("Earth's trees, grass, flowers could not grow on my street, but the rose of the syphilis bloomed by night and day" [Gold 17]). Compare Babel's "A Sequel to the Story of a Horse," a combination of the pathos of the revolution with a grotesque and cynical remark about a heaven whose "old man [ . . . ] doesn't have a kingdom, but a bordello with all the trimmings" when "there is enough gonorrhoea on the earth already" (CS 199).

Short sentences are the predominant form of description for both Gold and Babel when they intend to provide a total visual impression of a scene or place. "A sweatshop holiday. Egypt's slaves around a campfire in the shadow of the pyramids. They drank wine even then. Thousands of years ago. And talked as now. The Bible records it. And their hearts were eased by it. And Moscowitz played the Babylonian harp" (G 116). It will suffice to put this next to such sentences by Babel as: "In the corner broad-shouldered Jews who resembled fishermen or apostles suffered aloud over their prayer books" ("The Rebbe," 125). Or compare with the whole of "The Cemetery in Kozin," with sentences such as: "Assyria and the mysterious decay of the East in the tall-weeded fields of Volhynia. Grey stones, ground smooth, with three-hundred-year-old characters on them" (150). Both Gold and Babel make historical leaps in their parallels, combining different historical eras of Jews. Gold unites Egyptian captivity and the Babylonian exile in a more explicit (more hypotactic) way ("even then . . . as now"); Babel refers to Babylon-Assyria in a more metaphorical, more condensed paratactic structure. At the end of Babel's text, another rhetorical element, typical of both writers, can be discovered: a strange intervention by the narrator's voice, an exclamation with a triply repeated sequence of "O . . . ." "O death, O profit-seeker, O avaricious thief, why hast thou not just once taken pity of us?" (150). Gold also applies this threefold exclamation several times, and, quite similarly to Babel, finishes his novel in this way: "O workers' Revolution . . . you are the true Messiah / ... / O Revolution that forced me to think, to struggle and to live.[24] O great Beginning! . . ." (G 309). Ideological conformity is less and less foreign to Babel in his late works. See the final sentences of "Karl-Yankel" (1931) or those of "The Journey" (1932) where false pathos appears. (Babel wrote these short stories nearly at the same time as Gold wrote his.) It would go beyond the scope of this paper to analyze how deeply Babel elaborates in *Red Cavalry* the metaphor of the Messianic revolution so common at the turn of the century.[25]

To continue with the less formal but more thematic similarities between the two writers, some basic elements of their similar *Weltanschauung*, especially their attraction and admiration for marginal men and women, gangsters and prostitutes, must also be mentioned. Nigger and OneEye may be psychologically and sociologically more exact versions of the Jewish gangsters than Benya Krik, who is more "*bogatyr*"-like, legendary and anecdotal—perhaps for the simple reason that Gold grew up among these people while Babel the writer takes the narrative position of an outsider in Odessa as well as in the Red Army, as Shklovsky already noticed.[26] (By the way, Nigger has a dovecote on the roof; see "The Story of My Dovecote" above.) It is worth noting that Gold's panorama of the Jewish lower social strata is very reminiscent of Semion Yushkevich, especially his Odessa novel, *The Street* (*Ulitsa*, 1911).

As for the way the two authors see women, Babel writes a lot about prostitutes and women extending comfort through sex from the very beginning ("Doudou," "Ilia Isaakovich and Margarita Prokofievna," and elsewhere). He discovers new qualities in the lonely, self-denying female characters much more common in French ("Maupassant") than in Russian or Jewish literature. Babel's whores are likened to the Madonna (in "The Widow," Sashka spreads her "outsized body" as she leans over the dead body of her lover, a commander killed in battle, and calls him "My Jesus Christ"), or they are shown simultaneously as lovers, sisters (in both senses: as nurses and members of the family),[27] as well as mothers. They are ambivalent Carnival characters (in the Bakhtinian sense of the Carnival), high and low, virgin and whore, saintly and vulgar at the same time. Similarly to carnival figures, the feminine "qualities and quantities" that Babel's women are endowed with are extreme or exaggerated: Sashka, the "lady of all the squadron," has an "immoderate body" (203); "her monstrous breasts swung behind her back" (216); "Sashka approached, her breasts dangling" (221). Gold's prostitutes have the same autonomy and anatomy: dignity and an abundantly feminine appearance. "She was eating an apple. She munched it slowly with the dignity of a whole Chamber of Commerce at its annual banquet. Her lap spread before her like a table" (G 17).

In Gold's city scenes, the war and pogrom situations of Babel occur—*mutatis mutandis*—with an astonishing frequency: an impersonal description of a street scandal (in the chapter "Summer Toadstools," Part 8) is reminiscent of the way Babel observes the rape of a virgin by a gang of Makhno's soldiers in the Civil War story "At Our Brother Makhno" (1924).

Gold is akin to Babel not only where his sensual-erotic attitude to women is concerned but also in his seeking out feminine qualities in the reality of the world (what I called the "eroticization of reality" in a different context). Despite the fact that the English language does not have gendered nouns, making it impossible for Gold to play word games as poetically as Babel does (for example, in the description of a church garden in "Pan Apolek"), Gold nevertheless manages to get across the feminine connotations of images. "Darkness, the old mother, has not forgotten my East Side. We are at peace in her womb" (G 123). Compare Babel's metaphor: "The night consoled us in our sorrows, a light wind fanned us like a mother's skirt" (CS 169) or "The evening placed its motherly palms on my burning forehead" (CS 123). The cosmic expansion of focus so characteristic of Babel's poetic language (sun, moon, stars participating in the events and basic elements of the metaphors) turns up also in Gold's text: "The pimps sleep. The cops sleep. The old Talmud dreamers sleep. The Rocky Mountains, the Atlantic Ocean, my Christie Street and Bronx Park are in the darkness" (Gold 123).

Gold even created a Gedali of his own in his novel in the character of the old Hasidic Jew Reb Shmuel: "His large blue eyes were calm with spiritual certainties" (Gold 191).

Finally, in Gold's approach to Jews and Jewishness, one finds a similar ambiguity and duality characteristic of the hesitant identity of assimilated Jews, which accounts for Babel's prominent place in world literature. In his "childhood" stories, Babel depicts his Hasidic forefathers as funny people. His narrator does not keep a great distance, but his tone implies some irony well compensated by the heroic hyperbole of fairy tales. Later, in *Red Cavalry*, the opposite extreme of his mental attitude also appears: a sense of self-hatred becomes tangible in the short story "Berestechko" (CS 161–62), where the Hasidic shtetl appears as a smelly, gloomy, rotting, and airless ghetto. Like Babel, Gold is critical of his family's observance of religion and the synagogue in general: "meaningless Hebrew for hours, bad air," "people gossiped, yawned, belched, took snuff, talked business and spat on the floor. Bored" (Gold 182). Babel belonged to the same generation of assimilated Jews: according to his 1920 *Diary*, he could not find the appropriate place in the prayer book in the synagogue.[28] At the same time, for Gold, all his European roots and Jewish tradition in general are very precious. He wants to escape from the ghetto atmosphere and, as a true Socialist, he rejects religion. But—here is a pattern again, this time a well-known psychological and sociological one—he seeks a new Messiah in Communist devotion.

## Henry Roth and Isaac Babel

*Call It Sleep* is a most important landmark in child-focused narration in the Jewish literature of assimilation. Critical surveys emphasize
that "the conflict between ordinary language and the language of imagination" is evident in Bialik, Shakhar, and Roth.[29] The general problem
of the "inadequacy of language" in expressing visions is well known, as
illustrated by the literary attempts to reproduce child's consciousness by
Boris Pasternak in *Luvers' Childhood* or Andrei Bely in *Kotik Letaev*. The
question before us is whether there are elements of child's consciousness
that are specific to child narrators in Jewish literature. The questions raised
by child narration—"utter the unutterable," "who am I"—are, in reality,
philosophical and psychological identity problems. For Jewish authors the
self-identification of the child hero—with his impartiality and his naive in-
comprehension on the one hand, and his imaginative-intuitive, paratactic
contemplation of the world on the other—stands for the choice of cultural
identity, the future of their people. What follows is an attempt to juxtapose
Henry Roth and Babel in the specific context of the vernacular Jewish literature preoccupied with a child's perspective.

It is easy to find a parallel to the patriotic song scene from Gold's
novel that I analyzed above in Roth's *Call It Sleep*. David tries to overcome his fear by singing a pathetic song: "My country 'tis of Dee, / Sweet
land of liberty / Of Dee I sing / Land where our fodders died!"[30] Of
course, even if the USA is David's country indeed, and even if com-
pared to Russia, it is a land of liberty, still, since "his fathers" did not
die there, he has no roots there. There is an obvious, paradoxical contradiction between the words and the life of a Jewish boy. Roth deepens
the paradox here by his special way of narration. He records the poor
pronunciation of the boy whose mother-tongue (*mameloshn*), is Yiddish.
Even if we were to disregard the circumstance that children often have
only a vague understanding of the lyrics of songs, which mean little to
them, and they are therefore inclined to distort or mispronounce these
words,[31] the "misspelled" text in this case underlines the distance or
even gulf between the song, its language, and its singer (the boy). This
distorted language is turned into a new method by Roth: he develops a
special English to differentiate it from the "natural" Yiddish, which is
represented here by correct English. The "distorted" English is not only
"phonetic" (spelled the way it is pronounced), but in all its structures

(grammatical, syntactical) it is an oral version of child language, or later, for instance, at the end of the novel, the idiom of the man in the street. Roth's specific multilingualism has been widely discussed in critical literature ever since 1934.[32] The problem as to how Henry Roth creates several languages in English has been discussed at length by many. To the best of my knowledge, though, this kind of stylization has never been linked to Babel's method as yet. Babel, in a very similar manner, invented a "Russian-Yiddish" for his Odessa Jews in his *Odessa Tales*, and a special, phonetically distorted Russian to create a sense of separateness from the Cossacks in *Red Cavalry*. Babel was a master, if not *the* master, of the *skaz* technique, a basic element of the new prose in the 1920s.[33]

Let us stick to the text of the song for one more moment in Henry Roth. There is a hidden allusion here to the most important metaphor dominating the novel—that of the father's character. The allusion in the song to the father's death mirrors the boy's genuinely Freudian desire. His father is the cause of all his troubles, and his fear of his father evolving into an extreme anxiety comes across in the novel as something associated with the supernatural paternal threat. Of course, apart from the authentic psychological situation of the family, there is also a manifest "Lord and His people" metaphor encoded in this father-and-son relationship. Judaism is a paternalistic religion; this is the reason why the father-and-son relationship is so predominant in the literature of Jewish assimilation. In *Call It Sleep*, this controversial relationship starts with a hostile rejection by the father ("not my son"), continues with the son being punished, and nearly comes to a tragic end. The son cannot get close to his father, looks for other relationships, losing his inner balance in his fear, and nearly dies. After the cathartic end, the father accepts his son, but for the son everything remains open and continues to be problematic according to the last sentence of the novel: "One might as well call it sleep."

Babel's father characters are not all so awe-inspiring or cruel but are usually loving and ready for sacrifice; they mean the world to their sons. The plural is justified since Babel's father characters are not always the same: in "Awakening" the son must leave his home because of his hysterical father. "Bobka held me tightly by the hand, so that I should not run away. She was right. I was thinking of escape" (67). This "escape" was Babel's last word in his "childhood cycle," "The Story of My Dovecote," at least until the 1936 edition of his writings.

The problem as to how Babel and Roth both create mythological worlds from the child's point of view, out of elements that are not under-stood by them, is a complex issue that cannot be discussed in detail in the present paper. Suffice it to say here that in this mythology, associative connections are made between images and phenomena perceived visu-ally and not logically. In David's mind, for instance, a marriage and a funeral become connected by the same coach that is being used on both occasions—this completely carnivalesque (Bakhtin's term) understanding of the interconnection between life and death is uncannily reminiscent of Babel's. David's friendship with Leo, a Polish-Irish Christian boy, brings elements of Christianity into his world. He falls in love with Leo. This kind of love / friendship between young children is a pattern present al-ready in Grigorii Bogrov's work, but in his *Zapiski evreia*, there is a fasci-nating and very genuine relationship developed into an odd triangle, with the Jewish boy being attracted to brother and sister alike, as enamoured, in a sense, of Misha as of Olga. This androgynous or platonic love encom-passes everything that represents health, a natural life and freedom com-pared to the Jewish way of life. The contrast of street (that is freedom) with home (that is suffocating prison), the same as between "free" children in the street with the closed, ghetto-like life in the family and the Kheder, is another pattern that turns symbolic in the text of nearly every Jewish writer of assimilation (Bogrov in *Notes of a Jew*, Babel in "Awakening," Aleksandr Kipen in "Izhe esi na nebesi . . . ," Henry Roth in *Call It Sleep*, and their Hungarian counterpart Karoly Pap in his novel *Azarel*,[34] and so forth). In David's microcosm the incomprehensible culture of Christian-ity along with separate islands of knowledge of Judaism produce a naive mixture of superstitions, esoteric reasoning, and traditions. The emerging instinctive and original mythology derived from similar or overlapping elements of Judaism and Christianity offers a universal meaning valid in all cultures, and gives rise to such categories of assimilation as tolerance, betrayal, religion, mythology, and ritual. In a broader context, both Babel and Roth, with their dually rooted mythology based both on Judaism and Christianity, are linked to the concept of messianic redemption. Babel places it in the political context of Communist revolution (the rabbi's son on the one hand, and his apostolic Cossacks, on the other). Roth's solution is personal salvation: David's Christ-like self-sacrifice on electric cables is committed in the guise of the Prophet Isaiah, where he is at the same time the acting hero and the victim of the crucifixion, the little "*Had Gadia*" from the Seder song offered to the Almighty (with an evident reference to the story of Abraham and Isaac ascending the hill to be offered as a sacrifice by his father).

Babel, too, shows how a child's fantasy may serve as an escape route and his shelter from reality. The storyteller imagines himself a member of the Jewish self-defense armed with a gun, although not so much to protect his humiliated father as to fascinate Galina, to draw the girl's attention to himself. We saw that the same motif of compensation, the "dream of the weak about being strong," featuring a Jew with a gun also occupies the center of the action in Semion Gekht's *The Man Who Forgot His Life*.[35] Gekht's 14-year-old protagonist falls in love with a Russian girl, the daughter of a cruel anti-Semitic policeman. This Romeo and Juliet story[36] is set during the Civil War. The boy, just to prove his bravery to the girl who admires the handsome Cossacks in their smart, colourful uniforms, enters the headquarters of the Ukrainian nationalist army of Semion Petliura, notorious for its anti-Jewish violence, and is executed. Babel, by contrast, does not allow his little protagonist to realize his dream, thus depriving him of a heroic destiny—and the readers of a negative catharsis. In fact, from the point of view of the reader's response, the approach chosen by Babel is psychologically more provocative as well as frustrating: he renders an authentic case history of how a nervous illness develops in young Jews. Instead of a gun-toting, macho protector, what the reader sees here is a boy with a nervous disorder that is characteristic mainly of women. The last sentence is a poetic overstatement; a rhetorical tool to keep the sympathy of the reader alive: "And now, when I remember those sad years, I find in them the beginning of the ailments that torment me, and the causes of my premature and dreadful decline" (CS 49).[37]

Mental / nervous disorder or the concurrence of traumatic psychological change with physical (psychosomatic) illness is also a typical problem of assimilation. At the end of the novel *Azarel* by Károly Pap, little Azarel, falling ill, learns the same lesson as the one learned by Henry Roth's lonely David: "Trust nothing. Never believe. Don't play" (Roth 130).

### Overstatement, Exaggeration, Fantasy, Creativity: "First Love" and "In the Basement"

Poetic overstatement or hyperbole is one of the main elements of the fantasy-based lies of Babel's child heroes, and it constitutes one of the defining features of his style.

"I was a deceitful boy. This was the result of reading. My imagination was always inflamed" (CS 49). Fantasy and lying stand for creative writing, as the short story "In the Basement" made it apparent. The ability to make up lies also helps in early adulthood: the young protagonist of the short story "My First Fee" is rewarded with fabulous sex for stirring up emotions in a prostitute with his imaginative, bookish lying. In this regard, "My First Fee" may be considered as a direct continuation of the story "In the Basement."

Overstatement, as Bruno Bettelheim explains in his book on fairy tales, manifests the basic requirement of children for understanding the world. Children cannot accept the mixture of positive and negative values in reality; ambivalence is very unsettling for them. They must imagine everything in polarities,[38] in binary antagonisms to make them clear; this is their way of creating order in the chaos (Bettelheim 102).

Similar to fairy tales, fantasy is also a healing experience for the psyche, not simply because it offers a refuge or escape from reality, but because it provides an opportunity to ponder different problems of the self (Bettelheim 95).[39] Or, expressed in terms of literary psychology, literature is a confrontation with reality where one faces reality in the form of models and in a metaphorical way. When the young boy in Babel's "In the Basement" recites Shakespeare—the funeral speech of Anthony—one must ask the question why he loves those lines "more than anything else in life" (CS 55). Does he want to find shelter in a time and space far from his own, in ancient Rome? Certainly this is the simplest explanation. But Babel's *ars poetica* as expressed here is that literature makes us understand the fundamental fact that nothing is certain or unambiguous in this world, everything depends on the way we speak about it. Language, rhetoric, narration are everything, because they carry our relationship to reality. This is the main message of the speech of Anthony for the boy who aspires to be a writer. This decoding is confirmed by a sudden ironical parallel to Anthony's words in the final scene. The boy, ashamed of the family scandal taking place in the presence of his friend, wants to vanish from this world, and he submerges himself in a barrel of cold water. His grandfather stands over him, saying: "I go to take castor oil that I should have something to put on your grave . . ." (CS 59) It is not easy to see the connection that the boy is a successor of this sarcastic grandfather in his literary aspirations: the old Levy Itzkhok spent all seventy years of his life describing his neighbours. The manuscript, "A

Man with No Head," is a mimetic diary of his life, rich in highly colorful personalities; thus he has written a chronicle. The basic discrepancy
between life and literature (documentary chronicle versus fiction) is the
relevant contradiction here.[40]

In "First Love," Babel found a further pattern of child behaviour
that became a method later on in his oeuvre; this is the secret observation
of persons, "peeping" from a hidden place. "Peeping" and eavesdropping
are peculiar forms of the child's-eye view (or child's hearing), a typical
situation of watching, collecting life experience. The boy watches the object of his love in all forms of erotic intimacy with her husband. This
perspective is a characteristic situation for Babel's short stories of different periods, including "Through the Peephole" (1916), "Evening" (1925),
"The Song" (1925) (in the *Red Cavalry* stories), "My First Fee" (1933), and
"Dante Street" (1933), where the stories' characters listen to the noises of
lovemaking.

Bettelheim points at another general psychological problem that
appears crucial in the Jewish literature of assimilation. The fundamental
suggestion of fantasy stories and fairy tales, he explains, is that everyone
who stays true to his principles and himself comes to a happy end, and
everyone who usurps someone else's place will come to a bad end. This
means that autonomous personalities are those who have their own order
of values and act correspondingly (Bettelheim 194). That is why the issue
of identity is so problematic in the case of Jewish children in assimilated
families or at the early stages of assimilation: the system of values is unde-
fined; not even opposite values are formulated clearly enough to be chosen
from, and there is no bipolarity of values ("either one or the other"). The
old, traditional identity (of the observant Jew) becomes hidden, rejected,
lost by the first generation, while the new identity is hard to establish. It
is the job of the second generation to find it, the generation represented in
literature by the child who cannot become a self-confident grown-up and,
in a way, retains some childish qualities for ever.

Dual identity and extreme sensitivity may produce a maladjusted
personality, as is strongly evidenced by the short story "In the Basement."[41]
Nevertheless, this negative psychological trait is very differently evaluated
in literary characters, especially in the 20th century. These features may
be attributed to literary characters favored by the author: hypersensitiv-
ity may go hand in hand with mental and psychical wealth, the ability
to grasp the world artistically in its totality, while a person's ambiguous

identity may serve as a source of tolerance, open-mindedness, cultural hybridity (multiculturalism), flexibility, and a keen eye.

It is important to emphasize that self-hatred is often a sign of the author's doubts.[42] Self-hatred is an issue that certainly comes through only in the child narrative. The overwhelming burden of the traditional Jewish way of life, the suffocating atmosphere of the ghetto, and the excitingly different qualities of gentiles are depicted with greater authenticity and without didacticism from the impartial perspective of the child.[43] Cultures that are in a relationship of antagonism and tension can coexist peacefully side by side, mixed or separated, only in the mind of the child who is still unfettered by the necessity of making his choices.[44]

In Babel's case, the coexistence of ambivalent values in the author's approach, his carefully kept distance from both of the antagonistic opposites (stay or escape, reject or love, home or prison, Jews or gentiles, be faithful or critic, and so forth), also results in a grotesque view of the Jewish milieu. In general, the grotesque is not an organic element of the child perspective, but in Babel's case the opposing poles are articulated with childish exaggeration (see above), with pathos as the basic attitude. Anthony's speech in the "upper" registers versus the basement's "low" atmosphere, the rich Jewish family versus the poor one, the members of the family at once as heroic and foolish figures, are all mixtures of the tragic and the comic.[45]

# 11

## Text, Intertext, Context
Babel, Bialik, and Others

EFRAIM SICHER

**STALINISM CENSORED THE WORK** and repressed the author, but the text and its context could not be totally destroyed. The first unexpurgated collection of Babel's stories in Russian, *Detstvo i drugie rasskazy*, published in Israel in 1979 and smuggled into the USSR, where it circulated clandestinely for some years, showed Babel's stories were clearly organized around themes central to Jewish culture and history. Most, but not all, Russian editions of Babel's work, however, deemphasize this aspect of Babel's cultural identity by publishing the stories in order of their publication, rather than by series, thus ignoring both the actual dates of composition and the author's conception of his work as a whole. Moreover, a context was ignored that was unmentionable and almost forgotten for the seventy years of Soviet rule.

I am indebted to Robert Alter and to Hamutal Bar-Yosef for useful comments on an earlier version, as well as to the Leonid Nevzlin Center for Russian and East European Jewry, Hebrew University of Jerusalem, for their encouragement and support. All references to Babel's works in Russian are to *Детство и другие рассказы*, ed. E. Sicher (Jerusalem: Sifriyat Aliya, 1979), henceforth *Detstvo*; the English translation is taken from *Collected Stories*, ed. Efraim Sicher and trans. David McDuff (London: Penguin Books, corrected edition, 1998), henceforth *Collected Stories*. References to Bialik's poems in Hebrew are taken from שירים (Tel-Aviv: Dvir, new edition, 1996), henceforth *Shirim*; Russian translation, *Стихи и поэмы* [1922] (Tel-Aviv: Dvir, new edition, 1964), henceforth *Stikhi i poemy*. The Hebrew transcription has been forced into compliance with the transliteration rules for Russian and follows the modern Israeli pronunciation, not the Ashkenazic one in which Bialik wrote.

Part of the reason for reluctance to fully reconstruct what remains of the corpus after the NKVD confiscated Babel's manuscripts and papers at the time of his arrest in May 1939 may have been a conservative orthodoxy that established the last printed edition in the author's lifetime as authoritative. We do know that the last Russian edition of Babel's stories before his arrest, *Rasskazy* (Moscow: Goslitizdat, 1936), was severely excised and expurgated. Another reason, however, may be that there has been resistance, both after the rehabilitation of the writer during the Thaw and during perestroika under Gorbachev, to fully readmit Babel into the canon of Russian literature. Even before his rehabilitation, the "non-person" Babel was mentioned along with the Hebrew poet Khaim-Nakhman Bialik as responsible for the corruption of the Russian language.[1] All too often after his official rehabilitation in 1954, Babel was identified with the fictional Jewish intellectual Liutov, who cannot accept the violence of the revolutionary struggle and cannot easily part from his Jewish past. Doubts were expressed about the readmission of Babel into the canon of Soviet literature at the time of the publication of a selection of his works in 1957.[2] There was, moreover, fresh censorship in the form of expurgation of phrases deemed to be obscene or offensive to the Russian national character in the edition that appeared in Moscow in 1966, which gave a somewhat expanded selection of Babel's works. Only a few years before the fall of the communist regime, at the height of glasnost, the publication of Babel's *1920 Diary* met opposition because of offensive remarks in the Diary about the Russian national character; it eventually appeared in censored form in *Druzhba narodov*, and only at the end of the Soviet period was it fully published, in 1990.[3] Some attempts were made to restore censored passages in Russian post-Soviet editions of Babel's stories, but, objectively, it would be nearly impossible to distinguish between Babel's fastidious stylistic revisions in the thirties and changes imposed by the censorship, implemented by editorial dictates, or influenced by political caution. For example, the original ending of "My First Love" ("Pervaia liubov") looked back to Tsarist pograms as one cause of the boy's neuroses and the narrator's present-day "waning" (*Detstvo*, 57), something quite unacceptable to the Soviet doctrine that the Revolution had solved all Jewish troubles and put an end to anti-Semitism. The end of communism did not spell the end of Babel's troubles. As the new freedom guaranteed free speech also to Russian nationalists, Babel drew fire as a Jew identified with the Bolshevik takeover that had destroyed the Russian heritage; he was dubbed the "Marquis de Sade" of the October Revolution, gloating on blood and cruelty.[4]

The texts require restoration and recovery, but so does the corpus in which they can be placed. Apart from the *Red Cavalry* series, Babel did not succeed in fulfilling his evident intention to publish his childhood stories as a book, to be entitled *Story of My Dovecote* (*Istoriia moei golubiatni*), though some stories appeared under this title. Nor did all the Odessa stories appear together in Babel's lifetime. To the end, Babel did not retract his conception of thematically linked series of stories, such as the Odessa Tales (*Odesskie rasskazy*) or Childhood stories (the projected book *Istoriia moei golubiatni*), which he continued to work on during the thirties, and he fought against cuts in his published work. Other projects seem to have been aborted or abandoned, such as Petersburg 1918 (*Peterburg 1918*), or Etchings (*Oforty*); there seems to have been a book in the making about the Cheka (or possibly a trilogy of plays that would include *Maria*) and a novella about a reformed gangster called Kolya Topuz. Ideological constraints and increasingly limited publishing opportunities during Stalin's terror made it impossible to realize plans for new books of stories, though the plans for New Stories (*Novye rasskazy*) were included in the publication schedule of the state publishing house Sovetskii pisatel' for 1939, which would have included stories of "heroes of our times," including childhood and other stories that appeared in journals in the first half of the thirties (despite pressure from critics on Babel to produce politically correct material).

Another example of loss of the corpus is the loss of the proposed book on collectivization, *Velikaia krinitsa*, apparently conceived as a linked series of separate stories, on the model of *Red Cavalry*, and promising to be no less controversial for its stark portrayal of forced collectivization in the Ukraine in 1929–1930, which led to mass deportation and famine. Given the fate of the *kulaks* and the destruction of traditional life in Ukrainian villages depicted in the two surviving stories, it is quite remarkable that Moscow journals could announce further chapters from *Velikaia krinitsa* (though this was doubtless partly a continuation of the delay tactics Babel seems to have been engaged in with Polonsky, the editor of *Novyi mir*, who died in 1932). Debts incurred from not delivering manuscripts for which he had taken advances did not deter Babel from his mastery of silence, declared famously at the 1934 Soviet writers' conference, even under political pressure and family duress. When the bailiffs (including the young lawyer-in-training Boris Slutsky) came to his apartment in 1938, they found nothing worth confiscating.[5]

In addition to text, we must discuss context. The Odessa in which Babel grew up was a thriving center of modern Jewish culture.[6] This is where the Russian-Jewish press began with *Rassvet* (1860–1861), *Tsion* (1861–1862), and *Den'* (1869–1871), besides the Hebrew periodical, *Hamelits* (1860). Osip Rabinovich helped found Russian-Jewish letters in Odessa and was a leading polemicist in the *Haskalah* (Jewish enlightenment movement), as were Lev Levanda and Grigory Bogrov. At the turn of the century, Semen Iushkevich and "Karmen" were writing novels and feuilletons in Russian, and the future Revisionist Zionist leader Vladimir (Zeev) Jabotinsky was writing in the local Russian press; his novel set in this period, *The Five* (*Piatero*), appeared in Paris in 1935 (an English translation appeared in 2005). In Odessa, Yiddish and Hebrew letters were reborn: Ben-Ami (pseudonym of I. M. Rabinovich) and Akhad Ha'am (pseudonym of Asher Ginzberg), among others, were prominent in the debate over the Jewish national revival. Until the reestablishment of Soviet rule in February 1920, publishing houses such as Bialik's Moriah were producing Hebrew and Yiddish books, and there was a plethora of Jewish political activity ranging from the Zionists to the socialist Bund.

During Babel's childhood, after his return from Nikolaev in 1905, where the family had been living since 1898, Babel would likely have heard Bialik, by then the Hebrew poet laureate, read his poetry or lecture; the years 1905–1911 were the most fruitful in Bialik's career. Babel, who was tutored at home in the Bible and Hebrew, probably knew enough Hebrew to read Bialik in the original, but he would certainly have been familiar with the many Russian translations of the best known poems of the Jewish national poet in Russian translation and, like most of his generation, would have known by heart Bialik's Kishinev pogrom elegy "In the City of Massacre" ("Be'ir heharigah"), which inspired many to join the local Jewish Defense League, as the boy in Babel's story "First Love" imagines doing.

Babel later recalled meeting not only Bialik, but also Mendel Moikher-Sforim (pseudonym of S. J. Abramovich) before the death of the "grandfather of Yiddish literature" in 1917. Babel grew up in a Yiddish-speaking family at a time when roughly one-third of Odessa's population was Jewish. Typically for his assimilated middle-class background, Babel spoke Russian as his first language, but was quite at home in the cosmopolitan world of Yiddish-speaking Odessa Jews. Babel apparently joined a

Zionist youth movement and was active in a Jewish welfare organization.[7] Yiddish is playfully inserted into the subtext of Babel's stories, for example, in "Shabos-Nakhamu" (1918), adapted from a Yiddish folk-tale about the legendary eighteenth-century jester Hershel Ostropoler, and is stylized in the speech of Yiddish speakers, such as Gedali (in the *Red Cavalry* story of that name). His love of the best-known Yiddish writer of the day, Sholom Aleichem (pseudonym of S. Y. Rabinovich), endured throughout his life, and he not only edited two volumes of Sholom Aleichem's works in Russian, translated by his Odessa friend Simon Hecht, but also wrote *Wandering Stars* (*Bluzhdaiiushchie zvezdy*, directed by G. Gricher; published 1926, released 1927), a reworking of Sholom Aleichem's novel of the same title, *Blondzhende stern* (1909–1910), and wrote the captions for *Jewish Luck* (*Evreiskoe schaste*, 1925, directed by G. Gricher; camera: Eduard Tisse), an adaptation of the Menachem-Mendel stories starring the famous Yiddish actor Solomon Mikhoels. His translation of a story by the Yiddish modernist writer, Dovid Bergelson, appeared during the Thaw when both Babel and Bergelson were posthumously rehabilitated. Indeed, Babel's affinity, in spirit rather than style, with Yiddish modernists such as Bergelson, Peretz Markish, or Der Nister (pseudonym of Pinkhas Kahanovich) is a topic that merits further discussion.[8]

The Odessa dialect, with its mix of Russian, Yiddish, and Ukrainian, peppers Babel's Odessa stories with its pungent aphorisms. Even today Odessisms and Odessa lore still leave their mark on popular Russian song, and Odessa has achieved something of an afterlife in post-Soviet fiction, for example, the Odessa-born poetess Irina Ratushinskaia's *Odessity* (*The Odessans*, 1996) or Rada Polishchuk's *Odesskie rasskazy, ili putanaia azbuka pamiati* (Odessa Tales, or the Incoherent Alphabet of Memory, 2005).[9] Odessa lore, literature, and language offer a further dimension to the intertextuality of Babel's Russian prose; indeed this meeting-point of Jewish, Ukrainian, and Russian cultures, mixed with heavy French, Italian, and Greek influences, gave birth to a putative "southern school" of Russian literature, later quashed under Stalin's monolithic hammer, but not before Babel, Olesha, Kataev, Paustovsky, Ilf and Petrov, and others had breathed some warm Odessa sunshine into Moscow literary circles.

Contemporary Jewish readers who had grown up before the Revolution would have easily deciphered what I would term the "double bookkeeping" of Babel's *Red Cavalry* stories. Linguistic interference encodes in the text a referentiality that can be deciphered by readers who are both bilingual or multilingual and versed in reading subtexts, as Jews were after centuries of cultural repression in various lands. Indeed, the Jews' trilingual culture in Tsarist Russia afforded insiders many a joke and pun. The contemporary readers of the Hebrew poets Bialik and Saul Chernikhovsky, or of Mendel Moikher-Sforim (who began writing in Hebrew, switched to Yiddish, then returned to Hebrew) and Sholom Aleichem, were attuned to the playful intertextuality of Yiddish and Hebrew. These modernists often parodied or inverted the meaning of familiar biblical verses and Talmudic phrases that were already enriched with subtle resonances by their reworking through the ages, especially among the newly rediscovered medieval Hebrew poets of Muslim Spain. Now such referentiality measured the distance between the traditional Jewish home and the acculturated enlightened secular Jews who could appreciate the full irony of the context of modernity. For Bialik this was the measure of poetry in modern Hebrew.

Babel's generation, which had grown up in assimilated homes or had broken with their traditional background to join the revolutionary movements, was further distanced from the referenced biblical and traditional sources by the destruction of the *shtetl* in pogroms, revolution, and war, as well as by the edicts against Jewish religious communities in 1918 and the ban on Hebrew. Intertextuality became a secret code known to the initiated who had grown up before the Revolution and were attuned to the Jewish cultural polysystem,[10] but its meaning was lost a generation later when Russification and Stalinist terror erased the institutions of both Judaism and secular Yiddish culture. In Babel's *Red Cavalry* story "Gedali," for example, to introduce interference of a Jewish language (stylized Yiddish) and reference to Jewish texts (Maimonides, Rashi) is to refer to a condemned culture. Murray Baumgarten speaks of "inter-reference" in "Gedali" as a cultural cross-reference that challenges the discourse of the Revolution and points to moral irony.[11]

A few examples must suffice. In "Gedali," Liutov looks around Zhitomir on a Friday evening for "the shy star": "*ia ishchu robkoi zvezdy*" (*Detstvo*, 125). The "shy star" tells him the Sabbath has begun at sundown and Jews are going to the synagogue to pray. The shy star is a referential sign of a lost Jewish traditional way of life ruined by pogroms and war. Liutov has turned his back on the Jewish past but he is nevertheless drawn to it: he recalls his grandfather's volumes of ibn Ezra, the medieval Spanish Jewish Bible commentator, and his grandmother lighting Sabbath candles, shielding her eyes as she chanted the prayers as if she were telling fortunes. The enchanted waves on which his child's heart rocked were the waves of the Talmud, commonly referred to as a sea. This is a situation that bears remarkable similarity to that of Bialik's wandering lone intellectual in "On the Threshold of the Study House" ("'Al saf bet hamidrash," 1894), who returns to the ruined *shtetl* that he had abandoned for the secular world of the city only to find everything dead and rotting. The difference is that the attraction of the wind or light of secular enlightenment has been replaced by the red star of Bolshevism.

Just before sunset the narrator finds Gedali locking up his Old Curiosity Shop, a Dickensian reference that evokes the old-fashioned romance of a bygone age. In his *1920 Diary*,[12] Babel does not record the name of the Jewish storekeeper with whom he had tea and who wished there were one good government. Yet there is a reference to the destruction of Judea in the name of Gedaliah, whose assassination around 585 BCE marked the end of Jewish sovereignty after the destruction of the First Temple. Liutov's verbal duel with Gedali opens a double perspective on the historical dimensions of the situation, as well as indicating the narrator's split loyalty to the bittersweet Jewish past and to the revolution that has helped destroy it.

> "The revolution—we will say yes to it, but will we say no to the Sabbath?" Thus begins Gedali entwining me in the silken throngs of his smoked eyes. "Yes, I hail the revolution, yes, I hail it, but it hides from Gedali and sends ahead of it nought but shooting. (*Collected Stories*, 117; slightly revised)[13]

Liutov's revolutionary discourse opposes the justice of the revolution to the blindness of the bourgeoisie, but the irony is that he cannot see what the old Jewish shopkeeper blinded by Poles in a pogrom sees: the contradictions of a violent revolution that dispossesses the battered Jews in the name of workers' justice. Gedali's Judaic version of messianism—an impossible "International of Good People"—is a direction Liutov does not take. Gedali is unable to understand why the Jews are suffering at the hands of both Revolution and Counter-Revolution. Why are the Jews who welcomed their delivery from the hands of the Poles and White Cossacks treated as enemies and subjected to looting and requisitions by the Reds? Where is the universal salvation promised by the communists?

Liutov gives Gedali no answer, and the historical injustice done to the Jews, needless to say, cannot be detailed given the circumstances of publication in Soviet Russia in the mid-twenties, accompanied as it was by General Budenny's raving against Babel's "bawdy babbling."[14] But the subtext could be read by anyone who was attuned to the Yiddish allusions in the Russian text[15] or to the intertext of modern Hebrew poetry. Anyone who had read Bialik in the various Russian translations by Jabotinsky, Briusov, Ivanov, Sologub, and others, or in the Hebrew original, would realize that to return in memory to the "rotted Talmuds of my childhood," "*istlevshie talmudy moego detstva*" (*Detstvo*, 125),[16] is to return to the "rotting faded green parchments" of childhood memory in Bialik's poem "On the Threshold of the Study House" ("Al saf bet hamidrash," 1894): "*gvilim balim viyerokim yirkevu bekhavit.*" It is to return also to the dead world of the grandfather's study, to the dusty ancient tomes of the rotted Talmuds of a cultural past, and to seek comfort in the starry night above the cemetery in Bialik's "Before the Book-Cupboard" ("Lifnei aron hasefarim," 1910):

> Do you still remember? I have not forgotten—
> In an attic, inside the deserted Study House
> I was the very last to remain,
> On my lips died the fluttering prayer of my forefathers.
> And in a concealed corner there, beside your Ark,
> Before my eyes the Eternal Lamp spluttered.
>
> (my translation)[17]

The lamp is the eternal flame (*ner tamid*) in the Temple or before the Holy Ark housing the Torah scrolls in synagogues, and, as in much of Bialik's poetry, the poet's language is replete with intricate references to Biblical Hebrew that invert religious meanings and secularize them in a modern context—the Ark (*aron*) is equally in Hebrew the Book Cupboard that houses the poet's cultural heritage whose lamp is spluttering and dying. The return of the Jewish intellectual to the Jewish bookshelf, after secular and Russian values have replaced the eternal lamp of religion, comes when the flame of Judaism has almost been extinguished. In Babel's story, the return to this *topos* of modern Hebrew literature can only be ironic, since, twenty-five years later, war and revolution have destroyed any remaining life in the Jewish *shtetl* and the nostalgic return in memory to the Jewish bookshelf and rituals of the narrator's childhood has been rendered all the more impossible by Liutov's ideological rift from his Jewish home and his enlistment in the communist cause that is helping to uproot it.

The star had inspired Bialik with romantic longing, but it also evoked the mystical pining of the *Shekhinah* (Divine Presence), as in "Sunset" ("'Im dimdumei hekhama," 1902). The star was in addition a guide through the despair of exile and alien culture, as in "A Lonely Star" ("Kokhav nidakh," 1899), where the poet prays to the star for his soul to be enlightened:

> Enlighten, oh Star, my soul that despairs
> Of idolatry and harsh exile.
>
> (my translation)[18]

The ironic play on the light of secular enlightenment, on the one hand, and the alien culture ("idolatry") of Diaspora suggests the failure of acculturation to alleviate the sufferings under the star of exile evident in Bialik's day.[19] In "Gedali" the star is the object of the uprooted wandering Jew's nostalgic search for Jewish values—for Jewish tea and the pensioned-off God, which can't be had where orphans are crying. In both Bialik and Babel reference to the collective memory of destruction recalls the cultural heritage and collective identity that the returning Jewish intellectual has lost.

It must be said that the passionate summer night of heathen lust can attract Bialik's lonely wanderer as much as the Sabbath Bride, whose central place in the Sabbath eve liturgy has made it canonical in Hebrew poetry. The prayer to the "shy stars" ("*hakokhavim hatznu'im*") in "One Summer Evening" ("Haya 'erev hakayits," 1908) is undermined by the sacrilegious and hedonistic atmosphere of Bialik's poem in which the young man is lured away from his Jewish home and spiritual values by the wanton eroticism of a Hellenistic culture. In the Hebrew of Bialik's poem, the term describing the stars *(tsanu'a)* can mean both shy and modest, so that in this intertext Liutov's search for a shy star ("*robkoi zvezdy*") reads all the more ironically since it represents the inauguration of the Sabbath—Jewish time—which beckons him, but also functions as a cultural sign for the lost past for which he yearns. If Bialik responds to the imagery of Russian symbolism and reinvents modern nature poetry in the holy tongue,[20] Babel's modernist prose in *Red Cavalry* sets romantic summer nights in Volhynia in a landscape of corpse-strewn fields and describes the Sabbath queen mounting her throne in a singularly modernistic image. Bialik's verse would in any case have been on the lips of Babel's generation, but to allude to Bialik, however obliquely, is to speak in a "hidden language"[21] that in turn remembers the intertext of Hebrew poetry through the ages and the renascence of Jewish cultural identity before the Revolution; it does so, moreover, from the retrospect of repression and loss of the original cultural referents.

As in "Alone" ("Levadi," 1902), Bialik's assimilated intellectual sees little but dark despair in *shtetl* Judaism in "On the Threshold of the Study House." The new spirit (or "wind") has carried away the young generation, attracted by the "light" of the secular enlightenment. The return comes when all is dead or dying, as in Bialik's "Upon My Return," a poem whose Hebrew title, "Betshuvati," plays on the Hebrew term for religious repentance. "On the Threshold of the Study House," dated the ninth day of the Hebrew month of Av, 1894 (the fast day for the Destruction of Jerusalem), was written after the closure by the Tsarist authorities in January 1892 of the famous Volozhin yeshiva, where Bialik had studied. Bialik can be said to be writing out of both personal and national bereavement, yet his attitude toward the past remains typically ambivalent. Two decades and a world war later, Liutov revisits Zhitomir, a town forever associated with Bialik's childhood, and finds the Jewish *shtetl* ruined and doomed. His remembrance of his own grandfather and grandmother is more nostalgic perhaps because there can be no "return." Now the Bolshevik Revolution has claimed the loyalty of the Russian-speaking Jew, and there is no place in the new order for the Jewish past or its traditions.

Liutov's dilemma would have been familiar to readers of Bialik. Like the uprooted Jewish intellectual (*talush*) of turn-of-the-century modern Hebrew literature, a cousin of the "superfluous man" (*lishnii chelovek*), he is torn between two worlds, "the Jewish world which he had left with no possibility of return, and the new world," the world of Russian culture, which rejected him, leaving him "isolated, dejected, and uprooted."[22] The "uprooted" is a term taken from the title of a 1904 story by I. D. Berkowitz and appears in the work of Berkowitz, Berdichevsky, Schoffman, and Gnessin against the background of disillusion after the 1904–1905 pogroms and frustration at the absence of an outlet for the wave of nationalism that swept East European Jewry. The question asked by M. Z. Feierberg in his novella, *Whither?* (*Lean?*, 1899), had been, where was the way forward for the Jewish intellectual who had turned his back on ibn Ezra and Maimonides but had not found a new world? For Feierberg the answer lay in the resettlement of the Holy Land. This question now found a cruel expression of despair in the ex-Bundist Russian Army deserter Yosef

Khaim Brenner's novel *Shekol vekishalon* (1920; translated as *Breakdown and Bereavement*, 1970). Brenner tells of a Russian-Jewish intellectual's displacement and disillusion, his impotence and insanity, in the return to Zion. This was the book that Kafka's Hebrew teacher, Puah Bentovim, gave him and whose title gave Kafka such trouble—how could the Zionist dream be expressed in breakage and failure?[23] The year of publication of Brenner's pessimistic novel was the year Babel met an enthusiastic Zionist called Akiva Govrin who has left a rather spurious memoir of this encounter,[24] in which Babel declaims Bialik and takes an eager interest in modern Hebrew literature, as well as admiring Jewish youth who were training in agricultural work. Babel records in his *1920 Diary* a meeting in Sokal with an outspoken Zionist youth, "ein [aus]gesprochener Nationalist,"[25] yet Babel's own assessment of the aspirations of Jewish youth in Galicia and Volhynia seem to be limited to brief references in his *1920 Diary* to Jewish men and women who have left good Jewish homes to join the Revolution, or an ironical description in the drafts of the *Red Cavalry* stories of Jewish "midgets" who enlisted in the Red Army because of their convictions.

At work here is a Bakhtinian "dialogization," both synchronically in the subtext and diachronically in the historical context. Throughout the *Red Cavalry* cycle, historical details pinpoint the repetition and ironies of history, as when a Jew is executed in "Berestechko" by Cossacks after they have passed the watchtower of the legendary Cossack hero Bohdan Khmelnitsky, the infamous scourge of the Jews in 1648, where he lost the battle with the Poles. The massacres by Khmelnitsky's Cossacks spurred the tide of messianism among East European Jews that gave rise, after the failure of the Shabtai Tsvi movement, to Hasidism, which flowered in this very region at the end of the eighteenth century and beginning of the nineteenth century. A fragment of a letter in French from the Napoleonic Wars is followed by a speech by the Bolshevik commander who hands over power to plundered, victimized Jews. But Liutov is blind to that context, just as the Cossacks are deaf to the ironies of the songs of Cossack glory. Jewish time and revolutionary time are not operating in the same historical context, yet both are messianic within their different constructions of the world. In "Crossing the Zbrucz," Liutov, as yet unnamed, beds down next to a sleeping Jew amid indescribable filth, unaware this is the debris of a pogrom. The Hasidim, for their part, seem oblivious to the destruction of their world, a building battered by history, in Gedali's metaphor in "The Rebbe," which, he says, is eternal like the memory of a mother. The desolation of war framed by the window in the rebbe's room provides mute comment on the timeless eternity of the Jews making Sabbath and it sharpens the dichotomy between two worlds, two histories.

Liutov finds the "shy star," but his self-identification as an Odessa Jew elicits the *rebbe*'s ironic comment on Odessa as the glorious star of the exile (*Detstvo*, 134). This was a city scorned by traditional Jews as a hotbed of secular assimilation, around which, as the Yiddish saying had it, the fires of hell burned for seven miles. The *rebbe* belongs to the Chernobyl dynasty, which boasted members of the famed Twersky family, yet Babel gives the *rebbe* the family name of Bratslavski and names the *rebbe*'s renegade son "Ilia," that is, Elijah, who, in Jewish lore, will herald the messiah. The *rebbe*'s son smokes on the Sabbath (a gross profanation of the day of rest obvious to anyone familiar with Jewish religious law) and is likened to Spinoza and to a Jesus surrounded by apostles—both heretical apostates in Jewish eyes. He has, like Liutov, rebelled against his Jewish past and joined the revolution. If for Gedali Hasidism was eternal like the memory of a mother, a mother, Ilia Bratslavski tells us, is a minor episode when there is a revolution going on. The Jewish reader will immediately pick up the reference to the Bratslav Hasidim, also known as the "Dead Hasidim" because they had no *rebbe* since the death a century earlier of Nakhman of Bratslav. This was at the time the most messianic of Hasidic sects, and one of the best-known Yiddish stories of Nakhman is "The Rabbi's Son," about a thwarted messiah, widely available at the time in Martin Buber's German translation.[26]

At the end of "The Rebbe" Liutov leaves the dead world of the impoverished, tormented Hasidim and returns to his identity as a journalist on the propaganda train whose bright lights and printing machines beckon him away from the *rebbe*'s Sabbath table; he turns his back on the Jewish past and looks toward the revolutionary future, lit brightly by the red star. The irony, of course, is that the red star shines brightly in *Red Cavalry* only in folksong and propaganda slogans. The reality is much darker: ill-equipped and half-educated peasants and Cossacks are fighting for ideals they barely understand and for a goal—Warsaw and world revolution—that was never reached.

The cultural and ethnic ambivalence of the contrast between the two worlds is reinforced by the sacrifice Liutov must make for his camaraderie with the Cossacks. In "My First Goose" ("Moi pervyi gus'"), the killing of a virgin white goose serves as a surrogate for "messing up" a lady, carried out in a travesty of Jewish ritual slaughter. Again, referents to a Jewish cultural code unlock the subtext of "double book-keeping."

The following story, "The Road to Brody" ("Put' v Brody"), begins with the narrator's conscience being pricked by the "chronicle of daily atrocities," yet these are unnamed in the text, which describes no "atrocities" apart from the raids on beehives. They are in fact detailed elsewhere as the shooting of prisoners in the Diary entry for August 30, 1920,[27] in "Squadron Leader Trunov," and in a brief story unpublished in Babel's lifetime, "There Were Nine" ("Ikh bylo deviat'"). And in an article Babel wrote for *Krasnyi kavalerist* under the pen-name of Kirill Liutov, "The Knights of Civilization," there is an account of a pogrom that actually calls on the Red soldiers to avenge the victims ("Rytsari tsivilizatsii," *Krasnyi kavalerist*, August 14, 1920). A similar angry description of a pogrom by White Cossacks in Komarov is given in another article, "The Unbeaten Killers" ("Nedobitye ubiitsy," *Krasnyi kavalerist*, September 17, 1920). Vengeance, however, was usually denied to the Jews. It is surely no accident that two stories of vicious Cossack vengeance should flank "Cemetery in Kozin" ("Kladbishche v Kozine"), a poetic vignette of the graves of *unrevenged* Jewish victims of Budenny's Cossack predecessor, the same Khmelnitsky who waged war in this region against the Poles and massacred a number of Jewish communities. History repeats itself, and not only the Poles and White Cossacks were perpetrators of anti-Jewish violence that swept the Ukraine, Belarus, and Galicia in 1918–1920 and claimed some 210,000 lives.[28] It is a historical fact that, though the communist authorities generally investigated and punished offenders, Cossacks of the Sixth Division of the First Horse Army, whose divisional commander appears in *Red Cavalry*, participated in pogroms during the retreat from Poland in October 1920 in the Berdichev region.[29]

The traditional Hebrew elegy suggested repose and melancholy; justice for victims of crusades and pogroms was left to divine vengeance. The "lachrymose conception of Jewish history" (in S. W. Baron's phrase) was still being expressed in responses to the pogroms of 1918–1920 in such dirges as Shimon Branfeld's *Sefer dm'aot* (Book of Tears, 1923), though Perets Markish's modernistic and iconoclastic poem, *Di kupe* (*The Heap*, 1922) breaks from this tradition.[30] The Kishinev pogrom of 1903 did change Jewish responses to catastrophe, and in Bialik's major poem on the atrocities, "In the City of Massacre" ("Be'ir heharigah," 1904), the poet is summoned to the cemetery only to be commanded to hold his tongue and witness the terror in silent horror. Babel's "Cemetery in Kozin," in the spirit of the post-Kishinev generation, emphasizes collective memory, memory of rabbinical dynasties and of the unavenged victims of Khmelnitsky, Budenny's legendary predecessor. As an unspoken commentary, "Cemetery in Kozin" is well placed: halfway through the *Red Cavalry* cycle, between two tales of particularly harsh Cossack revenge. The ending echoes the Jewess's cry at the close of "Crossing the Zbrucz," when the sleeping Jew is revealed to be the corpse of a pogrom victim. Why has death not spared the Jews once? The knowledgeable reader might have smiled sadly, recalling Bialik's similarly despairing cry "until when?" in his pogrom poem, "On the Slaughter" ("Al hashkhita," 1903), which recorded the poet's outrage that no vengeance could avenge the blood of the victims:

> "Who cries Revenge! Revenge!—accursed be he!
> Fit vengeance for the spilt blood of a child
> The devil has not yet compiled . . . [31]

In the Soviet period, pogroms and anti-Semitism could only be presented as part of a class struggle under the Tsarist regime, yet we can see here a mute testimony to injustice that is informed by Bialik's angry response to unspeakable atrocity. In the framing of Babel's story and in its intertextual rereading of the post-Kishinev lament in Hebrew poetry, we sense a Jewish modernist response comparable to the stark horror of the avant-garde Jewish artist Issachar-Ber Rybak's 1918 Pogrom series, or the frustrated redemption of Marc Chagall's *The Cemetery Gates* (1917).

The dialectic of Liutov's stormy and ancient imagination continues throughout *Red Cavalry* as we journey across the heartland of East European Jewry that had been battered by pogroms and deportations, war and revolution, and has now become a battleground between Poles and Bolsheviks. Throughout, Liutov is unable to solve his identity crisis or resolve the contradictions between the violence of the revolution he follows and the humane values of the Jewish past he has abandoned. The dilemma is not new. In a not dissimilar meditation, Bialik addresses the silent stars in recalling the dead Jewish past in "Before the Book Cupboard," but Liutov, in addressing himself in "The Rebbe's Son" to a Russian by the name of Vasili, effectively distances any Jewish viewpoint through the naming of a Russian addressee, presumably the ruthless political commissar who tells his story in "Konkin." Liutov recalls the Friday evening at the *rebbe*'s and tells the story of Ilia Bratslavski, whom he first saw there. Ilia is Liutov's alter ego, yet the cultural referents in Ilia's last possessions make a strong statement on the failure of Hebrew communists to wed Judaism and communism:

> Here everything was dumped together—political pamphlets and the commemorative booklets of a Jewish poet. Portraits of Lenin and Maimonides lay side by side. Lenin's nodulous skull and the tarnished silk of the portraits of Maimonides. A strand of female hair had been placed in the resolutions of the Sixth Party Congress and in the margins of communist leaflets swarmed crooked lines of Hebrew verse. (*Collected Stories*, pp. 226–27; translation slightly revised)[32]

These impossible contradictions rain down on Liutov, who receives Ilia's last breath as a brother. The first edition of *Red Cavalry* closes with Ilia's futile death, impotent and forgotten. Robert Alter points to this as a quintessential response in a transitional period of Jewish culture to the chasm between two worlds, akin to M. D. Berdichevsky, but aestheticized into what Yeats called "a terrible beauty."[33]

The selection of "The Rebbe's Son" and other *Red Cavalry* stories, in a Hebrew translation approved by Babel himself, for the first and last issue of the Hebrew communist journal *Genesis* (*Breshit*, 1926), the only translations in the volume, sums up the situation of Jews who wished to combine the ideals of the Hebrew prophets and the revolution. These Hebrew communists, among them hardliners such as the editor and translator Moshe Khyog (pseudonym of Grigorii-Tsvi Plotkin) or the Trotskyite Shimon Haboneh (Trebukov), who condemned the dead world of the *shtetl*, as well as Yocheved Bat-Miriam, who later became a well-known poetess in the land of Israel, naïvely believed they could write of the new communist life in Biblical Hebrew. Akhad Ha'am's cultural Zionism was anathema to them, and they rejected the path of Bialik, who had managed to leave Russia through Gorky's intercession in 1921. The Hebrew communists apparently still believed that the contradiction in Ilia Bratslavsky's last effects between Maimonides and Lenin could be resolved.[34] The journal appeared (with the assistance of a representative of the Palestine Communist Party in Moscow, Yosef Barzilai) through the initiative of Khyog and Haboneh, both crazy idealists, and despite the fact the journal had to be printed in Berlin because Hebrew printing in the Soviet Union was strictly controlled by the Jewish section of the Communist Party (Evsektsiia), who regarded it as a reactionary language of the clerics

**FIGURE 11** Cover of *Breshit* (Iosif Tchaikov, 1926).

and bourgeoisie! Nevertheless, Iosif Tchaikov's futuristic design for the front cover, similar to the one he did for a Kiev Yiddish journal, likewise entitled *Beginnings* (*Beginen*, 1919), expresses the idealistic hope for a new, universal Soviet future in the modern city. Together with Marc Chagall, Natan Altman, Issachar-Ber Ryback, Boris Aronson, and others, Tchaikov, a graphic artist and sculptor trained in Paris, was associated with the Kiev *Kultur-lige*, a group of avant-garde Jewish artists founded in spring 1918. Its publishing house brought out a thirty-four-page collection of Babel's stories[35] that gives no name of translator (one wonders whether the Yiddish version could be the work of Babel himself). Incidentally, it is indicative of the fate of the Ilia Bratslavskys of this world that Tchaikov later did conformist work, designing posters that lauded Stalinism. The distance between the postrevolutionary hopes for a new society, which avant-garde Jewish artists invested in the *Kultur-lige* and elsewhere, were soon eclipsed by communist control of the *Kultur-lige* and other cultural organizations and by the gradual repression of free artistic expression, culminating at the end of the twenties in the Markish and Kvitko affairs in Yiddish literature and the Zamiatin and Pilniak affairs in Russian literature.

When we consider Ilia Bratslavsky's lonely death, we may ask what hope Babel's stories might represent for the post-Kishinev generation of Jews looking for some realization of the prophetic vision of a just society. And to what extent could there be a social and cultural identity for Russian-speaking Jewish intellectuals who might move freely between Russian and Yiddish culture? The real Ilia Bratslavskys, like Shlomo-Ya'akov Nepomniashchi, apparently a Cheka agent, believed that the contradiction could be resolved in Ilia Bratslavsky's last effects between Maimonides and Lenin by rejecting the bourgeois past.[36] Others, however, became disillusioned. Eliezer Steinman, who wrote a manifesto called "The Hebrew Communist" ("Hakomunist ha'ivri"), published in Odessa in 1919, left Russia in despair in 1924, while others learnt to accommodate themselves with the regime. Several Hebrew poets languished in camps or exile.[37]

Part of the answer may be found in the publication history of the *Red Cavalry* stories. The first drafts for the stories were apparently written during or shortly after the Soviet-Polish campaign, others during 1921–1923, and the stories appeared in Odessa newspapers and in Moscow literary journals in 1923–1925. Some of the drafts did not materialize into stories, while a few that had appeared, such as "Grishchuk" or "At Batko Makhno's" ("U bat'ki Makhno"), were never incorporated into the published book.

The drafts suggest a broader treatment of the First Horse Army, and Dmitri Furmanov, the commissioning editor for *Red Cavalry* at Gosizdat, records in his diaries that Babel had planned a collection of some fifty stories.[38] What is clear is that the changing political circumstances, as well as Babel's own stylistic development away from descriptive journalism to modernist vignettes, made for an ironic distancing from the alienated Jewish intellectual who may have hoped his ideals might come true in 1918–1919, but must be disappointed by the mid-twenties, when the *Red Cavalry* stories appeared in Moscow. The end of war communism and retreat from the international revolution gave way to the consolidation of a centralized Soviet state under Stalin; the *Red Cavalry* stories appeared at a time when the failures of war and revolution had to be toned down in line with the official revision of history, particularly the battles at Tsaritsyn, and with the rising cult of legendary heroes, such as Budenny. Babel may himself have harbored great hopes for the socialist state under construction and there is genuine excitement in his correspondence with his family abroad at the enormous changes that were transforming Soviet Russia, but by the mid-twenties he also felt cramped by the increasing restrictions on artistic freedom and the stifling atmosphere in Moscow as the hardliners took control.[39]

It is important to note that *Red Cavalry* appeared alongside other Civil War novels that also depicted conflicted intellectuals, for example, Furmanov's own *Chapaev*, Fadeev's *The Rout* (*Razgrom*), or Serafimovich's *The Iron Flood* (*Zheleznyi potok*), but it shared concerns and modernist leanings with some contemporary Hebrew and Yiddish writing, for example the theme of the price Jews paid for Bolshevik victory. Haim Hazaz's Hebrew tale of a *shtetl* during the Civil War, "From Here and There" ("Mizeh umizeh," 1924), features a verbal duel between the town's old Jews and the militant Jewish commissar very similar in tone and content to Liutov's confrontation with Gedali.[40]

In his *1920 Diary*, Babel seems not to have fully thought through the relationship of the Revolution to his own identity and his humanitarian values. He relates how he pretends to be a Russian, but then bares his soul to his fellow-Jews,[41] yet he apparently witnesses in silence the Cossacks' pillaging of Jewish religious articles, looting of *shtetls*, and rape of Jewish women;[42] elsewhere he notes how the Cossacks forced Jews to cook unkosher meat for them on the ninth of Av (which fell that year on July 25), the fast that recalls the destruction of the Temple.[43] Historical sensibilities resound here in a clear reference to a major paradigm in Hebrew poetry and liturgy, and while Babel, an assimilated Odessa Jew, is distant from Jewish traditions, he identifies with the collective memory of persecution and the experience of the destruction of the *shtetl*.[44] Babel chides himself to be strong, but by September, after the defeat on the Vistula, when the campaign is clearly lost and the Reds are in retreat, he is sick and exhausted, only too pleased to find refuge with a Jewish family on the Jewish New Year.[45]

A new ending to *Red Cavalry*, the story "Argamak," added to the 1931 edition, suggests that, unlike Ilia Bratslavsky, the narrator can ride with the Cossacks, though not before making enemies. One more story, "The Kiss" ("Potselui," 1937), was never included in the collection, but indicates, in a reworking of the Chekhovian tale of the same name, a more ambivalent conclusion to Liutov's dilemma, in a tale of military retreat and romantic disappointment. By then the dialectic of hope and despair, understood in its cultural context and intertextual referencing, has been played out. Boris Ehrlich, the Red Army officer in *The Jewess* (*Evreika*), an unfinished novella Babel was working on from around 1927, has none of Liutov's Jewish complexes. After his father's death, Boris brings his mother and sister from the dying *shtetl* to a new life in Moscow. What will be the family's future is unclear, and the manuscript breaks off on a note of trouble brewing over the reek of garlic and onion from gefilte fish in the communal apartment.

A no less ambiguous statement on the outcome of dual identity, Jewish and Soviet, Hebrew and communist, is found in the ending of "Karl-Yankel" (1931). This story, which was, to Babel's embarrassment, republished within a few months in a Paris émigré newspaper, tells of one of the public trials of Jewish ritual circumcision that were held in the Soviet Union until the end of the twenties as part of the campaign against religion. But it is also a trial that marks the end of the ethos of Jewish Odessa. The baby, named "Karl" for the founder of Marxism by his communist father, concerned about his acceptance in the Party, and circumcised as "Yankel," named by the religious grandmother in Yiddish for the Jewish patriarch Jacob, represents that impossible fusion of the old and the new that we saw in Ilia Bratslavsky. A Kyrgyz woman nurses the child, in parody of the Brotherhood of the Soviet Peoples, and promises he will grow up to be a pilot, in the spirit of the Soviet future. But the narrator thinks of his own childhood, growing up on the streets of Odessa:

From the window I saw running into the distance the streets traversed by my childhood and youth—Pushkin Street led to the railway station and Lower Arnaut Street ended at the park by the sea.

I grew up on these streets, now it was the turn of Karl-Yankel. But nobody fought for me as they are fighting for him. . . . Almost nobody bothered about me. (my translation)[46]

Pushkin Street clearly speaks for the Russian literary tradition and the cultural memory of Pushkin's exile in Odessa in 1823–1824 (as in the epiphany at the end of "Di Grasso"), but Lower Arnaut Street is where Bialik lived until 1921, as every Odessa Jew knew. The duality of the narrator's cultural identity embedded in these literary addresses is an anachronism in the thirties, not a symbiosis, and the story closes with the ironic hope that Karl-Yankel will be happier than the narrator was.

"It cannot be," I whispered to myself, "that you would not be happy, Karl-Yankel. . . . It can't be that you wouldn't be happier than me. . . ." (my translation)[47]

Ostensibly, the story mouths the clichéd slogans of allegiance to the Party line, but, at least in the unexpurgated first published version, the ambivalence of the authorial position is unmistakable: the Galician Hasidic rabbis come to see Judaism on trial; the ridiculous figure of the old attorney for the defense, Lining, attempts to show the evidence is fabricated; the bloodied and beaten *mohel* (ritual circumciser) Naftula reminds the public prosecutor that he too was circumcised and born Zusman—all this reminds us of the fate of Jewish Odessa in what was, sequentially, the last story in the Odessa series, following "Froim Grach" and "End of the Old Folks' Home" ("Konets bogadel'ni").[48] This was a final end of a world that could henceforth be referenced only in the subtext and in the intertext of cultural memory.

# 12

## Staging Babel's *Maria*—For Young American Audiences, Seventy Years After

CARL WEBER

**IT WAS IN 1961**—the year that the Berlin Wall cemented the split of the world into two mutually hostile systems for the foreseeable future, or so it seemed at the time—when I first encountered a text by Isaac Babel, a slim paperback titled *Budjonnyjs Reiterarmee* (Berlin: Malik-Verlag, 1926). I was immediately captivated by the power and compass of his writing, by his aptitude for portraying events in the fullness of their multifaceted reality, with all the ambiguities and abrupt turns from horrifying cruelty to grotesque and often farcical behavior that the author had witnessed while serving with the Red Army cavalry during the Polish campaign of 1920. A few years later, an at the time completely unknown play by Babel, *Maria*, received its first-ever production in Italy (1964), and some years thereafter premiered in both of the German Cold War states. I immediately got ahold of the German translation and rediscovered all the riches that had so fascinated me in Babel's *Red Cavalry* stories. There was, in addition, the unusual dramatic structure he employed to unfold his narrative of an odd collection of people who were caught in the turmoil and harshness of 1920 civil-war Petrograd. Coming from all walks of life, they had been swept by the Revolution way down, or up, from their previous station in Russian society. The work combined a story brimming with vibrant, colorful characters in highly controversial circumstances with a particular epic dramaturgy—one is tempted to call it "film-like"—that made me keen on staging the play. By then I was living and working as a director in New York City, and so I tried to interest off-Broadway producers and artistic directors of nonprofit theaters, with whom I had worked before, in Babel's daring text—an attempt, I must admit, that was rather quixotic, since there was not yet an English translation available. I could only try to recapitulate the play's complex narrative and explain what made it so fascinating, in the hope some producer might be impressed by my passion for the text and encouraged to commission a translation. In the cold war climate of the time there was little enthusiasm to be expected for the production of a play that was quite evenhanded in its depiction of the early Soviet system, not to mention that it was hardly a commercially promising project.[1]

More than thirty years had to pass until I was at last offered the occasion to explore on stage the story of Maria that so vividly intrigued my imagination when I first encountered the text. In 2003, Professor Gregory (Grisha) Freidin approached the Stanford Drama Department and inquired if we might be interested in presenting Babel's *Sunset* for a Symposium entitled "The Enigma of Isaac Babel" that he was preparing for 2004. When I proposed *Maria* in its place, Grisha Freidin immediately accepted. Thus began a close and immensely pleasurable collaboration during which we researched and discussed every conceivable aspect of the text and arrived at a stage version of Peter Constantine's translation,[2] which served for the play's American premiere at Stanford in February 2004.[3]

Approaching the production, the first question I had to ask myself was: How should we present Babel's narrative to a twenty-first century American audience? Most in this audience are young, and their knowledge of Russian history and the early Soviet society during the post-Revolutionary Civil War and its Polish campaign is minimal, if at all extant. Most of Babel's characters would appear to our audience quite mystifying when judged by their utterances and interactions. On the surface, the play's story is clearly told, but the underlying conditions and motivations of the characters would not be easily recognizable for contemporary spectators unfamiliar with the social and political milieu surrounding the narrative. Obviously, the production's most important task was to unfold Babel's story—in our particular interpretation—as transparently as possible. This entailed a lucid demarcation of the time frame, given the way it often moves in peculiar nonsequiturs. For example, the opening scene, in which we witness the seedy activities of a gang of black marketeers and their boss, Isaac Dymshits, is separated by a considerable number of days, if not weeks, from Scene 2, which appears to be starting the completely different story of the former Czarist general Mukovnin's family. Scene 3 happens later that same evening, when the storylines of the previous two scenes have converged. Scenes 4, 5, 6, and 7 all play out during one evening and night, several days after Scenes 2 and 3, and they lead to the conclusion of the Mukovnin family's story. Finally, Scene 8 introduces a completely new set of characters, and it takes place at least four to six weeks after the previous events, when a time of grim winter and darkness has given way to early spring and bright sunshine. It seemed to me essential that we clearly establish the unexpected shifts in the play's time frame.

One particular concern was how the production would accentuate the cinematic structure of Babel's text. He does not waste much time on a detailed exploration of the characters' psychology but delineates their behavior in a quick succession of scenic moments that often are linked or, rather, juxtaposed, similar to cuts in a film. Often we are observing what amounts to an on-stage equivalent of close-ups and zooming, all evidence of Babel's extensive experience of writing for the movies. His dramaturgy demands from the actors that they play their characters' interactions moment-by-moment, each one for its own sake, with little harking back to previous scenes and no anticipating of subsequent events, quite like the way performers work in film where scenes usually are shot in a nonsequential, nonlinear fashion.

Babel's dramaturgy also calls for a staging that facilitates the film-like "flow" of his play, with the narrative's swift dialectical movement and its precise framing for each moment. Our solution was the use of a revolving stage that carried four sets, which accommodated, with a few appropriate adjustments, all required locations of the play. Between scenes, a half-curtain, made of a very light fabric, was rapidly closed and opened again. It left the upper segment of the stage frame open so that the walls, when moving with the revolve, remained visible during the scene shifts and thus helped to achieve a continuous visual flow of the show. The revolve turned also within one of the scenes, from one segment of the space to another, at times in response to an actor's crossing the stage; another attempt to support the cinematic pacing of the performance.

The half-curtain served as well as a projection surface. Thanks to the extensive archives of Stanford's Hoover Institute, we discovered many photos from the Petrograd of 1918–1920. They enabled us to project pictures of the city's street life between scenes, images that documented the harsh, inhospitable environment confronting citizens in the period of Babel's narrative. Before the final scene, when a working-class family, the purported winners of the Revolution and the Civil War, take over the apartment of the former general Mukovnin, the projection showed instead Bolshevik posters in praise of the victorious Soviet republic, proceeding from Lenin's to Stalin's image and thus indicating what the future was holding in store for the city and the Soviet Union.

Of course, such staging techniques had been extensively tested during the late twenties and early thirties, mainly by Erwin Piscator and Bertolt Brecht in Berlin, where they evolved their practice of an "Epic Theater." Babel wrote *Maria* in 1933, while on an extended trip to Western Europe. He had been to Berlin in the late 1920s and then again in 1932 and early 1933. Given his interest in the theater, he surely must have been aware of the experiments conducted on the city's stages that counted among the most innovative in Europe. It made perfect sense to employ some of the Epic Theater devices in a production of Babel's play. They worked extremely well with its inscribed structure, and it is entirely plausible to assume that Babel might have had some such techniques in mind when he was composing his text. In fact, his dramaturgy comes remarkably close to several of the ideas Brecht elaborated in his writings on Epic Theater later in the thirties, and which he eventually implemented, and further experimented with, in the fifties with his Berliner Ensemble.[4]

If one accepts an apparently prevalent notion that Brecht's theater concept was inflexibly opposed to the one ascribed to Chekhov—an opinion I strongly disagree with—it might surprise that *Maria* also shows the influence of Chekhov's stage texts. Considering that Chekhov regarded his plays to be comedies—in contrast to the tragic and somewhat sentimental reading Stanislavsky appears to have espoused in his productions at the MkhAT—a "Chekhovian" approach is evident in the way Babel has serious, and often tragic, events being followed by bizarrely hilarious or grotesque moments. For instance, while Viskovsky (the former captain of the Imperial Horse-Guards turned black marketeer) is raping Lyudmila Mukovnina in an adjacent room, a certain Madame Dora, who fancies an absurd French accent, is trying to physically seduce the giggly and bashful Red Artillery man Kravchenko. In the same moment Filip, one of the black market crooks from Dymshits's gang, creeps into the room to filch a bit of food and a bottle of vodka. The next instant, Viskovsky and Kravchenko shoot at and, maybe, kill each other; we will never know, though, because Babel wants the scene to black-out before we might recognize the outcome. Another example: immediately after General Mukovnin has suffered what appears to be a seizure, if not a heart attack, the same Filip wolfs down some cooked potatoes while holding forth, to the Mukovnin family's baffled old Nanny, about the Polish campaign in a ludicrously ignorant manner. Such a construct of scenes by Babel offered another indication to the actors that every interaction needed to be played for its own sake—as it also was demanded by Brecht for his plays—and that any suggestion of a subsequent turn from farce to tragedy, or vice-versa, had to be avoided.

As in Chekhov—and Brecht, of course—Babel's characters are to a great measure conditioned by their class and motivated by their environment and economic needs, even when they themselves may be barely aware of it. Consequently, the perennially talked-about waiting for Maria's return—anticipating in a way Beckett's *Waiting for Godot*, in Oksana Bulgakowa's astute observation—is hardly a metaphysical condition, in the manner of Beckett (or Chekhov in his *Three Sisters*). Rather, it is the Mukovnin family's increasingly desperate desire for relief from very concrete economic and social hardships that Maria, with her frequently mentioned energy and political connections, is expected to provide. For our American middle-class audience in 2004, spectators who neither survived a devastating war in their own country nor had been expropriated by a revolutionary movement of ruthless force, it had to be difficult to fully apprehend the privations Babel's stage characters are trying to alleviate or escape from. European audiences, when they were watching the newly discovered play during the sixties and seventies, encountered a world that would not look particularly strange to them. World War II was still recent history. Life in a black-market economy, and being haunted by the constant dread of hunger or a lack of heating and electricity, were quite familiar experiences. In addition, such times tend to produce gallows humor and bitter laughter, which permeates Babel's scenes. We tried to make these aspects of the text as recognizable as possible by, paradoxically, representing them as unfamiliar, as one might present the habits and strange beliefs of an exotic tribe, rather than as the behavior and customs of a civilized society that shared European history and enlightenment. The fact that several of Babel's characters invoke the values of that humanistic tradition makes the discrepancy between their expressed convictions and their actual reality especially grotesque.

Theatergoing European audiences would probably be intrigued by the similarities between the waiting for Maria, who never arrives, and Beckett's characters' futile wait in the much later *Godot* in 1952. Certainly, the Red Army soldier's entrance in Scene 7, who announces Maria's failure to return, evokes uncannily the appearance of the boy at the end of Beckett's play who informs us that Godot is not going to come.

Directing a production in Europe, I might have hinted at this alluring parallel and made the insistence on useless waiting more palpable and tedious. But I question if this would have been effective, that is, recognized as a convincing metaphor by our audience, predominantly composed of students. There had been an acclaimed production at East Berlin's Deutsches Theater, in 1970, which strongly emphasized a pervasive mood of tiresome and frustrated expectation. It must have provoked potent associations for an audience who, since the erection of the Berlin Wall, had become accustomed to endless waits for visits from their West German relatives, for permission to travel out of the country, or for other occasions of relief from East Germany's claustrophobic way of life, with its recurrent economic shortages and political and cultural restrictions. Such an interpretation, however, would hardly have struck a comparable chord with our spectators. After all, in Babel's play it is mainly the members of the Mukovnin household who are obsessed with waiting for Maria. Other characters comment on her beauty and her service with the Red Cavalry, but they don't appear to be much troubled by her absence.

The final scene of the play presented another problem for our American audience of 2004. In the event, they were watching a group of simple and uneducated people take over the site of culture and enlightenment that used to be the Czarist General Mukovnin's home. They are, if you will, a new class of "happy barbarians," as Grisha Freidin liked to describe them during the rehearsals, echoing Alexander Blok,[5] even though at least one of them doesn't seem particularly happy with the large new premises they have inherited from the Mukovnins. The survivors from the old class try to cash in their few remaining assets and to escape. Babel does not conceal his sympathy for the young members of the rising class. He has them occupying the stage, pregnant with new life and full of expectations—and he hardly could have done otherwise at the time of the play's writing if he hoped for a Moscow production. But he does not come down firmly in favor of one side or the other; he merely shows us their mutually exclusive predicaments and aspirations, leaving it to the spectators to draw their own conclusions. Furthermore, he wrote the play for an audience for whom these events were recent history and who would have understood the slightest hint that a telling gesture or peculiar inflection might have indicated. It is this subtlety, this density of allusions and ambiguity, that may well have been one of the reasons why the production of the play was prematurely abandoned by the Vakhtangov Theater in 1935—and Moscow had to wait until 1990 for its performance!

Seventy years after the play was penned, we were performing it mainly for young Americans who had grown up familiar with the designation of the Soviet Union as the "Evil Empire." Europeans, regardless of their attitude towards communism, and especially if they had lived within the satellite states of the Soviet empire or in proximity to its borders, would comprehend the context of Babel's play, that is, Petrograd shortly after the Bolshevik revolution. The older among them would understand the austere conditions depicted in the play as well as the Bolsheviks' genuine, if flawed and failed, effort to achieve social justice. It seemed important for our production not to demonize the early Soviet system and its supporters, nor to dismiss those who tried to adjust and make the best of the new, if harrowing, conditions of life. Our intention was to let the audience arrive at their own judgment. The jubilant but harshly unforgiving *Workers Oratorio* by Dmitry Shostakovich that we used as a lead-in to the last scene; the projected poster of Lenin with the opening words of the *Communist Manifesto;* other visual tributes to the revolutionary class; and, finally, a poster of Stalin triumphant were intended to put the play in its proper historical perspective—both in terms of its setting and its period of composition. I am still not sure if we provided enough contextual support for our audience so that they fully appreciated the hardships of the Russian civil war that often drive Babel's characters into a behavior that might strike a contemporary Stanford student as perplexing, repulsive, or even stupidly bizarre.

I had the occasion to watch a video recording of a fairly recent *Maria* production, directed by Mikhail Levitin at the Moscow Hermitage Theater, in 1996. The staging played clearly to an audience that was only all-too-familiar with its country's history. With such an audience, I could imagine enticing possibilities of a less realistic staging of the play, though one that would not necessarily arrive at a similarly cartoonish interpretation of the text. But such a performance for our Stanford audience of 2004, I feel, would not have done justice to Babel's attempt to show us a fair cross-section of Russian citizens in their desperate struggle to survive in harsh post-revolutionary Petrograd. And in a more general sense, I wished our production to share the play's empathy with the often appalling decisions people can arrive at for the sake of sheer survival.

Babel's text reminds me of a maxim voiced by Brecht's Mother Courage: "Corruption is our only hope. As long as it exists, even the innocent has a chance of getting justice."

Since the most important task of our production was to tell Babel's story as clearly as possible, we continually checked the translation against the Russian original, exploring all potential meanings a particular sentence might have had in the vernacular of the play's period. Thus, numerous alternative versions of specific lines were tested in rehearsal, in order to achieve the most revealing patterns of language and gestural behavior the actors would employ in a given interaction. With the company, we also watched documentary and feature films of the period, which provided samples of manners that were characteristic of Russians in the early twentieth century. They provided models that helped the actors in articulating their own gestural repertoire. It seemed important that our young American performers approached, as closely as possible, historically authentic behavior patterns.

Even though the performances were very well received, I still harbor some doubts about whether we made Babel's world of Civil War Petrograd fully accessible to our mainly student audience. The most rewarding comment about the production was a remark by Antonina Nikolaevna Pirozhkova. The companion of Babel's final years and the mother of his daughter Lydia, she, along with Lydia and Babel's other daughter, Nathalie, attended the final performance of *Maria*. She felt, so she told me, the presence of Babel's spirit on our stage.

# Notes

## Notes to Chapter 1

1. Eduard Beltov, "*Eto nuzhno ne mertvym-zhivym*," cited in Robert C. Tucker, *Stalin in Power: The Revolution from Above* (New York: Norton, 1990), p. 578.

2. Gregory Freidin, "Vopros vozvrashcheniia II: Velikii perelom i Zapad v biografii I. E. Babelia nachala 1930-kh godov," *Stanford Slavic Studies* 4–2 (1991): 195–204. See also Janina Salajczyk, "Polski epizod w biografii Izaaka E. Babla." *Zeszyty naukowe wyzszej szkoly pedagogicznej im. Powstancow slaskich w Opolu. Filologia rosyjska* IX. Seria A. (Opole, 1972), pp. 103–111.

3. This controversial issue is further discussed in G. Freidin's contribution to this volume. *Ed.*

4. Clara Malraux, *Le bruit de nos pas: Voiçi que vient l'été* (Paris: Bernard Grasset, 1973), pp. 285–87.

5. Quoted in Nadezhda Mandelshtam, *Hope against Hope*, trans. Max Hayward (New York: Atheneum, 1970), 11.

6. Ervin Sinkó, *Egy regény regénye: Moszkvai naplójegyzetek, 1935–1937* (Novi Sad, 1961). A Serbo-Croatian edition came out earlier as *Roman jednog romana: Biljeske iz moskovskog dnevnika od 1935 do 1937 godine* (Zagreb: Zora, 1955).

7. The late military historian Dmitrii Volkogonov, who had exceptional archival access, estimated that nearly a million were shot and five million arrested. Volkogonov, *Autopsy for an Empire* (New York: Free Press, 1998), p. 105. Higher and lower figures continue to be put forward in the absence of full documentation.

8. Lev Razgon, *True Stories*, trans. John Crowfoot (Dana Point, CA: Ardis, 1997), 267.

9. Two months after my detention by the KGB, two Soviet journalists, obviously with close connections with the secret police, attacked me in *Izvestia* as a "scrawny" woman who had previously written "a calumny about the status of national minorities in our country." The piece ends: "Why accord hospitality to hacks like these who come here as tourists. Wouldn't it be better to send hacks like these packing?" D. Dmitriev and A. Cherkasov, *Izvestia*, September 12, 1962, 3.

10. This reconstruction is drawn from the author's several interviews with Boris Souvarine in the 1960s and also: Boris Souvarine, "Derniers entretiens avec Babel," *Counterpoint* (Paris) 30 (1979).

11. Sergei Povartsov, *Prichina smerti-rasstrel: Khronika poslednikh dnei Isaaka Babelia* (Moscow: Terra, 1996); Vitalii Shentalinskii, *Raby svobody: v literaturnykh arkhivakh KGB: Babel, Bulgakov, Florenskii, Pilniak, Mandelshtam, Kliuev, Platonov, Gorkii* (Moscow: Parus, 1995).

12. http://www.stanford.edu/group/isaac_babel/bibliography/index.htm, accessed January 4, 2009.

## Notes to Chapter 2

1. Here and elsewhere, unless otherwise indicated, translations are by the author.

2. "Khodya" (Chink), 1923. Isaak Babel, *Sochineniia*, 2 vols., comp. and ed. Antonina Priozhkova, comment. Sergey Povartsov (Moscow: Khudozhestvennaya literatura, 1990), vol. 1, p. 98. This edition is hereafter cited as *Sochineniia*, followed by volume and page number.

3. See Isaak Babel, *Peterburg 1918*, ed. Efraim Sicher (Ann Arbor: Ardis, 1987). Among the Babel scholars, Sicher has been most consistent and meticulous in recognizing Babel's book projects. Babel used cycles to fill his need for an epic sweep while preserving the form of a short story in a manner similar to that employed by his contemporary poets, among them Alexander Blok and Osip Mandelstam, who arranged their lyric poems into larger cycles or books, creating a lyric *Bildungsroman* of sorts. On Babel's use of the epic frame, see Gregory Freidin, "Isaac Babel (1894–1940)," in George Stade, ed., *European Writers: The Twentieth Century* (New York: Scribners, 1990), p. 1993ff.

4. I. Babel, "Moi listki. Odessa," *Zhurnal zhurnalov* 51 (December 22, 1916), *Sochineniia* 1:64.

5. The Acmeist manifestoes of Gumilev, Mandelstam, and Gorodetsky.

6. Lev Lunts, "Na zapad!" *Beseda* 2 (1923).

7. On Babel's complex relationship with Gorky, see chapter 7 ("Spravka—rodoslov-naia" [Babel' i Gor'kii]) of Alexander Zholkovsky's *Poltora rasskaza Babelia: "Gui de Mopassan" i "Spravka/Gonorar." Struktura, smysl, fon* (Moscow: KomKniga, 2006). This edition is hereafter referred to as Zholkovsky 2006.

8. "L'Aveu" is one of the three stories that Babel translated for the three-volume *Collected Works of Maupassant: Sobranie sochinenii*, 3 vols., ed. I. Babel (Moscow: Zemlia i fabrika, 1926–27), vol. 1, pp. 34–43. The other two were: "Le Mal d'André" and "Idyll." See also E. Pogorelskaia, "I. E. Babel—redaktor i perevodchik Giui de Mopassana," *Voprosy literatury* 4 (2005).

9. For more on Babel's uses of Nietzsche, see my "Justifying the Revolution as an Aesthetic Phenomenon: Nietzschean Motifs in the Reception of Isaac Babel (1923–1932)," in Bernice G. Rosenthal, ed., *Nietzsche and Soviet Culture: Ally and Adversary*, Cambridge Studies in Russian Literature (Cambridge: Cambridge University Press, 1994), pp. 149–73.

10. Cf. Zholkovsky 2006, pp. 17, 135, and elsewhere.

11. No wonder, then, that the Marxist theoretician, critic and literary entrepreneur, Aleksandr Voronsky, the proponent of the view of art as a higher form of the "cognition of life," championed Babel in the 1920s.

12. See also Gabriella Safran's discussion of Babel's early fiction as a response to Maxim Gorky's search for a new type of Russian-Jewish writer in her "Isaak Babel's El'ia Isaakovich as a New Jewish Type," *Slavic Review* 61(2): 253–72, esp. p. 258.

13. Viktor Shklovsky was the first to elaborate Babel's *Odessa Stories* as an allegory of a Russian-Jewish "assault" on Russian culture. Babel, wrote Shklovsky, "is a brave man, I even think that 'he could spend the night with a Russian woman and the Russian woman would be satisfied.' Because the Russian woman loves eloquence." "I. Babel (Kritichesky romans)," *LEF*, no. 6 (1924): 153. On the phrase "refreshing blood" and a range of contemporary references implied by it, including the "tainted blood" of the Romanovs, see Olga Matich, *Erotic Utopia: The Decadent Imagination in Russia's Fin de Siècle* (Madison: University of Wisconsin Press, 2005), p. 274 and elsewhere.

14. For a review of responses to Babel's debut in 1922–1926, see my "Justifying the Revolution."

15. Babel's "Autobiography" is datelined "Sergiev Posad, November 1924" and was intended as a response, if oblique, to Budenny's attack on him in the September issue of *Oktiabr*, as well as a statement safeguarding the fate of the book *Red Cavalry*, which came out a year and a half later.

16. I. Babel's letter to Gorky, June 25, 1925. *Sochineniia* 1:242ff.

17. Ilya Ehrenburg, *Liudi, gody, zhizn*, ed. B. Ia. Frezinskii, 3 vols. (Moscow: Tekst, 2005), 1:517.

18. I owe this observation to Oksana Bulgakova.

19. Sergei Povartsov, "P'esa I. Babelia "Mariia": Opyt kommentariia," *Uchenye zapiski Moskovskogo oblastnogo pedinstituta (Sovetskaia literatura 10)*, 265: 77–87. Povartsov traces *Maria* back to Babel's 1918 piece "O gruzine, kerenke i general'skoi dochke" ("About a Georgian, Kerensky Rubles, and a General's Daughter").

20. In its journal publication, "The Story of My Dovecote" was accompanied by a note indicating that it was the "beginning of an autobiographical prose fiction" (*nachalo avtobiograficheskoi povesti*). *Krasnaia nov* 4 (1925): 33.

21. See my biographical essay, "Isaac Babel (1894–1940)," ed. G. Stade, in *European Writers: The Twentieth Century*, vol. 11 (New York: Charles Scribner's Sons), pp. 1885–1914.

22. Nevsky's original name was officially restored in January 1944.

23. Viktor Shklovsky, "I. Babel: Kritichesky romans," p. 155.

24. The only known publications after the closing of *Novaia zhizn'* were his sketch "Na stantsii" (*Era*, July 17, 1918), "Na Dvortsovoi ploshchadi," and "Kontsert v Katerinien-shtadte," the latter two subtitled "diary" and published in *Zhizn' iskusstva* on November 11 and 13, 1918, respectively. His next publication, "Na pole chesti," a free reworking of Gaston Vidal's *Figures et anecdotes de la Grande Guerre* (Paris, 1918), appeared in the Odessa journal *Lava* 1(July 1920), when Babel was at the Polish front.

25. *Zhizn iskusstva* (Petrograd), November 13, 1918. *Sochineniia* 1:199–201.

26. "During my disappearance, la vie made me thrash about this way and that, I departed, came back, was ill, got drafted . . . I am leaving for Yamburg today to open a peasant university." I. Babel's letter to Anna Slonim (December 7, 1918). In his "Autobiography" (1924), Babel mentions his work for the Commissariat of Enlightenment (his reference to opening a peasant university in Yamburg).

27. According to the recollections of L. N. Livshits (the wife of Babel's friend Isaac Livshits), Babel returned to his parents' home in Odessa in May 1919. I. E. Babel, *Pis'ma drugu: iz arkhiva I. L. Livshitsa*, ed. E. I. Pogorel'skaia (Moscow: Gosudarstvennyi literaturnyi muzei, 2007), 107.

28. See Vladimir Iaskov, "Khlebnikov. Kosarev. Kharkov," *Volga* 11 (1999); http://magazines.russ.ru/volga/1999/11/, accessed August 11, 2002.

29. Nathalie Babel, Introduction, in Nathalie Babel, ed., *Isaac Babel: The Lonely Years 1925–1939 (Unpublished Stories and Private Correspondence)*, trans. Andrew R. MacAndrew and Max Hayward (Boston: Verba Mundi, David R. Godine, 1995), p. xv. Hereafter, this edition is referred to as *The Lonely Years*.

30. Elena Pilsky (née E. S. Kuznetsova; died in 1972), "Venok pamiati Babelia," *Novoe Russkoe Slovo* (NY), June 8, 1966, p. 3.

31. Piotr Pilsky, "Isaak Babel'," in his *Zatumanivshiisia mir* (Riga: Gramatu Draugs, 1929), pp. 157–64.

32. Babel's "Na pole chesti" (1920) was prefaced by an awkward phrase that could only have been written by a person without firsthand military experience (italics are mine, GF): "Present stories are the beginning of *my* notes about war. Their *content is borrowed* from the books written by French soldiers and officers who participated in battles. . . . *Sochineniia* 1:80.

33. According to Babel's sister Mary, her brother concealed from his family his plans to join Budenny. His schoolmate and lifelong friend Isaac Livshits, then also a figure in the Odessa literary and publishing scene, was supposed to come along but his parents locked him up in a room as soon as they found out about the upcoming adventure. One may assume that the elder Babels would have done the same for their offspring. Sergei Povartsov, "Podgotovitelnye materialy dlia zhizneopisaniia Babelia Isaaka; http://magazines.russ.ru/voplit/2001/2/povar.html, accessed November 26, 2002.

34. Isai Lezhnev, "Novaia p'esa Babelia 'Mariia'," *Teatr i dramaturgiia* 3 (1935): 56.

35. Babel's letter to his sister Mary dated May 12, 1925 (*Sochineniia* 1:241). Babel's letter to Kashirina dated October 6, 1927, in Tamara Ivanova, "Glava iz zhizni: Vospominaniia, pis'ma I. Babelia," *Oktiabr* 5–7 (1992), 7, 170ff. See also the entry in Viacheslav Polonsky's 1931 diary about Babel's unpublished pieces ("Voronsky tells me they are all counterrevolutionary"). Viacheslav Polonsky, "'Mne eta voznia ne kazhetsia chem-to ser'ezno literaturnym . . .' (Iz dnevnika Viach. Polonslkogo. Mart-Aprel 1931 goda)," publication by A. A. Abroskina, *Vstrechi s proshlym, Federalnaia arkhivanaia sluzhba Rossii. Rossiiskaii gosudarstvennyi arkhiv literatury i iskusstva* (Moscow: Russkaia kniga, 2000), p. 309.

36. The most comprehensive story of Babel's relationship with Tamara Ivanova (Kashirina) is narrated by her, along with Babel's letters to her, in "Glava iz zhizni: Vospominaniia, pisma I. Babelia," *Oktiabr* 5, 6, and 7 (May, June, and July, 1992).

37. Babel's letter to Anna Slonim dated July 22, 1927, still unpublished, contained the following: "Evg. Borisovna rented a small house on the outskirts of Paris. I have settled in a tiny room on the ground floor of this same house. Evg. Borisovna knew practically everything; I told her what others had neglected to inform her about. She and I will try to live a quiet life of work; I do not know if we are destined to be happy but we shall struggle to do work." Manuscript Collection of the Russian State Library, Fond 660, k. 1, ed. khr. 6.

38. See, e.g., Babel's letter to Tamara Ivanova (Kashirina) dated January 26, 1928 (*Oktiabr* 7, 176), and Babel's letter to Efim Zozulia dated October 14, 1938, *Sochineniia* 1:358ff.

39. For the earliest such documented plea, see Babel's letter to I. Livshits, April 17, 1923 (*Sochineniia* 1:238).

40. See, e.g., Karl Marx, "On the Jewish Question" (1844). In Babel's own time, Marx's position became the foundation for a very popular sociological study by Werner Sombart, *Jews and Economic Life* (*Die Juden und das Wirtschaftsleben*, 1911), which Babel no doubt studied at the Kiev Commercial Institute. A similar position is expressed in Georg Simmel's famous essay "Stranger" ("Exkurs über den Fremden," 1908). Both Sombart and Simmel were known in Russia in the 1910s.

41. "The Road" was completed in 1931 (see Babel's letter to V. A. Reginin, October 13, 1931, in *Sochineniia* 1:318 and 459). "Evening at the Empress's" (Vecher u imperatritsy, *Sochineniia* 1:95–97) appeared in the Odessa *Siluety* 1, 1922. There may have been an intermediate, now lost, version of the story, alluded to by Viktor Shklovsky: "The third issue contains the story 'The Road.' Eleven years ago, it used to be shorter. It was published in Odessa. Without this beginning and without this ending. But as in this version, the telegraph operator did his killing by shooting a Jew in his face with a Mauser pistol. And the freezing traveler was warming himself in the Empress's library." Viktor Shklovsky, "O liudiakh, kotorye idut po odnoi i toi zhe doroge i ob etom ne znaiut: Konets barokko" (About the People Who Journey Along the Same Road But Are Not Aware of It: The End of the Baroque), in *Literaturnaia gazeta*, July 17, 1932. This may have been one of Shklovsky's intentional mystifications: Babel's "Evening" does not mention any telegraph operator.

42. In December–January 1917–1918, Odessa was ruled by Rumcherod, i.e., a joint Soviet of the Rumanian Front, Black Sea Fleet, and the City of Odessa. A "disintegration of the front" implied, among other things, that Babel did not desert and, more important, that the service rolls were unlikely to have survived.

43. Konstantin Paustovskii and V. K. Paustovskii, *Povest o zhizni (Kniga chetvertaia)*, in his *Sobranie sochinenii*, 9 vols., vol. 5 (Moscow: Khudozhestvennaia literatura, 1985), pp. 90ff.

44. The opening salvo was the ominous article signed by Semyon Budenny himself ("Babizm Babelia iz *Krasnoy novi*") published in *October* 3 (1924). Far more ominous was Budenny's renewed attack on Babel *and* his patron, Maxim Gorky, in *Pravda* in 1928 ("Otvet tovarishchu Gor'komu," October 26, 1928). According to a memoirist who interviewed Budenny about the polemic, Budenny recalled that in the end it was Stalin who intervened personally and asked Budenny to cease the public controversy,

as it was interfering with Stalin's campaign of "winning Gorky over to our side." Major General Mikhail Loshchits (ret.), "Besedy s chelovekom-legendoy: K 120-letiyu so dnya rozhdeniya S. M. Budennogo," *Krasnaya Zvezda* (Moscow), April 24, 2003, p. 4.

45. See Babel's letters to Anna Slonim dated October 27, 1928 and November 27, 1928, *Sochineniia* 1:288ff. and 291.

46. Gorky was aware of the actual threat of violence against Babel, contained in Budenny's assault on the young author. An earlier draft of Gorky's rebuttal letter contains direct references to it (see Sergey Povartsov's commentary in *Sochineniia* 1:455–56. See also G. S. Merkin, "S. Budenny i I. Babel (k istorii polemiki), *Filologicheskie nauki* 4 (1990): 97–102. On Babel's awareness of Stalin's ways, see Boris Souvarine, "Moi vstrechi s Isaakom Babelem," *Kontinent* 23 (1980): 343–78. See also Lazar Fleishman, "Ob odnom neraskrytom 'prestuplenii' Babelia," in I. Ia. Vigasin et al., eds., *Poetika, istoriia literatury, lingvistika: sbornik k 70-letiiu Viacheslava Vsevolodovicha Ivanova* (Moscow: OGI, 1999), pp. 382–406.

47. *Sochineniia* 2:367. "Nachalo" was first published on June 18, 1938, the second anniversary of Gorky's death, in *Literaturnaia gazeta* and, as "Iz vospominanii," in *Pravda*.

48. Bruno Jasenski, "nashi na Riv'ere," *Literaturnaia gazeta* (July 10, 1930), p. 3. A transcript of Babel's statement is in the Manuscript Collection (Otdel rukopisei) of the Gorky Institute of World Literature in Moscow, fond 86, op. 1, ed. khr. 6, pp. 1–5. See Gregory Freidin, "Vopros vozvrashchenii II: Velikii perelom i Zapad v biografii I. E. Babelia nachala 1930-kh godov," *Stanford Slavic Studies* 4-2 (1991): 190–240. See also Janina Salajczyk, "Polski epizod w biografii Izaaka E. Babla," in *Zeszyty naukowe wyzszej szkoly pedagogicznej im. Powstancow slaskich w Opolu. Filologia rosyjska* IX. Seria A (Opole, 1972), pp. 103–11.

49. Cf. Viktor Shklovsky writing in 1922: "But the hole in the tram post made by an artillery shell at the corner of Grebetskaya and Pushkarskaya is still there. If you don't believe that there has been a revolution, go there and thrust your hand into the wound. It is big—the post has been shot through by a shell from a three-inch gun." *Sentimental'noe puteshestvie*, in Viktor Shklovsky, *Eshche nichego ne konchilos*, ed. A. Galushkin and V. Nekhotin (Petersburg: Propaganda, 2002), p. 149.

50. Cf. Osip Mandelstam's 1921 poem "Concert at the Railroad Station" (Kontsert na Vokzale): "It is impossible to breathe, and the firmament is teeming with maggots/ And not a single star speaks" (*Nel'zia dyshat', i teverd' kishit cherviami/I ni odna Zvezda ne govorit . . .* ).

51. I am indebted to Ken Moss for this suggestion.

52. "The stranger is thus being discussed here, not in the sense often touched upon in the past, as the wanderer who comes today and goes tomorrow, but rather as the person who comes today and stays tomorrow. He is, so to speak, the *potential* wanderer: although he has not moved on, he has not quite overcome the freedom of coming and going. He is fixed within a particular spatial group, or within a group whose boundaries are similar to spatial boundaries. But his position in this group is determined, essentially, by the fact that he has not belonged to it from the beginning, that he imports qualities into it, which do not and cannot stem from the group itself." From Kurt Wolff, trans., *The Sociology of*

*Georg Simmel* (New York: Free Press, 1950), p. 402. Simmel's thought is echoed in Walter Benjamin's famous "The Storyteller: Reflections of the Work of Nikolay Leskov" (1936).

53. Cheka, as it was constituted in December 1917 and until August 1918, was subdivided into the Provincial Department (*Inogorodnii*), the Department for the Struggle against Counter-Revolution (*Dlia borby s kontr-revoliutsiei*), and the Department for the Struggle against Abuse of Power (*dlia borby s dolzhnostnymi prestupleniiami*). The Foreign Department proper (*Inostrannyi otdel*) was established in December 1920 "on the basis of one of the subdivisions of the Special Department" (*Osobyi otdel*), itself created in January 1919, with the purpose of fighting "counter-revolution and espionage in the Red Army." A. I. Kokurin and N. V. Petrov, comps., R. G. Pikhoia, eds., *Lubyanka: VChK-OGPU-NKVD-NKGB-MGB-MVD-KGB. 1917–1960. Spravochnik* (Moscow: Mezhdunarodnyi Fond "Demokratiia," 1997), pp. 9–10.

54. Another reason to doubt Babel's claim is the absence of any mention of his service for the Cheka from his NKVD dossier, including the transcripts of his interrogations and other statements. More recently Babel's assertion was questioned by the Cheka itself. In response to the official query by V. Kovskii, the Petersburg FSB (then MBRF) declared that neither Isaac Babel nor Ivan Kalugin could be located in their personnel rolls. V. Kovsky, "Sudba tekstov v kontekste sud'by," *Voprosy literatury* 1 (1995); http://www .auditorium.ru/books/277/Vopli95-1_chapter3.html, accessed April 10, 2004. This gives credence to the words of Evgeniia Gronfain who, wrote Nathalie Babel, "told me that his service with the Cheka was pure fabrication." Nathalie Babel, "Introduction," *The Lonely Years*, p. viii. None of this, of course contradicts the possibility that Babel may have done some translating for the Cheka on an ad hoc basis while in Petrograd in 1918–1919, but regular employment seems out of the question.

55. This "happy" passage has elicited considerable skepticism from the Babel scholars, among them, Milton Ehre, *Isaac Babel* (Boston: Twayne, 1986), 138–39.

56. In a letter to Tamara Kashirina (July 21, 1926), Babel refers to his Cheka friends en masse, describing how they swooped down on him and took him with them to the funeral of Felix Dzerzhinsky (*Oktiabr* 6, 196). Babel did have one very good friend in the upper echelons of the Cheka (by then the OGPU), Efim Grigorievich Evdokimov (1891–1940), whom he may have met during the Polish campaign when Evdokimov, a Cossack by birth and a onetime anarchist, served as the head of the Secret-Political Section of the Special Department of the All-Russian Cheka of the South-Western Front. A key Chekist behind the Shakhty trial, by 1932, Evdokimov was finishing his stint as the Head of the Cheka in Central Asia and was about to take charge of the Cheka for Trans-Caucasia. Evdokimov was a complex figure. Recovering from months of torture in the NKVD hospital, he is reported to have said that "he would have liked one thing—a bomb—in order to blow up the entire investigative branch of the NKVD, along with himself, that such an apparat, which cripples and destroys innocent people can only be qualified as fascist. . . ." "Doklad Komissii TsK KPSS Prezidiumu TsK KPSS po ustanovleniiu prichin massovykh repressii protiv chlenov I kandidatov v chleny TsK VKP (b), izbrannykh na XVII s`ezde partii (9 February 1956)," Almanac *Rossiia. XX vek. Dokumenty* 2 (2001); http://www.idf.ru/2/7.shtml, accessed April 10, 2004. Evdokimov and Babel were on the

same execution list, and Babel was shot on the same day as Evdokimov's wife and son. Evdokimov was posthumously cleared of all charges.

57. Writing to Viacheslav Polonsky on November 28, 1928, Babel still hoped that his position was beyond the reach of the cultural commissars from RAPP. The cultural revolution then going on could drive "nervous people to shoot themselves, but as to the merry folk, all they can do under the circumstances is to keep following their merry line." *Sochineniia* 1:291.

58. See also Elif Batuman's treatment of this story in this volume.

59. "We Russians have two souls: one, inherited from the nomadic Mongols, is the soul of a dreamer, mystic, sloth, convinced that 'Fate shall resolve all' . . . , and next to this impotent soul, there exists the soul of a Slav, it can flare up bright and beautiful, but it does not burn for long, goes out quickly, and is incapable of protecting itself from its congenital toxins that poison its strength. . . . Whence comes the cruelty, zealotry, mystical-anarchic sects—castrati, khlysty, . . . as well as drinking on a monstrous scale." Gorky, "Dve dushi," *Letopis'* 1 (December 1915): 1–12. Polemics around the controversial essay lasted for years, in part, because it encapsulated Gorky's thought about Russia and anticipated his *Untimely Thoughts* (1917) and "V. I. Lenin" (1924). The essay is enigmatically mentioned by Shklovsky in his "Babel: A Critical Romance" (1924) and served as the title for Kornei Chukovsky's brochure *Dve dushi Maksima Gor'kogo* (Petrograd, 1924).

60. The choice of the last name Madame *Bender*sky may have been a private joke, prompted by the serialization of the novels about the great deal-maker Ostap *Bender* in the same journal *30 dnei*. The wild popularity of *The Golden Calf* could not but irk Babel. Babel responded by following the Russian saying: "Some take to the priest, but others, the priest's wife." Ilya Ilf was present at a public reading of the story. See Sergei Bondarin, "Prikosnovenie k cheloveku," in A. N. Pirozhkova and N. N. Yurgeneva, eds. and comps., *Vospominaniia o Babele* (Moscow, 1989), pp. 99ff. Hereafter this edition is cited as *Vospominaniia*.

61. Jerry T. Heil, *The Russian Literary Avant-Garde and the Cinema (1920s and 1930s): The Film-Work of Isaak Babel' and Jurij Tynjanov*, 2 vols. (Ph.D. dissertation, University of California, Berkeley, 1984).

62. Tamara Ivanova (Kashirina), "Glava iz zhizni. Vospominaniia. Pis'ma I. Babelia," annot. Evgenii Peremyshlev, *Oktiabr* 5–7 (1992). Hereafter, this publication is cited as *Oktiabr*, followed by number of issue number and page. "Misha was about four, Isaac Emmanuilovich sent his diplomats to me asking for a permission to see his son. I refused categorically. Misha considered Vsevolod to be his father (he was not yet two when Vsevolod entered my life), loved him very much, and Vsevolod treated him very well. Did I have the right to complicate the child's life with this sort of dualism that was incomprehensible to him? I thought that I did not, and have never regretted that I rejected Babel's request to see his son." (*Oktiabr* 7, 185)

63. Cf. Shimon Markish's reading of "Karl-Yankel" as an "inflated and false" story meant to celebrate the wonders of Soviet nationalities policy. Shimon Markish, "Saak Babel," in his *Babel' i drugie* (Moscow and Jerusalem: Personal'naya tvorcheskaya masterskaya "Mikhail Shchigol," 1997), pp. 26ff.

64. "He, Benchik, went to Froim Grach, who already looked at the world with his one eye and was what he is. He said to Froim: 'Take me in. I want to moor by your shore. The shore I moor by will gain.'" This passage from "How It Was Done in Odessa" is a recapitulation of the memorable encounter between the young writer and the great man of letters that took place in the office of *Letopis* in 1916, as does this passage in "Father": "But I am alone in my business, the late Lyovka Byk [Tolstoy, *GF*] is dead, have no help from anywhere, and here I am all alone as happens only to God in heaven. . . . 'Benya Krik,' said Lyubka then, 'You have tried him out on Tartakovsky, what don't you like about Benya Krik?'"

65. In his 1925 Diary, Dm. Furmanov recorded his conversation with Babel: "as to Dzerzhinsky, he is full of admiration for him. 'What precision, what brevity, and how practical!' He then told me that he wanted to write a big book about Cheka. 'I don't know, though, if I can manage it—my view of Cheka is just too one-sided. The reason is that the Chekists that I know, they are, well, they are simply holy people, even those who did the shooting with their own hands. . . . And I fear [the book] may come out too saccharine. On the other hand, I don't know [enough]. I just have no idea of the mood of those who inhabited the cells. Somehow, I am not even interested. Still, I think I am going to do it.'" Manuscript Collection of the Institute of World Literature, fond 30, op. 1, ed. khr. 791. See also Sergei Povartsov, *Prichina smerti-rasstrel: Khronika poslednikh dnei Isaaka Babelia* (Moscow: Terra, 1996), pp. 18ff; and V. Kovsky, "Sudba tekstov v kontekste sudby," *Voprosy literatury* 1 (1995).

66. Valentin Kataev, who had a first-hand near-death experience with the Odessa Cheka in its heyday in 1919, presents a vivid picture of this organization and its activity in *Uzhe napisan Verter* (1979). See also a vibrant, if not altogether reliable contemporary account: N. I. Averbukh (Avenarius), *Odessakaya "Chrezvychaika": bolshevistsky zastenok* (Kishinev, 1920).

67. Stalin's letter to Lazar Kaganovich dated June 7, 1932, in O. V. Khlevniuk et al., eds. and comps., *Stalin i Kaganovich. Perepiska. 1931–1936 gg.* (Moscow: ROSSPEN, 2001), p. 149.

68. I. Babel, "Kontsert v Katerinenshtadte" (Concert in Katerinenstadt), subtitled "Diary" and published in *Zhizn' iskusstva* on November 13, 1918.

69. Based in part on Babel's Paris friend, General Count Alexey Alexeevich Ignatyev (1877–1954), in 1933 an employee of the Soviet trade mission in Paris; see Ignatyev's memoirs, *Pyatdesyat let v stroiu* (Moscow: 1940). The book was reprinted in 1948 and went through many editions, the last one by Voenizdat in 1988. Although Babel could not have seen the actual published book, he was no doubt familiar with Ignatyev's stories either from the Paris days in 1932–1933, when the Babels and the Ignatyevs saw each other socially or when Ignatyev relocated permanently to Moscow in 1937.

70. See, e.g., the memoirs of Babel's younger friend and protégé Semyon Gekht, "U steny Strastnogo monastryria v letnii den 1924 goda," in *Vospominaniya* 1989, p. 57.

71. See, e.g., Babel's letter to his mother and sister dated November 14, 1934, in Nathalie Babel, ed., *The Lonely Years*, pp. 263ff.

72. Sergei Povartsov draws a connection between some elements of the plot of *Maria* and another of Babel's 1918 Petrograd sketches, entitled "About a Georgian, Kerensky

Rubles, and a General's Daughter (A Modern Tale)," published in Gorky's *Novaia zhizn'* no. 83 (April 21, 1918). S. Povartsov, "P'esa Babelia "Mariia: opyt kommentariia," *Uchenye zapiski Moskovskogo oblastnogo pedinstituta (Sovetskaia literatura 10)* 265 (1970): 77–87.

73. See Babel's letter to Solomon Mikhoels, dated November 28, 1931. *Sochinenniia* 1:320.

74. Archive of the Museum of the Vakhtangov Theater. Correspondence of V. V. Kuza, no. 126. This seems to be the only letter by Babel that has survived the fire caused by a German bomb during World War II.

75. Babel's letter to Kaganovich of June 27, 1932. Andrei Artizov and Oleg Naumov, comps., *Vlast i khodozhestvennaya intelligentsiya: Dokumenty TsK RKP(b), VChK-GPU-NKVD o kulturnoy politike 1917–1953 gg* (Moscow: Mezhdunarodnyy fond "Demokratiia," 1999), p. 180, hereafter cited as *Vlast i khodozhestvennaya intelligentsiya*.

76. Kaganovich's letter to Stalin of June 23, 1932. *Stalin i Kaganovich. Perepiska: 1931–1936 gg* (Moscow: ROSSPEN, 2001), p. 189.

77. Rumors of Babel's decision to seek permanent residence abroad, to become a *nevozvrashchenets* (a crime that was equivalent to treason since the adoption of the Law on Non-returnees of November 29, 1929) began to circulate in Moscow in 1933. According to Antonina Nikolaevna Pirozhkova, Babel wrote to her with denials, expressing his surprise that she would take them seriously. For her recollection of Babel's correspondence, see A. N. Pirozhkova, *Sem' let s Isaakom Babelem: vospominaniia zheny* (New York: Slovo/Word, 2001), p. 13.

78. As the Commissar for the South Western front, Stalin pushed the offensive against Lvov in August 1920, in which the Cavalry Army of Voroshilov and Budenny played a major role—in direct contravention of the order issued by the commander-in-chief in Moscow (Kamenev) to abandon Lvov and move to support Tukhachevsky's forces outside Warsaw. When the First Cavalry Army, depleted by its repeated and unsuccessful assaults on Lvov, finally redeployed as ordered, the battle of Warsaw had been lost, and the Polish forces counterattacked, leading to the rout of the Red Army. Although "no single cause explains the Soviet debacle," writes Stalin's biographer Robert Tucker, "based upon the writings of Soviet military historians published after Stalin's death, his [Stalin's] insubordination was an extremely contributing factor." Robert C. Tucker, *Stalin as Revolutionary: 1879–1929: A Study in History and Personality* (New York: Norton Library, 1974), pp. 204–5. See also Dmitry Volkogonov, *Stalin: Triumph and Tragedy*, trans. Harold Shukman (Prima Publishing: Rocklin, CA, 1996), p. 361.

79. Alexey Tolstoy knew Maria Denisova, the prototype for Babel's Maria, and apparently interviewed her and used her stories as he was preparing the last edition of his trilogy. Thus, Denisova became, in addition to the Krandievsky sisters, a prototype for the two female heroines in Tolstoy's trilogy. Babel may have further hinted at his affinity with Tolstoy by giving one of his characters the name of Alexey Tolstoy's second wife (1907–1914), an avant-garde artist, Sofia Isaakovna Dymshits (1889–1963).

80. In 1937, Shchadenko (1885–1951) was appointed by Stalin as Deputy People's Commissar of Defense to head the all-important Personnel Department of the Red Army.

81. As she complained to her friend Vladimir Mayakovsky in the 1920s, Denisova

chafed under the traditional housewife role imposed on her by her husband and as a result, felt frustrated as an artist. There are indications that in his 1930 play *The Bath House*, Mayakovsky modeled the selfish Soviet bureaucrat Pobedonosikov and his unhappy, suicidal wife, Paula, on Shchadenko and Denisova. See the publication of unknown letters of Denisova addressed to Mayakovsky: V. N. Terekhina, "Razbilas o byt. Vladimir Mayakovsky: neopublikkovannye stranitsy zapisnykh knizhek i perepiski," *Chelovek* 1 (2000): 157–69.

82. Ibid., p. 166.

83. Vera Mukhina, "Krestianka" (1927), State Tretyakov Gallery, Moscow.

84. Here is the text of the ballad in my more literal translation: A Cossack rode through a valley, through Manchurian land, He rode by a green orchard, A ring shone on his hand. A Cossack lass gave him the ring when the Cossack rode away to war. She gave it to him, saying, "In a year I shall be yours. A year has come and gone." [Curtain.] And like an arrow, the Cossack galloped to his native village. He saw a hut in the foothills, and his heart began to pound. An old woman walked toward him, and tenderly spoke to him thus: "Your Cossack girl has betrayed you. She made another man happy." The Cossack lad turned his horse to the right and rode into a clear field. He took off his rifle from his shoulder and ended his life forever. And that young Cossack girl—she is still waiting and waiting for her Cossack lad. And that old woman—an evil witch—she had been bribed with money [to deceive the Cossack lad].

85. M. Gorky, "V. I. Lenin," in *Sobranie sochinenii*, 30 vols., vol. 17 (Moscow: GIKhL, 1949–1956), pp. 26ff.

86. Letter of May 2, 1933, in Nathalie Babel, ed., *The Lonely Years*, p. 232.

87. See Fleishman, "Ob odnom neraskrytom 'prestuplenii' Babelia."

88. See "Pis'mo Gor'kogo Babeliu o p'ese 'Mariia,'" in *Gor'kii i sovetskie pisateli. Literaturnoe nasledstvo*, vol. 70 (Akademiia nauk SSSR: Moscow, 1963), pp. 43–44.

89. Suggested by Carl Weber, who directed the Stanford University production of *Maria* in 2004. See his essay in this volume.

90. In a letter to his mother and sister dated February 24, 1934, Babel writes about "My itch for drama" (*The Lonely Years*, p. 250). He expressed similar sentiments a year later (February 24, 1935), in ibid., pp. 275–76.

91. These acclaimed productions included: Vsevolod Ivanov's *Armored Train 14–69* (1927); K. Trenev's *Lyubov' Yarovaya* (1926); Vs. Vishnevsky's *Pervaia konnaia* (First Cavalry Army, 1930); and, of course, Bulgakov's *Dni Turbinykh* (The Days of the Turbins, 1927), which after Stalin's personal intervention became the mainstay of the Maly Theater repertoire. According to Tatyana Stakh, Babel admired Bulgakov's play intensely: "He sat and watched the play that he had seen more than once with the kind of excitement as if he saw it for the first time." T. Stakh, "Kakim ia pomniu Babelia," in *Vospominaniia*, p. 155.

92. Robert Conquest, *The Great Terror, Revisited* (Oxford: Oxford University Press, 1990): 37.

93. Lezhnev, "Novaia p'esa Babelia 'Mariia'," pp. 46–57.

94. According to Mikhail Koltsov's testimony given under interrogation in the Lubyanka prison on April 9, 1939, "On the third day of the Congress, A. Gide conveyed via

Ehrenburg an ultimatum for A. S. Shcherbakov and me: either Babel and Pasternak are sent to Paris immediately or A. Gide and his friends leave the Congress . . . A. Gide said that only they could be trusted about the information regarding the USSR: 'they alone tell the truth, the rest are bought and paid for.'" Viktor Fradkin, *Delo Kol'tsova* (Moscow: Vagrius, Mezhdunarodnyi fond "Demokratiya," 2002), pp. 90–91. See also Boris Frezinskii, "Velikaia illiuziia: Parizh 1935 (materially k istorii Mezhdunarodnogo kongressa pisatelei v zashchitu kultury)," *Minuvshee: Istoricheskij al'manakh* 24 (1998): 166–239.

95. G. S. Faiman, "Liudi i polozheniia. K shestidesiatiletiiu diskussii o formalizme v iskusstve. Glazami NKVD," *Nezavisimaia gazeta* (Moscow), March 14, 1966, p. 5.

96. See Ervin Sinkó's entry in his diary for February 9, 1936. Ervin Sinkó, *Roman eines Romans; Moskauer Tagebuch*, trans. from Serbo-Croatian by Edmund Trugly (Köln: Verlag Wissenschaft und Politik, 1962).

97. G. Mochanov, "Spravka Sekretno-politicheskogo otdela GUGB NKVD SSSR ob otklikakh literatorov i rabotnikov iskusstva na stat'i v gazette 'Pravda' o kompozitore D. D. Shostakoviche," in *Vlast i khodozhestvennaya intelligentsiya*, p. 290.

98. "A. M. Gorky's letter to I. V. Stalin," ibid., pp. 300–302.

99. According to a secret report of the NKVD about the Writers' Union discussion, Boris Pasternak's speech, in which he condemned the campaign, was, in part, encouraged by Babel, who, having just returned "from Foros, was saying that Gorky was very unhappy about the struggle against Formalism." Babel told another writer, Lev Slavin, that "Gorky is very disturbed by the Formalism discussions, and for this reason: these discussions will be followed by personal attacks." Grigorii Faiman, "Liudi i polozheniia (Okonchanie). K shestidesiatiletiiu diskussii o formalizme v iskusstve. Glazami NKVD. O vtorom dne diskussii o formalizme v iskusstve," *Nezavisimaia gazeta* (Moscow), March 27, 1996, p. 5.

100. See the secret police report on Babel in July 1936 in *Vlast i khodozhestvennaya intelligentsiya*, pp. 316–18.

101. As he claimed in a letter to his Brussels relatives, Babel wrote the script for the film *Liotchiki* (Pilots, a.k.a. in the United States as *Men with Wings*) but, following his habit, asked not to have his name listed in the credits, a decision he came to regret when he saw the film's runaway success. A story of a flight school romance between a very young female cadet and her middle-aged flight instructor, the film in many respects resembles Babel's romance with Pirozhkova, who, born in 1912, was a little more than half his age.

102. Ervin Sinkó, *Roman eines Romans. Moskauer Tagebuch*, trans. Edmund Trugly (Verlag Wissenschaft und Politik: Köln, 1962), pp. 354–57.

103. "Dokladanaia zapiska nachalnika Glavnogo upravleniia kinematografii B. Z. Shumiatskogo chlenam Politbiuro TsKn VKP (b) o situatsii vokrug postanovki S. M. Eizenshteinom filma "Bezhin lug," *Vlast i khodozhestvennaya intelligentsiya*, p. 352. Among other things Shumiatsky wrote: "We have here an egregious attempt to appeal to foreign public opinion in order to preempt our evaluation of Soviet films."

104. Oksana Bulgakowa, *Sergei Eisenstein: A Biography* (Berlin, San Francisco: PotemkinPress, 2001), pp. 185–89.

105. I. Babel, "Lozh, predatelstvo, i smerdiakovshchina" (Lies, Treason, Smerdya-kovism), *Literaturnaia gazeta*, February 1, 1937.

106. Marietta Chudakova's article in this volume offers a rich reading of this story.

107. Gregory Freidin, "Fat Tuesday in Odessa: Isaac Babel's 'Di Grasso' as Testament and Manifesto," *The Russian Review* 40, no. 2 (April 1981): 101–21.

108. Curtis Cate, *André Malraux: A Biography* (New York, 1995), p. 264.

109. The letter, addressed to mother and sister, datelined "Moscow, November 3, 1937." Copy in possession of the author.

110. Babel's letter to E. D. Zozulia dated October 14, 1938. *Sochineniia* 1:358ff.

111. Pirozhkova, *Sem let s Isaakom Babelem* (New York: Slovo, 2000), p. 99.

112. A. Read and D. Fisher, *The Deadly Embrace: Hitler, Stalin and the Nazi-Soviet Pact 1939–1941* (London: Joseph, 1988), p. 49ff. See also Jonathan Haslam, *The Soviet Union and the Struggle for Collective Security in Europe, 1933–39* (New York: St. Martin's Press, 1984), pp. 86, 96, 127–28, and 144; and H. D. Philips, *Between the Revolution and the West: A Political Biography of Maxim M. Litvinov* (Boulder, CO, San Francisco, and Oxford: Westview Press, 1992), p. 154.

113. Zachary Shore, *What Hitler Knew: A Battle for Information in Nazi Foreign Policy* (Oxford: Oxford University Press, 2002), pp. 109ff.

114. Arkady Vaksberg, "Protsessy," *Literaturnaia gazeta* (May 4, 1988), p. 12. Vitalii Shentalinskii, *Raby svobody: v literaturnykh arkhivakh KGB: Babel, Bulgakov, Florenskii, Pilniak, Mandelshtam, Kliuev, Platonov, Gorkii* (Moscow: Parus, 1995). Sergei Povartsov, *Prichina smerti—rasstrel : khronika poslednikh dnei Isaaka Babelia* (Moscow: Terra, 1996).

## Notes to Chapter 3

1. On the Bolshevik policy toward the Jewish population, methods of the "establish-ment of the proletarian dictatorship on the Jewish street," see Zvi Gitelman, *Jewish Nation-ality and Soviet Politics: The Jewish Section of the CPSU* (Princeton: Princeton University Press, 1972); Mordechai Altshuler, *Ha-yevsektsia bi-vrit ha-moazot* (1918–1930) (Tel Aviv: n.p., 1980); Michael Beizer, *Evrei Leningrada, 1917–1939: Natsional'naia zhizn' i sovetizatsiia* (Moscow and Jerusalem: Mosty kul'tury-Gesharim, 1999); O. V. Budnitskii, *Rossiiskie evrei mezhdy krasnymi i belymi (1917–1920)* (Moscow: ROSSPEN, 2005), and others.

2. Viktor Sevskii, "Dva kazaka. I. Podtelkov," *Donskaia volna* 7 (1918): 3.

3. Loengreen (P. T. Gertso-Vinogradskyi), "V odnom dome (Sovetskie dni v Ros-tove)," *Donskaia volna* 8 (1918): 8.

4. Prince Gr. N. Trubetskoi, *Gody smut i nadezhd. 1917–1919* (Montreal: 1981), p. 49.

5. M. M. Prishvin, *Dnevniki. 1918–1919* (Moscow: Moskovskyi rabochyi, 1994), p. 282. Entry of Sept. 22, 1919.

6. Vladimir Amfiteatrov-Kadashev, "Stranitsy iz dnevnika," ed. S. V. Shumikhin, *Minuvsheie: Istoricheskyi almanakh* 20 (Moscow and St. Petersburg: Atheneum-Feniks, 1996), p. 537.

7. Gosudarstvennyi arkhiv Rossiiskoi Federatsii (GA RF), fond 440, opis' 1, edinitsa khraneniia 110, 10 and its reverse, 18 and its reverse. Dispatches of the Kiev branch of *Azbuka* from March 28 and April 3, 1919.

8. Hoover Institution Archives, Stanford University, Petr Vrangel Collection, Box 38, Folder 22.

9. GA RF, f.440, op.1, ed. khr.52.11 and its reverse. Bulletin no. 7 of the Propaganda Department of the Special Conference under the Staff of the Commander-in-Chief of the military forces of the South of Russia of 21 June 1919, Rostov-on-Don.

10. Prishvin, p. 329. Entry of Nov. 15, 1919.

11. Vladimir Amfiteatrov-Kadashev, pp. 543–44.

12. Ibid., pp. 593–94. Entries of May–June 1919.

13. S. A. Pavliuchenkov, *Voennyi kommunizm v Rossii: vlast' i massy* (Moscow: RKT-Istoriia, 1997), pp. 256, 259.

14. Pavliuchenkov, *Voennyi kommunizm*, pp. 259, 260.

15. Ibid., p. 259.

16. On pogroms in the Ukraine during the Civil War see E. G. Elias Heifetz, *The Slaughter of the Jews in the Ukraine in 1919* (New York: Seltzer, 1921); S. I. Gusev-Orenburgskii, *Kniga o evreiskikh pogromakh na Ukraine v 1919 g.* (Petrograd: Izdatel'stvo Z. I. Grzhebina, n.d.); and *Bagrovaia kniga: Pogromy 1919–1920 gg. na Ukraine* (Kharbin: Izdatel'stvo Dal'nevostochnogo Evreiskogo Obshchestvennogo Komiteta Pomoshchi Sirotam-Zhertvam Pogromov ["Decopo"], 1922); Nahum I. Shtiff, *Pogromy na Ukraine (v. Dobrovol'cheskoi armii)* (Berlin: Vostok, 1922); I. M. Cherikover, *Antisemitizm i pogromy na Ukraine, 1917–1918 gg. (K istorii ukrainsko-evreiskikh otnoshenii)* (Berlin: Ostjudisches Historisches Archiv, 1923); Joseph B. Schechtman, *Pogromy Dobrovol'cheskoi armii na Ukraine (k istorii antisemitizma na Ukraine v 1919–1920 gg.)* (Berlin: Ostjudisches Historisches Archiv, 1932); Nahum Gergel, "The Pogroms in the Ukraine in 1918–21," *YIVO Annual of Jewish Social Science* 6 (1951). The number of victims of the pogroms is not known with certainty. Figures ranging from 50,000 to 200,000 persons are cited in literature. Gergel considered it possible to document 50,000 to 60,000 Jewish deaths due to pogroms, but noted that, considering the lack of precise data, the actual number could actually well be twice that figure. The author of a recent study accepts the relatively lower figures (Henry Abramson, *A Prayer for the Government: Ukrainians and Jews in Revolutionary Times, 1917–1920* [Cambridge, MA: Harvard University Press, 1999], 110). See also Oleg Budnitskii, "Jews, Pogroms, and the White Movement: A Historiographical Critique," *Kritika: Explorations in Russian and Eurasian History* 4.2 (Fall 2001): 751–72; and Budnitskii, *Rossiiskie evrei*, pp. 275–343.

17. This was no news. The taking of large cities by the Cavalry Army, namely of Voronezh and especially of Rostov-on-Don, was accompanied by robbery, heavy drinking, and murder of civilians and even Communists. See S. Orlovskii, *Velikii god: Dnevnik konnoarmeitsa* (Moscow; Leningrad: Gosizdat, 1930), pp. 35–37; V. L. Genis, "Bataiskaia probka," *Voprosy istorii* 1 (1994): 153–58. One of Babel's comrades-in-arms was telling him "of the days when he spent 20 thousand, 30 thousand. Everyone has gold, everyone got it in Rostov, flung sacks with money over the saddles and off they went." Isaac Babel, "Dnevnik 1920 g. (konarmeiskii)," in *Sobranie sochinenii v 2 tomakh* (Moscow: Ald, 2002), vol. 1, pp. 463–64.

18. On the "political education" in the First Cavalry Army see Stephen Brown, "Com-

munists and the Red Cavalry: The Political Education of the Konarmiia in the Russian Civil War, 1918–20," *Slavonic and East European Review* 73.1 (1995): 61–81.

19. V. L. Genis, *"Pervaia Konnaia armiia: za kulisami slavy,"* *Voprosy istorii* 12 (1994): 68–69.

20. N. Prisiazhnyi, *Pervaia Konnaia armiia na pol'skom fronte (maloizvestnie stranitsy istorii)* (Rostov-na-Donu: Izdatel'stvo Rostovskogo Universiteta, 1992), p. 20.

21. A. G. Kavtaradze, *Voennye spetsialisty na sluzhbe Respubliki Sovetov* (Moscow: Nauka, 1988), p. 174; G. Iu. Gaaze, "Belye ofitsery i soldaty v nashykh r'adakh," *Sbornik vospominanyi k 4-y godovshchine RKKA* (Moscow: n.p., 1922), 81–83; N. A. Efimov, "Komandnyi sostav Krasnoi armii," *Grazhdanskaia voina*, vol. 2 (Moscow: n.p., 1928), 95.

22. Vladimir Fisher, "Zapisky iz mestechka (Ocherki nedavnego proshlogo)," *Na chuzhoi storone* VII (Berlin: Vataga, and Prague: Plamya, 1924): 115–16.

23. On Babel's service in the First Cavalry Army see Efraim Sicher, "The 'Jewish Cossak': Isaac Babel in the First Red Cavalry," in *Studies in Contemporary Jewry* IV, ed. Jonathan Frankel (Oxford: Oxford University Press, 1988), 113–34.

24. Babel, "Dnevnik 1920 g. (konarmeiskii)," in his *Sochineniia*, 2 vols., comp. and ed. Antonina Priozhkova, comment. Sergey Povartsov (Moscow: Khudozhestvennaya literatura, 1990), vol. 2, 426, 428. This edition is hereafter cited as *Sochineniia*, followed by volume and page number.

25. See Babel's notes on hatred of the Poles, who "tore beards," and on the horrors of the pogroms perpetrated by the Polish troops and the "White" Cossacks of *yesaul* Iakovlev who fought among the ranks of the army of Piłsudski, in Babel, "Dnevnik 1920 g. (konarmeiskii)," *Sochineniia* 2:422, 445, 486.

26. S. Orlovskii, *Velikii god*, p. 107. Entry of June 30, 1920.

27. Babel, "Dnevnik 1920 g. (konarmeiskii)," *Sochineniia* 2:484, 486–87. Entries of August 25 and 28.

28. Ibid., p. 437. Entry of July 18.

29. Ibid., p. 441. Entry of July 18.

30. Ibid., p. 481. Entry of August 21.

31. Ibid., p. 466.

32. Ibid., p. 487. Entry of August 29. Emphasis added.

33. Prisiazhnyi, *Pervaia Konnaia*, p. 13.

34. Genis, *"Pervaia Konnaia armiia,"* p. 72.

35. Genis, *"Pervaia Konnaia armiia,"* p. 71–72.

36. Fisher, "Zapisky iz mestechka," pp. 117, 119.

37. S. Orlovskii, *Velikii god*, p. 114.

38. There was a good reason for the brigade to be called Special. It was not part of any of the four divisions of the First Cavalry and was subordinate directly to the Revolutionary Military Committee of the army. It was comprised of over 30 percent Communists, which was double the army average.

39. Prisiazhnyi, *Pervaia Konnaia*, p. 17.

40. Brown, "Communists and the Red Cavalry," p. 86.

41. S. Orlovskii, *Velikii god*, p. 114. Orlovskii wrote afterward that "at the Cavalry Army we have a considerable number of the Jews not only engaged in political work but also in the rank political-military positions. They are also present among the commanders. Despite the really dire conditions they work in, they stand firm in combat and are well-liked by their comrades. Many received the order of the Red Banner for their part in the battles." Alas, Orlovskii failed to mention any specific names, save for a Jewish machine-gunner Merkin, whose "truly heroic work" he observed near Brody. Merkin with his machine gun "was advancing ahead of our lines and worked without an assistant, who ran away to God knows where." Ibid., p. 115. It is evident that the Red Army servicemen were irritated by the absence of the Jews precisely among the army ranks rather than among political workers. It is quite possible that the Jewish machine-gunner, who somehow appeared ahead of the attacking lines (if he indeed was not a figment of imagination of the secretary of the Revolutionary Military Council, just like the "liking by the comrades") was the only exception.

42. Genis, "*Pervaia Konnaia armiia*, " p. 72.

43. Prisiazhnyi, *Pervaia Konnaia*, p. 19.

44. Ibid., p. 20.

45. Genis, "*Pervaia Konnaia armiia*, " p. 73; Prisyzhnyi, *Pervaia Konnaia*, p. 19.

46. Genis, "*Pervaia Konnaia armiia*, " p. 73.

47. S. Orlovskii, *Velikii god*, p. 126.

48. A. Lysenko, *Iosif Apanasenko* (Stavropol: Stavropol'skoie knizhnoe izdatel'stvo, 1987), 340–41. This apologetic biography, published at the dawn of perestroika, simply omits the period from August 1920 to the beginning of 1921.

49. S. Orlovskii, *Velikii god*, p. 125.

50. In that instance the Red cavalrymen were mistaken—their new commander, Samokhin, was Russian. He had to flee from his own subordinates in haste.

51. Nikolai Rakitin, *Zapiski konarmeitsa* (Moscow: Federatsiia, 1931), pp. 191–92.

52. Genis, "*Pervaia Konnaia armiia*, " p. 74.

53. N. Gergel, "The Pogroms in the Ukraine in 1918–1921," *YIVO Annual of Jewish Social Science*, vol. 6 (1951): 244, 248.

## Notes to Chapter 4

1. D. Biriulin, "Pis'mo tov. Stalina—v massy!," *30 dnei* 12 (1931): 12–15.

2. Letter of October 13, 1931 from Babel to V. A. Reginin (editor of *30 dnei*), Isaak Babel', *Sochineniia* (Moscow: Khudozhestvennaia literatura, 1991), 1:318.

3. I. Stalin, "O nekotorykh voprosakh istorii bol'shevizma," originally published in *Proletarskaia revoliutsiia*, 1931, no. 6; in I. V. Stalin, *Sochineniia* (Moscow: Politicheskaia literatura, 1951), 13:84–102. Slutsky's article, "Bol'sheviki o germanskoi s.-d. v period ee predvoennogo krizisa," appeared in *Proletarskaia revoliutsiia* 6 (1930): 37–72.

4. The fate of Slutsky is noted in Robert C. Tucker, *Stalin in Power: The Revolution from Above, 1928–1941* (New York: Norton, 1990), p. 154; on the instructions to historical journals, see p. 156. One example of the practice of broader-circulation journals: the January 1932 issue of *Molodaia gvardiia*, an organ of the Komsomol, led with Stalin's letter followed by an editorial entitled "We Shall Expose Trotskyist Contraband!"

5. Biriulin, "Pis'mo tov. Stalina—v massy!," 15.

6. Babel', "Dnevnik 1920 g.," *Sochineniia*, 1:362–435.

7. One instance in which Babel claimed to be half-Jewish is described in the entry for July 5; on that occasion as on July 24 (among other times), he describes telling tales about the rosy future. For a discussion of his experience as propagandist and camouflaged Jew see my introduction to the English translation of the diary, Isaac Babel, *1920 Diary* (New Haven: Yale University Press, 1995); and "Kinship and Concealment in Red Cavalry and Babel's 1920 Diary," *Slavic Review* 53:3 (Fall 1994): 694–710.

8. I. Babel', "Giui de-Mopassan," *30 dnei* 6 (1932): 36.

9. I. Babel', "Vecher u imperatritsy," in *Peterburg 1918*, ed. Efraim Sicher (Ann Arbor: Ardis, 1989), 105–7. The story's first publication, subtitled "Iz peterburgskogo dnevnika," was in *Siluety* 1 (December 1922): 7.

10. I. Babel', "Doroga," *30 dnei* 3 (1932): 41; the story concludes on p. 43. Further references to the story, given in parentheses, are to this edition. Translations are my own, with some indebtedness to the two English versions: David McDuff, "The Journey," in Isaac Babel, *Collected Stories* (London: Penguin, 1994), 80–87; and Peter Constantine, "The Road," in *The Complete Works of Isaac Babel* (New York: Norton, 2002), 659–66.

11. L. Ovalov, "Pervoe vospominanie Katsnel'sona," *30 dnei* 10–11 (1932): 63–64.

12. David Bergel'son, "V den' budnichnyi," trans. A. Popovskii, *30 dnei* 7 (1934): 7–10.

13. G. Eikhler, "Kak my vziali Zimnii dvorets," *30 dnei* 11 (1934): 9.

14. Milton Ehre, *Isaac Babel* (Boston: Twayne, 1986), 138–39.

15. Efraim Sicher, *Jews in Russian Literature after the Russian Revolution* (Cambridge: Cambridge University Press, 1995), 73.

16. Vadim Kovskii, "Sud'ba tekstov v kontekste sud'by," in "Kak izdavali, kak izdaiut, i kak nado izdavat' I. Babelia," *Voprosy literatury* 1 (1995): 54–55.

17. On the service of Jews in the Cheka, see Yuri Slezkine, *The Jewish Century* (Princeton: Princeton University Press, 2004), 177; Slezkine is also a stimulating source on Babel's stories and on the relation of Jews to Bolshevism and to the Soviet state.

18. "Moi pervyi gus'," *Sochineniia*, 2:34.

19. There are no sources for Babel's service in the Cheka beyond his own words—-in a 1926 autobiographical profile and in a 1930 statement defending himself against charges of slandering the Soviet Union. Doubts about his Cheka service are voiced in Kovskii, "Sud'ba tekstov v kontekste sud'by," 53–58; on the 1930 episode, see Grigorii Freidin, "Vopros vozvrashcheniia II: Velikii perelom i zapad v biografii I. E. Babelia nachala 1930-x godov," *Stanford Slavic Studies* 4, no. 2 (1991): 6–15.

20. "Dvorets materinstva," *Novaia zhizn'*, March 31, 1918.

21. V. Desnitskii-Stroev, "Otkrytoe pis'mo gr. Uritskomu," *Novaia zhizn'*, April 16, 1918.

22. Shamil' Zloi, "P'slushaite, chei vy podannyi?" *Novaia zhizn'*, March 16, 1918. The adjacent Babel article is "O loshadiakh."

23. The trial was covered in *30 dnei* 3 (1931): 6–13, in a piece by I. Bachelis called "'Ikh interventional.'"

24. On the regime's promotion of the mentality of indebtedness to the state see Jeffrey

Brooks, *Thank You, Comrade Stalin! Soviet Public Culture from Revolution to Cold War* (Princeton: Princeton University Press, 2000), chap. 4.

25. Sheila Fitzpatrick, *The Commissariat of Enlightenment: Soviet Organization of Education and the Arts under Lunacharsky, October 1917–1921* (Cambridge: Cambridge University Press, 1970), 11.

26. A. B. Lunacharskii, *Sud'by russkoi literatury* (Leningrad: Rossiiskii institut istorii iskusstva, 1925), 53.

27. "Syn rabbi," *Sochinenia* 2:129.

28. Katerina Clark has a useful discussion of the history and usage of these terms in *The Soviet Novel: History as Ritual* (Chicago: University of Chicago Press, 1981), 15–24.

29. *Pravda*, November 22, 1935; quoted in Brooks, *Thank You, Comrade Stalin!*, 89.

30. "Rabbi," *Sochineniia*, 2:36.

31. See Maurice Friedberg, "Yiddish Folklore Motifs in Isaak Babel's Konarmija," *American Contributions to the Eighth International Congress of Slavicists*, ed. Henrik Birnbaum and Victor Terras (Columbus, OH: Slavica, 1978), 2:192–203.

32. "Dnevnik 1920 g.," 362–63.

33. "Gedali," *Sochineniia*, 2:30.

34. "Konets bogadel'ni," *30 dnei* 1 (1932): 25.

35. "Karl-Iankel," *Sochineniia*, 2:170. For further discussion of both this story and "The End of the Almshouse," see my "Jewish Ritual and Soviet Context in Two Stories of Isaac Babel," in *American Contributions to the Twelfth International Congress of Slavists*, ed. Robert A. Maguire and Alan Timberlake (Bloomington, IN: Slavica, 1998), 11–20.

36. "Evreika," *Peterburg 1918*, 206.

37. Ibid., 202.

38. Il'ia Il'f and Evgenii Petrov, *Zolotoi telenok*, ed. M. Odesskii and D. Fel'dman (Moscow: Vagrius, 2000), 314–15 (chap. 27). For a useful analysis of this incident and related issues, see Alice Stone Nakhimovsky, "How the Soviets Solved the Jewish Question: The Il'f-Petrov Novels and Il'f's Jewish Stories," *Symposium* 53, no. 3 (Summer 1999).

39. "Vecher u imperatritsy," 106.

40. *The Secret Letters of the Last Tsar, Being the Confidential Correspondence between Nicholas II and His Mother, Dowager Empress Maria Feodorovna*, ed. Edward J. Bing, preface by R. H. Bruce Lockhart (New York: Longmans, Green, 1938), 304.

41. Ibid., 305.

42. Sergei Povartsov, *Prichina smerti—rasstrel: Khronika poslednikh dnei Isaaka Babel'ia* (Moscow: Terra, 1996), 150–52. That Uritsky recanted his testimony is noted in a document excerpted in Vitaly Shentalinsky, *Arrested Voices: Resurrecting the Disappeared Writers of the Soviet Regime*, trans. John Crowfoot, intro. Robert Conquest (New York: Free Press, 1993), 71.

## Notes to Chapter 5

1. "Modernization in Comparative Perspective," in *Nation-Building and Citizenship* (New York: Wiley, 1974), pp. 404–34.

2. Clifford Geertz, "Art as a Cultural System," in *Local Knowledge: Further Essays in*

*Interpretive Anthropology* (New York: Basic Books, 1983), pp. 94–120; Edward Shils, *The Constitution of Society* (Chicago: University of Chicago Press, 1972), esp. chaps. 4, 8.

3. Moshe Lewin, "The Social Background of Stalinism," in *The Making of the Soviet System: Essays in the Social History of Interwar Russia* (New York: Pantheon Books, 1985), p. 260; Sheila Fitzpatrick, "The Bolsheviks' Dilemma: Class, Culture, and Politics in Early Soviet Years," *Slavic Review* 47.4 (1988): 559–613.

4. *O partiinoi i sovetskoi pechati. Sbornik dokumentov* (Moscow: Pravda, 1954), p. 173.

5. Quoted from Mikhail Heller and Aleksandr Nekrich, *Utopia in Power: The History of the Soviet Union from 1917 to the Present* (New York: Summit Books, 1986), p. 174.

6. *Kommunisticheskaia partiia sovetskogo soiuza v rezoliutsiiakh i resheniiakh s'ezdov, konferentsii i plenumov TsK* (Moscow: Izd. politicheskoi literatury, 1970), vol. 2, p. 360.

7. The "living newspaper" (*zhivaia gazeta*) was a generic hybrid that combined the public reading of the daily news with the factual and ideological elucidation of the local agitator. Although both it and the broader notion of the "living word" had pre-revolutionary roots, they acquired new significance after 1917. More than oral, colloquial news or language, they came to imply a mode of communication that was entirely novel, or revolutionary.

8. *Rossiiskii Gosudarstvennyi Arkhiv Literatury i Iskusstva* (RGALI), f. 2164, ed. khr. 1, 1.

9. I use the term "utopian mentality" here in the sense described by Karl Mannheim, that is, the total "infusion . . . into every aspect of the dominating mentality of the time" of an orientation that not only transcends existing reality but also "tend[s] to shatter, either partially or wholly, the order of things prevailing at the time." In Mannheim's vocabulary, "utopias" actually succeed in somehow transforming existing reality, while "ideologies" do not. "The Utopian Mentality," in *Ideology and Utopia: An Introduction to the Sociology of Knowledge* (New York: HBJ, 1936), pp. 192–263.

10. See André Mazon, *Lexique de la guerre et de la révolution en Russie* (Paris: Librairie Ancienne Honore Champion, 1920); S. O. Kartsevskii, *Iazyk, voina i revoliutsiia* (Berlin: Russkoe Universal'noe Izd., 1923); E. D. Polivanov, "O literaturnom (standartnom) iazyke sovremennosti," *Rodnoi iazyk v shkole* 1 (1927): 225–35; A. M. Selishchev, *Iazyk revoliutsionnoi epokhi: iz nabliudenii nad russkim iazykom polednikh let (1917–1926)* (1928; reprint, Letchworth-Herts, UK: Prideaux Press, 1971).

11. Ia. Shafir, *Gazeta i derevnia* (Moscow: Krasnaia nov', 1924); Selishchev, *Iazyk revoliutsionnoi epokhi*, chaps. 7–8; M. Rybnikova, "Ob iskazhenii i ogrubenii," *Rodnoi iazyk v shkole* 1 (1927): 243–55; I. N. Shpil'rein, *Iazyk krasnoarmeitsa* (Moscow: Gosizdat, 1928).

12. See Shafir, *Gazeta i derevnia*; Jeffrey Brooks, "The Breakdown in Production and Distribution of Printed Material, 1917–1927," in *Bolshevik Culture*, ed. Abbott Gleason, Peter Kenez, and Richard Stites (Bloomington: Indiana University Press, 1985), pp. 151–74. Not all of the peasant and working-class population rejected the new public discourse. Selishchev notes several cases of willing and successful acquisition, especially among the younger and more politically active citizens (*Iazyk revoliutsionnoi epokhi*, pp. 178–218).

13. Victoria E. Bonnell and Lynn Hunt, *Beyond the Cultural Turn: New Directions in the Study of Society and Culture* (Berkeley: University of California Press, 1999), p. 17. In his influential study of the origins of nationalism, Benedict Anderson singles out the newspaper and the novel as the two most influential forums for the creation and maintenance of what he calls "imagined communities" (*Imagined Communities: Reflections on the Origin and Spread of Nationalism* [London: Verso, 1983]). For equally compelling discussions of the role of language and narrative in making sense of reality, see Hayden White, "The Value of Narrativity in the Representation of Reality," in W. J. T. Mitchell, ed., *On Narrative* (Chicago: University of Chicago Press, 1980), pp. 1–23; and Jerome Bruner, *Acts of Meaning* (Cambridge, MA: Harvard University Press, 1990).

14. For commentary on the special regard for the writer and the intelligentsia in general, see Gary Saul Morson, "Introduction: Literary History and the Russian Experience," in *Literature and History: Theoretical Problems and Russian Case Studies*, ed. Gary Saul Morson (Stanford, CA: Stanford University Press, 1986), pp. 14–27.

15. Sheila Fitzpatrick, "New Perspectives on the Civil War," in *Party, State, and Society in the Russian Civil War: Explorations in Social History*, ed. Diane Koenker, William G. Rosenberg, and Ronald Grigor Suny (Bloomington: Indiana University Press, 1989), p. 6; Mark Von Hagen, *Soldiers in the Proletarian Dictatorship: The Red Army and the Soviet Socialist State, 1917–1930* (Ithaca: Cornell University Press, 1990), p. 8. Leon Trotsky also recognized the potential threat and benefit of this group of mostly rural, newly educated citizens (see "Zadachi voennoi pechati," in *Voprosy kul'turnoi raboty* [Moscow: Gosizdat, 1924], pp. 29–30).

16. *Magnetic Mountain: Stalinism as a Civilization* (Berkeley: University of California Press, 1995), p. 14.

17. Citing Soviet sources, Moshe Lewin offers the following demographic breakdown of Red Army soldiers: peasants, 77 percent; workers, 14.8 percent; others, 8.2 percent. "The Civil War: Dynamics and Legacy," in *Party, State, and Society in the Russian Civil War: Explorations in Social History*, ed. Diane Koenker, William G. Rosenberg, and Ronald Grigor Suny (Bloomington: Indiana University Press, 1989), p. 420, n. 13.

18. See *Soldiers in the Proletarian Dictatorship*, pp. 50–66, for a discussion of the state's increased concern for and monitoring of the numerous bands of partisan fighters who fought against both White and Red Armies in 1918–1919. Von Hagen argues that the movement was a response by rural peasant communities to the power vacuum in the countryside, in an effort to defend their local interests. It is worthy of note, also, that both Babel and Furmanov actually served in the capacity of reporter and political commissar, and that these fictional accounts are based on those experiences.

19. Dm. Furmanov, *Chapaev* (Moscow: Gosizdat, 1923), p. 12. This and subsequent quotes from *Chapaev* are taken from this first-edition volume. Page numbers will appear in parentheses following the text. All translations of *Chapaev* are my own.

20. In *The Complete Works of Isaac Babel*, ed. Nathalie Babel, trans. Peter Constantine (New York: Norton, 2001), p. 203. All subsequent translations come from this volume with page numbers appearing in parentheses after the text.

21. The most inflammatory reaction came from General Budenny himself, accusing

"citizen Babel" of offering petty insights worthy of a peasant "wench." Using the full rhetorical force of the language of state, he writes: "It is unimportant to him why and for what the First Red Cavalry Army, amongst the greatest weapons of the class struggle, fought. Despite the fact that the author was in the ranks of the glorious Red Cavalry, albeit at the rear, he did not notice—it passed by his ears, eyes and comprehension—either its heroic struggle, or its terrible inhuman sufferings and deprivations. Being by nature . . . ideologically alien to us, he did not notice its struggle of gigantic sweep" ("Babizm Babelia iz *Krasnoi novi'.*" *Oktiabr'* 3 [1924]: 196). In his response to Budenny's critique, Babel attributes the misunderstanding to his own shortcomings in making the complete shift from "historical truth" to a "literary form" ("A Letter to the Editor" [1924], in *Complete Works of Isaac Babel*, p. 362).

22. He had even considered leaving the book in the same first-person narrative he used in his wartime diaries (*Iz dnevnika pisatelia*, p. 35). Most reviews, in fact, characterize the work as being more akin to a journalistic memoir than a work of fiction. See [G. Kor.], "Chapaev," *Na postu* 4 (1923): 195; A. Lunacharskii, "Desiat' knig za desiat' let revoliutsii," *Sobranie sochinenii v vos'mi tomakh: literaturovedenie, kritika, estetika* (Moscow: Khudozhestvennaia literatura, 1964), vol. 2, p. 359; A. Kamegulov, "*Chapaev* Dm. Furmanova. Frontovye zapiski," *Literaturnaia ucheba* 6–7 (1933): 39. All reviews listed here cite this feature as a positive one, the last one in particular praising it, because it permitted Furmanov to "interrupt the picture of the artistic display of the civil war with . . . commentaries on military-strategic and political themes" (pp. 42–43).

23. Gregory Freidin has described Liutov's status in terms of "cultural marginality" twice over—as both Jew and intellectual ("Isaac Babel," in *Modern European Writers: The Twentieth Century*, ed. George Stade [New York: Scribner's, 1990], 1980).

24. Furmanov, *Chapaev*, pp. 85–86. See M. Gorky, "O russkom krest'ianstve" (Berlin: Izd. I. Ladyzhnikov, 1922), 43–44. On this essay and Gorky's attitude toward the Russian peasantry in general, see William Mills Todd III, "Gor'kij's Essay on the Peasantry: Framing the Mirror," in *Russian Literature* 24 (1988): 555–68.

25. See L. Iakubinskii, "O snizhenii vysokogo stilia u Lenina," *LEF* 1.5 (1924): 71–80; V. B. Shklovsky, "Lenin, kak dekanonizator," *LEF* 1.5 (1924): 53–56.

26. Writing in his 1920 diary, Babel offers a similarly ironic reflection on the incongruity of ideology and demographics: "The opening of the Communist club in the editorial office. There it is—the proletariat: these unbelievably emaciated Jewesses and Jews from the underground. Pitiful, fearsome tribe, forward march."

27. M. Bakhtin, *Problemy poetiki Dostoevskogo*, 4th ed. (Moscow: "Sovetskaia Rossiia," 1979), 222–25.

28. Liutov actually appears in all of the stories but his presence is less felt in a handful, including "Pis'mo," "Solntse Italii," "Konkin," "Sol'," "Prodolzhenie istorii odnoi loshadi," and "Izmena." Although by Bakhtin's definition Liutov's presence precludes the possibility of pure *skaz*, the relative remoteness of his voice gives rise to that "double-voiced discourse" that distinguishes the device for the Russian critic. Four of the six are written texts (private or official letters), "Pis'mo" is a letter dictated to Liutov, and "Konkin," assumes the form of an oral history retold in the voice of the original storyteller.

29. According to Bakhtin, a "hybrid" is " . . . an utterance that belongs, by its gram-matical (syntactic) and compositional markers, to a single speaker, but that actually con-tains mixed within it two utterances, two speech manners, two styles, two 'languages,' two semantic and axiological belief systems" ("Discourse in the Novel," in *The Dialogic Imagination: Four Essays*, ed. Michael Holquist and trans. Caryl Emerson and Michael Holquist [Austin: University of Texas Press, 1981], 304).

30. It also makes a third, "meta-literary" statement—that, in the end, it is only the writer (or implied author) who has the power to manipulate the language and symbols of both worlds, playing them off of one another, while at the time maintaining distance and enjoying a laugh. Babel makes light of this privileged position in his own autobiographi-cal sketch, where, after elaborating on his rigorous education as a young Odessan Jew, he is careful to note the "real" influences on his emergence as a writer: first, the patronage of Gorky, who encouraged him to go out and "live among the people," and secondly, his varied experiences "among the people," which, significantly, included such state-related employers as the military, the secret police, the *Narkompros*, and various state-run pub-lications. Only then, Babel writes, did "I learn to express my thoughts clearly and not in great length." Though the first biographical phase (the intellectual) is underplayed, it is really the one that enables his distance from (and influence over) the second two (the people and the state). Babel, "Aftobiografiia" (written November 1924) in *I. E. Babel': stat'i i materialy*, ed. B. V. Kazanskii and Iu. N. Tynianov, Mastera sovremennoi litera-tury no. 2 (Leningrad: Academia, 1928), 6–9.

31. "O sebe, o kritikakh i o svoei rabote," *Mastera sovremennoi literatury, stat'i i materialy: M. Zoshchenko*, ed. B. V. Kazanskii and Iu. N. Tynianov (Leningrad: Aca-demia, 1928), 11.

## Notes to Chapter 6

1. O. Mandel'shtam, "Burya t natisk (1922)," in B. A. Filippov and G. P. Struve, eds., *Sobranie sochinenii*, 4 vols. (Washington, D.C.: 1962–68), vol. 2 (2d ed.), 341, 343.

2. P. M. Bitsilli, "Bunin i ego mesto v russkoi literature" (1931), in *Tragediia russkoi kul'tury: Issledovaniia, stat'i, retsenzii* (Moscow: 2000), 421–23.

3. G. Adamovich, "O frantsuzskoi 'inquietude' i o russkoi trevoge" (1928), in *Litera-turnye zametki: Kn. 1* (St. Petersburg: 2002), 112.

4. Russian literature did not pay particular attention to color until after Chekhov. L. Pantellev notes correctly: "Chekhov is a black-and-white writer. One is struck by this especially when one turns to Chekhov after Bunin, so colorful, painterly, in which every page has so many different colors and hues. Chekhov does not use 'color,' but just a bit of coloration, as for example, in 'The Black Monk': It was a tender, soft combination of blue and green; in some spots the water looked like blue vitriol, in other spots, it seemed moonlight became so dense that it replaced water in the bay" (L. Pantellev, *Priotkrytaia dver'* [Leningrad: 1980], 523).

5. K. Chukovskii, "Rannii Bunin" (1915), *Voprosy literatury* 5 (1968): 83–84.

6. N. I. Berkovskii, "Chekhov: ot rasskazov i povestei k dramaturgii," in his *Litera-tura I teatr: Stat'I raznykh let* (Moscow: 1969), 79.

7. A. Chekhov, "Krasavitsy" (1883), in *Polnoe sobranie sochinenii* (Moscow: 1947), 7: 133.

8. All translations into English are by the editor. References to Babel are to the two-volume edition: I. Babel', *Sochineniia*, 2 vols. (Moscow: Sovetskii pisatel, 1990), ed. by A. Pirozhkova, comment. by S. Povartsov.

9. Adamovich, "O frantsuzskoi 'inquietude' i o russkoi trevoge," 113. Emphasis added.

10. I wrote about this at a greater length in my book *Masterstvo Iuriia Oleshi* (Moscow: 1972).

11. K. Chukovskii, "Rannii Bunin," 95.

12. Bunin, "Derevnia," in *Sobranie sochinenii*, 9 vols. (Moscow: 1965), 3:39–40. In Chekhov, too, in such stories in the 1890s as "Baby," "Murder," and others, one could discern, according to N. Berkovskii ("Chekhov," 71), "an anticipation of Isaac Babel's stories that deal with everyday life under the old regime."

13. O. Mandelshtam, "Literaturnaia Moskva: Rozhdenie fabuly" (1922). *Sochineniia*, 2 vols. eds. S. S. Averintsev and P. M. Nerler (Moscow: Khudozhestvennaia literatura, 1990), vol. 2: *Proza, Perevody*, pp. 278-81. Hereafter referred to as *Sochineniia*.

14. V. Shklovsky, "Babel': Kriticheskii romans," in *Gamburgskii schet* (Leningrad: 1928), 77.

15. O. Mandel'shtam, "Burya i natisk" (1923). *Sochineniia* 2:282–91.

16. E. Toddes, "Mandel'shtam i opoiazovskaia filologiia," in *Tynianovskii sbornik. Vtorye Tynianovskie chteniia* (Riga: 1986), 92–93.

17. Babel, in fact, anticipated Mandelshtam's program for Russian literature (as well as Lev Lunts's Serapion manifesto "To the West!") in his essay, "Moi listki: Odessa," published in November 1916 in the Petrograd *Zhurnal zhurnalov* (no. 49). Combining what would later be known as a Formalist analysis of the crisis state of Russian literature with a clear-eyed sociological insight—the ascendancy of the petty bourgeois culture in Russia—he wrote lucidly, perhaps even more lucidly than Mandelshtam, about the need for a new "Russian literary Messiah" who would bring some Odessan sunshine, in the manner of Maupassant, to dissipate the gloomy Gogolian-Dostoevskian mists of the Petersburg tradition. A permanent Petrograd resident since the fall of 1916, Babel quickly became a fixture in the literary milieu of the capital, absorbing, and contributing to, the ongoing discourse on the crisis of Russian letters. The similarity of his views with those of Osip Mandelshtam may have had something to do with the interest Babel expressed in the early 1920s in joining the Acmeists. See Nadezhda Mandelshtam, *Hope Abandoned*, trans. Max Hayward (New York: 1974), 55ff. *Ed.*

18. N. Ashukin, "Sovremennost' v literature," *Novaia russkaia kniga* 6 (1922): 4, 6. The article is dated: "Moscow, July, 1922." For more on this subject, see my Introduction to the publication of the correspondence between Maxim Gorky and Lev Lunts, *Neizvestnyi Gor'kii: k 125-letiiu so dnia rozhdeniia* (Moscow: 1994), 133–40.

19. Blok's *The Twelve* represents a snapshot of the kind of urban speech that Mandelshtam had in mind. Nikolai Leskov and, later, Maxim Gorky both were masters at using "overheard" urban speech (*razgovorchiki*). *Ed.*

20. "Chto ia imeiu ot nego  . . . segodnia zhivotnye shtuki, zavtra zhivotnye shtuki."

21. "For him ideology is a constructive device." D. S. Mirskii, *Uncollected Writing on Russian Literature* (Berkeley, CA: 1989), 204.

22. D. S. Mirskii, "I Babel'. Rasskazy. Gosudarstvennoe izdatel'stvo. 1925," *Blagonamerennyi* 1 (1926): 168. Emphasis added.

23. Viktor Shklovsky, "Babel': Kriticheskii romans," *Gamburgskii schet* (Leningrad: 1928), 77.

24. B. Vladimirskii, *Likuia i sodrogaias'* (Odessa: 1992).

25. P. S. Kogan, "Babel'," in a collection without a title: A. Sobol', "Pechal'nyj vesel'chak," D. Khait, "Mut'," Z. Vendrov, "Po evreiskim koloniiam" (Izdatelstvo P. A. Krasnogo i M. S. Shliaposhnikova: Kharkov, 1927), 3–4.

26. See, e.g., Iurii Tynianov, "200000 metrov Il'i Erenburga," *Zhizn' iskusstva* 6 (1924).

27. *Prozhektor* 10 (May 31, 1925): 6.

28. P. Rusin, "Makhovik: A Story," *Novyi mir* 4 (1935): 5.

29. Ibid., pp. 11, 19, 23.

30. N. Atarov, *Rasskazay* (Moscow: 1947), pp. 52–54.

31. A. Pis'mennyi, *Fart* (Moscow: 1980), p. 55.

32. I have argued this point in my "Skvoz' zvezdy k terniiam," in *Izbrannye raboty*, vol. 1, *Literatura Sovetskogo proshlogo* (Moscow: 2001), 1:357.

33. See my "Sud'ba 'samootcheta-ispovedi' v literature sovetskogo vremeni (1920-e—konets 1930-kh godov)," in *Izbrannye raboty*, vol. 1, *Literatura sovetskogo proshlogo* (Moscow: 2001).

34. Roskin, Stat'i o litereature i teatre (Moscow: Sovestkii pisatel', 1959), pp. 22–23.

35. Pustovskii, Gekht, Bondarin, and Fraerman were, at one time or another, protégés of Isaac Babel and were like him one-time members of the Odessa writers' community. *Ed.*

36. In a newspaper article in 1939, Roskin cited a description from Kozhevnikov as a example of new mastery: "Storm clouds smelled of the cellar (M. Chudakova, *Masterstvo Iuriia Oleshi* [Moscow: 1972], 51).

37. A. Roskin, Stat'i o litereature i teatre, 271.

38. Ibid., p. 317.

39. A. P. Chudakov, "Poetika pushkinskoi prozy," in *Boldinskie chteniia* (Gorky: 1981), pp. 62–63.

40. D. S. Mirskii, "I. E. Babel'. Rasskazy," *Sovremennyia zapiski* 26 (1925), in D. S. Mirskii, *Uncollected Writings on Russian Literature* (Berkeley, CA: 1989), p. 205.

41. I. Babel', "Di Grasso" (*Sochineniia*, vol. 2:238).

42. "Babel-stilist," in L. D. Rzhevskii, Prochtenie tvorcheskogo slova: Literaturovedcheskie problemy i analizy (New York: 1970), 79–81.

43. In his private correspondence with me, the editor of this volume, Gregory Freidin, wrote: "These [Soviet writers] would take the weighty gold piece of Babel's prose, shave off a granule and drop it into their thin gruel. It would have been inedible otherwise. St. Paul: 'a little leaven leaveneth the whole lump.'"

44. Emil' Mindlin, *Neobyknovennye sobesedniki: Literaturnye vospominaniia* (Moscow: 1979), 439–40.

45. I. Goff, "Zapakh lokrykh zaborov," in *Vospominaniia o Konstantine Paustovskom* (Moscow: 1983), 258.

46. M. Gorky, "Zametki o meshchanstvo," in *Nesobrannye literaturno-kriticheskie stat'i* (Moscow: 1941), 386. Emphasis added. The article was not reprinted in Gorky's lifetime.

47. *Rasskazy 1953 goda* (Moscow: 1954), 85.

48. Shimon Markish, *Babel' i drugie* (Moscow: 1997), 7.

## Notes to Chapter 7

1. Viktor Shklovsky remarks in passing on the affinity between the two writers, stressing the Orientalist Flaubert of *Salammbô*, and there are, in fact, Orientalist moments in Babel. See Shklovsky, "Isaac Babel: A Critical Romance," in *Modern Soviet Writers: Essays in Criticism*, ed. Edward Pearson and Edward J. Brown (London, Oxford, New York: Oxford University Press, 1973), pp. 295–300.

2. Gustave Flaubert, *Madame Bovary* (Paris: Garnier-Flammmarion, 1966), 55. The translation of this and all subsequent passages from the French is mine.

3. Isaac Babel, *The Complete Works*, ed. Nathalie Babel, trans. Peter Constantine (New York: Norton, 2002), 290. All subsequent quotations from Babel are from this volume.

4. Gustave Flaubert, *L'éducation sentimentale* (Paris: Flammarion, 1985), 429.

5. Babel picked up this image from Lermontov's well-known poem "Vykhozhu odin ia na dorogu" (1841), as Gregory Freidin observes in his essay, "The Other Babel," in this volume.

## Notes to Chapter 8

1. For references and discussion see Yuri K. Shcheglov, "Some Themes and Archetypes in Babel's *Red Cavalry*," *Slavic Review* 53.3 (1994): 653–70.

2. Alexander Zholkovsky and Mikhail Yampolsky, *Бабель/Babel* (Moscow: Carte Blanche, 1994).

3. On this intertextual connection see A. K. Zholkovsky, *Poltora Rasskaza Babelia: "Gui de Mopassan" i "Spravka/Gonorar". Struktura, Smysl, Fon* (Moscow: URSS, 2006), 149–67.

4. See A. K. Zholkovsky, "Dve obez'iany, bochki zlata," *Zvezda* 10 (2001): 202–14.

5. See Brian Boyd, *Vladimir Nabokov: The American Years* (Princeton, NJ: Princeton University Press, 1991), 108; M. Malikova, "'Pervoe stikhotvorenie' V. Nabokova. Perevod i kommentarii," in *V. V. Nabokov: Pro et Contra. Antologiia*, ed. B. Averin et al. (St. Petersburg: Izd. Russkogo Khristianskogo gumanitarnogo instituta, 1997), 769.

6. On Nabokov's "First Poem," see Malikova; for my argument in more detail, see A. K. Zholkovsky, "Dve obez'iany, bochki zlata . . . ," *Zvezda* 10 (2001): 202–14; A. K. Zholkovsky, "Poem, Problem, Prank," *The Nabokovian* 47 (Fall 2001): 19–28.

7. On Nabokov's deliberate fictionalization of his autobiographical narrative see Vladimir Nabokov, *Selected Letters 1940–1977*, ed. D. Nabokov and Mathew Briccoli (New York: Harcourt Brace Jovanovich, 1989), 69; quoted in Malikova, "'Pervoe stikhotvorenie' V. Nabokova," (763); and in John Burt Foster Jr., *Nabokov's Art of Memory and European Modernism* (Princeton, NJ: Princeton University Press, 1993), 179.

8. The comparison is, of course, conceived as purely typological. Apparently, close to nothing is known about Nabokov's reception of Babel's work, while Babel's only known reaction to Nabokov (as Sirin) seems to have been codedly enthusiastic, albeit purportedly critical. See G. Freidin's publication and discussion of Babel's 1933 reminiscences of his travels in France and Italy in his "Vopros vozvrashcheniia II: 'Velikii perelom' i Zapad v biografii I. E. Babelia nachala 1930-kh gg.," *Stanford Slavic Studies*, vol. 4, part 2 (1991), 214, 218.

9. Boyd, *Vladimir Nabokov*, 686.

10. See Zholkovsky and Yampolsky, *Бабель / Babel* (148–73). Less fictional and less radical in its intertextual subversion is Babel's "The Beginning" ("Nachalo," 1937), directly involving the recently deceased Gorky.

11. See Andrew Wachtel, *The Battle for Childhood: Creation of a Russian Myth* (Stanford: Stanford University Press, 1990).

12. On Jan. 3, 1944, Nabokov wrote to Edmund Wilson: "From the literary material produced during 25 years of the Soviet rule I could select about a dozen readable shorts (Zoshchenko, Kaverin, Babel, Olesha, Prishvin, Zamiatin, Leonov)" (*The Nabokov-Wilson Letters: Correspondence Between Vladimir Nabokov and Edmund Wilson, 1949–1971*, ed. Simon Karlinsky (New York: Harper and Row, 1979), 122); mentioned in Iu. Leving, *Vokzal—Garazh—Angar: Vladimir Nabokov i Poetika Russkogo Urbanizma* (St. Petersburg: Izdatel'stvo Ivana Limbakha, 2004), 155.

## Notes to Chapter 9

1. Louis Iribarne, "Babel's 'Red Cavalry' as a Baroque Novel," *Contemporary Literature* 14.1 (1973): 60.

2. Isaac Babel, "*Pan* Apolek," in *The Complete Works*, trans. Peter Constantine, ed. Nathalie Babel (New York: Norton, 2002), 220. Further references to this edition are by "TCB" and page number. Where the translations are my own, the references are to Isaac Babel, *Sobranie sochinenii*, 2 vols., ed. S. Povartsov (Moscow: Al'd, 2002), by "SS 2002," volume, and page number.

3. *Pan* Robacki calls Apolek "*pan* artist [*pan khudozhnik*]," lending plausibility to the idea that Apolek might call the narrator "*pan* writer" (222).

4. "My First Fee" ("Moi pervyi gonorar") is a longer version of "Answer to Inquiry" ("Spravka"). "Moi pervyi gonorar" is dated 1922–1928 and was not published during Babel's lifetime. "Spravka" exists only as an undated Russian typescript and as an English translation published in 1937. "Spravka" is usually considered to be an earlier variant of "Gonorar" (see Povartsov's note in SS 2002, 1:512), although Zholkovsky and Iampolski consider it to be the final version (on the grounds that Babel would never revise a story by making it *longer*). See Mikhail Iampolski and Alexander Zholkovsky, *Babel' / Babel* (Moscow: Carte Blanche, 1994), chap. 1, "Metaportret khudozhnika v iunosti." Further references to this volume are to "*Babel'/Babel*" or "BB."

5. Babel, like Stendhal, also aspired to a certain bureaucratic / fiscal quality in his fiction: "A short story ought to be precise, like a military report or a bank check." Quoted in

Alexander Zholkovsky, "Isaak Babel, Author of Guy de Maupassant," *Canadian Slavonic Papers*, 36.1–2 (March–June 1994): 90.

6. Giorgio Vasari, *The Lives of the Artists*, trans. Julia Conaway Bonandella and Peter Bonandella (Oxford: Oxford University Press, 1991), p. 291. For Babel's "formative" reading of the biography of Leonardo da Vinci, see Efraim Sicher, "Art as Metaphor, Epiphany, and Aesthetic Statement: The Short Stories of Isaak Babel'," *Modern Language Review* 77.2 (April 1982): 392.

7. Michel Jeanneret, *A Feast of Words: Banquets and Table Talk in the Renaissance*, trans. Jeremy Whiteley and Emma Hughes (Chicago: University of Chicago Press, 1991), 260–61.

8. A different way of viewing the role of Tolstoy and Maupassant is through the Bloomian framework of "anxiety of influence": see Zholkovsky, "Tolstoi i Babel', avtory Mopassana," chap. 2 in *Babel'/Babel*.

9. Lukács, *The Theory of the Novel*, trans. Anna Bostock (Cambridge: MIT Press, 1971), 78; Frederic Jameson, *Marxism and Form* (Princeton: Princeton University Press, 1974), 169–70.

10. The story of Marcel's *Figaro* piece easily suggests itself as a member of the "debut" genre discussed by Zholkovsky in his contribution to this volume.

11. See Gregory Freidin, "Isaac Babel" (1990), http://www.stanford.edu/gfreidin/Publications/babel/Babel_Scribners_Freidin1990.pdf. Further references are to Freidin, 1990. A version of this essay also appears in *Walter Benjamin to Yuri Olesha*, vol. 11 of *European Writers: The Twentieth Century*, ed. George Stade (New York: Scribner's, 1990), 1885–1914. "[Babel] was one of the first major Jewish writers, along with Franz Kafka, to develop and practice a particular literary idiom in the language of the dominant culture." Proust may perhaps be added to their number.

12. Marcel Proust, *Time Regained* (TR), trans. Andreas Mayor and Terence Kilmartin, rev. D. J. Enright (New York: Modern Library, 2002), p. 525. I have slightly modified the translation: cf. *Temps Retrouvé*, ed. Pierre-Louis Rey and Pierre-Edmond Robert (Paris: Gallimard, 1990), 348–49.

13. Miguel de Cervantes, *Don Quijote*, trans. Burton Raffel, ed. Diana de Armas Wilson (New York: Norton, 1999), 38. Further references are by page number to this edition. The other classic example of Sancho's "translation" of imitatio into mimesis is in the adventure of Mambrino's golden helmet (book 1, chaps. 21, 44–46). Don Quijote mistakes a brass barber's basin (*bacía*) for the golden helmet (*yelmo*); Sancho refers to the object as *baciyelmo* (basin-helmet), testifying to his double vision. For a discussion of Sancho as the "authorial consciousness" of *Don Quijote*, see Elif Batuman, "The Windmill and the Giant: Double-Entry Bookkeeping in the Novel" (Ph.D. diss., Stanford University, 2007), chap. 3.

14. I am grateful to Gregory Freidin for bringing to my attention an unpublished letter from Babel to I. L. Livshits (dated Molodenovo, April 24, 1932), in which Babel writes: "If you can, buy me the complete *Don Quijote* in the [illegible] edition, I really need it [*ochen' nuzhno*]." I am also indebted to Prof. Freidin for his extremely helpful comments on earlier drafts of this paper.

15. As Freidin puts it, writers like Babel played "the role of the *other* and the very center, and not the margins, of their country's culture" (Freidin, 1990). Manuel Durán tells a similar story about Cervantes: "Cervantes was . . . at the same time *inside* and *outside* the mainstream of Spanish life . . . he took part in the battle of Lepanto and wrote . . . two successful books . . . [but] he was always poor . . . and not infrequently in jail . . . a complete outsider would have rebelled or subsided into depression and silence. A complete insider would have seen only the rosiest aspects of Spanish life. It was his fate, and our gain, that he saw both sides" (Durán, "Cervantes' Harassed and Vagabond Life," in Roberto González Echevarría, ed., *Cervantes' Don Quixote: A Casebook* [Oxford: Oxford University press, 2005], 32).

16. Evidence for the theory of Cervantes's *converso* ancestry—first proposed by the important Hispanist Américo Castro in the 1960s—includes: the *converso* lineage of Cervantes's in-laws; Cervantes's affinity for Erasmus; the large number of physicians in Cervantes's immediate family; Talmudic and / or Kabbalistic references in *Don Quijote*; and Cervantes's unusually shabby treatment by the Spanish government. For a sympathetic presentation of the theory, see Ellen Lokos, "The Politics of Identity and the Enigma of Cervantine Genealogy," in *Cervantes and His Postmodern Constituencies*, ed. Anne J. Cruz and Carroll B. Johnson (London: Routledge, 1999), 116–33.

17. Jean Canavaggio, *Cervantes*, trans. J. R. Jones (New York: Norton, 1990), 142–45.

18. See "Avtobiografiia" (SS, 1:33). "The *Ivan-and-Maria*" takes place during "the first produce expedition in our nation in the summer of 1918" (667).

19. "The *Ivan-and-Maria*" and "The Story of My Dovecote" are typically not foregrounded in discussions of Babel's metaliterary narratives, but I consider them to be counterparts to the other three stories ("Guy de Maupassant," "In the Basement," and "My First Fee"), which *are* typically foregrounded. See Victor Erlich, "Art and Reality: A Note on Isaak Babel's Metaliterary Narratives," *Canadian Slavonic Papers* 36.1–2 (March –June 1994): 107–14. See also Iampolski and Zholkovsky, *Babel'/Babel*.

20. "Guy de Maupassant," "The *Ivan-and-Maria*," and "The Road" were published in the same journal (*30 dnei*), in the same year (1932). All three stories describe the jobs held by a young intellectual in and around Petrograd, in 1916–1918; these jobs involve either clerkship ("*Ivan-and-Maria*") or translation ("Maupassant," "The Road"). In terms of time and space, the stories are mutually reinforcing. In "*Ivan-and-Maria*," set in 1918, the produce expedition is staffed by "residents of Peski and Okhta"; in "Maupassant," set in 1916, the narrator lives in Peski.

21. The gap between military and civilian industries was particularly large in Petrograd, where a full 75 percent of the labor force was devoted to military production. S. O. Zagorsky, *State Control of Industry in Russia during the War* (New Haven: Yale University Press, 1928), 66.

22. Edouard Maynial, *La Vie et l'oeuvre de Guy de Maupassant* (Paris: Société du Mercure, 1907). The clerk years (1870–1878) played an important role in Maupassant's development as a writer and served as a lifelong source of material (ibid., 56–57). At his desk, Maupassant alternated between accounting and literary compositions, which he sent to Flaubert; Maynial writes of "*essais poétiques qu'il écrivait, aux heures de bureau, sur*

*le papier de l'administration, et qu'il soumettait le dimanche à son maître, Flaubert*" (ibid., 56). This alternation anticipates Babel's "Autobiography," in which the stint in the produce expedition is associated with Babel's "apprenticeship" to Maxim Gorky.

23.  Guy de Maupassant, "L'Aveu," in *Contes et Nouvelles*, 2 vols. (Paris: Laffont, 1988), 2:193–97.

24.  My explanation for this departure is that Babel's narrator, in his retelling, turns "L'Aveu" into a story about *himself.* As a commentary on his own situation, the most important element of the story is the young idealist's compromise. Céleste's pregnancy, having no real counterpart in Babel's plot, is accordingly elided. I part here from Zholkovsky, who suggests that, by removing the "cynical" pregnancy conversation, Babel "sanitizes Maupassant, effectively laundering his dirty deal" (*Babel'/Babel*, 94).

25.  Charles Rougle has noted the color changes, as well as the fact that Babel's Polyte hikes the price for Celeste's ride, from ten to fourteen sous; his interpretation of these "revisions" is that they indicate "a subjectivity in approach that goes beyond poetic license to become a rather eclectic interpretation of Maupassant himself" (179).

26.  Povartsov translates "*ce diable*" as "*etot proidokha*" (SS 2002, 1:203, n. 1).

27.  I am grateful to Gregory Freidin for this observation. For a discussion of the "etiological legends" surrounding the *ivan-da-mar'ia* in Slavic folklore, see Valeria B. Kolosova, "Ivan-da-marja," *Pro Ethnologia* 18 (2004): 87–95. See also Freidin's reading of "The *Ivan-and-Maria*" in this volume.

28.  In his paper in this volume, Gregory Freidin mentions the Gorky subtext in "*Ivan-and-Maria*," comparing Babel's Korostelev to Gorky's Smuryi (from *My Apprenticeship*). Korostelev also bears a close resemblance to Iakov Shumov, the stoker on Smuryi's boat: a former jailbird, monk, and hobo, who has been everywhere from Belgrade to Christopol, and who remains for Alesha a "locked chest." Shumov finally hires himself out to a member of the Skopets sect and vanishes to Siberia. Babel's Korostelev is a vision of Shumov thirty years later, back from Siberia, and containing within himself the secret of all Russia: "Russia! Russia!" Korostelev cries, banging his head on the floor (TCB, 677).

29.  See, for example, S. A. Rachinskii's much-quoted letter of January 6, 1878: "The novel lacks architecture. Two themes develop side by side, not connected in any way" (in Lev Tolstoy, *Pis'ma Tolstogo i k Tolstomu* [Moscow: Gosudarstvennoe izdatel'stvo, 1928], 223).

30.  The analogy between Levin and Sancho Panza is suggested by Viktor Shklovsky in his last book, *The Energy of Error*, which ascribes Levin's double vision to a Panzaic worldview: "Sancho Panza, if not Tolstoy's favorite hero, is in any case an opening [*vakansiia*] for his main hero . . . Sancho Panza's life consists of believing and not believing in Don Quijote." *Energiia zabluzhdeniia: Kniga o siuzhete* (Moscow: Sovetskii pisatel', 1981), 240.

31.  Anton Chekhov, *Diadia Vania*, Act 4, in *Polnoe sobranie sochinenii i pisem*, 30 vols., ed. N. F. Belchikov, D. D. Blagoi, L. D. Opul'skaia, et al. (Moscow: Nauka, 1986), vol. 13.

32.  Babel makes poignant use of the phrase "sky full of diamonds" in the 1920 diary, recording his conversation with a "plundered" Jewish family in Dubno: "I tell [them] yes, everything will be for the better . . . in Russia wonderful things are happening:

express trains, free food for children, theaters, the International. They listen with delight and mistrust. I think to myself: a sky full of diamonds will be yours [*budet vam nebo v almazakh*], everything will be turned upside down, everyone will be dislocated yet again" (TCB 407). Sonia's words, quoted in this context, represent the epitome of the empty promise. Babel is tormented by the thought that the Jewish family's sacrifices for the Revolution will remain unpaid (like Vania's and Sonia's sacrifices for the Serebriakovs) and that, in their lifetime, the credits will never balance the debits.

33. Babel does not name the sum of 55 kopecks—we must calculate it. The narrator starts out with 1 ruble 50 kopecks; after buying two pairs of doves, 40 kopecks remain.

34. In his haste to repudiate *The Headless Man*, the narrator does not realize that *Julius Caesar* is also the story of a headless man: Caesar's assassination leaves Rome without a head. Thus Brutus says of Antony that "he can do no more than Caesar's arm / When Caesar's head is off" (*Julius Caesar*, II.i, lines 180–81). For a general discussion of decapitation in Babel's works, see Gregory Freidin, "Fat Tuesday in Odessa: Isaac Babel's 'Di Grasso' as Testament and Manifesto," *Russian Review* 40.2 (April 1981): 109–12.

35. Is the rich church warden "stolen" from Tolstoy—perhaps from "Master and Man" ("Khoziain i rabotnik," 1895)? In this work, the "master," Vasilii Andreevich, is a church warden, and steals from the church strong-box in order to buy land. In both "My First Fee" and "Master and Man," two socially disparate people spend a night together, transcend their commercial relationship, and achieve brotherhood / sisterhood.

36. *Babel'/Babel*, 182. Iampolski ascribes the asthma to Babel's *own* asthma, which was, in real life, aggravated by the kerosene fumes that he inhaled while writing at night. The narrative frame within the story thus merges with the extra-textual frame of the writer's biography.

37. Proust, *Swann's Way* (SW), trans. C. K. Scott Moncrieff and Terence Kilmartin, rev. D. J. Enright (New York: Modern Library, 2002), 241–42.

38. Marcel imagines himself telling the Duchess of Guermantes about his future career as a writer: "Since I wished, some day, to become a writer, it was time I knew what I was going to write. But as soon as I asked myself the question . . . my mind would cease to function, my consciousness would be faced with a blank" (SW, 243). Marcel adds, a few pages later: "How often . . . in the course of my walks along the Guermantes way, and with what . . . melancholy, did I reflect on my lack of qualification for a literary career, and abandon all hope of ever becoming a famous author" (SW, 251).

39. Forty-year-old Dvoira (Deborah), with her goiters, is also made fun of at her own wedding. There is again hiccupping and a huge banquet. "The King" ends with Dvoira "edging her timid husband toward the door of their nuptial chamber, looking at him lustfully" like a cat toying with a mouse (TCB 139).

40. According to Shklovsky, the writers who understood this method were Tolstoy (who "would never have written *War and Peace* had he not been an artilleryman"), and Babel ("who reminded me of . . . Tolstoy"). "Thus Babel," writes Shklovsky, "he was in favor of freedom." Shklovsky's other comments on Babel in this passage are brief and rather cryptic: Babel is "extremely talented"; Babel handles his talent as delicately as the actor Davydov handles his top-hat; and "Babel does not swim in his works [*ne plyvet v*

*svoem proizvedenii*]." Viktor Shklovsky, *Tret'ia Fabrika*, in *Gamburgskii Schet* (St. Petersburg: Limbus, 2000), 120–21. English translation consulted: *Third Factory*, trans. Richard Sheldon (Ann Arbor: Ardis, 1977), 51–52.

## Notes to Chapter 10

1. Written in languages of surrounding nations. I do not speak of writers in Yiddish or Hebrew. For the definition and criteria of Russian-Jewish or "any"-Jewish literature, see my book: Zsuzsa Hetényi, *In a Maelstrom. The History of Russian-Jewish Prose (1860–1940)* (New York and Budapest: Central European University Press / Center for Jewish Publication Society, 2008). In Hungarian: Hetényi Zsuzsa, *Örvényben. Az orosz-zsidó próza története (1860–1940)* and *Az orosz-zsidó próza antológiája (1860–1940)* (In a Maelstrom, vol. 1, The History of Russian-Jewish Prose [1860–1940], and vol. 2, An Anthology of Russian-Jewish Prose [1860–1940]) (Budapest: Dolce Filologia, 2000).

2. "The room was hot and stuffy, and this always made me depressed and feel I wanted to escape to freedom." "The heat in the room kept increasing. . . . At that moment all seemed extraordinary to me and made me want to flee from it and yet remain for ever." "I cannot breathe, there is nothing to breathe, I must run outside to fresh air, to freedom, but I have no strength to raise my dropping head." Isaac Babel, *Collected Stories*, trans. David McDuff (New York: Penguin, 1994), 22, 24, 26–27. Hereafter, this edition is cited as CS, followed by the page number.

3. On the contrary, a good example of an unsuccessful angle of narration is "Karl-Iankel."

4. The same technique was already employed by Aleksander Kipen in "At the Crossroads" (1910). Kipen describes the soldiers and officers killing time at the outskirts of town, near a little synagogue, but at a distance from where the pogrom rages. Only its noises are heard and the tension is visible in the reactions and the faces of different people—soldiers, officers, passersby. After Kipen, a predecessor, we can mention also one successor: Friedrich Gorenstein in the short story "The House with a Turret" uses the child's eye and *Weltanschauung* (in the proper meaning of the German word) to depict the horror of the evacuation. The Jewish boy whose mother dies during the evacuation is not able to find the practical steps needed for life. The lack of visual concentration of the child makes him a victim, a role that psychologically provokes the reader's emotional participation. The turret becomes a symbol. Cf. Zsuzsa Hetényi, "Pasynki Rossii. Motivy marginal'nosti v proizvedeniiakh F. Gorenshteina," *Revue des études slaves* 75.1 (2004): 141–55.

5. In *Fascinating Fascism*, an essay on Leni Riefenstahl's photo book (New York Review of Books, February 8, 1975), Susan Sontag makes reference to Sartre, *La mort dans l'âme* (1949), quoting a description of Daniel's perception of the German occupation of Paris. As in the work of Babel, the description takes the form of an adolescent's overtly erotic experience. Sontag considers that the sexualization of its accessories is one of the manipulative techniques of fascism and totalitarianism—we could add: of Soviet totalitarianism. The force and even the violence within beauty, its incoherence and inaccessibility, the ambivalent fear it produces, are all elements that arouse admiration as Sontag proves: this extremely complex duality we find already in Babel.

6. See a detailed analysis of this scene as well as of "childhood stories" in an article I had the chance to read only recently: Gregory Freidin, "Isaak Babel," *European Writers: The Twentieth Century* (New York: Scribners, 1990), pp. 1885–1914. A copy is on the internet: http://www.stanford.edu/gfreidin/Publications/babel/Babel_Scribners_Freidin 1990.pdf. For the scene see especially p. 18.

7. This solution is not at all self-evident. An opposite settling can be found in David Aizman's "Flood of Blood" ("Krovavyi razliv," 1906). Aizman does not yet unify the two elements, the child's eye and the objective focus. The child, a girl violated and killed before her father, is only the innocent victim (a very old pattern to arouse the sympathy of the reader). The beauty of the young lad enthusiastically participating in the pogrom, and the festive atmosphere in the streets is shown by the author's voice as well.

8. The symbolist concept of the child as possessor of secret knowledge and language without words is elaborated in Andrei Bely's *Kotik Letaev*; not without influence on Boris Pasternak's *Luvers' Childhood*. Here I just mention a problem of literary continuity that shows how closely Babel's ornamental prose is correlated with the symbolists, their theory of hidden secrets of the world, the Russian prose of the 1910s, even more than that of Boris Pil'niak who is considered to be a direct follower of the ornamental-prose stream launched by Bely.

9. In the short story "Pogrom" (in *Early Grief*) Danilo Kiš portrays a Jewish boy left alone in the street at the end of the pogrom with a packet of noodles in his hand. It was given to him by a nice lady who kindly shared her loot with him after having robbed a Jewish shop. The boy is utterly confused as to what to do: whether he should take the packet of noodles home, or better throw it away? Danilo Kiš employs Babel's "binarity" regarding "staying" and/or "fleeing," but also adds new dimensions: what are the criteria of participation and betrayal, what is the right conduct from the point of view of survival?

10. For a detailed analysis of *Gedali*, see my article "Lavka vechnosti: K motivnoi strukture rasskaza 'Gedali' I. Babelia," *Studia Slavica Hung.* 36 (1989): 187–92.

11. Another wonderful example of the child's tolerant eye is Emile Ajar (Roman Gary): *La vie devant soi* (1975).

12. "Here everything was dumped together—the warrants of the agitator and the commemorative booklets of the Jewish poet. Portraits of Lenin and Maimonides lay side by side . . . in the margins of communist leaflets swarmed crooked lines of Ancient Hebrew verse . . . pages of the Song of Songs and revolver cartridges" (227).

13. "In this trunk there were dumb-bells, a lock of female hair . . . Uncle's prayer-shawl [tallit], horsewhips with gilt knobs and flower tea in boxes decorated with cheap pearls." The translator did not pay attention to the repetition of the detail, the lock of female hair, in the trunk of the rabbi's son; there he put "strand of female hair" (226).

14. A simple but illuminating example can be found in a Biblical phrase, Joshua 1:5: "I will not fail you or forsake you." Most translations say "and" instead of "or." Levinas translates "but": "I will keep you—I do not give you go but I do not abandon you" (*Je ne t'abandonnerai pas mais je ne te lacherai pas. L'impossible divorce est ici le supreme refuge*), cited in Benny Lévy, *Etre juif.* Paris: Verdier, 2003), 46. The neutral "and"-structure is

open to decoding and allows multiple interpretations. Here, instead of a calming promise, the ambivalent question of freedom and protection arises, which is very close to the ambivalence of the assimilation: going freely and getting lost, or staying bounded but protected.

15. The psycholinguistic interconnections of visual perception / imagery and that of intellectual forms / models were discovered by the *Gestalt*-theory at the beginning of the twentieth century. A new approach to the question is in Christopher Collins, *The Poetics of the Mind's Eye: Literature and the Psychology of the Imagination* (Philadelphia: University of Pennsylvania Press, 1991).

16. Here I use the term "primitive" to denote something elementary, initial, original, of an early stage of development.

17. Robert Alter points out that the same phenomena in the modern Hebrew prose of Mendele Mokher Seforim and others; see "From Pastiche to Nusakh," in *The Invention of Hebrew Prose: Modern Fiction and the Language of Modernism* (Seattle: University of Washington Press, 1988). When I found pairs and triplets in Babel's prose in 1977, using the philosophy of language by Sándor Karácsony, I did not yet discover that Babel follows a pattern deeply rooted in the mentality of the Hebrew language. Babel is part of a process or tradition that starts in Biblical Hebrew poetry and arrives at modernity. A brilliant example from the later period is David Albahari's postmodern, deconstructionist, but still "traditional" prose.

18. In the childish admiration for physical prowess, there lies a deeper juxtaposition, a further pattern, an older one: the traditional lifelong devotion of Jewish men, physically weak and fragile, to the study of religious texts no longer suffices as a model for the assimilated generations. Physically powerful Jews appear in Russian-Jewish literature well before Babel's Odessa "King," Benia Krik. The earliest novel where the issue emerges is Yaroshevsky's *In a Maelstrom* (1883)—an emblematic title that I have chosen for my book on Russian-Jewish literature.

19. Cf. the description of the procession in "The Story of My Dovecote," 39.

20. A. Kipen, "Izhe iesi na nebesi . . . ," *Evreiskii mir*, 1910, 3 columns, 58–64.

21. "Uzh i est' za shto, / Rus' moguchaia, / poliubit' tebia, / Nazvat' materiu," or "Snova mne slyshits'a pesnia rodimaia / Snova mne viditsia rodina-mat' / Ty-l' predo mnoi, nezhno liubimaia / Ty-l' predo mnoi opiat'?" "Iz besed o zhestokikh nravakh," in "Mimokhodom," *Nedelnaia Khronika Voskhoda* 50 (1897): columns 1406–7. The same can be found in the memoirs of Sandor Márai's *journal*, in July 1944. A Jewish boy whose grandparents were deported recites in his refuge a patriotic poem: "I am Hungarian, I was born Hungarian, / my nurse sang Hungarian songs to me, / My mother taught me prayers in Hungarian, / and to love you, my beautiful homeland." Márai Sándor, *Napló, 1943–1944* (Budapest: Helikon, 1998), 187. See later the same distorted language in the patriotic song of little David (Henry Roth, *Call It Sleep*).

22. Michael Gold, *Jews without Money* (New York: Carrol and Graf, 1996). Hereafter, this edition is referred to as Gold followed by page numbers. The first edition was published in 1930 (New York: Horace Liveright).

23. Michael Gold: *120 Million* (New York : International Publishers, 1929).

24. Another three-fold structure.

25. This was the central issue of my book *Csillagosok—keresztesek. Mítosz és messianizmus Babel Lovashadseregében* (Under the Star and the Cross: Myth and Messianism in Babel's *Red Cavalry* [Budapest: Tankönyvkiadó, 1992]). Some chapters have been reprinted in Russian in *Studia Slavica Hung.* 27 (1981), 31 (1985), 34 (1988), 36 (1989), 37 (1991–92), 38 (1993), and 43 (1998).

26. "Babel prikidyvaetsa inostrantsem, potomu shto etot priiom, kak ironiia, oblegchaet pismo." V. Shklovsky, I. Babel, "Kriticheskii romans," *LEF* 1925 2, no. 6: 155.

27. Zsuzsa Hetényi, "Eskadronnaia dama, vozvedennaia v madonnu. Ambivalentnost' v *Konarmii* I. Babel'ia," *Studia Slavica Hung.* 31 (1985): 161–69; in English: Zsuzsa Hetényi, "'Up' and 'Down,' Madonna and Prostitute: the Role of Ambivalence in *Red Cavalry*," *Acta Litteraria Acad. Sci.* 32, 3–4 (1990): 309–26. (Unfortunately a bad translation made by the journal at that time.)

28. "I can't find my place in the prayerbook." It would be better to write: "The" place in prayer book. Isaac Babel, *1920 Diary*, ed. Carol J. Avins, trans. H. T. Willets (New Haven and London: Yale University Press, 1995), p. 4.

29. Naomi Sokolov, "Discoveries of Reading: Stories of Childhood by Bialik, Shakhar, and Roth," *Hebrew Annual Review* 9 (1985): 321–42.

30. Henry Roth, *Call It Sleep* (New York: FSG, 1991), 62.

31. This distortion was used in the title of a Hungarian-Jewish novel showing Hungarian history from the point of view of a Jewish boy. The song in the novel is the "Pioneer March." Miklós Vámos, *Zenga zének* (Budapest: Szépirodalmi, 1983).

32. Cf. *New Essays on* Call It Sleep, ed. Hana Wirth-Nesher (Cambridge: Cambridge University Press, 1996); H. Wirth-Nesher, afterword in *Call It Sleep* (1991); Dan Miron, "A Language as Caliban," in *A Traveler Disguised*, ed. D. Miron (New York: Schocken Books, 1973). On the general problematic: Itamar Even-Zohar, "Russified Literary Models," in Materials of the Symposium, *The Dynamics of East European Ethnicity Outside of Eastern Europe* (Bellagio, Italy, 1977); M. Samuel, *In Praise of Yiddish* (New York: Cowles, 1971), to name only a few.

33. The *skaz* technique was identified with Leskov in the 19th century, was renewed by Evgenii Zamiatin, and was widely used in the 1920s also by writers like Boris Pil'niak and Mikhail Zoshchenko. *Skaz* is by definition of the Russian Formalist literary theorists of 1920s a stylization of the idiom of the lower strata of society, the function of which is to create a narrative structure distanced several times over. This distance separates the narrator both from the author and the characters (Babel from Liutov, Liutov from the Cossacks, and the Cossacks from the Jews), and the language defines the narrator's place among the social strata.

34. See my articles: Zsuzsa Hetényi: "Pik i tupik inoiazychnoi evreiskoi literatury. Isaak Babel i Karoi Pap" / "Success and failure in Jewish literature—Isaac Babel and Karoly Pap," *Studia Slavica Hung.* 43 (1998): 325–32; "Karoi Pap," *Jerusalem Review* 11 (2002): 280; "Delaite vsio, kak oni" / "Do everything as they do" (on assimilation, "Karoly Pap and his novel *Azarel*"), *Jerusalem Review* 12 (2002): 162–70.

35. Semion Gekht, Chelovek, kotoryi zabyl svoiu zhizn. / Prostoi rasskaz o mertvet-sakh i drugiie rasskazy, reprint edition by M. Wainstein (Jerusalem: Zikhron/Pamiat', 1983), pp. 17–127.

36. Again a pattern of Russian-Jewish literature, the love with a Christian girl. Bogrov was the first who used it in his *Notes of a Jew*.

37. Babel's narrator says: "The doctor found I had a nervous illness. 'This illness,' he said, 'occurs only in Jews and among Jews it occurs only in women.' . . . And now, when I remember those sad years I find in them the beginning of the ailments that torment me, and the causes of my premature and dreadful decline" (SC 49). Babel eliminated this passage from his later editions.

38. Bruno Bettelheim, *The Uses of Enchantment: The Meaning and Importance of Fairy Tales* (New York: Alfred A. Knopf, 1976), p. 102. Further references to this edition are given to Bettelheim and page number.

39. Bettelheim proves his statement by the mechanism of the *Arabian Nights*. He argues that only unrealistic stories can give solutions and satisfaction to children in their real problems; realistic ones suggest simplified answers.

40. As Bettelheim notices, the usual logic, connections of causes and consequences do not apply to the fairy tales, because the realm of the subconscious is exceptional, surprising. Nevertheless, the irrational is not only frightening but also evocative of hope (if there are exceptions, miracles, nothing is hopeless: B 86, 87). Fantasy plays the same role as fantastic elements in literature.

41. The first Jewish author to display Jewish self-hatred is again Grigorii Bogrov, cf. Shimon Markish, "Tretii otets-osnovatel'," *Ierusalimskii Zhurnal* 6 (2000): 228–89.

42. On Babel's self-hatred see the chapter on him, especially about his short stories such as "Berestechko" or his *1920 Diary*, in my book *In a Maelstrom*.

43. The difference is detectable in Bogrov's novel: in the chapters on childhood, his self-hatred is "authentic," while in chapters on the hero's married life it is didactic.

44. I propose a summary of methods in child-focused prose of Jewish assimilation and its general features in my book mentioned above (*In a Maelstrom*).

45. The polarity of stylistic layers also reaches extreme contrasts, but the grotesque is hidden in their semantic parallel. Antony's *funeral* speech is pronounced in a pathetic mood. "Before my eye—in the mist of the *universe*—hung the face of Brutus. . . . The Roman people, growling, advanced towards me" (55). At that moment the drunken uncle appears with second-hand furniture and starts to cry out curses in Yiddish. His "brazen voice caulked up all the holes of the *universe* . . . he promised that our eyes would fall out, that our children would begin to rot and decompose while yet in their mother's womb, that we would not be able to bury each other and that we would be dragged by the hair to a *common grave* . . ." (57, emphasis added). Not only the cosmic amplitude of the universe, but also the funeral context and the pathetic heat merge comically the high and the low, Rome and Shakespeare on one side, second-hand furniture and the drunken uncle on the other: literature and life contrasted, side by side.

## Notes to Chapter 11

1. А. Тарасенков, "За богатство и чистоту русского литературного языка," *Новый мир* 2 (1951): 214.

2. See А. Метченко, "Историзм и догма," *Новый мир* 12 (1956): 228; А. Нинов, "Литература и история," *Литературная газета*, 23 июня 1956; С. Штут, "У карты нашей литературы," *Новый мир* 9 (1956): 247; В. Соловьев, "Смелость подлинная и мнимая," *Литературная газета*, 14 мая 1957, 1; А. Сурков, "Борьба за идеалы коммунизма," *Правда*, 1 декабря 1957, 2; Д. Стариков, "Необходимые уточнения," *Литературная газета*, 10 апреля 1958, 2; В.Архипов, "Уроки," *Нева* 6 (1958): 187–99; А.Хватов, "... и доказательной!" *Литературная газета*, 17 августа 1958, 3; А.Макаров, "Разговор по поводу . . ." *Знамя* 4 (1958): 187–217; Ф. Панферов, "Кому нужен этот окрик?" *Октябрь* 5 (1958): 222–23; В. Щербина, "Ответ фальсификаторам," *Октябрь* 11 (1958): 92.

3. See Г. Белая, "Третья жизнь Исаака Бабеля," *Октябрь* 10 (1989): 185–97.

4. И. Яркевич, "Бабель как Маркиз де Сад русской революции," *Независимая газета*, 16 марта 1994.

5. Boris Slutsky, *Things That Happened (New Russian Writing*, 19), ed. G. S. Smith (Moscow: Glas, 1999), pp. 53–56.

6. See S. J. Zipperstein, *Imagining Russian Jewry: Memory, History, Identity* (Seattle: University of Washington Press, 1999), pp. 63–87; Ezra Spicehandler, "Odessa as a Literary Center of Hebrew Literature," in *The Great Transition: The Recovery of the Lost Centers of Modern Hebrew Literature*, ed. Glenda Abramson and Tudor Parfitt (Totowa, NJ: Rowman & Allanheld, 1985), pp. 75–90.

7. According to his sister, Meri Shaposhnikoff, cited in Judith Stora-Sandor, *Isaac Babel: L'homme et l'oeuvre* (Paris: Klincksieck, 1968), pp. 18–20.

8. See, e.g., Amelia Glaser, "The End of the Bazaar: Revolutionary Eschatology in Isaac Babel's *Konarmiia* and Peretz Markish's *Di Kupe*," *Jews in Russia and Eastern Europe* 2 (53) (2004): 5–32.

9. See also Robert A. Rothstein, "How It Was Sung in Odessa: At the Intersection of Russian and Yiddish Folk Culture," *Slavic Review* 60, 4 (2001): 781–801.

10. See Itamar Even-Zohar, "Interference in Dependent Literary Polysystems," *Poetics Today* 11, 1 (1990), pp. 79-83; special issue on Polysystems. See also Benjamin Harshav, *Language in the Time of Revolution* (Berkeley: University of California Press, 1993).

11. Murray Baumgarten, *City Scriptures* (Cambridge, MA: Harvard University Press, 1982), pp. 154–55.

12. Entry for July 3, in Isaac Babel, *1920 Diary*, ed. Carol Avins, trans. H. T. Willetts (New Haven: Yale University Press, 1995), pp. 1–2. The first entries are apparently dated June in Roman numerals, which is clearly a mistake for July.

13. —Революция—скажем ей да, но разве субботе мы скажем нет?—так начинает Гедали и обвивает меня шелковыми ремнями своих дымчатых глаз.— Да, кричу я революции, да, кричу я ей, но она прячется от Гедали и высылает вперед одну только стрельбу . . . (*Detstvo*, p. 126).

14. "Бабизм Бабеля из Красной нови," *Октябрь* 3 (1924): 196–97.

15. Gedali is a *zaidener mentsh* (literally, "silken man" in Yiddish) bound by the "silken throngs of his smoked eyes," or rather the leather straps of his phylacteries, a fusion of images that curiously recalls the Odessa Hebrew poet Saul Chernikhovsky's "To Apollo" ("Lenokhakh pesel apolo," 1899), where the straps of the phylacteries bind the poet in an imprisoning knot but also, in the closing pun, betroth him to Hellenism.

16. A phrase missing from later editions of Babel's works and from *The Complete Works of Isaac Babel*, trans. Peter Constantine, ed. Nathalie Babel (New York: Norton, 2002).

17.

התזכרו עוד?–אנכי לא שכחתי–
בעלית קיר, בתוך בית-מדרש שומם.
אני הייתי אחרון לאחרונים,
על-שפתי פרפרה ומתה תפילת אבות.
ובפנת סתר שם, על-יד ארונכם,
לעיני דעך כליל נר התמיד.

(*Shirim*, 207). The Russian translation reads:

Вы помните? Бывало, бейт-га-мидраш
Оденет тьма; все разошлись давно,
И в тишине предела—я один;
Дрожа, слетает с уст молитва дедов,
А там, в углу, близ вашего ковчега,
Мерцает тихо вечная лампада (*Stikhi i poemy*, p. 56).

18.

האר אפוא, כוכב, נפשי הנואשה
מעבודה זרה ומגלות קשה

(*Shirim*, p. 86).

19. The identification of Diaspora and alien culture is conveyed in a neat pun in Jabotinsky's Russian translation: "Озари же дух мой, опаленный срамом/ Блуда по чужбинам и по чуждым храмам" (*Стихи и поэмы*, p. 13).

20. See Hamutal Bar-Yosef, "Х. Н. Биалик и русская поэзия," *Ariel* (Russian edition) 3 (1990): 24–49; and her "Reflections on Hebrew Literature in the Russian Context," *Prooftexts* 16 (1996): 127–49.

21. On the "hidden language" of the Jews in Germany see Sander Gilman, *Jewish Self-Hatred: Anti-Semitism and the Hidden Language of the Jews* (Baltimore: Johns Hopkins University Press, 1986).

22. Nurit Govrin, *Alienation and Regeneration*, trans. John Glucker (Tel-Aviv: Ministry of Defense, 1989), p. 22.

23. See Ruth Wisse, *The Modern Jewish Canon: A Journey through Language and Culture* (New York: The Free Press, 2000), p. 87. There is no evidence that Babel read Brenner's novel, but Brenner was translated into Russian in Soviet Russian journals in the twenties.

24. "פגישות עם יצחק בבל" *מאזנים* 38, 1–2 (1973–1974): 42–49.

25. Entry for August 25, Babel, *1920 Diary*, p. 80.

26. Sicher, *Jews in Russian Literature: Writers and Artists between Hope and Apostasy* (Cambridge: Cambridge University Press, 1995), pp. 55–57; Maurice Friedberg, "Yiddish Folklore Motifs in Isaac Babel's *Konarmiia*," in *Modern Critical Views: Isaac Babel*, ed. Harold Bloom (New York: Chelsea House, 1987), pp. 191–98.

27. Babel, *1920 Diary*, p. 87.

28. И.Чериковер; И.Б. Шехтман, *История погромного движения на Украине*, 1917–21гг., 2 vols. (Berlin: Ostjüdisches historisches Archiv, 1923–1932); Peter Kenez, "The Pogroms of 1919–1921," in *Pogroms: Anti-Jewish Violence in Modern Russian History*, ed. John D. Klier and Shlomo Lambroza (Cambridge: Cambridge University Press, 1992), pp. 291–313.

29. For historical documentation of atrocities committed against Jews see Oleg Budnitsky's essay in the present volume and his *Российские евреи между красными и белыми (1917–1920)* (Москва: РОССПЭН, 2005); see also Лидия Миликова; Ирина Зюзина, "Из погромной хроники Гражданской войны," *Еврейская Книгоноша* 1 (2005): 34–39.

30. On the modernist response to catastrophe in Hebrew and Yiddish in this period see David G. Roskies, *Against the Apocalypse: Responses to Catastrophe in Modern Jewish Culture* (Cambridge, MA: Harvard University Press, 1984).

31. Translated by A. M. Klein in *Complete Poetic Works*, ed. Israel Efros (New York: Histadruth Ivrith of America, 1948), vol. 1, p. 128.

וארור האומר: נקום!
נקמה כזאת, נקמת דם ילד קטן
עוד לא ברא השטן—

(*Shirim*, p. 152). The Russian translation reads:

Проклятье,—кто местью за ужасы воздал!

За кровь, за убийство младенца,—отмщений

И дьявол не создал!

("О резне," *Стихи и поэмы*, p. 23).

32. "Здесь все было свалено вместе—мандаты агитатора и памятки еврейского поэта. Портреты Ленина и Маймонида лежали рядом. Узловатое железо ленинского черепа и тусклый шелк портретов Маймонида. Прядь женских волос была заложена в книжку постановлений шестого съезда партии, и на полях коммунистических листовок теснились кривые строки древнееврейских стихов" (*Detstvo*, p. 229).

33. "The Jewish Voice," *Commentary* (October 1995): 41–42. The filtering of the extreme through the aesthetic is also what brings Babel into affinity with Flaubert, as Alter shows in his contribution to this volume.

34. See Jehoshua Gilboa, *A Language Silenced: The Suppression of Hebrew Literature and Culture in the Soviet Union* (Rutherford NJ: Fairleigh Dickinson University Press, 1982); Zvi Gitelman, *Jewish Nationality and Soviet Politics: The Jewish Sections of the CPSU, 1917–1930* (Princeton, NJ: Princeton University Press, 1972).

35. דערציילונגען (קיעוו: קולטור-ליגה) (1925).

36. Gitelman, *Jewish Nationality and Soviet Politics*, pp. 283–84.

37. On the fate of the Hebrew communists see Ruth Karton-Blum, "Hebrew Communist Literature in Soviet Russia," in *The Great Transition: The Recovery of the Lost Centers of Modern Hebrew Literature*, ed. Glenda Abramson and Tudor Parfitt (Totowa, NJ: Rowman & Allanheld, 1985), pp. 103–9.

38. See Ю.Андреев, "Заметки Фурманова о Бабеле," in *Из истории русских литературных отношений 17–20 веков* (Москва-Ленинград, 1959), pp. 402–6.

39. See, e.g., Babel's letter to his sister, Meri Shaposhnikov, May 12, 1925, which speaks of being oppressed by "a sickening professional environment devoid of art or creative freedom" (*The Lonely Years, 1925-1939: Unpublished Stories and Private Correspondence*, trans. Max Hayward, ed. Nathalie Babel [New York: Farrar & Straus, 1964], p. 61). Excerpt published in *Собрание сочинений в 4-х томах* (Москва: Время, 2006), vol. 4, p. 22. In 1925 Babel was a signatory of a petition to the Central Committee by "fellow travelers" protesting the increasing ideological attacks by Marxist critics.

40. See on such parallels Rina Lapidus, *Between Snow and Desert Heat: Russian Influences on Hebrew Literature, 1870–1970* (Cincinnati: Hebrew Union College Press, 2003), pp. 134–54. Haboneh (Trebukov) wrote an enthusiastic review of this story by Hazaz in *Breshit*, taking sides with the Jewish commissar against the old Jews.

41. See entry for July 4, Babel, *1920 Diary*, pp. 7–8.

42. Babel, *1920 Diary*, pp. 12, 81, 85.

43. Babel, *1920 Diary*, pp. 35–36.

44. Babel, *1920 Diary*, pp. 33, 43–44.

45. Babel, *1920 Diary*, p. 98.

46. Из окна летели прямые улицы, исхоженные детством моим и юностью —Пушкинская тянулась к вокзалу, Мало-Арнаутская вдавалась в парк у моря.

Я вырос на этих улицах, теперь наступил черед Карл-Янкеля, но за меня не дрались так, как дерутся за него . . . Мало кому было дела до меня . . . (*Detstvo*, p. 317).

47. —Не может быть, —шептал я себе, —чтобы ты не был счастлив, Карл-Янкель . . . Не может быть, чтобы ты не был счастливей меня . . . (*Detstvo*, p. 317).

48. The translation of the story in *The Complete Stories of Isaac Babel* is based on an excised version and it is not included in the section of Odessa Stories.

## Notes to Chapter 12

1. There was, however, a well-received production of Babel's earlier play, *Sunset*, with its sympathetic and often grotesquely comic presentation of Jewish gang-life in pre–World War I Odessa, by the Chelsea Theatre Center at the Brooklyn Academy of Music in the early seventies.

2. Isaac Babel, *The Complete Works*, trans. Peter Constantine, ed. Nathalie Babel (New York: Norton, 2002).

3. See Gregory Freidin's essay, "Two Babels—Two Aphrodites: Autobiography in *Maria* and Babel's Petersburg Myth," in this volume.

4. Babel and Brecht also had mutual friends, such as Mikhail Koltsov, mentioned in Gregory Freidin's chapter in this volume. They might well have met, either during

Brecht's two visits to Moscow, in May 1932 and spring 1935 (when Brecht wrote the poem "How the Workers of Moscow Took Possession of the Great Moscow Subway on April 27, 1935," in which he emphasized the contribution of women during the subway's construction; Babel lived at the time with Antonina Pirozhkova, who was one of the subway's head engineers). Or Babel and Brecht may have met while both attended the International Writers' Congress in Defense of Culture and Peace in Paris on June 21–25, 1935.

5. A crucial passage from Alexander Blok's famous 1918 essay, "The Collapse of Humanism," reads as follows: "Not only is it unnecessary to civilize the masses, there is no need to do so. If, nevertheless, we continue talking about making it possible for humankind to embrace *culture*, it is by no means clear who will make such an embrace possible for whom—the civilized folk for the barbarians or the other way around— because the civilized folk have become exhausted and lost their cultural integrity; in such epochs, the barbarian masses, who retain their freshness, happen to serve as unconscious guardians of cultural legacy." My thanks to Grisha Freidin for supplying me with this translation.

# Index

Note: Illustrations are indicated by page numbers in italic type.